Memorable
Neurology

Jonathan Heldt, M.D.

Also available from the same author:
Memorable Psychopharmacology
Memorable Psychiatry

The content of this book is not intended to be a replacement for proper medical training, nor is it intended to substitute for professional medical advice, diagnosis, or treatment. Always seek the advice of your physician or other qualified health provider with any questions you may have regarding a medical condition.

Editing and behavioral consultation provided by **Juliane Heldt, BCBA (Board Certified Behavior Analyst)**.

Revision 1.5. Last revised February 3, 2021.

ISBN: 0578520141
ISBN-13: 978-0578520148

DEDICATION

To **Dr. William Hemmerlin**. Thank you for showing me that anything is teachable with the right combination of passion for the learner, dedication to the craft, and ample servings of liquid nitrogen ice cream.

CONTENTS

Acknowledgments   i

1   Introduction   1

Neuroanatomical Foundations

2   The Nervous System   3

3   The Cerebral Cortex   21

4   The Cerebral Subcortex   35

5   The Cerebellum   53

6   The Brainstem   65

7   The Spinal Cord   77

8   The Peripheral Nervous System   95

9   The Special Senses   113

10   The Kitchen Sink   139

Clinical Applications

11	The Neurological Exam	155
12	Stroke	173
13	Intracranial Pressure	195
14	Myopathy	215
15	Neuromuscular Junction Disease	225
16	Motor Neuron Disease	235
17	Movement Disorders	247
18	Seizures	265
19	Neoplasms	283
20	Infections	303
21	Demyelinating Diseases	329
22	Peripheral Neuropathy	341
23	Headache	351
24	Neurocutaneous Disorders	363
25	Final Review	373

ACKNOWLEDGMENTS

To **Nick** for keeping me happy, warm, and well fed while working on this book.

1 INTRODUCTION

Before we begin, your author has something that he needs to disclose: he is not a neurologist. More than that, he doesn't even *like* neurology. Even on his best days, he finds the subject dense, tedious, and overly technical in a way that resists easy memorization and understanding. So what exactly makes him feel qualified to write a book on the subject when there are thousands of trained specialists that would be much more informed on the subject from whom you could learn?

In short, this book is written for people who feel the same way. Because learning neurology can be a painful experience at times, this book liberally uses mnemonics, visual aids, practice questions, and a few spoonfuls of sugar to help everything go down. With that in mind, this book will be helpful mostly for people who need a **basic understanding of the key concepts of neurology** but won't necessarily be pursuing neurology at a higher level, including medical students, nurses, nurse practitioners, physician assistants, and doctors in other specialties like psychiatry and internal medicine. If you are in the process of becoming a neurologist or want to gain a deeper understanding of the field, this book can absolutely serve as a helpful starting point. However, you will likely want to supplement your learning from additional sources before heading out to begin a career as a clinical neurologist, reflex hammer in hand.

This book is divided roughly into two halves. The first half covers the **anatomical foundations** upon which neurology rests. Learning the basic neuroanatomy of both the central and peripheral nervous system is essential for understanding the diseases that you will see in neurology, so neuroanatomy is where we will begin. The second half of the book will take everything that you've learned about neuroanatomy and turn it on its head by showing the **clinical pathology** of what can go wrong. "But wait!" you might say. "I don't want to wait until halfway through the book to learn about *actual* diseases!" Fear not. This book takes an unapologetically clinical perspective throughout, with a focus on pathology from the very beginning. Even in early chapters, important information about relevant disease processes will be sprinkled throughout to allow you to immediately apply what you're learning.

As you go through the book, you will soon realize that, when it comes to classifying neurologic disorders, there is often **more than one way to slice the bread**, meaning that many diseases will not fit neatly into a single category but rather will be classifiable in several ways. For example, Guillain–Barré syndrome is a disease in which someone's immune system attacks their own nerves by removing the protective sheath around them following an infection, leading to dysfunctional neuronal transmission in the peripheral nervous system. Does that make Guillain–Barré syndrome an autoimmune disease? A demyelinating disease? A post-infectious disease? A peripheral neuropathy? The answer to all of these questions is, basically, *yes*. Because nature does not carve neatly at the joints, it is not always possible to neatly categorize its disorders into mutually exclusive chapters. However, rest assured that we will cover all the important major diseases in due time.

As you read, look for boxes like the one below to highlight the **most clinically relevant information.** If you are short on time, you can rapidly review the information by only looking at the boxes. Each box will also contain a memory aid to help you to get the information to stick. By design, some of the mnemonics and analogies may be silly, shocking, or amusing. This is done in service of making the information more accessible, as provoking an emotional response is a good way of getting information to stick. Nothing in this book is intended to stigmatize, trivialize, or humiliate anyone struggling with any of the disorders mentioned. Instead, the goal is to make the necessary clinical information more accessible to their healthcare providers.

> **Concepts in boxes** are particularly **high-yield**!
>
> An **easy way** to remember them will be in **italics** below.

Before we begin, it's worth pointing out that this book assumes that the reader is familiar with **basic concepts from anatomy, physiology, and cell biology**. Make sure that you have an introductory understanding of things such as action potentials, neurotransmitters, and hormones as well as a background in how various organ systems work, including the circulatory, respiratory, gastrointestinal, genitourinary, immune, endocrine, and musculoskeletal systems. If you feel rusty on any of these subjects, now is a good time to go back and do some reviewing on your own.

Now, let's get started…

2 THE NERVOUS SYSTEM

Neurology is the study of the **nervous system**, or the organ system consisting of all the **neurons** (or nerve cells) in the human body. Neurons are the building blocks of the nervous system in the same way that many bricks come together to make a house. Just as one brick isn't really useful for much, a single neuron on its own is kind of pointless. This is because the primary function of a neuron is to **communicate** with other cells, including muscle cells (telling them to contract), endocrine cells (telling them to release a specific hormone), and—most importantly—other neurons. Understanding how an individual neuron works will be crucial to understanding the nervous system as a whole, so let's start there.

THE NEURON

Like most cells in the human body, a neuron has a **cell body** (also known as a **soma**) where the nucleus, mitochondria, endoplasmic reticulum, and other organelles are housed. The entirety of a neuron's anatomy relates back to its primary function: to communicate. Like an antenna, the neuron needs an apparatus to both **receive and transmit signals**. Neurons communicate by passing along an electrical signal known as an **action potential**. A neuron *receives* signals by way of its **dendrites**, or spiny processes that shoot off from the soma like the branches of a tree to receive signals from other neurons or from the environment. The neuron then *transmits* signals by way of its **axon**, a long slender "tail" that passes along action potentials to other cells. Many axons are wrapped in a fatty substance known as **myelin** which acts to protect the nerve (like tape wrapped around an electrical wire) and to increase the speed of the action potential. A drawing of a typical neuron is found below:

When the signal reaches the **terminal** end of the axon, it causes the release of **neurotransmitters** which then diffuse across the space between cells (known as a **synapse**) and bind to receptors on the dendrites of nearby neurons. By activating these receptors, a new action potential is generated, thereby passing the signal from the **pre-synaptic neuron** to the **post-synaptic neuron** and beginning the cycle anew.

A visual depiction of a synapse is found below:

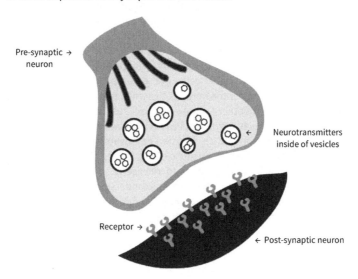

The process of releasing neurotransmitters into the synaptic cleft is found below, going from left to right:

Neurotransmitters are not made on demand when an action potential arrives at a synapse, as manufacturing these chemicals takes time which would slow down the near-instantaneous speed that allows the nervous system to operate as quickly and efficiently as it does. Instead, prior to their release, neurotransmitters are stored in lipid bubbles known as **synaptic vesicles**. When an action potential arrives at a synaptic terminal, it causes an influx of **calcium** ions into the pre-synaptic neuron. Calcium then stimulates a group of protein complexes known as **SNARE proteins** that help guide the vesicles to the cell membrane. Once there, they fuse with the membrane and release their contents into the synapse in a process known as **exocytosis**. You can remember the steps leading to neurotransmitter release by thinking of them being like a group of soldiers marching into battle. **Call**-cium is the battle **call**, and **SNARE** proteins are the battle **drums** marching the neurotransmitters into the synapse.

> **Neurotransmitter release** relies upon an influx of **calcium** into the **pre-synaptic nerve terminal**, which then activates **SNARE proteins** to mediate **vesicle fusion** with the cell membrane.
>
> *Call*-*cium is the battle **call**, and **SNARE** proteins are the battle **drums**.*

THE NERVOUS SYSTEM

While a single neuron is so small you need a microscope to see it, a bunch of neurons grouped together can be visible to the naked eye. A group of neurons running together like this is known as a **nerve**. Together, all of the neurons in the human body comprise the **nervous system** which works to take in information about the environment and then use that information to coordinate the actions of the entire organism.

The nervous system is divided into two parts: the **central nervous system**, which includes the brain and spinal cord, and the **peripheral nervous system**, which consists of all the neurons outside of the central nervous system. The peripheral nervous system is further subdivided into the **somatic nervous system**, which consists of both **sensory** and **motor** nerves carrying information and making movements about which we have conscious awareness, as well as the **autonomic nervous system**, which regulates vital functions such as one's heartbeat, breathing, digestion, urination, and other processes of which we have little conscious awareness. The autonomic nervous system is itself split into two systems: the **sympathetic nervous system** and the **parasympathetic nervous system**. The sympathetic nervous system has an *activating* effect on the body (also known as the "fight or flight" response) while the parasympathetic nervous system promotes more homeostatic processes such as eating and digesting (the so-called "feed and breed, then rest and digest" response). We'll now go over each of these systems in more detail.

THE CENTRAL NERVOUS SYSTEM

The **central nervous system** (sometimes abbreviated CNS) is divided into two main parts: the brain and the spinal cord. The **brain** is the "capital city" of the nervous system and acts as the primary organ that coordinates activity among all the different parts of the body. The brain is divided into three parts: the **cerebrum**, the **cerebellum**, and the **brainstem**. From there, the central nervous system continues on as the **spinal cord**, as seen below:

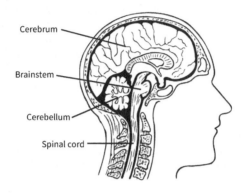

THE CEREBRUM

The cerebrum is the largest part of the brain and is responsible for higher order functions such as learning, memory, communication, sensation, and movement. The outermost layer of the cerebrum, known as the **cerebral cortex**, is made up of neuronal cell bodies. Because the cell bodies themselves are not covered in myelin like the axons are, they have a greyish appearance to the naked eye, so someone thought to give them the imaginative name of "**grey matter**." Underneath the grey

 matter lies the myelinated axons connecting these neurons to one another. Myelin is a fatty substance that appears white, so naturally these axons are called "**white matter**." The cerebrum is split into left and right hemispheres by a deep "canyon" known as the **longitudinal fissure** that runs down the middle of the brain. However, a white matter tract known as the **corpus callosum** exists that connects these two halves of the brain together and allows them to communicate. (You can think of this as the cor-*plus* callo-*sum* to remember that it *adds* the two halves of your brain together.)

The **corpus callosum** connects the **right and left hemispheres** which are separated by the **longitudinal fissure**.

*The cor-**plus** callo-**sum adds** the two halves of the brain together.*

For the most part, similar regions in the left and right parts of the brain do similar things. However, this isn't always the case, as some specific functions are found only on one side or another. Neurologists will often make reference to a **dominant hemisphere** and a **non-dominant hemisphere**. The dominant hemisphere is the one that controls your dominant hand (for most people, the right hand). However, because neurons controlling voluntary muscles cross over from left-to-right and right-to-left on their way down to the peripheral nervous system (for reasons we will talk about further in Chapter 6), the dominant hemisphere ends up being on the *opposite* side as the dominant hand (so a right-handed person has a left-dominant hemisphere, and vice versa). Besides controlling the dominant hand, the dominant hemisphere has a few other jobs to perform, most notably understanding and producing **language**. Up to 99% of right-handed individuals have their language centers in their left cerebral hemisphere, while only around 70% of left-handed individuals do. This makes handedness an important consideration when discussing an individual patient's clinical presentation. (This is why neurologists will often begin talking about a patient by saying, "This is a 76-year-old *right-handed* male..." The fact that he is right-handed means that it is exceedingly likely that his language centers will be located on the left side of his brain, as opposed to a left-handed individual where this is less likely.)

Below the cerebral cortex is the **cerebral subcortex**. The subcortex contains a few key structures that each perform a variety of functions, including fine-tuning movement, directing sensory information to the correct part of the brain, and taking care of such vital processes as eating, drinking, and social bonding.

THE CEREBELLUM

Tucked away in a little space behind the cerebrum is the **cerebellum**, a "little brain" that helps to coordinate complex movements, balance, and posture. (If you're not falling over as you read this, it's probably because your cerebellum is working.) In contrast, someone with a dysfunctional cerebellum will have imprecise, erratic, and uncoordinated movements. So don't let it's "little" status fool you—the cerebellum plays a big role in movement despite its diminutive size.

THE BRAINSTEM

If the brain is the capital city, then the **brainstem** is the "bridge" connecting the brain to the "highway" of the spinal cord. While learning to associate the brainstem with the word "bridge" early on is helpful, it threatens to obscure the fact that the brainstem is so much more than *just* a bridge. Indeed, the brainstem is not just an inert lump of tissue over which other more important neurons cross. Instead, the three parts of the brainstem—the **midbrain**, **pons**, and **medulla oblongata**—perform a variety of functions all their own, with many of these being among the most vital and basic to survival such as breathing, sleeping, and maintaining a heart beat. The brainstem is so essential for survival that most medical practitioners will only consider someone "brain dead" once it is clear that the brainstem has stopped functioning. (Compare this to someone who has suffered a widespread loss of cerebral tissue, who may technically still be considered "alive" because their heartbeat and respiration are continuing on their own due to an intact brainstem.)

THE SPINAL CORD

The **spinal cord** is the final part of the central nervous system. It acts as a "highway" connecting neurons traveling between the brain and the organs in the rest of the body. Like the brain, the spinal cord is made up of both grey matter and white matter. However, the pattern here is reversed, with the grey matter on the *inside* and the white matter on the *outside*.

Like any highway, the spinal cord travels in a central location. When it comes time to go to their final destinations in the muscles, skin, and organs scattered throughout the body, these nerves form "exits" from the central highway around the level at which their target organ lies. Like a real highway exit, these nerves have both an "on-ramp" and an "off-ramp," with motor nerves getting *off* the highway exiting on the *anterior* side of the spinal cord while sensory nerves getting *on* the highway enter on the *posterior* side. These **nerve roots** join together to form two-way "side streets" known as **spinal nerves** that go on to innervate the target organs directly. (Some nerves exit directly from the brain rather than first traveling in the spinal cord. These are known as **cranial nerves**.) Together, cranial nerves and spinal nerves collectively form the peripheral nervous system, which is where we will now turn our attention.

*Note the resemblance to highway **on-ramps** and **off-ramps**.*

Nerves from the brain cross the **brainstem** and travel via the **spinal cord** to the level of their target organ. They then exit the spinal cord as **peripheral nerves**.

Some words to associate for now:
Brain – Capital city
Brainstem – Bridge
Spinal cord – Highway
Peripheral nerves – Side streets

THE PERIPHERAL NERVOUS SYSTEM

The **peripheral nervous system** is made up of all the nerves connecting target organs to the central nervous system. These nerves have one of two functions: either they are **sensory nerves** transmitting information about the environment *up to* the central nervous system, or they are **motor nerves** carrying instructions *down from* the central nervous system to enact out a certain response. Nerves carrying sensory information are also known as **afferent** nerves while those carrying motor signals are also called **efferent** nerves. You can remember the difference between afferent and efferent nerves by thinking that **A**fferent nerves **A**scend to **A**lert the brain while e**F**ferent nerves **F**low down to e**F**fect change. The afferent division is the simpler of the two, and it is where we will head next.

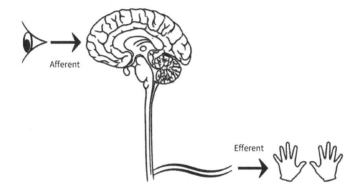

Afferent nerves carry **sensory information** up to the central nervous system while **efferent nerves** carry **motor signals** down from the central nervous system.

*A*fferent nerves *A*scend to *A*lert the brain while
e*F*ferent nerves *F*low down to e*F*fect change.

THE AFFERENT DIVISION

The **afferent division** acts to relay information about the environment to the central nervous system so that someone can respond appropriately to their situation. Sensory information comes in a few different varieties including **touch, pain, temperature, vibration,** and **proprioception** (with proprioception being one's sense of the position of their body parts in space, as in your ability to tell if someone has lifted your arm up or down even if your eyes are closed). We also have additional other sensory modalities that instead come from specialized **sense organs,** like the eyes and ears, that are specifically structured to provide unique forms of information about the environment. These **special senses** are **vision, hearing, balance, smell,** and **taste** (each of which we will cover in more detail in Chapter 9).

While seemingly a simple concept, the sense of touch requires some additional explanation. The sense of touch is really *two* senses: **crude touch** (also known as non-discriminative touch) and **fine touch** (also called discriminative touch). Crude touch can only tell you whether or not you are being touched, while fine touch involves nerves that are sensitive enough to distinguish between two contact points in the same area. You can test this on yourself using two pin points both on the tip of your finger and on the back of your hand. With your eyes closed, you will be able to tell the difference between two points with your finger much better than with the back of your hand, as your fingertips are better of the two at fine touch.

There are two types of neurons carrying sensory information from the skin. The first kind, known as **protopathic** neurons, carries information about **crude touch**, **pain**, and **temperature**. In contrast, the second kind, known as **epicritic** neurons, carries information about **fine touch**, **vibration**, and **proprioception**. Protopathic and epicritic neurons have a few key differences. First, they travel in different parts of the spinal cord (this will become important when we talk about the various forms of spinal cord injury in Chapter 7). In addition, epicritic neurons are **myelinated**, meaning they have that insulating sheath wrapped around them to enable action potentials to travel more quickly down axons, while protopathic neurons are **unmyelinated** and carry action potentials much more slowly (this will come into play clinically when talking about demyelinating diseases in Chapter 21). For now, just remember the distinction between the two by thinking of **proto**pathic nerves as carrying the "lower" or "baser" senses that likely developed first (which makes sense as "**proto**-" means "primitive") while epi**critic** should make you think of a snobby **critic** who thinks he is better than everyone else with his "finer" or "more sophisticated" senses.

Protopathic neurons carry information about **crude touch**, **pain**, and **temperature** while **epicritic neurons** carry information about **fine touch**, **vibration**, and **proprioception**.

Proto means *"primitive"* so the **proto**pathic senses are more **basic**, while a snobby epi**critic** thinks he has **more sophisticated senses** than everyone else.

While these different sensory modalities travel *separately* in the spinal cord, they travel *together* in the peripheral nervous system as cranial and spinal nerves. Each spinal nerve (and some cranial nerves) is responsible for innervating a specific area known as its **dermatome**. (For example, the spinal nerve that exits from the spinal column below the tenth thoracic vertebra innervates the area around the belly button.) We'll go over dermatomes in more detail in Chapter 8.

THE EFFERENT DIVISION

While the afferent division helps to bring information about the environment *into* the central nervous system, this would be pointless without the ability to *respond to* this information. (For example, just being able to *see* a swarm of bees flying towards you doesn't really help that much. It is only if you are able to *act* on this information by running away that the information confers any advantage.) This is where the **efferent division** comes into play. By enabling an organism to not just be *aware* of its environment but to *respond* to it as well, the efferent division completes the function of the nervous system.

The efferent division acts in two distinct ways that form the basis for a *further* subdivision of the nervous system. The **somatic nervous system** involves sending signals to muscles throughout the body to enable **voluntary movements** such as walking, eating, stretching, and working with our hands. In contrast, the **autonomic nervous system** effects changes in bodily processes that we do *not* have conscious awareness of or control over, including our heart rate, blood pressure, and release of certain hormones. We'll talk about the somatic nervous system first.

THE SOMATIC NERVOUS SYSTEM

The somatic nervous system involves all of the skeletal muscles over which we have direct voluntary control. (It's worth pointing out that many of these muscles can involve *both* voluntary and involuntary control. For example, the muscles we use to breathe or blink will contract without our conscious input most of the time. However, if we choose to, we can hold our breath or shut our eyes.)

Similar to the afferent division and its dermatomes, different muscles in the body are innervated by specific cranial and spinal nerves, with the muscle groups that a particular motor nerve innervates known as its **myotome**. Efferent nerves carry signals down from the brain to the muscles and meet them at the **neuromuscular junction**, or the point at which the axon of a motor neuron terminates onto the muscle. When an action potential arrives at the neuromuscular junction, it triggers an influx of **calcium** ions into the neuron. The neuron then releases a neurotransmitter known as **acetylcholine** (ACh) into the synapse between the neuron and the muscle. Acetylcholine binds to a specific type of acetylcholine receptor known as a **nicotinic receptor** on the muscle itself, which causes the muscle to depolarize and contract. (The process is overall quite similar to what happens at most synapses except that the post-synaptic cell is a muscle cell rather than another neuron.) We will talk about diseases specific to the neuromuscular junction in more detail in Chapter 15.

THE AUTONOMIC NERVOUS SYSTEM

In contrast to the somatic nervous system (where there is usually some degree of conscious control over the impulses that are sent down), the effects of the **autonomic nervous system** are not things that we can control directly and, in some cases, are not even visible to us. (For example, can you tell whether your pancreas is secreting insulin at this exact moment?) For this reason, the autonomic nervous system can be initially more difficult to comprehend. It is best thought of as our body's attempt to take care of the basics (like digesting food and circulating blood through our bodies) so that our conscious awareness can be reserved for more complicated things like cooking dinner or doing math.

The autonomic nervous system is itself divided into two opposing forces: the **sympathetic nervous system** and the **parasympathetic nervous system**. These systems should be familiar to you if you've studied physiology, but we'll briefly review them here, starting with the parasympathetic nervous system.

PARASYMPATHETIC NERVOUS SYSTEM

The **parasympathetic nervous system** is activated when the body doesn't have any immediate stresses to face down and is able to focus on **homeostatic activities** like resting, eating, urinating, defecating, and reproducing (**"feed and breed**, then **rest and digest"**). The parasympathetic nervous system largely arises from nerves coming directly from the brain as well as the spinal nerves coming out of the sacral vertebrae and is therefore said to have **craniosacral** outflow.

> The **parasympathetic nervous system** is activated in the **absence of immediate stressors** and promotes **homeostatic functions** such as feeding and reproducing.
>
> Think *"**feed and breed**, then **rest and digest**."*

The parasympathetic nervous system uses the neurotransmitter **acetylcholine** at all of its synapses (both the one near the spinal cord and the one closer to the target organ). However, despite the same *neurotransmitter* being found at both synapses, different *receptors* are found in each of these synapses. At the first synapse acetylcholine binds to a **nicotinic receptor**, while at the target organ it binds to a

different kind of receptor known as a **muscarinic receptor**. This becomes clinically important because certain drugs and diseases affect one type of acetylcholine receptor but not the other, leading to different presentations depending on which are involved. You can remember the effects of *muscarinic* receptor activation using the mnemonic **SLUDG-E BM**, with BM being a common medical abbreviation for a bowel movement (making this mnemonic an unpleasant but highly relevant mental image). SLUDG-E BM stands for **S**alivation, **L**acrimation (excessive tear production), **U**rination, **D**iaphoresis (excessive sweating), **G**astrointestinal hypermotility, **E**mesis, **B**radycardia (slow heart rate), and **M**iosis (constricted pupils). (The M at the end of the mnemonic should remind you that these are the effects of acetylcholine at *Muscarinic* receptors, not nicotinic.)

Muscarinic acetylcholine receptors are responsible for most of the **efferent effects** of the **parasympathetic nervous system**.

*SLUDG-E BM: (with the **M** reminding you of the **M**uscarinic receptor)*
Salivation
Lacrimation
Urination
Diaphoresis
Gastrointestinal hypermotility
Emesis
Bradycardia
Miosis

In contrast, the effects of nicotinic receptors largely involve the **motor system** (remember that nicotinic receptors are the ones at the neuromuscular junction) and the higher processes of the brain, where nicotinic receptors are involved in things like **memory** and **behavior**. You can remember this by thinking of **Nic's muscle memory.**

Nicotinic acetylcholine receptors are involved in the **motor system** and in **higher cognitive processes** such as memory and behavior.

*Think of **Nic's muscle memory**.*

THE SYMPATHETIC NERVOUS SYSTEM
In contrast to the parasympathetic nervous system and its "feed and breed, then rest and digest" functions, the **sympathetic nervous system** is used to generate a **"fight or flight"** state in response to a threat (whether that is a physical threat like a swarm of bees or a more social one like giving a speech in public). If the central nervous system recognizes a threat, the sympathetic nervous system kicks into high gear and makes the heart beat faster, the airway open wider, and the pupils dilate (among many other things) to enable us to either fight the threat or run away from it. While the *para*sympathetic nervous system has craniosacral outflow, the sympathetic nervous system largely arises from nerves coming off of the spinal cord in the thoracic and lumbar regions and is therefore said to have **thoracolumbar** outflow.

> The **sympathetic nervous system** is activated in the **presence of immediate stressors** to enable a **physiologic response to the threat**.
>
> Think *"fight or flight."*

In contrast to the parasympathetic nervous system (which uses the same neurotransmitter at both synapses, even if the *receptor* differs between the two), the sympathetic nervous system uses a different neurotransmitter at each synapse. At the synapse near the spinal cord, acetylcholine binds to a *nicotinic* receptor. However, at

the synapse near the target organ, a different neurotransmitter known as **norepinephrine** is used. This is true across all organs in the body that respond to the sympathetic nervous system with the sole *exception* of **sweat glands**! At sweat glands, acetylcholine is used again, with a *muscarinic* receptor. (This explains why **D**iaphoresis is the **D** in SLU**D**G-E BM. While normally sweating is a *sympathetic* function, because it involves the muscarinic acetylcholine receptor, widespread activation of muscarinic receptors will include sweating in addition to the other *para*sympathetic effects.)

For future reference, a quick review of the neurotransmitters and receptors used in the parasympathetic, sympathetic, and somatic nervous systems is found below, with N standing for nicotinic receptors and M standing for muscarinic. (We haven't talked about anterior horn cells yet, but we'll go over them in Chapter 7 when we discuss the spinal cord.)

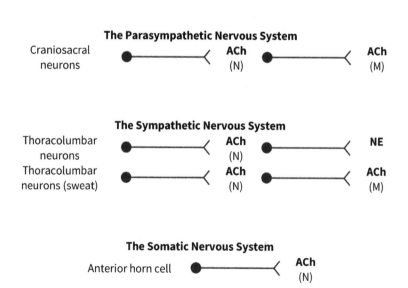

GLIAL CELLS

We first learned about the nervous system at the level of the neuron, then we zoomed out to look at the nervous system on the scale of the whole person. To finish off, we're going to jump back to the microscopic level to talk about other cells belonging to the nervous system that are *not* neurons but are still essential for neuronal functioning. Just as you need more than just bricks to make a house (with additional materials like mortar and rebar being required to support the structure of the building), neurons rely on a variety of support cells to function. These support cells are collectively known as **glial cells** (from the Greek for "glue") and come in a few varieties.

OLIGODENDROGLIA AND SCHWANN CELLS

Myelin is not made by the neuron itself. Instead, it is created by two types of glial cells: **oligodendroglia** (each one of which provides myelin for *multiple* neurons in the *central* nervous system) and **Schwann cells** (which live in the *peripheral* nervous system and only myelinate a *single* neuron each). Diseases of these myelin-producing cells can result in poor signal transmission and inadequate nerve functioning. One fact that will become important when we talk about nervous system tumors is that oligodendroglia have a characteristic "fried egg" appearance under the microscope as seen below. File this away as a bit of trivia for now, but it will come into play later.

Oligodendrocytes myelinate multiple neurons in the **central nervous system** and have a **fried egg** appearance when examined under a microscope.

Think of them as ol-egg-odendroglia.

Schwann cells myelinate a **single neuron** in the **peripheral nervous system.**

Sch-wann cells can myelinate only wann (one) cell at a time.

ASTROCYTES AND SATELLITE CELLS

Astrocytes and **satellite cells** are the **support staff** of the nervous system. They help to provide nutrients to neurons, maintain a clean and non-toxic extracellular environment, regulate blood flow, and repair neurons following an injury—all in all, pretty helpful little guys. Like with the myelin-producing cells, they differ between the two halves of the nervous system, with astrocytes being found exclusively in the *central* nervous system while satellite cells are found in the *peripheral* nervous system. To remember the location and function of astrocytes and satellite cells, connect **astros** (stars) and **satellites** with the mental image of **space**. This

will help you think of these cells as being located in the *space* around the neuron where they help to support the *stars* of the show.

> **Astrocytes** and **satellite cells** help to **support neurons** in a variety of ways.
>
> *Astros (stars) and satellites are found in the space between neurons.*

EPENDYMAL CELLS

The **ependyma** is a thin layer of cells lining the **ventricular system**. (We will talk more about the ventricular system in Chapter 10, but by way of a brief introduction it is a series of cavities inside the brain and spinal cord through which a liquid known as **cerebrospinal fluid** flows.) Ependymal cells are involved in not only producing the cerebrospinal fluid but also helping to circulate it and absorb it back into the system. To link the ependyma to its role regulating cerebrospinal fluid, try to imagine dipping an e-**pen**-dyma in (cerebrospinal) **fluid** to write.

> The **ependyma** is a thin layer of cells lining the **ventricular system** where it is involved in **producing, circulating, and absorbing cerebrospinal fluid.**
>
> *Visualize dipping an e-**pen**-dyma in (cerebrospinal) **fluid**.*

MICROGLIA

Microglial cells are found in the central nervous system where they help to protect the brain and spinal cord from infectious diseases by, basically, eating them (a process known as **phagocytosis**). In this way, microglial cells are part of both the nervous system and the immune system.

PUTTING IT ALL TOGETHER

To recap: the nervous system is made up of specialized cells known as **neurons** as well as various supporting cells known as **glial cells**. The main function of a neuron is to communicate which it does by sending electrical signals known as **action potentials** to muscles, glands, and other nerves.

The nervous system is divided between the **central nervous system** (consisting of the brain and spinal cord) and the **peripheral nervous system** (everything else). The peripheral nervous system itself is divided between the **afferent division** (which carries sensory information) and the **efferent division** (which carries motor signals). The efferent division is divided into the **somatic nervous system** (which innervates skeletal muscles over which we have conscious control) and the **autonomic nervous system** (which innervates internal organs over which we have little conscious awareness). Finally, the autonomic nervous system is itself further subdivided into the **sympathetic nervous system** ("fight or flight") and the **parasympathetic nervous system** ("feed and breed, then rest and digest"). Whew! A visual recap of the organization of the nervous system is found below.

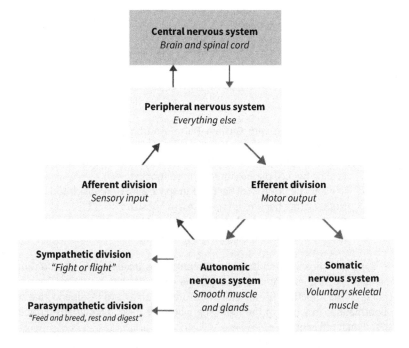

We've covered a lot of ground here, and unfortunately not a lot of it is going to be *immediately* relevant in a clinical sense. Nevertheless, it is important to absorb all of the concepts here because they will come back to haunt us in later chapters. Don't feel like you need to have complete understanding yet, as learning more about the anatomy and pathology of the nervous system in the rest of the book will reinforce and deepen your comprehension of these concepts as we continue our journey through the nervous system.

REVIEW QUESTIONS

1. A 43 y/o F who works on a farm accidentally ingests an unknown quantity of an insecticide. Upon arrival to the hospital, she is suffering from severe nausea with copious vomiting, diarrhea with fecal incontinence, excessive tear and saliva production, and diffuse sweating across her entire body. On examination, her pupils are narrow and non-reactive to light as seen in the image below:

   Which of the following signs and symptoms seen in insecticide poisoning is *not* also seen in cases of extreme parasympathetic nervous system excitation?
   A. Nausea and vomiting
   B. Diarrhea
   C. Lacrimation
   D. Salivation
   E. Diaphoresis
   F. Miosis

2. A 46 y/o F is diagnosed with Guillain–Barré syndrome, a disease in which the immune system attacks the myelin sheath of peripheral nerves. Which of the following actions or processes is *least* likely to be affected by this disease?
   A. Feeling her cell phone vibrating in her pocket
   B. Sensing the position of her hand in space with her eyes closed
   C. Noticing that her arm is too close to a hot stove
   D. Being able to tell whether she is being poked by one needle or two
   E. Taking a kickboxing class

3. An 8 y/o M is hospitalized due to a *Streptococcus pneumoniae* infection of the meninges, or the membranes covering the central nervous system. During the course of the infection, he sustains widespread damage to his ependymal cells. Abnormalities in which of the following would be most directly attributable to ependymal cell injury?
   A. Nervous tissue of the brain
   B. Nervous tissue of the spinal cord
   C. Peripheral nerves
   D. Arterial blood
   E. Venous blood
   F. Cerebrospinal fluid
   G. None of the above

4. A 53 y/o F begins taking amitriptyline, a potent antidepressant with strong anticholinergic effects at muscarinic receptors. Which of the following side effects is she *least* likely to experience?
   A. Blurred vision
   B. Dry mouth
   C. Constipation
   D. Rapid heart rate
   E. Excessive urination

1. **The best answer is E.** Some insecticides contain organophosphates, a poison that causes acetylcholine to build up in synapses across the body. This leads to the characteristic SLUDG-E BM signs and symptoms due to hyperactivation of muscarinic receptors. Because acetylcholine is the neurotransmitter found in synapses across the parasympathetic nervous system, signs and symptoms of organophosphate poisoning often resemble a state of parasympathetic nervous system excitation (answers A–D, F). One exception to this is sweating, which is related to the *sympathetic* nervous system. While the sympathetic nervous system generally uses norepinephrine (rather than acetylcholine) as its primary neurotransmitter, in the case of sweating the neurotransmitter at both of the synapses involved is acetylcholine.

2. **The best answer is C.** A demyelinating disease will primarily affect those processes that travel on myelinated, rather than unmyelinated, neurons. This means that vibration (answer A), proprioception (answer B), and discriminative touch (answer D) are all likely to be impaired. Neurons controlling voluntary movement are also myelinated, so some degree of motor weakness is likely to be observed as well (answer E). The primary processes that would not be affected are non-discriminative touch, heat sensation, and pain sensation, as these signals travel on unmyelinated neurons.

3. **The best answer is F.** Ependymal cells can be found lining the ventricular system, or the series of cavities through which cerebrospinal fluid flows in the brain. Because of this, damage to ependymal cells can cause dysfunction in cerebrospinal fluid flow and volume, including an excessive build-up of fluid in the ventricular system known as hydrocephalus. While dysregulation of cerebrospinal fluid may have downstream effects on nervous tissues and/or the blood vessels traveling through them (answers A–E), the most direct effect of ependymal damage will be on cerebrospinal fluid itself.

4. **The best answer is E.** Another question on acetylcholine! This time however we are looking at what happens when acetylcholine's effects are reduced rather than increased. To understand what is happening here, assume that anticholinergic effects will be the exact opposite of what is seen in the SLUDG-E BM mnemonic, with constricted pupils turning into dilated ones (answer A), salivation turning into dry mouth (answer B), gastrointestinal hypermotility turning into constipation (answer C), and bradycardia turning into tachycardia (answer D). Excessive urination is unlikely to be seen with use of anticholinergic drugs, with urinary *retention* being more common.

3 THE CEREBRAL CORTEX

Now that we have talked about the organization of the nervous system as a whole, it's time to talk in more detail about its individual components. We will begin with the **central nervous system** before moving onto the peripheral nervous system. Our first stop will be the **brain** which is the "capital city" of the entire nervous system, as it is the organ that most sensory information is sent up *to* and where most motor impulses come down *from*. At first glance, the brain can seem like a giant amorphous blob, especially given that it has a physical consistency not unlike Jell-O or uncooked tofu. Yet within this lump of nervous tissue lies a surprisingly high degree of structure and organization. This is because **neurons that serve similar purposes tend to cluster together**, and for this reason the brain can be described in terms of **distinct anatomical regions**, each with a specific function or set of functions. This organization forms the basis for the field of **neuroanatomy** which will be our focus for the first half of this book.

To begin our study of neuroanatomy in earnest, we will look first at the cerebrum. Because the cerebrum is the largest part of the brain by size, it is easier to break it down further rather than covering it as a single entity. For this reason, we will start first with the *outer* region known as the **cerebral cortex** before discussing the deeper underlying structures known as the **subcortex** in the next chapter. In this way, we'll be working from the outside in, like peeling an apple. The cerebral cortex is largely made up of **grey matter** (which, as you'll recall from the previous chapter, consists of neuronal cell *bodies*, as compared to white matter which consists of myelinated neuronal *axons*). The neuronal cell bodies contained in the grey matter of the cerebral cortex play key roles in many of the "higher functions" that make us human, including making plans, performing actions, learning information, sensing our environment, and feeling emotions. (This contrasts with many of the structures in the subcortex which perform functions that are more basic to survival such as hunger, thirst, and sleep.) The cerebral cortex is itself divided into four lobes known as the **frontal lobe**, **parietal lobe**, **occipital lobe**, and **temporal lobe**. Each of these carries out distinct functions, as we will discover next. You can remember the order of the four lobes from front-to-back and top-to-bottom with the acronym **FPOT**.

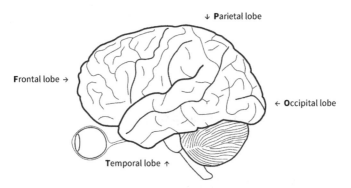

The **cerebral cortex** is responsible for **higher cognitive functions** and is divided into **four lobes**, each of which has unique functions.

*From front-to-back and top-to-bottom, the lobes are **FPOT***:
F*rontal lobe*
P*arietal lobe*
O*ccipital lobe*
T*emporal lobe*

THE FRONTAL LOBE

The **frontal lobe** is found just behind the forehead and is the "brainiest" part of the brain. In particular, a region at the front of the frontal lobe called the **prefrontal cortex** (essentially the front-most part of the front-most part of the brain) is involved in **executive functions** such as decision-making and planning. For example, when you are making a complex decision, you may try to weigh the potential benefits ("This job has a much higher salary…") as well as the downsides ("…but the commute would be so much longer."). When doing this, you are primarily using your prefrontal cortex. The frontal lobe is also involved in planning complex tasks that require multiple thoughts and ideas to be held in mind at once, such as a chef keeping track of a multiple dishes or an architect drawing up plans for a new house.

Another important task of the prefrontal cortex is to **say "no" to other parts of the brain**. The brain is a complex organ with many different parts which each have their own goals and priorities, so it shouldn't come as a surprise that these parts will end up disagreeing with each other at times. For example, if you sit down to a meal with friends while you are hungry, one part of your brain (the hypothalamus, which we will learn about in the next chapter) will give off hunger signals, tempting you to immediately start eating all the food around you. However, when you notice that not everyone's food has arrived yet, your prefrontal cortex steps in to inhibit this initial impulse, bringing your behavior in line with social norms and allowing you to avoid the social embarrassment of bad manners. In contrast, people who have sustained damage to their frontal lobe often become unable to override their baser instincts, leading to impulsive, inappropriate, and even aggressive behavior.

Finally, the back of the frontal lobe contains the **primary motor cortex** from which efferent signals in the **somatic nervous system** originate to control **voluntary movement**. Most actions that you do voluntarily and with some degree of conscious effort, such as hitting a ball with a racket or giving someone a high-five, are based off of an initial signal that is generated in your motor cortex. (This signal is not sent directly to your muscles. Rather, it is altered and refined in the basal ganglia, which we will talk about in the next chapter.) Various parts of the body are mapped to specific places in the motor cortex in a predictable way, with the lower extremities being controlled from the *medial* part of the brain (closer to the longitudinal fissure) while the upper extremities and facial muscles are controlled from the *lateral* part. This becomes clinically relevant because the medial part of the motor cortex is supplied by a different artery than the lateral part, so you can often successfully figure out the location of a stroke based on which muscle groups have become unresponsive (with weakness of the lower limbs suggesting a different artery than weakness of the upper limbs). To remember that the motor cortex lies in the front part of the brain, think of the brain as being like a standard car with the motor (engine) in the front.

The **primary motor cortex** lies in the **frontal lobe**.

*It's **like a car**: the **motor** is in the **front**.*

THE PARIETAL LOBE

The **parietal lobe** lies just behind the frontal lobe and is separated from it by the **central sulcus**, a deep groove making a "canyon" between the two lobes. The parietal lobe is involved in processing **sensory information** from different parts of the body.

Neurons carrying each of the main sensory modalities we talked about earlier (both protopathic neurons carrying crude touch, pain, and temperature as well as epicritic neurons carrying fine touch, pressure, and proprioception) travel from the body to the **primary somatosensory cortex** which lies just behind the central sulcus. The somatosensory cortex is similar to the motor cortex in that specific parts of the body are mapped to specific areas of the brain, with the same overall pattern (lower parts more medial, upper parts more lateral). The image below shows a rough approximation of how various body parts are mapped to the motor and sensory cortices, with motor on the left and sensory on the right. You'll notice that some parts of the body are bigger than others. This is because the number of sensory neurons does *not* necessarily correlate with the physical size of the organ! For example, while the hand is smaller than the leg, it is more densely innervated and sensitive to stimuli (especially fine touch) so it takes up more real estate in the parietal lobe.

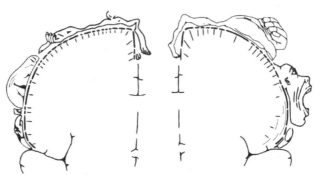

*The localization of various body parts to the **primary motor cortex** (left) and the **primary somatosensory cortex** (right).*

More than just responding to each of the senses on an individual basis, the parietal lobe is also involved in maintaining an **awareness of one's environment**. This can be seen in people who suffer damage to their non-dominant parietal lobe, as they often show signs of **hemineglect** or a general ignorance of sensory information coming from one side. For example, if you ask them to draw a clock, they may draw the numbers entirely on the one side only. This is not because the nerves carrying this sensory information are damaged but rather because the part of the brain set up to gather them (the parietal lobe) cannot receive them properly. To remember the association of the parietal lobe to sensation and awareness, think of it as the **pariah**-tal lobe. A **pariah** is an outcast who could be quite **sensitive** to criticism, just as the pariah-tal lobe is quite sensitive to sensory information coming from the body.

The **parietal lobe** is the site of the **primary somatosensory cortex**.

*The **pariah**-tal lobe is quite **sensitive** (**sensory**).*

THE OCCIPITAL LOBE

The occipital lobe is the smallest of the four lobes and is found in the back-most part of the brain. It is quite specialized in its function and primarily serves as the site of the **visual cortex**. In contrast to sensory information from the body (which goes to the parietal lobe), special sensory information from the **eyes** instead travels to the occipital cortex where the information is processed into conscious awareness (the picture that we actually "see"). You can remember that the occipital lobe is the place of the visual cortex by thinking that **oc**ular information (such as the pictures that you see through bin**oc**ulars) goes straight back from the eyes to the **oc**cipital lobe.

The **occipital lobe** is the site of the **visual cortex**.

Sensory information from binoculars goes to the occipital lobe.

When the occipital lobe is damaged, varying degrees of visual impairment or even blindness can occur. This is illustrated in a rare but fascinating disorder known as **Anton's syndrome**. Someone with Anton's syndrome is completely blind as a result of damage to the occipital lobe. However, if asked they will adamantly deny that they are blind and will simply make up answers to any questions that they are asked involving sight. While Anton's syndrome is extremely rare, its usefulness in demonstrating the function of the occipital lobe makes it often show up on test questions. To remember the syndrome, make **ANTON** stand for **A**dmit **N**ot **T**o **O**ccipital **N**on-function.

Damage to the occipital lobe can result in a state of **cortical blindness** known as **Anton's syndrome**.

ANTON: Admit Not To Occipital Non-function.

THE TEMPORAL LOBE

The final lobe of the cerebrum is the **temporal lobe** which is the lowest part of the cortex, located to the sides just above the **ears**. This placement makes sense, as the temporal lobe is the site of the **auditory cortex**. Like the visual cortex in the occipital lobe, the auditory cortex receives special sensory information from the ears and processes it into the sound that we actually "hear." You can remember the association of the temporal lobes with hearing by thinking that the **tempo**-ral lobe helps you to hear the **tempo** of music. (The temporal cortex has a variety of other functions in addition to processing sound, including being a primary site where emotions are generated and memories are stored. We will talk about these later on in this chapter when we discuss the limbic system.)

The **temporal lobe** is the site of the **auditory cortex**.

The **tempo**-*ral lobe helps you hear the* **tempo** *of music.*

LANGUAGE CENTERS

Comprehending and producing language is an incredibly complex task, so it should come as no surprise that it involves multiple regions of the brain. A few areas of the brain in particular have been found to be particularly important in the use of language. These **language centers** are spread throughout the various lobes of the cerebrum, although they work together as a coherent unit. It's important to note that language centers are not only involved in speech but also play a role in any form of language-based communication, including reading, writing, and signing.

The first language center we will discuss is **Broca's area** which is located in the **frontal lobe** of the dominant hemisphere and is responsible for language **production**. Someone who sustains damage to Broca's area will have trouble producing language, a type of condition known as an **expressive aphasia**. While some people with an expressive aphasia are completely mute, most are able to speak but may put forth great effort to produce even a few words. (For example, when asked to repeat the sentence, "The orange cat walked through the open door," someone with an expressive aphasia may only be able to say, "Cat............ door..........") To remember the association of Broca's area with an expressive aphasia, think of a **pull string doll** that is supposed to talk when you pull the string. If the doll is **Broca** (broken), then it won't talk.

Broca's area is responsible for **language production**. Damage to this region results in an impaired ability to produce language known as an **expressive aphasia**.

*Think of a **pull string doll** that will talk when you pull on its string.*
*If this becomes **Broca** (broken), then the doll **won't talk**.*

The second area involved in language is **Wernicke's area** which lies at the part of the brain where the **temporal and parietal lobes** meet. Wernicke's area is responsible for language **comprehension**, so someone with damage to this area will have difficulty understanding the words that are being said to them, a type of condition known as a **receptive aphasia**. Someone with a receptive aphasia may still be able to speak with the normal rhythm, tone, and musical flow that most speech has, although the content of what is being said is often nonsensical and may even incorporate made-up words known as **neologisms** (as in the sentence "Shemucker froos be sunt."). You can remember the association of receptive aphasia with Wernicke's area by thinking that someone with receptive aphasia can still be quite **Wer**-dy (even if the words don't actually make sense most of the time).

Wernicke's area is responsible for **language comprehension**. Damage here results in an impaired ability to comprehend language known as **Wernicke's aphasia**.

*Someone with **Wer**nicke's aphasia can still be quite **Wer**-dy.*

A bundle of axons known as the **arcuate fasciculus** connects Broca's area to Wernicke's area and allows someone to use what is being said to them to inform what they say back. Someone with a damaged arcuate fasciculus will be able to both speak and understand language, but they will not be able to accurately repeat something that is spoken to them (known as a **conduction aphasia**).

The **arcuate fasciculus** connects Wernicke's area to Broca's area. Damage to the arcuate fasciculus results in a **conduction aphasia**.

*Without an **accurate** fasciculus, you cannot **accurately** repeat what someone just said.*

Finally, someone who sustains damage to multiple parts of their language centers may develop a **global aphasia** in which both language production and comprehension are profoundly impaired. Keep the various forms of aphasia in mind, as they can be key to localizing a lesion (for example, someone who comes into the hospital for a stroke and is unable to speak has likely sustained damage in a different part of the brain compared to someone who is unable to understand what you're saying to them).

THE LIMBIC SYSTEM

Our final stop in this chapter is the **limbic system**. "Limbic" is Latin for "border," and this region is so-named because it lies at the border between the cerebrum and lower structures like the brainstem. The limbic system is not an *anatomically* distinct region but rather one whose various parts are united by a shared *function*: specifically, regulation of **emotion, memory, motivation,** and **behavior**. Because the boundaries of this system are functional rather than anatomic, there are many parts of the brain that could technically be classified as being in the limbic system. However, for the sake of simplicity we will limit our discussion to just a core few that are universally considered to be a part of the limbic system: the **amygdala**, the **hippocampus**, the **mammillary bodies**, the **nucleus accumbens**, and the **anterior cingulate cortex**. While some of these structures lie in areas that we haven't talked about yet (such as the subcortex and the brainstem), overall they all contribute to the "higher order" cognitive processes of emotion, memory, and behavior, so we will cover them here.

THE AMYGDALA

The **amygdala** is a paired group of neuronal cell bodies lying on the inner part of the **temporal cortex** that determines our **emotional response to stimuli**. For example, if a mountain lion suddenly jumps out at you from behind the bushes while you are out camping in the woods, you will likely feel an immediate rush of fear. This is because your amygdala has judged this situation to be potentially dangerous and has activated parts of your body (such as the sympathetic nervous system and its "fight or flight" response) to take action. More than just being involved with our *immediate* response to stimuli, the amygdala is directly involved in the formation of **long-term memory and decision-making**. The next time someone asks you to go walking in that part of the woods, the memory of the mountain lion will likely pop into your mind and factor

into your decision to accept or decline their invitation. The amygdala exerts a powerful effect on our lives through its effect on our emotions. You can remember the function of the amygdala by thinking of it as the **emo**gdala to associate it with our **emo**tional response to certain stimuli.

The **amygdala** is involved in determining our **emotional response to stimuli** as well as forming **long-term emotional memories**.

*The **emo**-gdala is strongly involved in our **emo**-tions.*

Damage to the amygdala can result in **Klüver-Bucy syndrome**. One of the most common findings in Klüver-Bucy syndrome is a **diminished or absent fear response** to frightening stimuli (often described as a "docility" or "tameness"). There is also an **inability to form new memories or recall old ones** which further underscores the amygdala's role in memory formation. Klüver-Bucy syndrome can also present with

hyperorality (a tendency to put non-food objects in the mouth) and **hypersexuality**, two features that are also shared with disorders involving the frontal lobe.

THE HIPPOCAMPUS

The **hippocampus** is a pair of seahorse-shaped structures that, like the amygdala, lies on the inner side of the temporal cortex and is involved in the formation of memories. In particular, the hippocampus is involved in **consolidating short-term memories into long-term ones**. All of us have the ability to keep track of information for a short amount of time (such as needing to keep a phone number in mind only long enough to dial it). Without the need to remember this for more than a few seconds, this information is quickly forgotten. In contrast, if the information is deemed important (for example, if it is the phone number of someone that we are very attracted to) then we will be much more likely to commit that information to long-term memory. Someone who sustains bilateral damage to their hippocampi will often experience a profound inability to form new emotional memories. The hippocampus is also one of the first structures to show evidence of damage in disorders like Alzheimer's disease in which loss of memory plays a key role. You can remember the function of the hippocampus by thinking of going to a school dance and seeing that someone has brought a hippopotamus as their date. If you see a "**hippo** on **campus**," you will almost certainly **remember** it.

The **hippocampus** is involved in **forming new memories** and **recalling old ones**.

*If you saw a "**hippo** on **campus**," you would almost certainly **remember** it.*

THE MAMMILLARY BODIES

The **mammillary bodies** are a pair of round structures that lie on the underside of the brain (not the cortex!) and are connected to both the amygdala and the hippocampus. Given the involvement of both of these structures, it shouldn't be too surprising that the **mam**millary bodies are closely involved with the process of **mam**ory.

A pair of round mammillary bodies as seen on autopsy.

The **mammillary bodies** are connected to both the **amygdala** and the **hippocampus** and play a key role in **memory formation**.

*The **mam**millary bodies are important for **mam**ory formation.*

On a clinical level, the mammillary bodies are perhaps most notable for their role in **Wernicke-Korsakoff syndrome**, a disorder that prominently features impaired memory formation, including both **anterograde amnesia** (an inability to form new memories) and **retrograde amnesia** (a loss of previously formed memories). Wernicke-Korsakoff syndrome is often associated with a long history of excessive alcohol intake, as chronic exposure to alcohol can result in a deficiency of vitamin B_1 (also known as thiamine). Atrophy of the mammillary bodies is often seen in these patients with neuroimaging or on autopsy.

THE CINGULATE CORTEX

Sitting on the inside of the canyon formed by the longitudinal fissure, just above the corpus callosum, lies the **cingulate cortex**. The cingulate cortex does not belong to any one lobe but rather spans various lobes, like a belt. (In fact, the word "cingulum" is Latin for belt.) The front-most part of the cingulate cortex, or the **anterior cingulate cortex**, is often considered to be a part of the limbic system. In particular, it seems to play a large role in **error recognition**. This can involve many different kinds of errors, whether it is a physical error (like seeing a color out of place in an otherwise perfectly organized box of crayons) or a moral error (such as seeing a rich person steal money from a

beggar on the street). Recognizing something as an error prompts the anterior cingulate cortex to generate a strong emotional response which then motivates us to act on the situation (such as moving the crayon to its right place or confronting the

thief). Because of its key role in error recognition, the anterior cingulate cortex frequently comes up when discussing various psychiatric conditions such as obsessive-compulsive disorder in which error recognition plays a large role. You can remember the function of the **A**nterior **c**ingulate **c**ortex by thinking of someone being disgusted and exclaiming, "**Acc!**" when coming upon an error.

The **anterior cingulate cortex** is involved not only in **recognizing errors** but also in **motivating** us to act to fix them.

*Think of someone coming across an **error** and exclaiming, "**Acc!**"*

THE NUCLEUS ACCUMBENS

Like the mammillary bodies, the **nucleus accumbens** is *not* located in the cortex. However, because it contributes to higher cognitive functions, it is often considered to be a part of the limbic system. In particular, the nucleus accumbens appears to play a key role in governing **motivation and reward**. Activities such as eating food, having sex, and using addictive drugs like nicotine or heroin have direct effects on the nucleus accumbens, leading to pleasurable feelings that increase the chance that someone

will engage in more of that same behavior in the future (a process known as **reinforcement**). While reward-oriented behavior is not in and of itself pathological, the nucleus accumbens has been found to play a role in addiction and other behavioral disorders. You can remember the function of this region by remembering that the nucleus **accum**bens helps you to **accum**ulate money and other rewards.

The **nucleus accumbens** governs **motivation** and **pleasure** and appears to play a key role in processes like **addiction**.

*The nucleus **accum**bens helps you to **accum**ulate money and other rewards.*

PUTTING IT ALL TOGETHER

And thus concludes our whirlwind tour of the cerebral cortex! We've covered four lobes (the **frontal**, **parietal**, **occipital**, and **temporal** lobes) as well as two systems (the **language centers** and the **limbic system**) that span those lobes. It's important to take another moment and point out that in this chapter we have focused exclusively on the functions of each lobe that are found in the *cortex*! However, each lobe has additional *sub*cortical structures that have their own functions, so don't go around thinking that the entirety of the temporal lobe is there *only* to allow you to hear the tempo of music. There are many more functions that are associated with the cerebrum than just the ones in the cortex, which we will learn about more in the next chapter.

REVIEW QUESTIONS

1. A 68 y/o left-handed F is recovering from a recent stroke. During an appointment, a physical therapist notices that she consistently does not use assistive devices that are placed on her left side and will even ignore the therapist's motioned instructions when he is standing to her left. She responds appropriately to objects placed to her right. The patient denies any difficulties understanding instructions when she is asked. Later, when the physical therapist is reviewing some forms that the patient filled out, he notices that the left half of the page is often blank, with only the right half filled out. Which of the following areas of the brain did this patient most likely sustain damage from her stroke?
   - A. Left frontal cortex
   - B. Right frontal cortex
   - C. Left parietal cortex
   - D. Right parietal cortex
   - E. Left occipital cortex
   - F. Right occipital cortex
   - G. Left temporal cortex
   - H. Right temporal cortex
   - I. More than one of the above
   - J. None of the above

2. A 55 y/o M is brought to his primary care doctor's office by his wife. The patient denies that there is anything wrong. However, his wife insists that over the past 3 months there has been a noticeable change in his behavior. He retired 2 years ago and initially spent his time attending to his garden. However, recently he has begun eating large amounts of candy and other sweet food, including two large tubs of ice cream that his wife had bought for a party. He has taken to stockpiling candy bars in his closet where he thinks his wife cannot find them. His wife says that he has been "throwing tantrums like a 5-year-old" when he does not get his way. He narrowly avoided having the police called on him after he was found in the mall putting his hand down his pants in the middle of a walkway. This patient's changes in behavior are most consistent with abnormalities in which of the following regions?
   - A. Frontal cortex
   - B. Parietal cortex
   - C. Occipital cortex
   - D. Temporal cortex
   - E. None of the above

3. A 70 y/o right-handed M experienced a stroke one year ago. Initially he presented with loss of motor control of his right arm and leg, but this recovered with time and physical therapy. However, since his stroke he has been unable to engage in conversation and often looks puzzled and confused when others speak to him. Following an evaluation with a speech and language pathologist, he is diagnosed with Wernicke's aphasia. Given the nature of his deficits, which of the following

tasks is he *most* likely to be able to perform?
- A. Pointing at the correct picture when someone says "Show me a lion"
- B. Being able to order a pizza when he gets hungry
- C. Answering the question "Why did they go up the hill?" after being told the story of Jack and Jill
- D. Being able to sing the melody of a song that he knows from childhood
- E. Repeating the sentence "She blazed around the dusty field"

4. A 12 y/o M has had recurrent seizures over the past year. Electroencephalography reveals bursts of neuronal activity originating in the occipital lobe without subsequent spread to other areas of the brain. Which of the following is the most likely sign or symptom that would appear during a seizure for this patient?
- A. Repetitive behaviors such as twisting, turning, or grimacing
- B. Hearing loud sounds despite being in a quiet area
- C. Sudden episodes of blurred vision
- D. Feeling electrical sensations running down one's arms and legs
- E. Inability to speak

5. A 44 y/o M with a long history of alcohol use is brought to the hospital by an ambulance after he was found wandering into traffic on a busy city street. He is admitted to the hospital and given intravenous fluids as well as oral thiamine. Several days later, he is discharged to a local substance abuse rehabilitation program. However, the staff there begin reporting that he has trouble engaging in treatment due to high distractibility, poor attention, and disorganized behavior. He is referred for neuropsychological testing which reveals significant deficits in both short-term and long-term memory. Which of the following limbic structures has most likely been damaged in this patient?
- A. Amygdala
- B. Hippocampus
- C. Mammillary bodies
- D. Nucleus accumbens
- E. Anterior cingulate cortex

1. **The best answer is D.** This vignette describes a case of hemineglect as evidenced by the patient's lack of awareness of information in one half of her sensory field. Given the parietal lobe's role in processing sensory information, damage to the parietal lobe is responsible for most cases of hemineglect, typically on the side opposite of the neglect. While the patient is left-handed, that does not mean that she is right dominant, as around 70% of left-handed individuals are still left dominant, making this still the most likely situation (answer C).

2. **The best answer is A.** This patient's behavior shows a startling lack of self-inhibition that is consistent with deficits in the part of the brain that says "no": the frontal lobe. This case describes a disease known as frontotemporal dementia in which damage to the frontal and temporal lobes accumulates over time. While both the frontal and temporal lobes are implicated, the patient's behavior as described in this case are clearly due to insufficient inhibition from the frontal lobe rather than damage to the temporal lobe (answer D). The parietal cortex is involved in attention, awareness, and receiving somatosensory signals (answer B) while the occipital cortex is the site of visual processing (answer C); neither would account for the behavioral changes described in this vignette.

3. **The best answer is D.** Receptive aphasia results in deficits in language comprehension. For this reason, any tasks that involve understanding the content of what someone else is saying will be impaired, including language comprehension (answers A and C) and repetition (answer E). However, receptive aphasia tends to produce deficits in speech production as well. While patients with this condition are still able to speak, the words they produce are often nonsensical, making it difficult to complete tasks like ordering a pizza (answer B). In contrast, the flow, rhythm, and musical tone of language is often preserved, so someone with this condition will often still be able to sing a melody.

4. **The best answer is C.** This vignette describes a case of occipital lobe seizures characterized by recurrent episodes of visual abnormalities, which can include blurriness, blindness, and hallucinations. Repetitive movements would be most likely in a seizure involving the motor cortex in the frontal lobe (answer A) , while sudden sensory abnormalities would be more likely observed in a parietal lobe seizure (answer D). Auditory hallucinations are more often related to a seizure in the temporal cortex (answer B), while speech impairment would likely involve the language centers, none of which are located in the occipital lobe (answer E).

5. **The best answer is C.** A deficiency of thiamine, often related to chronic alcohol abuse, is well-known to damage the mammillary bodies, a pair of structures involved in memory. While the hippocampus is also involved in memory, its role more specifically involves consolidating short-term memories to long-term ones, in contrast to this patient who had pronounced deficits in both short-term and long-term memories (answer B). The amygdala is involved in generating fear and other emotions (answer A), while the nucleus accumbens is involved in reward-driven behavior (answer D). Finally, the anterior cingulate cortex appears to be involved in error recognition (answer E).

4 THE CEREBRAL SUBCORTEX

As we go deeper into the brain, we reach the structures that lie underneath the cortex, fittingly called the **subcortex**. While much of the subcortex is made up of white matter, there are pockets of grey matter in this area as well that carry out some vitally important functions. The jobs that these subcortical structures perform are perhaps less sophisticated than the complex decision-making and executive-functioning done by the cortex, but what they lack in sophistication they more than make up for in necessity. Indeed, many of the subcortex's functions are ultimately

more important for survival, including the **epithalamus** and **hypothalamus** which regulate such basic functions as hunger, thirst, and sleep. The subcortex also plays a key role in fine-tuning signals coming to and from the cortex, with the **thalamus** sorting sensory information on its way to the parietal cortex and the **basal ganglia** smoothing out motor signals coming down from the frontal cortex. We'll go over each of these regions and their primary functions in more detail in this chapter.

As we discuss these regions, you may see the word **nucleus** pop up from time to time (for example, the caudate nucleus or the subthalamic nucleus). It's important not to confuse this with the DNA-filled *cell* nucleus! In neurology, the term "nucleus" is used to describe a cluster of neuronal cell bodies that are grouped together and share a similar function. The term nucleus is specifically used for clusters that are located in the *central* nervous system, while the term **ganglion** is used to describe similar neuron clusters when they are found in the *peripheral* nervous system.

THE THALAMUS

The **thalamus** acts as a **relay station for sensory information** by routing afferent neurons traveling from various areas of the body to the appropriate part of the cerebral cortex, such as sending information from the body to the primary somatosensory cortex in the parietal lobe, visual information from the eyes to the visual cortex in the occipital lobe, and auditory information from the ears to the auditory cortex in the temporal lobe. (In fact, the only major form of sensory information that does *not* pass through the thalamus is the sense of smell, which instead goes directly to the cerebral cortex and subcortex.) In this way, the thalamus acts like your brain's version of a telephone operating **switchboard** to make sure that relevant **th**en**th**ory information gets where it needs to go. This function is illustrated when damage to the **th**alamus occurs, as this often produces **th**evere **th**en**th**ory defici**th**.

> The **thalamus** acts as a **relay station** for **sensory information** traveling to the cerebral cortex.
>
> *The **thalamus** is all about **thenthation**.*

The manner in which afferent neurons pass through the thalamus is neither messy nor disorganized—quite the contrary, in fact! Like other parts of the brain, the thalamus is not a single uniform area but instead consists of specific nuclei where the cell bodies of neurons serving similar purposes have gathered together. We won't go over all of these nuclei but will instead try to focus on the most clinically relevant.

 The **ventral posterolateral nucleus** and **ventral posteromedial nucleus** are both involved in relaying sensory information to the primary somatosensory cortex in the parietal lobe. In particular, **V**entral **P**ostero**L**ateral nucleus receives sensory information from the arms and legs, which means that neurons coming up from **V**ery **P**ainful **L**imbs will go through the **VPL**. In contrast, the **V**entral **P**ostero**M**edial nucleus receives input from the **face and mouth**, so a **V**ery **P**ainful **M**outh will pass through the **VPM**.

> The **ventral posterolateral nucleus** receives sensory information from the **arms and legs**, while the **ventral posteromedial nucleus** receives sensory information from the **face and mouth**.
>
> *Ventral PosteroLateral nucleus = Very Painful Limbs*
> *Ventral PosteroMedial nucleus = Very Painful Mouth*

While the ventral posterolateral and ventral posteromedial nuclei process somatosensory information, two other nuclei in the thalamus process special sensory information from the **eyes and ears**. The Lateral Geniculate Nucleus is the primary relay center for **visual information** and is therefore important for checking yourself in the mirror to make sure you are Looking Good Naked. In contrast, the Medial Geniculate Nucleus serves the same purpose for **auditory information** and is therefore important for hearing someone Making Great Noise.

The **lateral geniculate nucleus** receives **visual information** from the **eyes**, while the **medial geniculate nucleus** receives **auditory information** from the **ears**.

*Lateral Geniculate Nucleus = Looking Good Naked (**visual** pathway)*
*Medial Geniculate Nucleus = Making Great Noise (**auditory** pathway)*

More than just relaying specific types of sensory information, the thalamus also appears to play a key role in determining a person's overall level of consciousness, awareness, and wakefulness. Indeed, in cases of severe damage to the thalamus, a permanent state of unresponsiveness known as a **coma** can result.

THE BASAL GANGLIA

The **basal ganglia** are a collection of subcortical nuclei that are highly involved in **regulating voluntary motor movements**. (For the record, they should probably be called the basal *nuclei* because they are in the central nervous system, although due to the traditional nature of the medical field this terminology change hasn't really caught on.) The primary role of the basal ganglia is to either **amplify or diminish an initial signal from the motor cortex** based on a variety of inputs. Recall that the prefrontal cortex is involved in decision making and planning. When the prefrontal cortex "decides" to do something, it sends signals to the motor cortex (located in the frontal lobe just in front of the central sulcus) to initiate these movements. This signal then passes through the basal ganglia which refines the request by amplifying signals to the muscles it thinks will get the job done best and inhibiting signals to muscle groups that are not needed.

Compared to the impulses generated in the motor cortex, we are not necessarily *conscious* of the changes in movement produced by the basal ganglia. For example, when we decide to pet a dog, we are likely conscious of the *initial* decision to begin the action, as it is generated first in the frontal cortex. However, we are then unaware of all the minute adjustments that the basal ganglia make to ensure that the action is smooth and that we are not petting the dog too soft or too hard. If we begin talking to someone or doing some other task while petting the dog, we likely will stop being overtly conscious of our actions even though the movement itself (your hand going back and forth) continues. This is largely due to the actions of various structures in the basal ganglia.

The basal ganglia consist of several structures that all sit deep in the brain, as seen below. The specific parts of the basal ganglia include the **caudate** and the **putamen** (which together form the **dorsal striatum**), the **globus pallidus** (which is divided into an internal and external part), the **subthalamic nucleus**, and the **substantia nigra** as seen below:

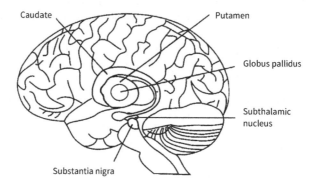

These structures do not operate independently but rather work as part of two interconnected pathways (known as the **direct pathway** and the **indirect pathway**) that each act to modify signals from the motor cortex. These pathways both end up at the thalamus before looping back to modify motor signals in the cortex, showing the key role that sensory information plays in regulating movement. For example, if we are petting the dog so hard that we are causing it discomfort, we can pick up on this via sensory information traveling through the thalamus. By getting input from the thalamus, our basal ganglia can modify the strength of our movement to be softer and more in line with what we are trying to do in the first place: pet the dog and make it happy.

The specific way that the basal ganglia modifies movement depends largely on whether it goes through the direct pathway or the indirect pathway. The **direct pathway** is the more straightforward of the two and generally has an amplifying or **excitatory effect** on the initial motor signal (for example, if we are not petting the dog hard enough and need to pet it harder). The direct pathway travels from the **C**ortex to the **S**triatum into the **I**nternal globus pallidus and finally to the **T**halamus which sends the signal back to the cortex for further refining. You can remember this sequence by thinking that the direct pathway **C**omes **S**traight **I**nto the **T**halamus.

In contrast, the **indirect pathway** takes a longer route through the basal ganglia and generally exerts a diminishing or **inhibitory effect** on the initial motor signal (for example, if we are petting the dog too hard and should back off a little). The indirect pathway starts out similarly to the direct pathway in that the signal is generated in the **C**ortex and travels to the **S**triatum. However, it then exits the direct pathway into the *External* globus pallidus before traveling to the **S**ubthalamic nucleus, the **I**nternal globus pallidus, and finally the **T**halamus. You can remember this route by thinking that the indirect pathway **C**omes **S**traight, **E**xits, then **S**idesteps **I**nto the **T**halamus.

A visual summary of both the direct and indirect pathways is found below. A ⊕ sign indicates an *excitatory* effect, while a ⊖ sign indicates an *inhibitory* effect. The logic here follows the rules of math when multiplying positives and negatives, so the two inhibitory neurotransmitters in the direct pathway cancel each other out and produce an overall excitatory effect, while the three inhibitory neurotransmitters in the indirect pathway produce an overall inhibitory effect.

The **direct pathway** in the basal ganglia works to **amplify the initial signal** from the motor cortex, while the **indirect pathway** exerts an **inhibitory** effect.

The **direct pathway** **C**omes **S**traight **I**nto the **T**halamus:
Cortex → Striatum → Internal GP → Thalamus.

The **indirect pathway** **C**omes **S**traight, **E**xits, then **S**idesteps **I**nto the **T**halamus:
Cortex → Striatum → External GP → STN → Internal GP → Thalamus.

So what exactly are all of these individual structures in the direct and indirect pathways *doing*, anyway? Let's go over each component one by one.

THE STRIATUM

In both the direct and indirect pathways, the initial signal from the motor cortex first travels to the **striatum** (specifically the *dorsal* striatum) which is itself composed of two things: the **caudate nucleus** and the **putamen**. These two structures then work to amplify or inhibit the signal. The **caudate nucleus** is highly involved in any form of **goal-directed activity** and plays an important role in other cognitive functions such as memory and sleep as well. For this reason, you can think of the **cau**date as the most **cau**gnitive part of the basal ganglia. In contrast, the **putamen** is more exclusively dedicated to **motor functions** and appears to play a role in both preparing and executing voluntary movements. This is illustrated clinically in patients who develop bleeding in the area of the putamen (known as a **putaminal hemorrhage**) who will often present with weakness or even complete paralysis of muscles throughout their body. So whenever you see the word "putamen" on an exam, look for the answer involving **M**otor functions and "**put-an-eM**" for **M**otor.

> The **dorsal striatum** is composed of both the **caudate** and the **putamen**.
> The **caudate** is involved in both **motor** activity as well as more **cognitive functions**,
> while the **putamen** is primarily involved in **motor** activity.
>
> *The **cau**date nucleus is the most **cau**gnitive part of the basal ganglia.*
>
> *When you see **put-am-en** on an exam, "**put-an-eM**" for Motor.*

THE GLOBUS PALLIDUS

The direct and indirect pathways both continue with the **globus pallidus**. The globus pallidus actually has two components: an *in*ternal part (GPi) that has *in*hibitory effects on the motor signals passing through it as well as an *ex*ternal part (GPe) that has *ex*citatory effects. The globus pallidus takes the signal from the striatum and passes it along to the thalamus, which then sends the information back to the cortex to fine-tune the movement.

> The **globus pallidus** has an **internal** part that is **inhibitory** as well as an **external** part that is **excitatory**.
>
> *It's easy to remember! **In**ternal is **in**hibitory, **ex**ternal is **ex**citatory.*

THE SUBTHALAMIC NUCLEUS

The **subthalamic nucleus** (or STN) is found only in the indirect pathway where it serves to ultimately **inhibit movements**. (This is because, despite releasing an *excitatory* neurotransmitter, the subthalamic nucleus acts on the *inhibitory* internal globus pallidus to ultimately produce inhibition of movement.) The subthalamic nucleus's inhibitory effects are illustrated in a movement disorder known as **hemiballismus** which involves dramatic swinging and flailing of the limbs after damage to the subthalamic nucleus occurs.

These movements occur because the inhibitory effect of the indirect pathway has been removed, resulting in excessive movements. While rare, hemiballismus often shows up on tests, so it's helpful to think of someone swinging their arm while throwing a **ball** during **Su**nday **N**ight Football to remember hemi**ball**ismus and the **Su**bthalamic **N**ucleus.

Hemiballismus is a disorder involving **involuntary flailing movements** of the limbs. It is related to damage of the **subthalamic nucleus**.

*The flailing arm movements look like **throwing a football**, so you can think of **Su**nday Night **football** to associate hemi**ball**ismus and the **Su**bthalamic **N**ucleus.*

THE SUBSTANTIA NIGRA

The final part of the basal ganglia, known as the **substantia nigra** (Latin for "black substance"), is located not in the subcortex but in the midbrain of the **brainstem**. It is not immediately involved in either the direct or indirect pathway but still plays a role in modifying movement by acting on the striatum directly. The substantia nigra uses the neurotransmitter **dopamine** to influence the basal ganglia. Dopamine is best thought of as being like **grease**: it does not *cause* movements but rather *facilitates* them. This means that someone with reduced production of dopamine in the substantia nigra (such as a person who has Parkinson's disease or who is taking dopamine-blocking medications) will be much less able to initiate movements, leading to muscle stiffness, rigidity, and slowness.

In summary, if you remember nothing else about the basal ganglia, remember that they are generally involved in **refining motor signals**. As such, abnormalities involving the basal ganglia often produce **movement disorders** (which we will talk about further in Chapter 17). You wouldn't expect to find full-on weakness or paralysis of muscles resulting from a lesion in the basal ganglia, however, because they are not directly involved in *producing* motor signals (that's what the motor cortex does). Instead, dysfunction of the basal ganglia leads to **uneven, uncoordinated, and rough movements** that are either excessive (if damage to a part of the indirect pathway occurs, as in hemiballismus) or insufficient (if damage to a component of the direct pathway occurs, as in a putaminal hemorrhage).

Basal ganglia dysfunction leads to **uneven and uncoordinated movements**.

*A broken basal **ganglia** leads to **gangly** movements.*

THE INTERNAL CAPSULE

If you think about it, the components of the basal ganglia are basically a bunch of bureaucrats: if left to their own devices, they would take the initial signal generated by the motor cortex and talk about it, debate it, and modify it until the cows come home. However, what happens when the motor cortex gets fed up with all the basal ganglia's red tape and *just wants to send a signal to the muscle it wants to already*? For this, the motor cortex can use the **internal capsule**, a V-shaped collection of white matter that brazenly travels right through the middle of the basal ganglia on its way to the spinal cord (probably flashing a middle finger to onlookers while doing so) so it can travel to the muscles directly. The V-shape makes the internal capsule easy to split up into three sections: the **anterior limb**, the **posterior limb**, and the **genu** making up the bend between them.

We'll start with the posterior limb. The posterior limb contains a pathway known as the **corticospinal tract**, so-named because it carries motor impulses from the cortex to the muscles via the spinal cord. You can remember this by thinking of a

PoLICe man (**Po**sterior **L**imb of the **I**nternal **C**apsule) going rogue and flipping the bird to the basal ganglia as it drives by on its way to the spinal cord. Policemen also need to move, so an injury to the posterior limb of the internal capsule generally results in **contralateral hemiparesis** (weakness of muscles on the opposite side of the body) or even **hemiplegia** (complete loss of movement, as in someone who is paraplegic or quadriplegic).

The **posterior limb of the internal capsule** contains the **corticospinal tract** which sends motor signals directly to the muscle groups, **bypassing the basal ganglia**.

*Think of a **PoLICe** man flipping the bird as he bypasses the basal ganglia to remember the **Po**sterior **L**imb of the **I**nternal **C**apsule.*

The bend in the middle of the internal capsule is known as the **genu** (Latin for "knee"). The genu contains the **corticobulbar tract** which travels to the midbrain to supply voluntary muscles of the face via the **cranial nerves**. You can remember the function of the corticobulbar tract by thinking of a **gen**i**u**s who gets an idea in their **cranium**. What happens? A light **bulb** goes on! This will help you associate the cortico**bulb**ar tract (found in the **genu** of the internal capsule) with **cranial** nerves.

The **genu** of the **internal capsule** contains the **corticobulbar tract** which sends motor signals to facial muscles via the **cranial nerves**.

*Think of a **genius** who gets an idea in their **cranium**, making a light **bulb** go on!*

Finally, the **anterior limb** of the internal capsule contains a variety of nerve fibers connecting different parts of the brain, and due to this heterogeneity there is typically not a singular function that can be ascribed to the anterior limb.

THE EPITHALAMUS

The **epithalamus** (Greek for "above the thalamus") is mostly made up of white matter, although it also contains the **pineal gland** which secretes the hormone **melatonin**. Melatonin is released at night in response to low light levels and helps to regulate **sleep-wake cycles** by inducing a tired feeling. Due to its location above the vertical gaze center in the medial longitudinal fasciculus (a pair of nerve tracts that control eye movements which we will talk about further in Chapter 9), a tumor of the pineal gland (known as a **pinealoma**) can cause an inability to move the eyes upward, leading to a state of downward trending eyes (or "sunset eyes") known as **Parinaud's syndrome**. You can remember the meaning of Parinaud's syndrome by thinking of it whenever you are examining someone whose **peering is odd**.

*This patient with a **pineal gland tumor** is being asked to look up but cannot.*

A **pineal gland tumor** is one cause of **Parinaud's syndrome**, a condition involving the **inability to look up**.

*Consider **Parinaud's** syndrome when you find someone's **peerin' odd**.*

THE HYPOTHALAMUS

The **hypothalamus** (Greek for "below the thalamus") is found—wait for it—*below the thalamus*. It is made up of a collection of nuclei that each perform various activities important to survival, including regulation of **body temperature, hunger, thirst, sleep,** and **interpersonal bonding**. In addition, the hypothalamus has direct control over the release of hormones from the **pituitary gland,** which we will discuss next. In this way, the hypothalamus acts as a **bridge between the nervous system and the endocrine system**. We'll go over each of these functions one-by-one.

TEMPERATURE REGULATION

The **Anterior hypothalamic nucleus** helps to initiate **Cooling** mechanisms such as sweating and panting (think of an **A/C** unit cooling down a house on a hot day) and is connected to the **parasympathetic** nervous system. In contrast, the **posterior hypothalamic nucleus** works to **heat up** the body through shivering and other mechanisms ("You've got a **hot posterior!**") and is connected to the **sympathetic** nervous system.

The **anterior and posterior hypothalamic nuclei** work to **regulate body temperature** by cooling down and heating up the body, respectively.

*The Anterior hypothalamic nucleus is for Cooling (A/C = Air Conditioning). The Posterior hypothalamic nucleus is for Heating ("You've got a **hot posterior!**").*

FOOD INTAKE

Activation of the **lateral hypothalamic nucleus** leads to a sensation of **hunger** (the lateral nucleus will make you **fatter**-al). In contrast, activation of the **ventromedial nucleus** is associated with a feeling of satiety (eating a ventro-**meal** will make you

full). Several hormones act on these two nuclei to influence the feeling of hunger. **Ghrelin** (released by the stomach when it anticipates a meal) acts on the lateral nucleus to induce hunger while **leptin** (released by fat cells to indicate that current fat stores are adequate) acts on the ventromedial nucleus to induce satiety. You can remember the function of each of these hormones by thinking that **ghrelin** is released when the stomach is **growlin'** while lep-**thin** will make you **thinner**.

The **lateral and ventromedial hypothalamic nuclei** regulate **food intake** by creating sensations of hunger and satiety, respectively.

*The **lateral** nucleus will make you **fatter**-al.*
*The ventro-**meal** nucleus will make you feel **full**.*

Ghrelin and **leptin** are hormones that act on the hypothalamus to **increase and decrease hunger**, respectively.

*Ghrelin is released when your stomach is **growlin'**.*
*Lep-**thin** will make you **thin**ner.*

CIRCADIAN RHYTHM

We've already talked about the role of the pineal gland in regulating the sleep-wake cycle, but the hypothalamus plays a role here as well. In particular, the **suprachiasmatic nucleus** acts as an internal clock that regulates a variety of processes in a consistent daily cycle known as the **circadian rhythm**. The suprachiasmatic nucleus communicates with other regions of the brain (including the pineal gland and other nuclei in the hypothalamus) to regulate body temperature and the production of certain hormones according to this 24-hour cycle. The circadian rhythm appears to be internally set, which is why **jet lag** exists (as someone's circadian rhythm is set to a different part of the world than the one they're currently in). To remember the function of the suprachiasmatic nucleus, remember that someone who doesn't get enough sleep is likely to be grumpy. If you get enough sleep, however, you can be charming and **chiasmatic** (charismatic).

The **suprachiasmatic nucleus** maintains a consistent **daily biological cycle** known as the **circadian rhythm**.

*If you get enough **sleep**, you can be charming and **chiasmatic** (charismatic).*

WATER BALANCE

Control over **thirst** and **water intake** is located in the hypothalamus. The **supraoptic nucleus** produces a hormone called **vasopressin** that works to maintain fluid balance by decreasing urine volume in the kidneys when the hypothalamus detects that the osmolality of the plasma is too high (this effect gives vasopressin its older name: **antidiuretic hormone**). In this way, vasopressin has the effect of diluting the blood by retaining more water and thereby lowering concentrations of sodium and other electrolytes. Vasopressin is one of two hormones that is produced in the hypothalamus and released in the **posterior pituitary** (the other being oxytocin, discussed next). To remember the function of the supraoptic nucleus, think about looking ("-optic") at the clouds above you ("supra-") to see if it's going to rain (water).

> The **supraoptic nucleus** produces **vasopressin** which helps to regulate **thirst** and **fluid balance**.
>
> **Look** ("**-optic**") at the clouds **above** you ("**supra-**") to see if it's going to **rain** (water).

SOCIAL BONDING

Besides vasopressin, the other hormone that is produced by the hypothalamus and released in the posterior pituitary is **oxytocin**. Oxytocin is involved in a variety of situations involving **interpersonal bonding and reproduction**, including hugging, skin-to-skin contact, sexual activity, and orgasm. In general, release of oxytocin during these events helps to promote trust, generosity, attachment, and other **prosocial behaviors**. It has specific functions in child rearing as well, as it helps the uterus to contract during birth and stimulates the release of breast milk after birth. Oxytocin is produced in the **paraventricular nucleus** of the hypothalamus, which you can remember by thinking that **Par**ental **V**iewing is **N**eeded for the "mature themes" that the **Pa**ra**V**entricular **N**ucleus is involved in.

> The **paraventricular nucleus** produces **oxytocin**, a hormone involved in **prosocial behaviors, sexual reproduction, uterine contraction**, and **breast milk release**.
>
> **Par**ental **V**iewing is **N**eeded for the "mature themes" of the **Pa**ra**V**entricular **N**ucleus.

HORMONE RELEASE

Finally, the hypothalamus interacts with the **pituitary gland** to release hormones that govern a variety of processes throughout the body. The pituitary gland is made up of two parts: the **anterior pituitary** and the **posterior pituitary**. We have already talked about the two hormones (vasopressin and oxytocin) that are produced in the hypothalamus, travel down the pituitary stalk, and are released in the posterior pituitary. In contrast, the hormones released by the *anterior* pituitary are not made in the hypothalamus. Rather, the hypothalamus releases its own hormones that then diffuse downstream to the pituitary gland to cause the release of *additional* hormones from the anterior pituitary. We will discuss this process further in the next section.

While these are not all the nuclei found in the hypothalamus, they are the most well-studied and clinically relevant. Remember the **six H's of the Hypothalamus**: Hot, Hungry, Hourly, Hydrated, Horny, and Hormonal.

> The **hypothalamus** performs a wide variety of **essential functions** in the body.
>
> The **six H's** of the *Hypothalamus*:
> *Hot, Hungry, Hourly, Hydrated, Horny, and Hormonal.*

Thalamus

Hypothalamus

Pituitary stalk

Anterior pituitary

Posterior pituitary

THE PITUITARY GLAND

The nervous system is great at rapidly effecting change through lightning-fast transmission of action potentials. However, sometimes it needs to slow things down and create longer-lasting changes by releasing hormones throughout the body. This is where the **anterior pituitary gland** comes in. The anterior pituitary gland releases 6 hormones which you can remember using the mnemonic **FLAT PiG**:

F is for Follicle-stimulating hormone. Follicle-stimulating hormone (FSH) is highly involved in regulating the **reproductive processes** of both men and women. In men, follicle-stimulating hormone is involved in stimulating sperm production, while in women it stimulates the growth of ovarian follicles.

L is for Luteinizing hormone. Like follicle-stimulating hormone, **luteinizing hormone** (LH) is concerned primarily with **reproduction**. In men, this involves stimulating the production of testosterone, while in women a surge in the level of luteinizing hormone triggers ovulation.

A is for Adrenocorticotropic hormone. Adrenocorticotropic hormone (ACTH) acts on the adrenal cortex to stimulate the release of **cortisol**, a hormone that allows the body to respond to long-term stress by releasing sugar into the blood and altering electrolyte balance (including increasing serum levels of sodium). Cortisol is also very effective at reducing inflammation, making it a great treatment for a wide variety of neurologic conditions involving an overactive immune system (as we will see in later chapters).

T is for Thyroid-stimulating hormone. Thyroid-stimulating hormone (TSH) acts on the **thyroid gland** to stimulate the production of thyroid hormones which then work throughout the body to increase the basal metabolic rate, stimulate blood flow, raise the core body temperature, and increase the speed of metabolism.

P is for Prolactin. Prolactin is primarily involved in stimulating **breast development** and the production of **breast milk.**

i is for ignore. You can ignore this one (it's just there for the mnemonic!).

G is for Growth hormone. As its name implies, **growth hormone** (GH) stimulates the growth of various cells and organs throughout the body, leading to **muscle growth** and **bone lengthening**. The effects of growth hormone are illustrated dramatically in the following picture:

Too much growth hormone on the left, too little on the right.

Each of these six hormones is either stimulated or inhibited by an upstream hormone released from the hypothalamus. In this way, there is a **three-part axis** formed between the hypothalamus, the pituitary, and the target organ. A summary of each hormone axis is found in the table below:

First, the hypothalamus releases:	...to make the anterior pituitary secrete:	... which itself acts on the:	... causing it to release:
Thyrotropin-releasing hormone (TRH)	Thyroid-stimulating hormone (TSH)	Thyroid gland	Thyroid hormone
Corticotropin-releasing hormone (CRH)	Adrenocorticotropic hormone	Adrenal gland	Cortisol
Gonadotropin-releasing hormone (GnRH)	Follicle-stimulating hormone (FSH) and luteinizing hormone (LH)	Gonads	Testosterone and estradiol
Growth hormone-releasing hormone (GHRH)	Growth hormone (GH)	Liver and other organs	Insulin-like growth factor 1 (IGF-1)
Dopamine	Prolactin (*inhibited*, not secreted!)	Mammary glands	Breast milk

One exception worth noting here is the hypothalamic–pituitary–mammary axis, as the hormone released by the hypothalamus (in this case, dopamine) actually *inhibits* rather than stimulates the release of the downstream hormone! Other than that, however, the pattern is pretty consist across all six of the hormones released by the anterior pituitary.

The **anterior pituitary gland** releases **six hormones** that each play an essential role in the **endocrine system**.

FLAT PiG:
Follicle Stimulating Hormone (FSH)
Luteinizing Hormone (LH)
Adrenocorticotropic Hormone (ACTH)
Thyroid Stimulating Hormone (TSH)
Prolactin
Growth Hormone (GH)

PUTTING IT ALL TOGETHER

At first glance, the cerebral cortex appears to be the most complex and intricate part of the brain. However, the more you learn about the subcortex, the more it becomes clear that the cortex would be hopelessly lost without the guidance and support of the structures beneath it. The parietal, occipital, and temporal cortices wouldn't be able to receive sensory information without the **thalamus** there to route information to them. The frontal lobe could technically make movements on its own, but without the refining influence of the **basal ganglia** these motions would be clumsy and ineffective. Even the prefrontal cortex—the "smartest" part of the brain—would be inept at its primary task of making decisions without the **hypothalamus** maintaining the basic processes that are central to survival such as eating, drinking, and sleeping. For this reason, don't underestimate the sophistication of the regions in the subcortex, many of which will come into play when we transition into learning about clinical neurology.

REVIEW QUESTIONS

1. A 56 y/o F with a history of hypertension experiences a sudden sense of dizziness and loss of vision while bending down to pick up a magazine. She calls an ambulance and is taken to the hospital. On admission, her blood pressure is 186/102 with otherwise normal vital signs. A neurological exam including a full motor and sensory evaluation is normal except for loss of visual acuity in the right visual fields. Which of the following structures is most likely to have been damaged during this episode?
   A. Nucleus accumbens
   B. Lateral geniculate nucleus
   C. Medial geniculate nucleus
   D. Ventral posterolateral nucleus
   E. Ventral posteromedial nucleus

2. A 63 y/o M with a history of atrial fibrillation is admitted to the hospital following a stroke in a branch of the left middle cerebral artery that primarily affected the posterior limb of the internal capsule. Which of the following deficits is he most likely to have from this point forward?
   A. Weakness of his right facial muscles
   B. Weakness of his left facial muscles
   C. Weakness of his right arm and leg
   D. Weakness of his left arm and leg
   E. Numbness of his right facial muscles
   F. Numbness of his left facial muscles
   G. Numbness of his right arm and leg
   H. Numbness of his left arm and leg

3. A 21 y/o F college student goes to see her primary care doctor after noticing an increase in how often she needs to urinate. Over the past month, she has been waking up several times per night to use the bathroom which has caused some tension between her and her roommate. At present, she notes that she urinates about once per hour during the day and once every other hour at night. She notes that the urine is usually clear with no trace of yellow. She has been drinking copious amounts of water to offset an increase in her thirst that she has noticed over the same time period. Her doctor orders blood work which reveals elevated sodium levels and a normal glucose level. Imaging reveals a small tumor in the region of the hypothalamus. Which of the following hypothalamic nuclei appears to be most affected in this case?
   A. Anterior hypothalamic nucleus
   B. Posterior hypothalamic nucleus
   C. Lateral hypothalamic nucleus
   D. Ventromedial nucleus
   E. Suprachiasmatic nucleus
   F. Supraoptic nucleus
   G. Paraventricular nucleus

4. A 44 y/o M is involved in a motor vehicle accident and loses consciousness after he is hit in the right side of the head. Upon awakening in the hospital, he is confused and disoriented, with profound memory difficulties. Over the next several weeks, he begins to regain his mental abilities. However, he begins to experience odd movements. A neurologist orders a magnetic resonance imaging scan of his brain which shows a focal lesion in the external globus pallidus. Which of the following is *least* likely to describe his movements?

    A. Recurrent spasms of his hand
    B. Tremor in his arm
    C. Involuntary tensing of his fingers
    D. Inability to flex the wrist
    E. Painful contraction of the neck and shoulders

1. **The best answer is B.** The lateral geniculate nucleus, medial geniculate nucleus, ventral posterolateral nucleus, and ventral posteromedial nucleus are all located in the thalamus. Each processes a different kind of sensory information. Given that this patient presented with visual disturbances, a lesion in the lateral geniculate nucleus, which is responsible for vision, is most likely. The medial geniculate nucleus processes auditory information, so a lesion here would most likely present with deficits in sound processing (answer C). The ventral posterolateral nucleus and ventral posteromedial nucleus process sensory information from the limbs and face, respectively, so a lesion here would result in numbness of these areas (answers D and E). The nucleus accumbens is a part of the limbic system and is not directly involved in visual processing (answer A).

2. **The best answer is C.** The posterior limb of the internal capsule contains the corticospinal tract, a group of neurons traveling to skeletal muscles of the body. For this reason, ischemic damage to this area can result in contralateral weakness due to the crossing of these fibers in the medulla. Therefore, a stroke in the left posterior limb of the internal capsule would lead to weakness of the right extremities, not the left (answer D). Facial muscles are controlled by the corticobulbar tract which passes through the genu of the internal capsule, not the posterior limb (answers A and B). A stroke in the thalamus, rather than the internal capsule, would result in numbness (answers E—H).

3. **The best answer is F.** This vignette describes a case of diabetes insipidus related to dysfunction of the supraoptic nucleus of the hypothalamus. Under normal conditions, vasopressin helps to reduce urination and retain water in the bloodstream. When vasopressin is not produced, however, a state of excessive urination (polyuria) with resultant excessive drinking (polydipsia) can result. Around a quarter of all cases of central diabetes insipidus (those related to dysfunction of the brain rather than the kidneys) involve a brain tumor. The anterior and posterior hypothalamic nuclei are involved in temperature regulation and autonomic nervous system activation (answers A and B). The lateral and ventromedial hypothalamic nuclei are involved in regulation of hunger and satiety (answers C and D). The suprachiasmatic nucleus is involved in the circadian rhythm (answer E), while the paraventricular nucleus is involved in social bonding through the production of oxytocin (answer G).

4. **The best answer is D.** An injury in the external globus pallidus would lead to dysfunction of the indirect pathway. As the indirect pathway typically plays an inhibitory role in the motor pathway, this would likely result in excessive or unrestrained movements such as spasms (answer A), tremor (answer B), tension (answer C), and dystonia (answer E). Of the options listed, only wrist drop involves too little muscle contraction rather than too much.

5 THE CEREBELLUM

Sitting behind and below the cerebrum is what appears to be a miniature version of the brain known as the **cerebellum**. In many ways, the cerebellum bears more than a passing resemblance to the cerebrum: it has a familiar folded appearance that increases surface area, a pattern of grey matter on the outside and white matter on the inside, and several divisions into multiple lobes. Despite its appearance, however, the cerebellum isn't just a miniature copy of the cerebrum. Instead, it has its own unique functions, primarily in the realm of **balance** and **motor coordination**.

    The cerebellum itself does not *generate* motor impulses (recall that those come from the motor cortex in the frontal lobe, just like the engine in the front of a car). Instead, the cerebellum *coordinates* motor actions by taking into account proprioceptive information about the position of various parts of the body in space). For example, when climbing a set of stairs, your legs can't simply repeat the same action over and over. Instead, you need to know when to lift one leg up while putting

 the other down as well as the timing of alternating between the two legs. Your body does this automatically and instinctually by sending proprioceptive and other sensory information to the cerebellum. The cerebellum then compares the position of each body part with its intended movement and adjusts the motor signal in a way that irons out the kinks, resulting in a smooth and coordinated set of movements. This is why a commonly used exam technique known as the **finger-to-nose test** is a good demonstration of cerebellar function, as it relies on asking the patient to touch their finger to your moving finger and then back to their nose several times. Doing this tests the patient's ability to combine sensory information from their eyes (the location of *your* finger in space) as well as proprioceptive information from their body (the location of *their* finger in space) and integrate them into a smooth, coordinated movement (moving their finger to touch your finger). An inability to do this suggests some degree of dysfunction in the cerebellum. (We'll talk about this test and others in more detail in Chapter 11.)

The world's first finger-to-nose test.

CEREBELLAR ANATOMY

The cerebellum is divided into three lobes: the **anterior lobe**, the **posterior lobe**, and a narrow strip of tissue known as the **flocculonodular lobe**. An "unrolled" view of the cerebellum is seen below:

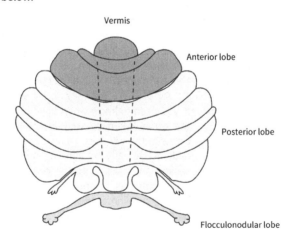

Vermis

Anterior lobe

Posterior lobe

Flocculonodular lobe

The anterior and posterior lobes perform the functions that we typically associate with the cerebellum, including both sending signals *to* and receiving signals *from* the cerebral cortex and spinal cord. The lateral aspects of the cerebellum coordinates the lateral parts of the body (primarily the arms and legs) while the medial aspect, known as the **vermis**, coordinates the trunk.

Compared to anterior and posterior lobes, the flocculonodular lobe is the odd one out. Rather than involving itself with coordinating the movements of the body, it instead works to coordinate **eye movements** and **balance** using sensory information about movement and spatial orientation from the **vestibular system** in the inner ear (we'll go over the vestibular system in more detail in Chapter 9). You can remember the function of the **flocc**ulonodular lobe by thinking of a **flock** of **see**-gulls being very **noisy** (using the noise to help you remember the vestibular system in the **ear**).

The **flocculonodular lobe of the cerebellum** is involved in coordinating **eye movements** and **balance** based on sensory information from the **vestibular system**.

*A **flocc** of **see**-gulls is very **noisy**! (Think of the vestibular system in the **ear**.)*

CEREBELLAR PEDUNCLES

The three lobes of the cerebellum connect to the rest of the body by way of three **cerebellar peduncles** (peduncles meaning "stalks" or "stem"), as seen below:

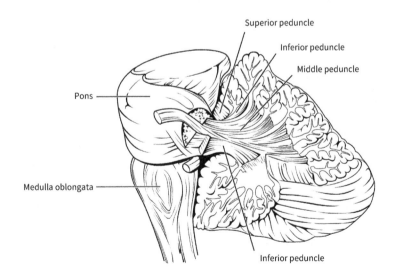

Each peduncle has its own function: the **superior cerebellar peduncle** *sends* information from the cerebellum to the cortex via the thalamus, while the **middle cerebellar peduncle** and **inferior cerebellar peduncle** both *receive* input (from the pons and spinal cord, respectively). It is this bidirectional flow of information that allows the cerebellum to accomplish its central goal of using sensory information to fine-tune the body's movement. One important point here is that the nerve tracts coming from the superior cerebellar peduncle cross from left-to-right and right-to-left so that, by the time they get to the brainstem, nerve fibers from the *left* side of the cerebellum are travelling in the *right* midbrain (and vice versa). You can remember this by thinking that the **S**uperior **C**erebellar **P**eduncle **S**ends **C**rossed **P**athways.

The **superior cerebellar peduncle sends signals** to the cortex, while the **middle and inferior cerebellar peduncles receive information** from the pons and spinal cord.

*The **S**uperior **C**erebellar **P**eduncle **S**ends **C**rossed **P**athways.*

However, while the superior cerebellar peduncle sends crossed pathways, the neurologic deficits seen in cases of unilateral cerebellar damage still end up being **ipsilateral** to (or on the same side as) the lesion. This is because motor signals from the cerebellum are **dirty double crossers**: they not only cross when they leave the cerebellum in the superior cerebellar peduncle but then cross *again* on their way down the medulla in the corticospinal tract (as we will find out in the next chapter).

Cerebellar damage produces neurologic deficits that are **ipsilateral** to the side of the lesion due to the fact that **cerebellar pathways cross twice**.

*Write it as **cerebe✕um** to remind yourself that it's a **dirty double crosser**!*

DEEP CEREBELLAR NUCLEI

Finally, we will briefly talk about four pairs of nuclei that lie deep within the cerebellum. While ordinarily the inside of the cerebellum is made of white matter, these four nuclei are an exception, as they are the cell bodies of the neurons that send output through the superior cerebellar peduncle. From lateral to medial, these four nuclei are the **dentate nuclei**, the **emboliform nuclei**, the **globose nuclei**, and the **fastigial nuclei** (although in humans the emboliform and globose nuclei are fused into one). You can remember these by thinking of **CDEFG**: the **C**erebellum contains the **D**entate, **E**mboliform, **F**astigial, and **G**lobose nuclei.

There are **four deep cerebellar nuclei** that send signals to the cerebrum through the **superior cerebellar peduncle**.

*CDEFG: The **C**erebellum has the **D**entate, **E**mboliform, **F**astigial, and **G**lobose nuclei.*

While there is more to learn about cerebellar anatomy (including some unique types of neurons that are only found here), on a clinical level these details don't come into play that often, so we will stop here.

CEREBELLAR DYSFUNCTION

One of the best ways of understanding the function of the cerebellum is to see what happens when it becomes *dys*functional. In contrast to injuries of the motor cortex or internal capsule, injuries of the cerebellum do *not* generally lead to motor weakness or paralysis! Instead, cerebellar damage is associated with specific deficits in the areas of **balance**, **posture**, and **coordination** that are collectively known as **cerebellar signs**. You can remember the cerebellar signs by thinking of a **dizzy ANT balancing 3 dys'es** (dishes). Let's go over the parts of this mnemonic bit by bit:

Dizzy is for Dizziness. Vertigo is a form of dizziness in which someone experiences a distinct sense that things are moving even when they are not (often described as a sensation of "room spinning"). Like a carnival ride, vertigo can be associated with a feeling of nausea. While there are many possible causes of vertigo, those that involve the cerebellum are often called **central vertigo** and tend to be accompanied by the other signs and symptoms we are about to discuss. (This is in contrast to cases of peripheral vertigo which are instead related to dysfunction of the inner ear, as we will talk about in Chapter 9.)

A is for Ataxia. The clinical term for a lack of coordination is **ataxia**, and it shouldn't be surprising based on what we have learned so far that ataxia is one of the key signs of cerebellar dysfunction. Ataxia can affect many different movements in various parts of the body, including the arms, legs, eyes, and even the muscles in the throat that

produce speech. The specific location of damage within the cerebellum largely dictates the movements that are affected, with damage to the *lateral* cerebellum producing *limb* ataxia, damage to the *vermis* causing *truncal* ataxia, and damage to the *flocculonodular lobe* causing *postural* instability due to the inability to control eye movements. Alcohol is a common cause of truncal ataxia which can be seen in the unsteady gait that many people develop when severely intoxicated.

N is for Nystagmus. Nystagmus refers to an involuntary twitch-like movement of the eyes (sometimes called "dancing eyes"). Under normal circumstances, the vestibular system in the ear helps to detect when the head is moving. The vestibular system then sends signals to the flocculonodular lobe of the cerebellum to move the eyes in response to this motion so that the eyes can maintain their gaze rather than being moved by the motion of the head. To see if this process is working, focus on the center of the image below, then shake your head back and forth a few times:

If your eyes were able to keep focused on the image despite the movement of your head, then congratulations! Your cerebellum is intact (as are a few other systems). Relative to their position in your head, your eyes were moving, but because they moved in a direction exactly *opposite* to the movement of your head, the overall effect was that your eyes were able to stay still relative to what they were looking at. In cases of nystagmus, however, this process has broken down such that the eyes try to move *even in the absence of head movement*. The eyes will usually catch themselves doing this and try to correct, but then just fractions of a second later they will begin doing it again, leading to the characteristic back-and-forth twitching motion of nystagmus. (Nystagmus is a hard concept to explain using just words, so to consolidate your learning, pull out your phone and look up some videos of nystagmus online.) Like with vertigo, cerebellar damage is only one possible cause of nystagmus, as injuries to other areas (such as the vestibular system) can produce this condition as well.

T is for Tremor. The cerebellum acts to smooth out movements, so dysfunction of the cerebellum is one possible cause of an involuntary, rhythmic, repetitive movement known as **tremor**. (To be clear, tremor can be caused by other things as well, which we will discuss further in Chapter 17.) Consider the image below, in which a person with cerebellar damage produced the bottom figure when asked to draw the top figure:

Balancing is for Balance. An inability to maintain a stable posture is a key cerebellar sign, and cerebellar damage places people at high risk of injuring themselves due to a fall. To compensate, people with cerebellar damage will often attempt to widen their stance or use their arms to balance themselves while walking, as seen below:

3 Dys'es is for Dysdiadochokinesia, Dysarthria, and Dysmetria. Finally, we will talk about the three **dys**'es of cerebellar dysfunction. **Dysdiadochokinesia** refers to an inability to engage in **rapid alternating movements** (for example, using your hand to screw in a light bulb). These sorts of motions require a high degree of motor coordination which will be lacking in someone with cerebellar damage. **Dysarthria** refers to an unsteadiness in the pitch or rhythm of **speech**. Because the cerebellum coordinates movements of the vocal cords as well (not just the arms and legs), someone with cerebellar dysfunction will have unsteadiness that can be *heard* rather than just seen. Finally, **dysmetria** refers to an inability to judge distances when moving, leading to either overshooting or undershooting the amount of movement required (such as when you embarrass yourself by trying to give someone a high-five and missing).

Cerebellar signs include **ataxia, nystagmus, tremor, imbalance, dysdiadochokinesia, dysarthria**, and **dysmetria**.

*Imagine a **dizzy ANT** failing to **balance 3 dys'es** (dishes):*
Dizziness (vertigo)
Ataxia
Nystagmus
Tremor
Balance problems
Dysdiadochokinesia
Dysarthria
Dysmetria

FRIEDREICH'S ATAXIA

Let's get clinical! Before moving on, we will talk about one disease that helps to illustrate the function of the cerebellum well. **Friedreich's ataxia** is a genetic disorder characterized by atrophy of the **spinocerebellar pathways** connecting the cerebellum to the spinal cord. This leads to a variety of cerebellar signs, including ataxia. However, damage isn't limited to just the spinocerebellar pathway, as patients with this condition often experience degeneration of the spinal cord (in particular, the parts carrying epicritic neurons) as well as a generalized **peripheral neuropathy**, both of which can make the ataxia worse and lead to even greater impairment. Friedreich's ataxia is also associated with **hypertrophic cardiomyopathy** (an enlarged heart) which is the most common cause of death in these patients. Various skeletal abnormalities are often seen, including **scoliosis** (abnormal curvature of the spine) and an **arched foot**. Finally, impaired carbohydrate metabolism or even full-on **diabetes mellitus** is a common finding in Friedreich's ataxia, although the reasons for this link are unclear. Friedreich's ataxia is an **autosomal recessive** disease in which mutations in the **frataxin gene** are passed to one's offspring. However, affected individuals often don't show signs of the disease until later childhood (usually around the age of 10). A suspected diagnosis can be confirmed by genetic testing which shows a **trinucleotide repeat sequence GAA** on **chromosome 9**.

Overall, you can encapsulate the most important features of Friedreich's ataxia using the mnemonic **CANDY** which stands for **C**ardiomyopathy, **A**taxia, **N**europathy, **D**eformities, and d**Y**abetes. You can connect this mnemonic to the disease itself by thinking of it as a **Fried Rich Ataxia**, with "fried" and "rich" meant to evoke visions of donuts, funnel cake, and other fried rich desserts. You can also connect the trinucleotide sequence GAA to this by thinking of a baby going **GAA GAA** over **CANDY**.

Friedreich's ataxia is an **autosomal recessive disorder** resulting in atrophy of **spinocerebellar pathways**. It is associated with **hypertrophic cardiomyopathy**, **diabetes mellitus**, and **skeletal deformities** including scoliosis and an arched foot.

*Fried rich ataxia should make you think of **fried rich desserts** and **CANDY**:*
Cardiomyopathy
Ataxia
Neuropathy
Deformities
d**Y**abetes

Friedreich's ataxia results from an expansion of the **trinucleotide sequence GAA** on **chromosome 9**.

*Think of a baby going **GAA GAA** over **CANDY**.*

PUTTING IT ALL TOGETHER

At first, the functions of the cerebellum can feel difficult to understand. However, we can gain a better understanding of the cerebellum by comparing it to the basal ganglia, another part of the brain that also modifies movements (rather than creating them). While both modify the motor signals coming from the cerebral cortex, the cerebellum specifically does so to promote **coordination** and **balance**. In contrast, the basal ganglia helps movements to be **smooth** and **fluid**. You can see this most dramatically in the disorders involving each of these areas, as people with a dysfunctional cerebellum (for example, someone intoxicated with alcohol) will likely be stumbling around and falling over, even if the individual muscle movements they're making are smooth and fluid. In contrast, someone with a dysfunctional basal ganglia (such as someone with Parkinson's disease) will often have slow, jerky, and stiff movements even if the movements are technically well coordinated. This is definitely a bit of an oversimplification, but it helps to illustrate the complementary roles that each of these systems plays in the motor system.

As we continue on throughout our study of the nervous system, we will see the cerebellum popping up from time to time. Whenever someone presents with any of the characteristic cerebellar signs we've talked about so far (as captured in the **dizzy ANT** failing to **balance 3 dys'es** mnemonic), you should immediately think of the cerebellum!

REVIEW QUESTIONS

1. A 24 y/o M is pulled over by a police officer after he was swerving erratically across the road while driving. A breathalyzer device estimates a blood alcohol content of 0.18, over two times the legal limit for driving. Which of the following tasks will this man likely have the *least* difficulty completing?
    - A. Sticking his tongue straight out from his mouth
    - B. Alternating his index finger between touching his nose and the police officer's moving finger
    - C. Speaking in a smooth and unbroken manner
    - D. Standing upright with his eyes closed for one minute without falling
    - E. Walking in a straight line by touching the heel of the stepping foot to the toes of the other foot
    - F. Repeatedly flipping his hands from palms-up to palms-down

2. A 12 y/o F comes to see her pediatrician. She has been having difficulty walking over the past year and experiences frequent falls if she does not steady herself using a nearby wall or banister. She has particular difficulty walking down stairs. Her speech is slurred, with difficulty enunciating words clearly. Family history is positive for an uncle with a similar condition. On exam, there is wasting of lower leg muscles bilaterally, with an inability to stand on her tip toes. She is scheduled to undergo surgery for scoliosis. An x-ray of the spine is below:

Which of the following features is *least* likely to be found on clinical investigation?
A.   Arched feet
B.   Impaired proprioception in the toes
C.   Loss of pain and temperature sensation in the hands
D.   Impaired glucose tolerance
E.   Progressive systolic dysfunction of the heart
F.   Trinucleotide repeats on chromosome 9 on genetic testing

3.   A 69 y/o F is brought to the hospital by ambulance after she calls 911 reporting the sudden onset of "world spinning" dizziness, blurry vision, and vomiting. She has a history of hypertension and diabetes mellitus. Neuroimaging revealed a stroke in the right posterior inferior cerebellar artery with ischemic damage to the right side of the cerebellum. Which of the following is *least* likely to be observed on clinical examination?
A.   Uneven tone and pattern of speech
B.   Subjective feeling of unsteadiness when walking
C.   Swaying of the body when standing upright with one's eyes closed
D.   Inability to mime screwing in a light bulb with her left hand
E.   Difficulty hopping on the right leg

1. **The best answer is A.** Alcohol has deleterious effects on the cerebellum, so any movements that require the balance and coordination that the cerebellum provides will likely be impaired in someone who is intoxicated. Point-to-point movement requires coordination between the eyes and the fingers and would likely be impaired during alcohol intoxication, known as dysmetria (answer B). Heel-to-toe walking is also likely to be impaired (answer E). Standing upright without falling requires coordination between multiple senses, including vision and proprioception, and is likely to be impaired as well (answer D). Unsteadiness of speech, known as dysarthria, is a sign of cerebellar dysfunction (answer C). Inability to perform rapid alternating motions, known as dysdiadochokinesia, is a characteristic cerebellar sign (answer F). In contrast to the other motions, sticking one's tongue out is a simple movement that does not require the coordination abilities of the cerebellum and is likely to be preserved during alcohol intoxication.

2. **The best answer is C.** This vignette describes a case of Friedreich's ataxia, an autosomal genetic disease involving a GAA repeat on chromosome 9 (answer F). Aside from various cerebellar signs resulting from damage to the spinocerebellar pathways, Friedreich's ataxia involves a variety of other signs and symptoms encompassing various organ systems, including musculoskeletal deformities such as scoliosis and arched feet (answer A), difficulties in glycemic regulation (answer D), and cardiomyopathy (answer E). Epicritic sensation is affected, resulting in impaired vibration, proprioception, and fine touch (answer B). In contrast, protopathic sensation is generally spared.

3. **The best answer is D.** A cerebellar stroke will produce cerebellar signs on the side ipsilateral to the lesion due to the double crossing of cerebellar pathways (once in the superior cerebellar peduncle and again in the medulla oblongata). For a right cerebellar stroke, dysdiadochokinesia is likely to be observed in the right hand, not the left. Ataxia in the right leg would be expected (answer E). Dysarthria (answer A), ataxia (answer B), and impaired balance (answer C) could all be observed in a unilateral cerebellar stroke as even unilateral dysfunction can lead to deficits in these processes.

6 THE BRAINSTEM

The **brainstem**: our final frontier in the brain! The brainstem is rather appropriately named, as visually it really does look like the *stem* of a flower or a piece of broccoli from which the brain itself has grown. On a functional level, we established in Chapter 2 that the brainstem acts as a "bridge" connecting the cerebrum and cerebellum to the spinal cord and the rest of the body. However, we also learned that the brainstem is much more than *just* a bridge, as it has a wide range of functions all its own. In this chapter, we will discover those functions in more detail and map them to specific anatomical regions.

The brainstem isn't a single homogenous structure but instead is split into three parts: the **midbrain, pons,** and **medulla oblongata** (or just "medulla"). The midbrain is the uppermost part of the brainstem and receives nerve tracts from the cerebral cortex as well as subcortical structures including the thalamus, basal ganglia, and internal capsule. These nerves then continue down the midbrain into the pons, which is found in the middle, and then into the medulla at the bottom before finally exiting the skull as the spinal cord. You can see this relationship illustrated on the next page.

The nervous system likes to keep things organized, and the midbrain is no exception! The nerves traveling through the midbrain, pons, and medulla are grouped in such a way that specific types of nerves travel together in pre-ordained "lanes." For example, nerve tracts carrying motor signals travel towards the middle of the brainstem, while those carrying epicritic sensory information travel more to the side. Pay attention to how these structures are organized, as this will come into play in later chapters when we talk about how damage in different parts of the brainstem will present clinically.

All three parts of the brainstem contain **motor and sensory pathways** traveling between the spinal cord and the brain. While each part of the brainstem contains unique nuclei that carry out specific activities, the three parts of the brainstem can also work together to perform several functions as well. For example, all three parts help to regulate states of **consciousness** (including alertness and awareness) through a shared group of interconnected nuclei known as the **reticular formation**. The reticular formation plays a vital role in deciding which sensory signals are sent upwards to the brain for conscious processing and which are considered irrelevant and therefore ignored. For example, someone living in an apartment on a busy city street is still able to sleep through the night despite the barrage of sensory information that this involves (such as the sound of cars honking or the brightness of the street lights outside). This is because the reticular formation is helping to filter out irrelevant stimuli and prevent them from breaking the state of unconsciousness. However, if something *unexpected* happens (such as someone **tickling** them while sleeping), the reticular formation determines that this isn't just the usual background noise and sends the signal into conscious awareness, waking the person from their sleep. In this way, the re-**tickler** formation helps govern which information is consciously processed and which is ignored.

The **reticular formation** is involved in **conscious awareness** and **sensory filtering**.

*Like someone **tickling** you, activation of the re-**tickler** formation will wake you up.*

The **three parts of the brainstem** all contain **motor and sensory pathways** in addition to housing the **reticular formation**.

SAM: Sensory, Awareness, and Motor.

Let's now dive into each of the three parts of the brainstem in more detail.

THE MIDBRAIN

The **midbrain** is the uppermost part of the brainstem and is often divided into a few main regions: the **tectum** on the dorsal side, the **cerebral aqueduct** in the middle, the **tegmentum** on the ventral side, and two **cerebral peduncles** jutting out from the tegmentum. When slicing horizontally across the midbrain to make a cross-section, an image not unlike a teddy bear's face appears (flip the book upside-down to see it!). We can use the shape of this teddy bear's face to describe the relevant neuroanatomy.

Hello!

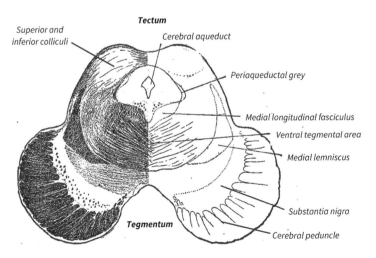

Superior and inferior colliculi
Tectum
Cerebral aqueduct
Periaqueductal grey
Medial longitudinal fasciculus
Ventral tegmental area
Medial lemniscus
Substantia nigra
Tegmentum
Cerebral peduncle

The "chin" of the bear is the **tectum** which contains two paired structures that are both involved in processing **special sensory information**. The higher pair (the **superior colliculi**) are involved in controlling eye movement in response to **visual information**, while the lower pair (the **inferior colliculi**) are involved in relaying **auditory signals** to the thalamus (and in particular the medial geniculate nucleus). We'll talk about both the superior and inferior colliculi further in Chapter 9.

In the middle is the "nose" of the bear, or the central **cerebral aqueduct**. This is a cavity that contains cerebrospinal fluid and forms part of the ventricular system which will be discussed further in Chapter 10.

The "bridge of the nose" is the **medial longitudinal fasciculus**, a structure that is heavily involved in **eye movement**. Specifically, the medial longitudinal fasciculus serves as the connection point between the three cranial nerves that innervate the various muscles surrounding the eyes. Like the inferior and superior colliculi, we will talk about the medial longitudinal fasciculus more in Chapter 9.

The bulk of the bear's "upper face" (roughly where the eyes and forehead would be) is made up of the **tegmentum**. The tegmentum contains much of the aforementioned **reticular formation** as well as sensory fibers traveling from the spinal cord to the thalamus. In addition, there are three colorful structures to note. The area immediately surrounding the cerebral aqueduct (the "snout") is known as the **periaqueductal grey** and contains a collection of cell bodies that plays an important part in the perception and regulation of **pain**. Next, the "eyes" of the bear are made up of the paired **red nuclei** which play a role in **motor functioning** (although to a much lesser extent than the neurons traveling in the "ears" which we will discuss in a bit). Finally, at the *base* of the "ears" lies the **substantia nigra** (Latin for "black substance") which, as you'll recall from Chapter 4, forms part of the basal ganglia (and in fact is the only part of the basal ganglia that lies *outside* of the cerebrum). Recall that the substantia nigra is not involved with initiating movements *directly*. Instead, it provides the basal ganglia with dopamine which acts as "grease" to facilitate movements throughout the body.

The "face" of the tegmentum also contains the **ventral tegmental area**, a collection of cell bodies that, like the substantia nigra, produces dopamine. However, while the dopamine produced in the substantia nigra goes on to modulate movement via the basal ganglia, the dopamine from the ventral tegmental area instead goes to the cerebral cortex and limbic system where it helps to govern **reward-driven behaviors**. (Knowing what you know, see if you can figure out which specific part of the limbic system is most strongly linked to the ventral tegmental area!)

Finally, the tips of the "ears" of the midbrain (known as the **cerebral peduncles**) consist largely of motor neurons traveling from the motor cortex to skeletal muscles (the **corticospinal tract**) and the muscles of the face via the cranial nerves (the **corticobulbar tract**). Two cranial nerves branch off of the midbrain as well: cranial nerve III (the **oculomotor nerve**) and IV (the **trochlear nerve**), both of which are involved in **eye movement**. For this reason, damage to the anterior part of the midbrain can lead to an inability to move the eyes in particular directions (we'll talk about which ones specifically in a future chapter). For now, you should associate these "ears" with *motor* functions (just as you associate the "chin" with *sensory* functions).

A cross-section of the **midbrain** shows the four main parts: the **tectum** on the dorsal side, the **cerebral aqueduct** in the middle, the **tegmentum** on the ventral side, and two paired **cerebral peduncles** forming lobes to either side.

*The mid-**bear**-ain has a face like a **bear**.*

To put this all together, you can use the mnemonic **IMPRESS** which stands for the Inferior colliculi, Medial longitudinal fasciculus, Periaqueductal grey, Red nucleus, Eye movement cranial nerves, Substantia nigra, and the Superior colliculi. You can connect this to the midbrain by thinking that the midbrain is at the **top** of brainstem, having beaten out the pons and the medulla—an **IMPRESS**ive feat!

The **midbrain** has several **unique areas** in addition to the **motor, sensory, and awareness functions** it shares with the other parts of the brainstem.

IMPRESS:
Inferior colliculi
Medial longitudinal fasciculus
Periaqueductal grey
Red nucleus
Eye movement cranial nerves
Substantia nigra
Superior colliculi

THE PONS

Moving down from the midbrain, we next hit the **pons**. Within the pons lies the continuation of the tracts carrying **motor and sensory information** between the brain and the spinal cord (its "bridge" function). It also communicates with the cerebellum via the **middle cerebellar peduncle**. However, the pons also contains a few unique structures that perform several vital functions. Let's use the word **PONS** itself to illustrate them:

P is for Pneumotaxic and apneustic centers. The pons contains the **pontine respiratory center** which is one of the three areas (the other two being in the medulla) that help to regulate the rate and depth of breathing. The pontine respiratory center is itself made up of two subareas. The first is the **pneumotaxic center** which stops inspiration when the lungs have stretched too far. The second is the **apneustic center** which helps to promote inspiration when the lungs are empty. Cycling between the pneumotaxic center and the apneustic center creates the usual rhythm of breathing.

O is for Ocular movement. Within the pons is the **paramedian pontine reticular formation** which will become important when discuss the process of sight in Chapter 9, as a lesion here produces a weakness of eye movements known as **gaze palsy**.

N is for Neurotransmitters. The pons contains two major sites of neurotransmitter production. The first is the **locus ceruleus** which produces **norepinephrine**, a neurotransmitter that you should be familiar with already through its role in the **sympathetic nervous system**. The second is the **raphe nucleus** which produces **serotonin**, a neurotransmitter involved in **mood** and **emotion**.

S is for Sleep. Finally, the pons contains structures important to the aforementioned reticular formation and is in particular a major contributor to the **sleep cycle**.

> The **pons** contains **motor and sensory pathways** in addition to performing several important functions including control of **breathing**, **sleep**, **eye movements**, and **neurotransmitter production**.
>
> *PONS:*
> *Pneumotaxic and apneustic centers*
> *Ocular movements*
> *Neurotransmitter production*
> *Sleep*

The middle four cranial nerves branch off of the pons: cranial nerve V (the **trigeminal nerve**), VI (the **abducens nerve**), VII (the **facial nerve**), and VIII (the **vestibulocochlear nerve**). We'll cover these in more detail in Chapter 8.

CENTRAL PONTINE MYELINOLYSIS

The various functions that the pons performs are illustrated in a disease known as **central pontine myelinolysis**. In this condition, the myelin sheaths of nerves in the pons becomes damaged due to **rapid correction of hyponatremia** with intravenous fluids. This results in changes in respiratory function (by damaging the pneumotaxic and apneustic centers), paralysis (from injury of the motor pathways passing through the basilar pons), ataxia (by disrupting the connections between the pons and the cerebellum), and changes in consciousness (from impairing the reticular formation). Central pontine myelinolysis is a deadly disease with a poor prognosis. While some survivors make a full recovery, others are left with lasting neurologic deficits. It can be avoided by making sure to correct hyponatremia slowly. You can remember this condition by thinking of the rhyme, "From low to high, the pons will die."

> **Central pontine myelinolysis** results in symptoms of pontine dysfunction including **respiratory dysfunction, paralysis, ataxia**, and **changes in consciousness**. It results from **overly rapid correction of hyponatremia**.
>
> *From **low to high** (sodium), the **pons will die**.*

THE MEDULLA OBLONGATA

The **medulla oblongata** is the lowest part of the brainstem. Like the midbrain and pons, the tracts carrying **motor and sensory information** continue here. The medulla also contains several **reflex centers**, most of which involve either keeping good things in (the **swallowing reflex**) or pushing bad things out (the **vomiting, coughing,** and

sneezing reflexes). The vomiting reflex lies in an area known as the **area postrema** which initiates this process when it detects a potential toxin in the mouth. You can remember the function of the area **postrema** by thinking of it as **p.o. streamer** (with p.o., or *per os*, being medical jargon for "by mouth").

> The **area postrema** regulates **vomiting** and other responses to **potential toxins**.
>
> *A **p.o. streamer** (postrema) will have a **stream of vomit** exiting **by mouth**.*

 The medulla also contains the **nucleus solitarius** which receives input from the tongue about **taste** and is involved in the **gag reflex**. In addition, the nucleus solitarius is involved in the **baroreceptor reflex** that regulates **blood pressure**. While most people think that you need a fancy sphygmomanometer to measure blood pressure, your body is actually quite adept at measuring it naturally using pressure sensors in various arteries throughout the body. This information is sent to the nucleus solitarius which then regulates both heart rate and vascular tone using the sympathetic and parasympathetic nervous systems. Because of its dual function, a lesion at the nucleus solitarius can result in a characteristic combination of **loss of taste** as well as instability of **blood pressure** and other vital signs. You can remember this by thinking of it as the nucleus **sole-lick**-tarius. Imagine being asked to **lick** the **sole** of someone's foot. This would likely make you want to **gag** and would cause your **heart rate and blood pressure to go up**.

> The **nucleus solitarius** is involved in **taste sensation**, the **gag reflex**, and regulation of **blood pressure**.
>
> *The nucleus **sole-lick**-tarius is like licking the sole of someone's foot. The **taste** would make you **gag**, and your **heart rate** and **blood pressure** would increase.*

In addition, the medulla oblongata contains the **nucleus ambiguus** which connects to the muscles involved with **speech** and **swallowing**. Damage to the nucleus ambiguus can lead to **dysphagia** (difficulty chewing), **dysarthria** (trouble speaking), and **dysphonia** (a hoarse voice). You can remember the function of the nucleus ambig-**uh-uh's** by pronouncing it with two uh's at the end, which should help to remind you of someone giving a **speech** who keeps saying lots of uh's.

The **nucleus ambiguus** controls the muscles involved in **speech** and **swallowing**.

*Think of the nucleus ambig-**uh-uh**'s when someone is having trouble giving a **speech**.*

Vitally, the **cardiovascular center** lies within the medulla, with the sympathetic and parasympathetic nervous systems working here to increase and decrease the heart rate, respectively. The rest of the **respiratory center** is also found in the medulla, with the **dorsal respiratory group** starting the process of inspiration and the **ventral respiratory group** controlling expiration. You can remember these core functions of the medulla oblongata by thinking of someone getting a **medul** pinned onto them as a reward—the **medul**(la) goes right over their **heart** and **lungs**.

"Cross my heart."

The **medulla oblongata** contains the **cardiovascular and respiratory centers**.

*Think of someone getting a **medul** (medulla) placed over their **heart and lungs**.*

Like the other parts of the brainstem, the medulla shoots off a few cranial nerves of its own: cranial nerve IX (the **glossopharyngeal nerve**), X (the **vagus nerve**), XI (the **spinal accessory nerve**), and XII (the **hypoglossal nerve**).

Finally, at the end of the medulla, the **pyramidal decussation** occurs. This is a key part of understanding the motor pathway, so pay close attention! At the pyramidal decussation, the nerve fibers in the motor pathway cross over from left-to-right and right-to-left. This right here is the reason why damage to the *left* side of the brain produces weakness on the *right* side of the body and vice versa. (Efferent motor pathways are not the only ones that decussate in the medulla—epicritic sensory signals also cross over here, as we will discuss further in the next chapter when talking about the spinal cord.) So what exactly do *pyramids* have to do with the motor pathway? If you use your imagination a little bit, the motor neurons running along the anterior side of the medulla kind of jut out from the landscape like pyramids. This led to their being called "**pyramidal tracts**."

Medulla oblongata

Pyramidal decussation

Spinal cord

After the pyramidal decussation, the brainstem ends and the spinal cord officially begins! To remember the functions of the medulla, use the mnemonic **SCARPH** which stands for the nucleus **S**olitarius, **C**rossing of motor and epicritic pathways, nucleus **A**mbiguus, **R**espiratory center, area **P**ostrema, and the **H**eart (or cardiovascular) center. You can remember this by thinking that the medulla is the **lowest** part of the brainstem, so it is closest to the neck where you would wear a SCARPH.

The **medulla oblongata** contains several areas that perform **unique functions**.

SCARPH:
*Nucleus **S**olitarius*
***C**rossing of motor and epicritic pathways*
*Nucleus **A**mbiguus*
***R**espiratory center*
*Area **P**ostrema*
***H**eart (cardiovascular) center*

PUTTING IT ALL TOGETHER

And with that, we have officially crossed the "bridge" from the brain to the spinal cord! As with so much in neurology, the best way to put all of this information together is to use it clinically. We will do this in earnest a few chapters from now when we talk about strokes, as ischemic damage in different parts of the brainstem leads to clinically distinct presentations. For now, let's head to the spinal cord.

REVIEW QUESTIONS

1. A 43 y/o M with a history of excessive alcohol intake and malnutrition presents after a fall in which he lost consciousness for approximately one minute. By the time he arrived at the hospital, he had regained consciousness. Initial neurological exam is unremarkable. Laboratory analysis reveals hyponatremia, hypokalemia, and abnormal liver function tests. Intravenous fluids are started which result in improvement in his electrolyte abnormalities within 24 hours. Several days later, he suddenly develops diffuse muscle weakness, including poor respiratory effort. This weakness progresses to complete paralysis of all muscles except for eye blinking and movement. An MRI scan of his head reveals the following:

Which of the following mechanisms likely accounts for the neuronal damage observed in this case?
   A. Ischemic damage in the midbrain
   B. Ischemic damage in the pons
   C. Ischemic damage in the medulla oblongata
   D. Osmotic demyelination in the midbrain
   E. Osmotic demyelination in the pons
   F. Osmotic demyelination in the medulla oblongata
   G. Autoimmune destruction in the midbrain
   H. Autoimmune destruction in the pons
   I. Autoimmune destruction in the medulla oblongata

2. A 52 y/o F is undergoing chemotherapy for breast cancer. During her initial treatment, she develops severe nausea and vomiting. Before her next treatment, she is prescribed ondansetron, an anti-nausea medication. The anti-nausea effect of ondansetron can most likely be explained by its interaction with chemical receptors in which part of the brainstem?
   A. Nucleus ambiguus
   B. Area postrema
   C. Pyramidal decussation
   D. Ventral tegmental area
   E. Paramedian pontine reticular formation
   F. Nucleus solitarius

3. A 37 y/o M military veteran is seen in a pain management clinic. He suffers from chronic pain due to multiple points of embedded shrapnel from exposure to an improvised explosive device while serving overseas. Despite several years of treatment involving medications, physical therapy, and alternative practices, he remains disabled by his pain. His pain management specialist offers to enroll him in a clinical trial of a new treatment for chronic pain involving implantation of a neurostimulator, or a device that is surgically inserted into the brain that activates neurons in nearby areas. Implantation of the neurostimulator into which of the following areas is most likely to result in pain relief for this patient?
   A. Periaqueductal grey
   B. Substantia nigra
   C. Medial longitudinal fasciculus
   D. Apneustic center
   E. Red nuclei

1. **The best answer is E.** This vignette describes a case of central pontine myelinolysis, a potentially deadly condition in which overly rapid correction of hyponatremia results in demyelination of neurons in the pons due to osmotic fluid shifts. Ischemic damage (answers A—C) and autoimmune mechanisms (answers G—I) are not believed to be involved. Damage to the midbrain (answer D) or medulla (answer F) would produce different signs and symptoms.

2. **The best answer is B.** Many chemotherapy drugs are notorious for causing severe nausea by activating chemoreceptors in the area postrema of the medulla oblongata. Ondansetron is believed to block this effect by antagonizing serotonin receptors in this area. None of the other areas listed are thought to be involved in the vomiting reflex, with the nucleus ambiguus involved in speaking and swallowing (answer A), the pyramidal decussation involved in the crossing over of the motor pathway (answer C), the ventral tegmental area involved in reward-driven behaviors (answer D), and the paramedian pontine reticular formation involved in eye movements (answer E). The nucleus solitarius is involved in the gag reflex which shares a similar purpose as the vomiting reflex (to keep potentially toxic substances out of the body); however, the mechanisms and neuroanatomical centers by which they do so are different (answer F).

3. **The best answer is A.** The midbrain contains the periaqueductal gray, a nucleus that plays a critical role in modulating pain perception. Indeed, several studies have shown that the periaqueductal gray appears to be the most promising site for deep brain stimulators in patients with chronic pain. The substantia nigra and red nuclei are involved in movement (answers B and E), the medial longitudinal fasciculus helps to control eye movements (answer C), and the apneustic center helps to regulate the respiratory cycle (answer D).

7 THE SPINAL CORD

If the brain is the capital city and the brainstem is the bridge, then the **spinal cord** is the highway on which nerves travel to and from their destination. Just as cars exit from the highway to take side streets, nerves traveling in the central nervous system branch off of the spinal cord and exit the vertebral column when they get close enough to their destination, at which point they continue their journey as **peripheral nerves**.

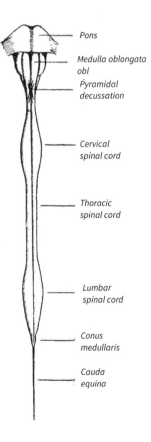

Pons

Medulla oblongata obl

Pyramidal decussation

Cervical spinal cord

Thoracic spinal cord

Lumbar spinal cord

Conus medullaris

Cauda equina

The spinal cord is traditionally divided into three regions, with the **cervical** spinal cord in the neck, the **thoracic** spinal cord in the chest, and the **lumbar** spinal cord in the abdomen. As you can see in the image to the right, there are enlargements in both the cervical and lumbar regions that correspond to the increased number of nerves shooting off here to go to the arms and legs, respectively. After the lumbar enlargement, the spinal cord begins to thin, creating a tapered region known as the **conus medullaris**. The spinal cord officially ends around the first or second lumbar vertebrae. However, even after the spinal cord ends, many of the nerves that have branched off from it continue to run downwards in a cluster of nerves known as the **cauda equina** (Latin for "horse's tail," which makes sense given its appearance). This highlights an important point, and one that is easy to get confused about: the place where a nerve branches off of the spinal cord is *not* necessarily the same place where it exits from the vertebral column! Instead, these nerves generally continue to travel in the vertebral column for a while before exiting. This is why there are spinal nerves from the sacral and coccygeal regions (around the pelvis) even though the spinal cord ends in the lower back, as these nerves exit the spinal *cord* before its termination at L1/L2 but do not exit the *vertebral column* until the sacral region.

The spinal nerves that exit from the spinal cord are **mixed nerves** consisting of both sensory and motor neurons (remember that the side streets are two-way streets). While the two kinds of neurons intermingle for most of the length of the nerve, close to the spinal cord the two types separate, with **M**otor (**E**fferent) neurons exiting on the **V**entral side of the spinal cord and **S**ensory (**A**fferent) nerves entering on the **D**orsal side (like the "on-ramp" and "off-ramp" of a highway). You can use the phrase "**ME Very SAD**" to keep this pattern straight in your head. The cell bodies of the *sensory* nerves lie *outside* the spinal cord in clusters known as **dorsal root ganglia** while the cell bodies of *motor* nerves lie *inside* the spinal cord in a region known as the **anterior horn**. We'll go over both sensory and motor pathways in more detail later in this chapter.

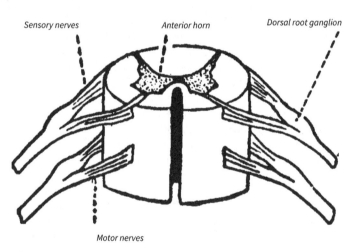

Sensory nerves   Anterior horn   Dorsal root ganglion

Motor nerves

Afferent sensory tracts are located in the **dorsal spinal cord**, while **efferent motor tracts** are located in the **ventral spinal cord**.

ME Very SAD:
Motor (Efferent) on the Ventral side, Sensory (Afferent) on the Dorsal side.

SPINAL CORD ANATOMY

The spinal cord is not a disorganized tangle of nerves thrown together in a haphazard fashion. Instead, the spinal cord features a surprising degree of organization owing to the fact that, as in the other parts of the nervous system we have discussed so far, **nerves that do similar things tend to travel together**. This allows us to understand and name the various parts of the spinal cord that we see.

When you cut horizontally across the spinal cord to make a cross-section, the first difference you'll notice is the separation between grey and white matter. Unlike the cerebrum (where the grey matter is on the outside and the white matter is on the inside), the spinal cord features the *opposite* arrangement, with the white matter on the outside and the grey matter making a "butterfly" in the middle.

While the composition of the grey and white matter changes down the length of the spinal cord, overall this butterfly-like appearance remains remarkably similar throughout, as seen below.

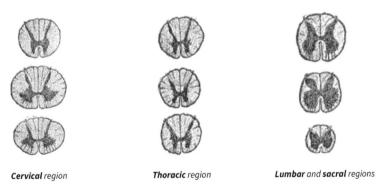

Cervical region   *Thoracic* region   *Lumbar* and *sacral* regions

Within the grey and white matter are further subdivisions based on function. To understand these, we'll need to look at the various pathways traveling through the spinal cord in more detail, starting with the sensory pathways.

THE DORSAL COLUMN—MEDIAL LEMNISCUS PATHWAY

As we talked about in Chapter 2, there are two types of sensory neurons, with **protopathic neurons** carrying **crude touch**, **pain**, and **temperature** and **epicritic neurons** carrying **fine touch**, **vibration**, and **proprioception**. We'll focus on the epicritic neurons for now.

Epicritic neurons travel in the **dorsal column** of the spinal cord (the part between the two upper wings of the butterfly). The dorsal column is further split up into two parts, with information coming from the *lower* body being carried *medially* in the **gracile fasciculus** and information from the *upper* body being carried *laterally* in the **cuneate fasciculus**. The fact that the gracile fasciculus is medial to the cuneate fasciculus will become clinically important when talking about spinal cord injuries. You can remember this by thinking that, most of the time, your arms are lateral to your legs. It is the same way in the dorsal column of the spinal cord. You can also use the phrase, "**Walk grac**efully and **eat** with your **hands**" to correlate your legs to the **grac**ile fasciculus and your hands to the cun**eate** fasciculus.

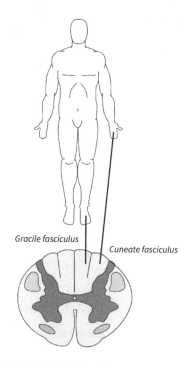

Gracile fasciculus

Cuneate fasciculus

Sensory information about **fine touch**, **vibration**, and **proprioception** travels on **epicritic neurons** in the **dorsal column**, with signals from the **lower body** in the **gracile fasciculus** and signals from the **upper body** in the **cuneate fasciculus**.

*Walk grac*efully *and **eat** with your **hands**.*

These neurons travel in the dorsal column of the spinal cord until they hit the medulla where another cluster of cell bodies known as the **dorsal column nuclei** (made up of both the **nucleus gracilis** and **nucleus cuneatus**) lies. After synapsing here, these neurons **cross over** from left-to-right and right-to-left (just like the motor fibers we talked about in the previous chapter). From there, these neurons continue their journey on a bundle of axons (now known as the **medial lemniscus**) before hitting the ventral posterolateral nucleus of the **thalamus** (remember both that the *th*alamus is for *th*ensthory information and that the VPL is the site where a *Very Painful Leg* is sensed). From the thalamus, the signal is finally passed on to its target: the **somatosensory cortex** in the parietal lobe. This entire pathway is known as the **dorsal column—medial lemniscus pathway**.

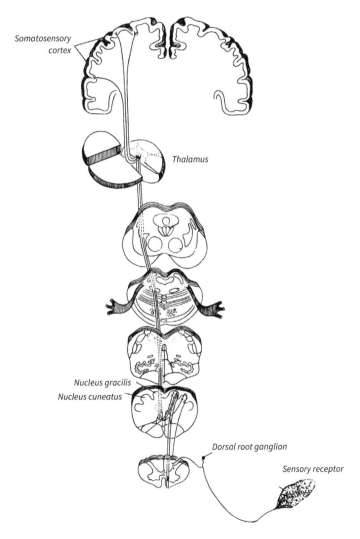

Somatosensory cortex

Thalamus

Nucleus gracilis
Nucleus cuneatus

Dorsal root ganglion

Sensory receptor

THE SPINOTHALAMIC TRACT

Take a step back and consider that the dorsal column—medial lemniscus pathway is just one of the *two* possible routes that sensory information can take through the central nervous system. The other route, known as the **spinothalamic tract**, carries information about **crude touch, pain,** and **temperature** and has its own way of doing things. Peripheral nerves carrying these sensory modalities initially enter the spinal cord on the dorsal side. They first enter an area known as the **posterolateral tract** or **Lissauer's tract**. Lissauer's tract is an interesting quirk of the spinothalamic tract. Neurons in Lissauer's tract often head up or down a spinal level or two, seemingly for no reason other than to confuse students! This is why sensory loss related to a spinal cord injury can often be "off" a level or two from what you would expect.

Anyway, after passing through Lissauer's tract, these neurons then enter into one of two areas that are contained in the upper wings of the butterfly: the **substantia gelatinosa** and the **nucleus proprius**. (The substantia gelatinosa is named for the "goopy" gelatin-like texture of this tissue caused by the lack of myelin in these nerves.)

Unlike the nerves traveling in the dorsal column (which wait until the medulla to cross over), the nerves in the spinothalamic tract cross over soon after entering the spinal cord in a bundle known as the **anterior white commissure**. You can remember this by thinking of **F**ine touch, **V**ibration, and **P**roprioception as **F**eeling **V**ery **P**atient (they are fine waiting until the medulla to cross over) while **N**on-discriminative touch, **T**emperature, and **P**ain are **N**ot **T**hat **P**atient and want to cross over *immediately*.

Protopathic neurons cross over immediately in the **anterior white commissure** of the spinal cord while **epicritic neurons** cross over in the **medulla oblongata**.

Fine touch, Vibration, and Proprioception are Feeling Very Patient while Non-discriminative touch, Temperature, and Pain are Not That Patient.

Because the dorsal column—medial lemniscus pathway and the spinothalamic tract cross over at different places, a patient with damage to their spinal cord can have **crossed findings** with numbness of crude touch, pain, and temperature on the right half of their body and numbness of fine touch, vibration, and proprioception on the left (or vice versa). This occurs if the injury is located after the spinothalamic tract has crossed over but *before* the dorsal column–medial lemniscus pathway has crossed.

After crossing over in the anterior white commissure, the nerves in the spinothalamic tract travel upwards in the white matter surrounding the anterior horn of the spinal cord, with the information from lower in the body being carried on the most lateral aspect while information from the upper body is carried more medially. (Note that this is the *opposite* pattern of what we saw with the dorsal column—medial lemniscus pathway, where information from the legs was *medial* to information from the arms!) They then travel to the brainstem where they *don't* cross over in the medulla (as they have done this already in the spinal cord, as they're **N**ot **T**hat **P**atient). They then synapse in the **thalamus** before completing their journey in the somatosensory cortex in the **parietal lobe**.

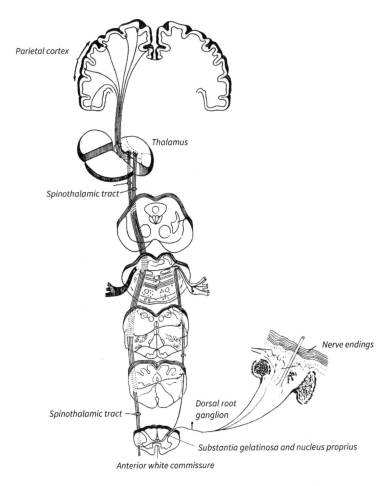

Parietal cortex

Thalamus

Spinothalamic tract

Nerve endings

Spinothalamic tract

Dorsal root ganglion

Substantia gelatinosa and nucleus proprius

Anterior white commissure

Let's use a mnemonic to put together everything that we've learned about the spinothalamic tract. The phrase "List Some Proper Avenues for Sending Temperature and Pain" can help you to remember this sequence from the time of entry into the dorsal aspect of the spinal cord to the point of arrival in the cerebral cortex.

The **spinothalamic tract** carries **protopathic sensations** from the body to the brain.

List Some Proper Avenues for Sending Temperature and Pain:
Lissauer's (posterolateral) tract
Substantia gelatinosa and nucleus Proprius
Anterior white commissure
Spinothalamic tract
Thalamus
Parietal lobe

THE CORTICOSPINAL TRACT

Now that we have covered both sensory pathways, we will now shift our attention to the motor pathway that makes up the other half of information flowing through the spinal cord. The vast majority of motor signals travel through the spinal cord in the **corticospinal tract**. The corticospinal tract is divided into two parts: the **lateral corticospinal tract** and the **anterior corticospinal tract**. The lateral corticospinal tract is the larger of the two, accounting for around 90% of all the motor neurons traveling through the spinal cord. In general, motor neurons going towards the upper extremities travel more *medially* while those going to the lower extremities are found more *laterally*. (This also follows the opposite pattern of the one seen in the gracile fasciculus and the cuneate fasciculus in the dorsal column! You can remember the distinction by thinking that the pattern in the dorsal column just makes *sense*, which should remind you of *sensation*.)

When it is their time to exit the highway and take side streets to their final destination, nerves in the lateral corticospinal tract synapse onto motor neurons in the **anterior horn** of the spinal cord (the bottom half of the butterfly's wings). This marks the position of a clinically important divide between **upper motor neurons** and **lower motor neurons**. The neurons that carry the motor signal at any point from the motor cortex in the cerebrum up until the anterior horn cell are considered *upper* motor neurons, while those that carry the signal down from the anterior horn cell to the muscle itself are considered *lower* motor neurons. On a clinical level, damage to upper motor neurons produces different signs and symptoms compared to damage to lower motor neurons (a concept we'll revisit in much more detail in Chapter 16).

After picking up the signal from the upper motor neurons in the anterior horn, lower motor neurons then exit the spinal cord as the ventral nerve root (remember **ME V**ery **SAD**) before joining afferent nerves from the dorsal root to form a spinal nerve. And with that, the motor pathway is done! (If you've made it this far, use your corticospinal tract to give yourself a high-five.) A visual summary of the corticospinal tract is found on the next page. To remember this pathway, think of a teacher reviewing the motor pathway who says, "**F**lexing **I**nvolves **P**yramids." However, if a student hasn't read the part of the previous chapter going over the pyramidal tracts, they may be confused and say, "**C**ome **A**gain?"

The **corticospinal tract** carries **motor signals** from the brain to the body.

"Flexing Involves Pyramids." "Come Again?"
Frontal lobe
Internal capsule
Pyramidal decussation
Corticospinal tract
Anterior horn

Motor cortex in frontal lobe

Internal capsule

Corticospinal tract

Pyramidal decussation

Lateral corticospinal tract

Anterior horn

Ventral nerve roots

EXTRAPYRAMIDAL TRACTS

The corticospinal tracts (along with the corticobulbar tracts carrying motor signals to the face as we discussed in Chapter 4) are collectively known as the **pyramidal tracts**. Just outside of the pyramidal tracts are four **extrapyramidal tracts** that do not control voluntary movements directly but rather help to **fine-tune movement** by working closely with the **basal ganglia**. The neurotransmitter **dopamine** is involved in the extrapyramidal system, so abnormalities in dopamine can lead to changes in involuntary motor processes such as tone and posture. To remember the function of the extrapyramidal tracts, think of a group of musicians playing some **fine tunes** *outside* the pyramids (as opposed to the tomb-like silence *inside* the pyramids).

SPINAL REFLEXES

Thus far, we have primarily talked about neurons traveling between the brain and the rest of the body by way of the spinal cord, including both motor neurons traveling on efferent pathways and sensory neurons traveling on afferent pathways. However, the spinal cord also contains connections between afferent and efferent neurons that *don't* involve the brain at all and are instead contained entirely *within* the spinal cord itself. These connections are responsible for several **spinal reflexes** that occur without conscious effort. Someone who receives a sensory stimulus (say, by accidentally stepping into a fire) will activate sensory neurons in the skin. Signals from these neurons will first travel along their axons to their main cell bodies in the dorsal root ganglion before entering the spinal cord. While some of these neurons will continue up into the brain via the spinothalamic tract, others will instead synapse with **interneurons** (or neurons that connect neurons to each other) that then synapse directly onto motor neurons in the anterior horn. These neurons will send motor signals to leg flexors that will then act to quickly withdraw the foot from the fire. Because this reflex arc only involves a few neurons and takes place entirely at the level of the spinal cord, it can occur with lightning-fast speed. In fact, the person may find that they have already moved their foot by the time their brain registers any conscious sensation of pain!

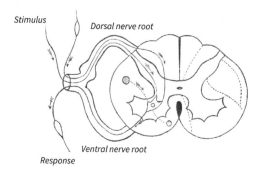

Stimulus

Dorsal nerve root

Ventral nerve root

Response

A number of **stretch reflexes** can activate certain muscles in response to the muscle being stretched. Anyone who has been to a doctor will likely recognize that these are commonly tested. As we will cover in Chapter 11, stretch reflexes are helpful for localizing where damage to the spinal cord has occurred, as each specific reflex maps to a particular level of the spinal cord. Absence of a particular reflex suggests damage to some aspect of the reflex arc (either the sensory nerves sensing the stretch, the motor nerves carrying the signal, or the spinal cord connecting them) at or around this level.

Okay, let's recap what we've learned about the anatomy of the spinal cord using the image on the next page. Feel free to refer back to this as needed!

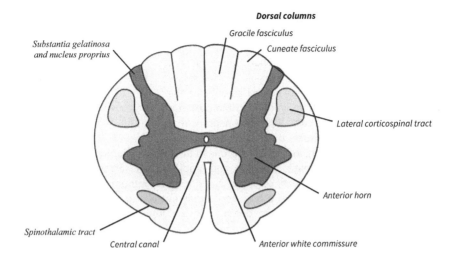

SPINAL CORD PATHOLOGY

Let's reinforce everything we've learned about the anatomy of the spinal cord so far by taking a closer look at what happens when something goes wrong. Injuries to the spinal cord can come from various sources, from mechanical injuries like a car crash to infectious diseases like polio. When looking at the effects of spinal cord injuries, the column-like nature of the spinal cord introduces a unique wrinkle. Unlike the brain, it's no longer enough to simply say *what part* of the spinal cord we are talking about. Instead, we need to specify at *what level* of the spinal cord the damage has occurred. While the *nature* of the deficits can help us to figure out the structures involved, the *location* of the deficits in the body will help us figure out the level.

The simplest kind of spinal cord injury to understand is a **complete spinal injury** in which all function below the level of the lesion is lost. For example, someone who sustains a complete injury at the level of their chest will likely lose all sensory and motor ability in their legs (but will retain these abilities in their arms). This is because the spinal nerves for the upper extremities have already exited the spinal cord in the neck, while those traveling to the legs have yet to depart.

In cases of **incomplete spinal injury**, however, only a part of the spinal cord has been damaged, so some functions will be lost while others will be retained. It is the specific *distribution* of abilities and deficits across various parts of the body that allows us to localize where in the spinal cord the injury has occurred. We will now talk about a few prototypical spinal cord injuries. If you have grasped the concepts so far, you should be able to guess what deficits will be seen from a lesion in a particular part of the spinal cord with enough time and effort!

ANTERIOR CORD SYNDROME

An injury to the front half of the spinal cord causes a loss of **motor function** as well as **crude touch, temperature, and pain** sensation below the level of the lesion. Recall that the spinothalamic tract not only travels in the anterior portion, it also crosses there in the anterior white commissure. While the lateral corticospinal tract is found in the posterior portion of the spinal cord, the motor neurons that emerge from these tracts then go to the *anterior* horn of the spinal cord, leaving them prone to this form of injury as well. However, the key here is that fine touch, vibration, and proprioception remain intact, as epicritic neurons travel in the *dorsal* columns! Anterior cord syndrome can be caused by a stroke of the anterior spinal artery, particularly in the mid-to-upper thoracic spinal cord, as collateral blood supply doesn't join the anterior spinal artery until lower down in the thorax.

POSTERIOR CORD SYNDROME

The posterior spinal cord is primarily made up of the dorsal columns, so when an injury occurs here, the primary deficits are in the sensory modalities of **fine touch, vibration, and proprioception** below the level of the injury (with crude touch, temperature, and pain sensation as well as motor function all remaining intact). Due to the loss of proprioception, people with posterior cord syndrome often develop a "stomping" gait as a way to compensate for their inability to sense limb posture and position. Posterior cord syndrome is rarely caused by direct mechanical injury to the spine. Instead, metabolic or inflammatory insults are more often at fault. For example, infection with syphilis can lead to demyelination of the dorsal columns, resulting in a permanent posterior cord syndrome known as **tabes dorsalis**.

CENTRAL CORD SYNDROME

An injury to the center of the spinal cord that leaves the periphery largely intact causes greater weakness of the **arms** compared to the legs (remember that the motor neurons traveling to the arms are *medial* to those traveling to the legs!). Sensory loss below the level of the injury is often seen as well due to the proximity of the spinothalamic tract to the center of spinal cord, although some degree of **sacral sparing** is often seen (as sacral fibers are located most *lateral*, away from the center). Common causes of a central cord syndrome include tumors (such as an ependymoma or astrocytoma) which can arise from *within* the spinal cord.

One frequently tested cause of central cord syndrome is **syringomyelia**, a condition in which a fluid-filled cavity (or cyst) forms within the spinal cord. The classic presentation of syringomyelia involves a **bilateral loss of motor strength** as well as **crude touch, pain, and temperature sensation** in the chest, back, and upper arms (often referred to as a "**cape-like distribution**"). This is due to the cyst forming from the cerebrospinal fluid-filled **central canal** and impinging upon the **anterior white commissure** and **spinothalamic tract** (which explains why fine touch, vibration, and proprioception, all of which travel in the dorsal columns, are spared). This also explains why protopathic sensation in the lower extremities is not affected, as these neurons travel more laterally in the spinothalamic tract than those coming from the upper extremities. You can remember the association of **syr**ingomyelia and a **cape**-like distribution by thinking of it as "**Cape Syr**" (like the movie "Cape Fear").

Syringomyelia typically presents as a **bilateral weakness and loss of crude touch, pain, and temperature** in a **cape-like distribution**.

*Think of "**Cape Syr**" (like the movie "Cape Fear").*

BROWN-SÉQUARD SYNDROME

Brown-Séquard syndrome (also known as **spinal hemiplegia**) occurs when one-half of the spinal cord—either the right or the left—is injured more than the other. For this reason, motor function as well as fine touch, vibration, and proprioception are compromised on the *same* side as the lesion, while crude touch, temperature, and pain are compromised on the *opposite* side as the lesion. (Remember that, of all the motor and sensory nerves in the spinal cord, only those carrying **N**on-discriminative touch, **T**emperature, and **P**ain are **N**ot **T**hat **P**atient and want to cross over immediately, which is why these are the specific deficits that are found *contra*lateral to the lesion.) While Brown-Séquard syndrome can occur due to any process that injures the spinal cord, the most common cause is direct penetrating trauma as in a gunshot or stab wound. You can remember this by thinking that **B**rown-**S**équard is what happens when someone tries to **B**ack**S**tab you but only does it **halfway**.

Motor weakness

Loss of fine touch, vibration, and proprioception   *Loss of crude touch, pain, and temperature*

Brown-Séquard syndrome is a **unilateral spinal cord injury** resulting in **ipsilateral motor weakness** and **epicritic numbness** as well as **contralateral protopathic numbness.**

Brown-Séquard is when someone tries to BackStab you but only does it halfway.

SUBACUTE COMBINED DEGENERATION OF THE SPINAL CORD

Subacute combined degeneration of the spinal cord involves a gradual loss of myelin in both the **dorsal *and* lateral columns** of the spinal cord. Demyelination of the dorsal columns leads to loss of fine touch, vibration, and proprioception resulting in **poor balance and falling**, while demyelination of the lateral columns containing the corticospinal tract leads to loss of motor function resulting in **muscle weakness** in the arms and legs. (Compare this to posterior cord syndrome which is more specific to the dorsal columns, leading to loss of epicritic sensation with sparing of motor function.) The "combined" part of the name really is the key to understanding this condition, as it is essentially two forms of spinal cord injury in one! The most common cause of subacute combined degeneration is a **deficiency of vitamin B₁₂** which you can remember by thinking that B**12** leads to not *1* but *2* forms of spinal cord damage!

Subacute combined degeneration of the spinal cord results in **demyelination** of both the **dorsal and lateral columns. Vitamin B₁₂ deficiency** is a common cause.

Lack of B12 leads to not 1 but 2 forms of spinal cord injury!

CAUDA EQUINA SYNDROME

While intuitively it would make sense that the nerves coming out of the cauda equina (the "horse's tail" at the lowest end of the spinal cord) would go to the lowest end of the body (the feet), in reality these nerves instead travel to the pubic and anal areas. (We'll go over why in the next chapter.) For this reason, **cauda equina syndrome** leads to deficits in both **motor and sensory function** in the **pelvic region**, including loss of bowel and bladder control, muscle paralysis and hyporeflexia in the lower body, and numbness around the perineum (sometimes called **"saddle anesthesia"** because the numbness is in the same area that would be in contact with a horse's saddle). It's easy to use some mental imagery to connect an injury in the **horse**'s tail with a **saddle** distribution.

An injury to the **cauda equina** leads to **bowel and bladder incontinence, muscle paralysis** in the lower body, and **saddle anesthesia**.

*Connect the **horse**'s tail (cauda equina) with numbness in a **saddle** distribution.*

PUTTING IT ALL TOGETHER

And with that, it's time to exit the central nervous system and head for the peripheral nervous system! Before we go, let's review each of the three main pathways that we have covered in these chapters: the **spinothalamic tract** made up of small unmyelinated protopathic fibers carrying crude touch, temperature, and pain sensation; the **dorsal column—medial lemniscus pathway** made up of large myelinated epicritic fibers carrying fine touch, vibration, and proprioceptive information; and the large myelinated fibers of the **corticospinal tract** carrying motor signals from the brain. Each of these three pathways involves **three neurons** between the brain and the rest of the body. Let's go each one-by-one.

Protopathic neurons enter the spinal cord through the dorsal side and synapse in the **substantia gelatinosa** or **nucleus proprius** (often going up or down a level or two in the **posterolateral or Lissauer's tract**). These fibers then cross over in the **anterior white commissure** *immediately* before traveling in the **spinothalamic tract** in the lateral spinal cord. They continue up the spinal cord and through the brainstem before synapsing again in the **ventral posterolateral nucleus** of the **thalamus**. From there, the third neuron travels to the **parietal lobe** of the cerebral cortex. Use the phrase "**L**ist **S**ome **P**roper **A**venues for **S**ending **T**emperature and **P**ain" to remember this sequence!

Epicritic neurons also enter the spinal cord through the dorsal side, but rather than synapsing and crossing right away, they instead travel in the **dorsal columns**, with fibers from the legs traveling medially in the **gracile fasciculus** and fibers from the arms traveling laterally in the **cuneate fasciculus**. These neurons synapse in the **nucleus gracilis** and **nucleus cuneatus** in the medulla before crossing over to the other side. They then travel in the **medial lemniscus** to the **ventral posterolateral nucleus** of the **thalamus** where they synapse again. For the final leg of their journey, they travel from the thalamus to the **parietal cortex**. Luckily, no mnemonic is needed to remember the order here, as the unique components (the dorsal columns and medial lemniscus) are right there in the name **dorsal column—medial lemniscus pathway**.

Finally, **motor** neurons travel from the **anterior lobe** of the cerebral cortex via the **posterior limb of the internal capsule** and into the brainstem. At the level of the medulla, they cross over in the **pyramidal decussation** and then continue on in the spinal cord as the **corticospinal tract**. These nerves then synapse on an interneuron entirely within the spinal cord which itself synapses onto the third and final neuron in the **anterior horn** (the lower wing of the butterfly). This lower motor neuron then exits the spinal cord on its anterior side and continues its journey to the muscle as a spinal nerve. The mnemonic "**F**lexing **I**nvolves **P**yramids"/"**C**ome **A**gain?" can help you keep this sequence in your mind.

*The **central nervous system** on the left and the **peripheral nervous system** on the right.*

92

REVIEW QUESTIONS

1. A 27 y/o F is brought to the hospital for a neurological evaluation. She is noted to have significant motor weakness in both her right arm and right leg, with an inability to make a fist with her right hand or raise her right foot off of the ground. Sensory exam is notable for loss of fine touch and vibration on the right side, with loss of pain and temperature on the left. Which of the following is the most likely event that precipitated this presentation?
   A. Sudden onset following a focal bacterial infection
   B. Slow onset due to a nutritional deficit
   C. Rapid onset following significant blood loss during childbirth
   D. Onset at birth due to a genetic mutation
   E. Immediate onset following complete transection of the spinal cord during a motor vehicle accident

2. A 52 y/o F comes to the hospital after sustaining second-degree burns on her right hand. While cooking dinner, she did not notice that her hand was touching a pot of boiling water. On exam, she is noted to have absent pain and temperature sensation in both arms as well as the back and shoulders, with motor weakness in a similar distribution. Pain and temperature sensation is normal throughout the lower extremities. Vibration and proprioception are intact throughout as well. Magnetic resonance imaging of the back is most likely to reveal abnormalities in which region of the spinal cord?
   A. Anterior
   B. Posterior
   C. Center
   D. Periphery
   E. Left
   F. Right

3. A 78 y/o M makes an appointment to see a nurse practitioner. He reports no significant medical history. On exam, the nurse practitioner notices that his ability to sense the position of his toes with his eyes closed is impaired. He does not detect a vibrating tuning fork when it is applied to his feet. Which of the following pathways is most likely damaged?
   A. Gracile fasciculus
   B. Cuneate fasciculus
   C. Spinothalamic tract
   D. Posterolateral tract
   E. Lateral corticospinal tract
   F. Anterior corticospinal tract
   G. Extrapyramidal tracts

1. **The best answer is A.** This vignette describes a case of Brown-Séquard syndrome in which one-half of the spinal cord (either the right or left side) is injured. This results in a characteristic combination of ipsilateral motor weakness, ipsilateral loss of epicritic sensation, and contralateral loss of protopathic sensation. While Brown-Séquard syndrome is most classically associated with stab injuries to the back, it can occur as a result of any lesion that preferentially affects one side of the spinal cord over the other (in the case of this vignette, a focal bacterial abscess that impinged on one side but not the other). Systemic causes of spinal cord damage such as nutritional deficits (answer B), shock (answer C), and genetic diseases (answer D) would be expected to affect both sides of the spinal cord equally. Complete transection of the spinal cord would result in bilateral loss of all movement and sensation in areas below the lesion (answer E).

2. **The best answer is C.** This patient's loss of motor strength and protopathic sensation occurs in a cape-like distribution which combined with the intact epicritic sensation should immediately make you think of syringomyelia. Syringomyelia is often caused by a cyst forming in the central canal of the spinal cord, which is why the dorsal columns on the periphery are generally spared (answer D). While anterior spinal cord syndrome involves the same combination of deficits as syringomyelia (motor weakness with intact epicritic sensation), the cape-like distribution helps to differentiate this, as an anterior cord syndrome would instead show these deficits below the level of the lesion (answer A). The intact epicritic sensation effectively rules out posterior cord syndrome (answer B). A spinal injury on either the right or left side would present as Brown-Séquard syndrome (answers E and F).

3. **The best answer is A.** The gracile fasciculus is the part of the dorsal columns that carries sensory information about fine touch, vibration, and proprioception from the lower extremities to the brain. While the cuneate fasciculus also carries this information, it connects to the upper extremities, not the lower (answer B). The spinothalamic tract and posterolateral tract both carry crude touch, pain, and temperature sensation (answers C and D), while the lateral and anterior corticospinal tract carry motor signals to voluntary skeletal muscles (answers E and F). Finally, the extrapyramidal tracts carry motor signals to non-voluntary muscles involved in fine-tuning other movements to improve posture and muscle tone (answer G).

8 THE PERIPHERAL NERVOUS SYSTEM

If the spinal cord is the highway connecting the brain to the rest of the body, then the **peripheral nervous system** is made up of the many side streets connecting the highway to the small cities and towns scattered across the countryside. On a functional level, the peripheral nervous system has two main subdivisions, with **afferent** and **efferent** neurons serving completely different purposes (despite traveling together on the same nerves). The efferent division of the peripheral nervous system is divided into the **somatic nervous system**, which innervates skeletal muscles to exert voluntary control over body movements, and the **autonomic nervous system**, which exerts unconscious control over various muscles and glands via two opposing systems. These two systems are the **sympathetic nervous system**, which kicks in the "fight or flight" response, and the **parasympathetic** nervous system, which activates when it is time to "feed and breed, then rest and digest." (If any of this feels unfamiliar to you, take a few moments to review Chapter 2!)

In this chapter, we will take our understanding of the peripheral nervous system to the next level by looking not only at the organization of the system as a whole but also at some of the individual nerves within it, including the twelve **cranial nerves** that branch off of the brain to supply the structures of the face, neck, and shoulders as well as the **spinal nerves** that emerge from the spinal cord to supply the rest of the body. Just to be clear, we will not necessarily talk about *every single peripheral nerve in the entire body*, as this is more in the realm of anatomy and would require a whole book on its own! However, we will go over enough so that you are able to understand what happens on a clinical level when diseases of the peripheral nervous system arise.

CRANIAL NERVES

The **cranial nerves** are a collection of peripheral nerves that branch off directly from the brain rather than from the spinal cord like the rest of the peripheral nervous system. There are 12 cranial nerves, the first two of which exit out of the cerebrum while the other 10 exit from different parts of the brainstem. (Technically speaking there are 24 cranial nerves as each one comes in a pair, with one going to the left and one going to the right. However, for the sake of simplicity we will refer to each of them in the singular.)

*The **cranial nerves** coming off of the **brain** and **brainstem**.*

The cranial nerves are **frequently tested**, both in a clinical sense (as they are a key part of the standard neurological exam that we will learn about in Chapter 11) as well as in an educational sense (as they frequently show up on board exams). For this reason, a variety of mnemonics exist to memorize them, a popular version of which goes, "**O**oh, **O**oh, **O**oh, **T**o **T**ouch **A**nd **F**eel **V**ery **G**reen **V**egetables, **AH**!" which represent the cranial nerves in order:

Ooh is for Olfactory. The **olfactory nerve** is a **sensory** nerve that is responsible for the sense of **smell**. Unlike most other sensory nerves, the olfactory nerve does *not* pass through the thalamus before going to the cortex but rather goes to parts of the cerebral cortex and subcortex directly (which may explain why our response to smells tends to be much more immediate and emotional compared to other sensory modalities).

Ooh is for Optic. The **optic nerve** is a **sensory** nerve that is responsible for **eyesight**. Like the olfactory nerve, it branches off of the brain directly (rather than the brainstem). We will cover the process by which light entering the eyes is converted into a conscious visual image in more detail in Chapter 9.

Optic nerve

Ooh is for Oculomotor. The **oculomotor nerve** is a **motor** nerve that branches off of the midbrain. It is one of three cranial nerves that are responsible for **eye movement** (the other two being the trochlear nerve and the abducens nerve). Together these nerves control the six muscles known as the **extraocular muscles** (as seen on the next page). The oculomotor nerve innervates four out of these six muscles, making it by far the biggest contributor to extraocular movement. This nerve also contains the nerve fibers going to the **pupillary sphincter** (which constricts the pupils to change the amount of light entering the eye) as well as those going to the **ciliary muscle** (which changes the shape of the lens to allow the eye to focus on nearby objects), making it a powerful contributor to multiple functions in the eyes.

To is for Trochlear. The **trochlear nerve** is a **motor** nerve that controls the **superior oblique** muscle which is responsible for moving the eyes at a downward medial angle. Interestingly, the superior oblique exists as a "pulley" system of sorts (as seen on the next page) which is why it pulls the eye at an angle rather than in a simple left-right or up-down direction.

Touch is for Trigeminal. The **trigeminal nerve** is a **mixed** nerve (meaning that it contains both motor and sensory neurons) that carries sensory information from the **face** as well as motor signals to the muscles responsible for **chewing**. The trigeminal nerve splits into three branches which each serve a different function: the **ophthalmic nerve** (sensation from the upper third of the face), the **maxillary nerve** (sensation from the middle third of the face), and the **mandibular nerve** (sensation from the lower third of the face as well as motor control over chewing).

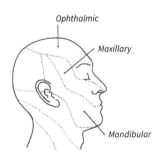

And is for Abducens. The **abducens nerve** is a **motor** nerve that is the third and final nerve responsible for extraocular movements. It controls the **lateral rectus** muscle that makes the eye look outward towards the ears (rather than inward towards the nose). You can remember which cranial nerves move which extraocular muscles by thinking of the phrase **LR₆SO₄** which, despite being non-sense, has a strange way of sticking in the brain.

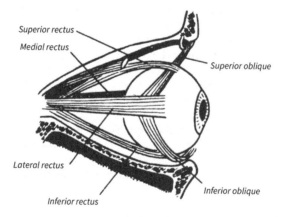

The **trochlear nerve** supplies the **superior oblique**, the **abducens nerve** supplies the **lateral rectus**, and the **oculomotor nerve** supplies the rest.

LR₆SO₄:
Lateral **R**ectus is the **6**ᵗʰ cranial nerve, **S**uperior **O**blique is the **4**ᵗʰ cranial nerve.

Feel is for Facial. The **facial nerve** is a **mixed** nerve that splits into separate branches as it progresses, with the temporal, zygomatic, buccal, mandibular, and cervical branches each traveling to various regions controlling the muscles of **facial expression** from the forehead down to the chin. The facial nerve also carries sensory information about **taste** from the anterior **two-thirds** of the tongue. Finally, a branch of the facial nerve travels to the **stapedius**, a small muscle (in fact, the *smallest* one in the human body!) that helps to stabilize and reduce the noise traveling on the stapes bone in the inner ear. Dysfunction of the facial nerve is known as **Bell's palsy** and results in a loss of motor ability on one side of the face. A change in taste and an increased volume of auditory sensations (known as **hyperacusis**) may both occur as well given the facial nerve's role in taste sensation and noise reduction. The loss of function on only a single side of the face is often quite noticeable, making it **clear as a Bell** that something has gone wrong with the facial nerve.

Bell's palsy is a form of **facial nerve dysfunction** that results in **unilateral loss of facial muscles, changes in taste sensation**, and **hyperacusis**.

*When half the face is not working, it's **clear as a Bell** what's going on.*

Very is for Vestibulocochlear. The **vestibulocochlear nerve** is a **sensory** nerve that carries two different types of sensory information from the inner ear. It splits into two main divisions: the **cochlear nerve**, which carries information about **sound** from the cochlea, and the **vestibular nerve**, which carries information about **balance and spatial orientation** from the vestibular system.

Vestibular system

Vestibulocochlear nerve

Cochlea

Green is for Glossopharyngeal. The **glossopharyngeal nerve** is a **mixed** nerve, although its sensory functions far outweigh its motor roles (as it innervates only a single muscle: the stylopharyngeus, which assists in **swallowing**). Its primary responsibility is to convey sensory information from the **inside of the mouth** as well as **taste** from the **posterior third of the tongue** (remember that the facial nerve covers taste from the anterior two-thirds!). One of its keys roles is to detect the presence of objects in the mouth that shouldn't be there and to initiate the **gag reflex** (the motor component of which is carried out by the vagus nerve, discussed next).

Vagus nerve

Glossopharyngeal nerve

Vegetables is for Vagus. The **vagus nerve** is a **mixed** nerve that is quite unique for a cranial nerve. While the function of most of the cranial nerves is localized to primarily the areas around the head and neck, the **vagus nerve** breaks this pattern by innervating organs across the entire body, including the **heart**, **lungs**, and **gastrointestinal tract**. (In fact, the only major organ that *doesn't* receive signals from branches of the vagus nerve in some way is the adrenal gland!) Specifically, the vagus nerve is responsible for controlling **parasympathetic output** to these organs, putting them in a state where they support the organism "feeding and breeding, then resting and digesting." The vagus nerve also relays **sensory signals** (including information about the physical state, chemical composition, ambient temperature, and fluid make-up) from these organs back to the brain, allowing it to further fine-tune the autonomic response. Like most cranial nerves, the vagus nerve does have a few functions specific to the head and neck, including innervating a few of the core muscles used for actions such as **speaking** and **swallowing** as well as the motor component of the **gag reflex**. Overall, the vagus nerve is a hugely important nerve given its widespread effects throughout the body!

A is for Accessory. The **accessory nerve** (also called the spinal accessory nerve) is a **motor** nerve that supplies two muscles in the neck: the **sternocleidomastoid** (which turns the head from side to side) and the **trapezius** (which shrugs the shoulders).

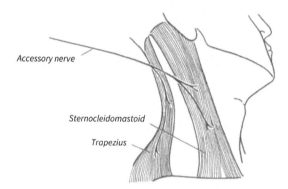

H is for Hypoglossal. Finally, the **hypoglossal nerve** is a motor nerve that innervates nearly all muscles involved with movement of the **tongue** (which makes sense as "glossal" comes from the Greek word for tongue). It is not involved in taste sensation (recall that this function is covered by the facial and glossopharyngeal nerves).

It can be helpful to remind yourself of the general function of each of the cranial nerves (specifically, whether it is a sensory nerve, a motor nerve, or both). You can use the phrase "**S**ome **S**ay **M**arry **M**oney **B**ut **M**y **B**rother **S**ays **B**ig **B**rains **M**atter **M**ore" to match the function of the nerve, with words beginning with **S** being **S**ensory nerves, those beginning with **M** being **M**otor nerves, and those beginning with **B** representing nerves with **B**oth motor and sensory functions.

The **twelve pairs** of **cranial nerves** exit the central nervous system from the **brain and brainstem** to supply areas around the **head and neck.**

Ooh, Ooh, Ooh, To Touch And Feel Very Green Vegetables, AH!
Olfactory
Optic
Oculomotor
Trochlear
Trigeminal
Abducens
Facial
Vestibulocochlear
Glossopharyngeal
Vagus
Accessory
Hypoglossal

Some Say Marry Money But My Brother Says Big Brains Matter More:
Sensory
Sensory
Motor
Motor
Both
Motor
Both
Sensory
Both
Both
Motor
Motor

Finally, it can be helpful to remember where in the brain each of the cranial nerves exits from. You can remember this using the "Rule of 4s": the **first 4** come out of the **brain and midbrain**, the **middle 4** exit from the **pons**, and the **last 4** originate in the **medulla.** (We'll go over the clinical implications of this in much more detail in Chapter 12.)

SPINAL NERVES

As the central nervous system exits from the skull and becomes the spinal cord, it continues to shoot off nerves supplying the rest of the body. These paired nerves are known as **spinal nerves** and are made up of both sensory and motor neurons. Spinal nerves are named according to which region of the spine they come from, with 8 pairs of **cervical nerves**, 12 pairs of **thoracic nerves**, 5 pairs of **lumbar nerves**, 5 pairs of **sacral nerves**, and 1 pair of **coccygeal nerves**. These spinal nerves emerge from the vertebral column in between two vertebrae. Just to make things confusing, all spinal nerves are named for the vertebra *above* where they exit *except* for cervical nerves 1 through 7 (this is because there is no vertebra above C1, as it exits between the first vertebra and the skull). Each region of the spine sends out nerves to specific parts of the body, with the cervical nerves innervating the **neck**, upper **chest**, and **upper limbs**; the thoracic nerves innervating the **trunk** and **back**; the lumbar nerves innervating the **upper legs** and **buttocks**; the sacral nerves innervating the **hips**, **thighs**, **legs**, and **feet**; and the single pair of coccygeal nerves innervating the skin on the back of the **coccyx**.

Recall from Chapter 2 that the specific area of the skin innervated by a particular spinal nerve is known as its **dermatome**. The specific dermatome of every single spinal nerve is far beyond our scope here, but you should be broadly familiar with the general area covered by each type of spinal nerve as seen below:

When learning about dermatomes, it can initially be kind of confusing. At first it makes sense, with the first few cervical dermatomes proceeding in an orderly fashion down the neck. However, things begin to break down quickly. Why do C5 and C6 innervate the *lateral* portions of the arm while C8 and T1 innervate the *medial* parts? Why does L1 cover the skin over the buttocks, but the genitals and anus aren't covered until the sacral nerves? Why is the area covered by S2 (the back of the legs) *higher up* than what is covered by S1 (the foot)? If you try to apply the order of the dermatomes to a human in a standing (bipedal) position, it won't make sense. However, if you apply it to a human who is in a *bent over* (quadrupedal) position with their hands towards the floor facing outwards so that the thumbs are towards the head, things start to come together a little more. Suddenly it's clear why the anus is innervated by a lower spinal nerve than the legs: it's farther back.

We will also discuss **myotomes**, or the muscles groups innervated by a specific spinal nerve. It's important to keep in mind that the dermatome and myotome for a particular spinal nerve do not necessarily overlap, as a muscle may be innervated by a completely different spinal nerve than the skin overlying it! For example, the spinal nerve C6 innervates the biceps muscle in the upper arm as part of its *myo*tome but its *derma*tome covers the *hand*. Don't get confused on this point!

CERVICAL NERVES

The 8 pairs of cervical nerves emerge from the spinal cord in the neck and form two major networks of nerves. The first is known as the **cervical plexus** and is made up of the first four cervical nerves (C1-C4). Nerves from the cervical plexus innervate parts of the head and neck, particularly the skin over the **back of the head** and **muscles of the neck**. For this reason, injuries to the neck can result in sensory deficits in the back of the head as well as difficulty moving the neck.

The second network arising from the cervical nerves is known as the **brachial plexus** and lies in the deep tissue between the neck and the armpit. Nerves from the brachial plexus innervate the upper chest, shoulders, arms, and hands. For example, damage to C7 produces numbness in the hands (particularly the palms and the middle three fingers) as well as muscle weakness in the elbow, forearm, wrist, and fingers.

Nerves from both the cervical and brachial plexuses (specifically, C3-C5) also innervate the **diaphragm**, or the large flat muscle that helps to bring air into the lungs. You can remember this using the rhyme, "C3, 4, and 5 keep the diaphragm alive."

The **third through fifth cervical nerves** innervate the **diaphragm**.

*C3, 4, and 5 keep the **diaphragm** alive.*

*The **dermatome** of selected **spinal nerves** in the **cervical, thoracic,** and **lumbar regions.***

Damage to the brachial plexus is one cause of **wrist drop**, or an inability to extend the hand at the wrist. This is commonly (though certainly not always) due to dysfunction of C7 or its branches, including the **radial nerve**. The radial nerve originates in the brachial plexus and travels down the arm and forearm, supplying muscles along the way. You can remember this association by thinking that a **D**ropped w**R**ist can be caused by **D**amage to the **R**adial nerve.

> **Wrist drop** can occur due to damage of the **brachial plexus**, the **radial nerve**, or one of its branches.
>
> *A **D**ropped w**R**ist can be caused by **D**amage to the **R**adial nerve.*

Another finding known as a **winged scapula** can occur due to damage of the **long thoracic nerve** which branches off of C5, 6, and 7 and travels to the **serratus anterior muscle**. Damage to either the nerve or the muscle can lead to an unnatural protrusion of the shoulder blade, especially when raising the arms.

Wrist drop *Winged scapula*

THORACIC NERVES

The 12 pairs of thoracic nerves run between the ribs and are known as **intercostal nerves** (except for the last thoracic nerve which runs *under* the last rib, earning it the name **subcostal nerve**). The thoracic nerves supply the regions of the **chest** and **upper back**. You can remember the general distribution of dermatomes by keeping in mind a few landmarks. For example, if you know that **T4** innervates the skin near the nipples ("T4 does the **teat pore**") and **T10** innervates the skin around the umbilicus ("T10 does the belly but-**TEN**"), you can estimate approximately which thoracic nerve is involved in an injury resulting in pain or numbness in any region between them.

> **Dermatomal landmarks** in the **thoracic region** include the **nipple (T4)** and the **umbilicus (T10)**.
>
> *T4 does the **teat pore**, while T10 does the belly but-**TEN**.*

LUMBAR NERVES

The 5 pairs of lumbar nerves generally innervate the **lower back, outer buttocks**, and **front of the legs**. Like the cervical nerves, the lumbar nerves have a tendency to form mesh-like networks. The first few pairs form the **lumbar plexus** which innervates the muscles of the **thigh**, while the latter pairs combine with sacral nerves from the next vertebral region to form the **lumbosacral trunk** which together innervate the skin and muscles of the **buttocks and pelvis**. Lumbar nerves also innervate the muscles of the lower **leg and foot**, which is why damage to this region (and in particular the L5 nerve root) can result in **foot drop**.

There are a few helpful dermatomal landmarks to remember here. One is that **L1** helps to innervate the skin over the **Inguinal Ligament**, or the band that helps form the "V" leading from the abdomen to the pubic region. The other is that **L4** helps to innervate the thigh leading down to the **knee**, which you can remember by thinking that L4 is activated when you get down on **all fours** (L4s).

Dermatomal landmarks in the **lumbar region** include
the **inguinal ligament (L1)** and the **knee (L4)**.

*L1 does the 1nguinal Ligament, while **L4** is for when you get down on **all fours** (L4s).*

*The **dermatome** of spinal nerves in the **lumbar** and **sacral regions**.*

SACRAL NERVES

The 5 pairs of sacral nerves form a **sacral plexus** which goes on to supply the muscles of the **hip, thigh, leg**, and **foot** as well as innervate the skin on the **back of the leg** and the **anogenital** region. In particular, the second through fourth sacral nerves form the **pudendal nerve** which supplies parasympathetic input to the gastrointestinal, urinary, and reproductive systems. In this way, the sacral nerves have a much greater autonomic component compared to most spinal nerve regions. You can remember the significance of S2 through S4 by using the rhyme, "S2, 3, and 4 let the urine hit the floor" (or the alternative, "S2, 3, and 4 keep the penis off the floor").

COCCYGEAL NERVE

Finally, the single pair of coccygeal nerves arises from the conus medullaris and helps to provide sensation to the skin over the **coccyx.**

THE SYMPATHETIC TRUNK

Unlike the parasympathetic nervous system which largely has its output through just a few nerves in the cranial and sacral regions (like the vagus or pudendal nerves), the sympathetic nervous system instead forms a paired bundle of nerve fibers known as the **sympathetic trunk** that lies just lateral to the vertebral column for almost the entirety of its run, though it is particularly pronounced in the **thoracic** and **lumbar** regions. Because the sympathetic nervous system innervates the entire body, this means that some nerve fibers arising from the sympathetic trunk near the *spine* will actually turn around and start climbing back up the body to the muscles of the *face*!

This becomes clinically important when trying to determine the source of dysfunction in the sympathetic nervous system. One high-yield condition you must be able to recognize promptly is **Horner's syndrome**. When the upper part of the sympathetic trunk becomes damaged, it causes a unique set of findings in the face including a constricted pupil (**miosis**), a lack of sweating (**anhydrosis**), and a drooping eyelid (**ptosis**). (We haven't covered this in particular, but the superior tarsal muscle responsible for raising the upper eyelid receives its innervation not only from the facial nerve but from the sympathetic nervous system as well.) Horner's syndrome can be caused by any lesion that interferes with normal functioning in the sympathetic nervous system, and we will return to it a few times throughout this book. For now, just remember h**O**rner's syndrome by thinking of **Sympa** Claus saying, "H**O** h**O** h**O**!" This should remind you of pt**O**sis, mi**O**sis, and anhydr**O**sis as well as the **sympa**thetic nervous system.

*An example of **ptosis**.*

Horner's syndrome is a combination of **ptosis, miosis**, and **anhydrosis** caused by damage to the **sympathetic trunk**.

***Sympa** Claus says, "H**O** h**O** h**O**!" (pt**O**sis, mi**O**sis, and anhydr**O**sis).*

The location of the sympathetic trunk in the thoracic region explains why lesions in the chest can lead to sympathetic dysfunction. Another high-yield condition to learn is a **Pancoast tumor** which is an abnormal growth in the uppermost part of the lung that leads to Horner's syndrome. Initially it can seem strange to learn this ("Why does a *lung* tumor lead to issues in the *face*?"), but now that we know that the sympathetic trunk arises from the thoracic and lumbar regions (with some fibers turning around to head back up to the face), it makes much more sense. You can remember this diagnosis by making an acronym out of **PANCOAST**: a **P**ulmonary **A**pex **N**eoplasm **C**ausing **O**'s (pt**O**sis, mi**O**sis, and anhydr**O**sis) **A**ttributable to the **S**ympathetic **T**runk.

A **Pancoast tumor** is a **tumor in the lungs** that compresses the **sympathetic trunk**, leading to **Horner's syndrome**.

PANCOAST:
A *Pulmonary Apex Neoplasm Causing O's Attributable to the Sympathetic Trunk.*

PUTTING IT ALL TOGETHER

Peripheral nerves are tricky things. While we have talked about them as discrete objects, this is more to enhance your initial understanding than it is to give a precisely accurate picture of the true organization of these nerves. In reality, peripheral nerves rarely just exit from the central nervous system and proceed in an orderly fashion to their destination. Instead, these nerves form networks, take detours, join up with (and then depart from) nerves in other regions, and generally do everything they can to resist an easy understanding. This complexity is why many specific functions map to *several* spinal nerves instead of just one (like control over the diaphragm in C3-5 or the urinary bladder in S2-4), as these nerves often combine with other nerves on the way to the target organ.

Given this complexity, let's do what we can to keep things simple. We will do our best to maintain a laser-like focus on covering just enough of the peripheral nervous system to understand the diseases that result from dysfunction in the nervous system itself (rather than those resulting from anatomical abnormalities). This will mean leaving out even some disorders that are common in clinical neurology (such as carpal tunnel syndrome), as going over all of the potential diseases involving peripheral nerves would require not just an understanding of neurology but also a good degree of knowledge about the anatomy of the entire body. We will leave you to do that work with your anatomy books. For our current purposes, it is enough to know the specific functions of each cranial nerve and the general mapping of dermatomes and myotomes covered by each spinal region, and we will fill in additional details as we go.

REVIEW QUESTIONS

1. A 54 y/o M with no prior medical history is referred to a neurologist after he notices increasing weakness in his legs, with pain and cramping if he walks for more than a few minutes. He recently has had several episodes where he has the sensation of "choking" while trying to swallow food. After a thorough evaluation he is diagnosed with amyotrophic lateral sclerosis, a disease that causes degeneration of motor neurons. Which of the following nerves is *least* likely to be affected by this disease?
   A. Trigeminal nerve
   B. Facial nerve
   C. Vestibulocochlear nerve
   D. Glossopharyngeal nerve
   E. Hypoglossal nerve

2. A 27 y/o M sees a sports medicine specialist after he notices increasing weakness of his right wrist over the past week. He is a professional body builder and is distraught about the prospect of missing his normal workout routine as a result of this deficit. On exam, he is unable to extend his wrist as seen below:

   Physical examination shows atrophy of muscles in the forearm and hand, with preservation of the triceps. Which of the following regions is most likely to show signs of numbness on further examination?
   A. Neck
   B. Arm
   C. Forearm
   D. Hand
   E. Chest

3. A 51 y/o M sees his primary care doctor complaining of pain in his left shoulder and arm. He first noticed it one month ago, but it has slowly gotten worse since that time. He reports numbness and tingling in his left forearm and fingers. His only other symptom is a persistent cough which he attributes to smoking one pack of cigarettes every day for the past 30 years. He is diagnosed with musculoskeletal pain and sent home with instructions to rest his shoulder. One

week later, he presents to the emergency department of the hospital believing he is having a stroke. Vital signs are HR 118, BP 146/90, RR 28, and T 100.1°F. His oxygen saturation is decreased at 84%. A chest x-ray is obtained:

Upon further work-up, he is diagnosed with an apical lung tumor that has spread to the preganglionic neurons ascending to the cervical sympathetic chain. Which of the following signs and symptoms is *least* likely to be seen in this patient?

A. Weakness of the muscles of chewing
B. Unequal diameter of the left and right pupils
C. Asymmetry of muscles innervated by the facial nerve
D. Changes in facial sweat production
E. All of the following are equally likely to be seen

1. **The best answer is C.** Given that amyotrophic lateral sclerosis only affects motor neurons, any nerves that do not have a motor component will not be affected. Out of the listed cranial nerves, all but one have a motor component and are therefore candidates for being affected by amyotrophic lateral sclerosis, with the trigeminal nerve controlling the muscles of chewing, the facial nerve controlling the muscles of facial expression, the glossopharyngeal nerve controlling a muscle involving in swallowing, and the hypoglossal nerve controlling the muscles of the tongue. In contrast, the vestibulocochlear nerve has only a sensory component.

2. **The best answer is D.** Damage to C7, either at its root or in one of the nerves that it contributes to, is a potential cause of wrist drop as most of the muscles of wrist extension originate at this level. The sensory dermatome of C7 includes the hands. The neck is generally C3 and C4 (answer A), the arm and forearm is C5 and C6 (answers B and C), and the chest gets into thoracic territory (answer E).

3. **The best answer is A.** This vignette describes a case of Horner's syndrome related to a Pancoast tumor. A Pancoast tumor is a form of lung cancer that develops in the apex of the lung. Some of the neurons traveling through the lung apices ascend in the cervical sympathetic chain to return to the face. For this reason, a tumor in this location can lead to the specific facial abnormalities seen in Horner's syndrome, including ptosis (answer C), miosis (answer B), and anhydrosis (answer D). The muscles involved in chewing are not directly innervated by the sympathetic nervous system.

9 THE SPECIAL SENSES

Now that we have covered both the central and peripheral nervous systems, we have the tools necessary to learn about the pathways involved in each of the **special senses**, including **vision**, **hearing**, **balance**, **taste**, and **smell**. These senses each require a specialized organ to process, which results in the ability to take in more detailed information from the outside world and convert them into

rich, complex sensations such as sight or sound. Each of these senses relies upon an intricate pathway that carries the signal from the time the sense organ first picks it up to the point at which it is processed into conscious awareness in the cerebral cortex. Despite the complexity of these pathways, our task at hand is to make this process understandable, so proceed we must, starting with vision.

VISION

Vision allows us to interpret the patterns of light reflecting off of the objects surrounding us in order to make sense of our environment. Out of all the special senses, we will spend the most time on the visual system due to its sheer complexity. Our eyes are unique for a sense organ in that they do not just passively absorb information from the environment. Instead, the eyes play an active role in controlling what information is available by moving in different directions, focusing on some objects rather than others, and controlling how much light enters. (While one could argue that this applies to other special senses as well, such as moving the head to better hear a sound, this process is nowhere near as complex as it is in vision.) For this reason, we will need to examine several processes to understand vision: the **visual pathway** carrying sensory information from the eyes back to the brain, the centers controlling **eye movements**, and the nerves involved in **pupillary size**.

THE EYES

The **eyes** are a pair of specialized sensory organs whose primary function is to convert light from our environment into neural signals that can travel to the cortex and enter our conscious awareness. Light initially hits the **cornea** and then travels through the **lens** which focuses it onto the **retina** at the back of the eye. The retina is filled with **photoreceptor cells** that are responsible for translating light into a neural signal. These photoreceptor cells contain proteins known as **opsins** that absorb light and transmit them into neuronal signals.

There are two main types of opsins that are involved in creating a visual image: **cones** (which can discriminate between different wavelengths to generate color) and **rods** (which cannot distinguish between different colors but are better adapted to see at low levels of light). Rods and cones are spread all across the retina, although they are highly concentrated in an area known as the **macula**. (The macula covers the center of one's vision, with damage to the macula producing a loss of central vision.) The process of converting light into an action potential is incredibly complicated and is well beyond the scope of this book, but after a lot of processing, this visual information begins its journey to the brain on the second cranial nerve, also known as the **optic nerve**. (Interestingly, the point at which the optic nerve leaves the retina, known as the **optic disc**, does *not* contain photoreceptor cells and is considered a visual blind spot.)

The **retina** consists of **photoreceptor cells** containing proteins known as **opsins** that convert light into neural signals. **Cones** are responsible for **color vision** while rods can pick up on **lower intensity light**.

Cones add color to an image.

THE VISUAL PATHWAY

After departing from the eye, the optic nerve travels to the **optic chiasm** which is located just under the hypothalamus and pituitary gland. Visual information from the *medial* part of the retina **crosses over** here, while information from the *lateral* part of the retina stays on the same side. However, because the light has already crossed over once when entering the eye via the lens, the medial part of the retina actually receives light from the *lateral* visual fields. (The visual pathway is best understood visually, not through text! Follow along with the diagram on the next page as you read.)

Following the optic chiasm, visual information continues its journey via the **optic tract** which now contains visual information from *both* eyes corresponding to the *opposite* field of view (so the left optic tract contains visual information from the patient's right field of view and vice versa). The optic tract then travels to the Lateral Geniculate Nucleus of the thalamus (remember that this is involved in *Looking* **G**ood **N**aked) before traveling further via **optic radiations** to finally reach its destination in the visual cortex of the **occipital lobe**. Of note, the optic radiations on each side are divided into halves, with the **superior division** carrying visual information from the *upper* retina (or the *lower* part of the visual field, since the image is reversed when it enters the eye) while the **inferior division** carries information from the *lower* retina (or the *upper* part of the visual field).

To remember this pathway, think about the **image** of **2 Ch**arismatic **Tra**velers **L**ooking **G**ood **N**aked at the **Radia**nt **Oc**ean. This should remind you of the optic nerve (cranial nerve **2**), the optic **Ch**iasm, the optic **Tra**ct, the Lateral **G**eniculate **N**ucleus of the thalamus, the optic **Radia**tions, and finally the visual cortex in the **Oc**cipital lobe.

The **visual pathway** carries signals from the **retina** to the **occipital cortex**.

2 Charismatic Travelers Looking Good Naked at the Radiant Ocean:
Optic nerve (Cranial nerve 2)
Optic Chiasm
Optic Tract
Lateral Geniculate Nucleus of the thalamus
Optic Radiations
Occipital cortex

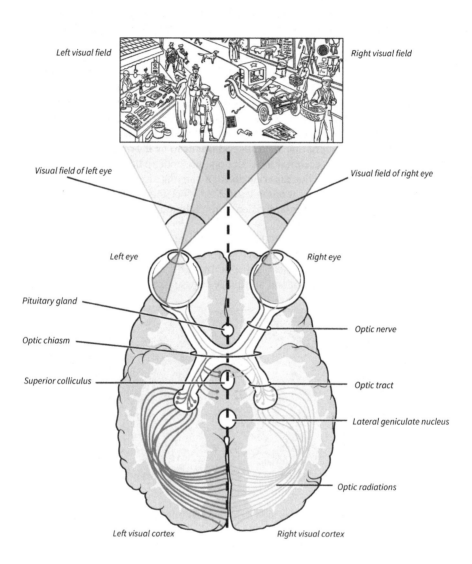

VISUAL FIELD DEFICITS

To help you put all of this information together, let's review what happens when damage occurs at various parts of the visual pathway. Because information travels from the retina to the occipital lobe in an organized way, we can predict how any given lesion will affect eyesight based on its precise location in the pathway. But first, some vocabulary! Loss of half of the visual field is known as **hemianopsia** (sometimes spelled hemianopia, without the s). **Homonymous hemianopsia** refers to when the *same* half of the visual field is lost in both eyes, while **heteronymous hemianopsia** means a *different* visual field is lost in each. Loss of a quarter of the visual field is known as **quadrantanopsia**.

Let's say that a person is standing in front of the following scene:

If they have complete eyesight, they will see approximately this, with each circle representing roughly the visual input from a single eye:

However, if a lesion occurs in the **right optic nerve** *anterior* to the optic chiasm, they will instead only be able to see this:

If damage occurs in the **optic chiasm** (for example, if a tumor of the pituitary gland got so large that it began compressing the nerves traveling here), it would result in **bitemporal hemianopsia** in which visual information is missing from the *lateral* fields of view (those closer to the temples of the head, giving this condition its name):

If instead the **right optic tract** were to become damaged, a **left homonymous hemianopsia** would result:

Damage to the **optic radiations** would produce **quadrantanopsia** in which a specific quadrant of the visual field is missing. Due to various crossings, damage to the *superior* division of the right optic radiations produces a loss of *inferior* visual fields…

… while damage to the *inferior* division produces a loss of *superior* visual fields:

Finally, damage to the visual cortex in the occipital lobe will produce either a homonymous hemianopsia or quadrantanopsia. The key defining feature here is that the center of the visual field is preserved, a phenomenon known as **macular sparing**.

Spend some time correlating each of the hemianopsias and quadrantanopsias discussed with the drawing of the visual pathway on page 116, and make sure you understand how damage to each area produces the specific deficits observed!

BRANCHES OFF OF THE VISUAL PATHWAY

Wait a minute, what about the **superior colliculi**? Didn't we learn that these were involved in the visual pathway previously when we talked about the midbrain? While it is true that some visual signals go to the superior colliculi, it is a *branching off* of the visual pathway rather than a *step along the way*. The superior colliculi essentially siphon off signals from the visual pathway and use them to move the eyes accordingly. (For example, if you see a shadowy figure out of the corner of your eye, your superior colliculi will send signals to the oculomotor, trochlear, and abducens nerves telling them to move your eyes in that direction.) In this way, the superior colliculi play a key role in eye movement in response to visual information.

It is also worth mentioning one more branch off the visual pathway. Specifically, a third type of photoreceptor (in addition to rods and cones) known as **melanopsin** generates visual signals that do not travel in the main visual pathway but instead go to the **pretectal olivary nucleus**. From there, they then travel to the **suprachiasmatic nucleus** of the hypothalamus where they help to regulate the circadian rhythm in response to environmental light. (Remember that you need sleep to be **chiasmatic**!)

EXTRAOCULAR MOVEMENTS

We already discussed the three cranial nerves that are responsible for extraocular movements (the oculomotor nerve, trochlear nerve, and abducens nerve) in Chapter 8. To improve our understanding, let's see what happens when each of these nerves becomes dysfunctional.

Loss of **oculomotor nerve** function results in a "**down and out**" positioning of the eyes. This is because the two remaining extraocular muscles each exert an unopposed pull on the eyes, with the lateral rectus pulling "out" (without the medial rectus to reign it in) and the superior oblique pulling "down" (without the remaining extraocular muscles to resist).

*Left **oculomotor** nerve palsy*
*with "**down and out**" positioning*

Loss of **trochlear nerve** function leads to paralysis of the **superior oblique** muscle which normally helps to pull the eye downward at an angle, leading to an "**up and in**" positioning of the eye when asked to look inward. This may cause someone with a chronic trochlear nerve palsy to develop a compensatory head tilt as a way of using their entire head to offset the upward drift of the eye.

*Left **trochlear** nerve palsy*
*with "**up and in**" positioning*

Finally, loss of **abducens nerve** function is probably easiest to understand, as its associated muscle (the **lateral rectus**) performs a simple function: pull the eye outwards towards the ear. For this reason, an abducens nerve palsy results in an eye that drifts inward by default and cannot be pulled outward.

*Left **abducens** nerve palsy*
*with **inability to abduct***

While extraocular movements can be brought under voluntary control, they also act automatically without our conscious input most of the time. This "autopilot" function for extraocular movements is coordinated largely by the **medial longitudinal fasciculus** (MLF) in the brainstem. The medial longitudinal fasciculus receives motor signals from the frontal cortex as well as information about the position of the head from the inner ear and uses that to generate **smooth and coordinated movements** of the

eyes. Damage to the medial longitudinal fasciculus results in a condition known as **internuclear ophthalmoplegia** (INO) in which the eye on the same side as the lesion cannot adduct or look inwards towards the nose. (The eye on the unaffected side can still look in that direction but will have nystagmus.) This causes **double vision** due to the eyes looking in two different directions. You can remember the association between the **M**edial **L**ongitudinal **F**asciculus and the **I**nter**N**uclear **O**phthalmoplegia by thinking of the phrase "This **MLF INO** (MILF I know) is so hot, I was **seeing double**."

Normal** patient asked to **look straight

Normal** patient asked to **look left

*Patient with **right internuclear ophthalmoplegia***
*asked to **look straight***

*Patient with **right internuclear ophthalmoplegia***
*asked to **look left**, with **nystagmus** in the left eye*

The **medial longitudinal fasciculus** controls the **extraocular muscles** to produce smooth and coordinated movements. A lesion here produces an **inability to adduct the ipsilateral eye** known as **internuclear ophthalmoplegia**.

*"This **MLF INO** (MILF I know) is so hot, I was **seeing double**."*

Two other structures are involved in coordinating extraocular movements. The first is the **paramedian pontine reticular formation** which, as we learned in Chapter 6, is located in the pons. Specifically, the paramedian pontine reticular formation helps to guide and coordinate *horizontal* eye movements. Damage to the paramedian pontine reticular formation produces a **contralateral gaze deviation** known as a **gaze palsy** in which the eyes deviate *away from* the side of the lesion (for example, damage to the *right* paramedian pontine reticular formation causes the patient to look *left*). You can remember this by thinking that **P**aramedian **P**ontine **R**eticular **F**ormation stands for **P**ee**P**ers **R**un **F**rom the lesion.

The **paramedian pontine reticular formation** in the pons helps to coordinate **horizontal eye movements**. A lesion here produces a **contralateral gaze deviation** known as a **gaze palsy** in which the eyes are fixed to the **opposite side as the lesion**.

Paramedian Pontine Reticular Formation = PeePers Run From the lesion.

The last structure involved in extraocular muscles lies in a part of the frontal lobe known as the **frontal eye fields**. The frontal eye fields communicate with extraocular muscles through the paramedian pontine reticular formation and are involved in both voluntary and involuntary eye movements. In contrast to the *contralateral* gaze deviation seen with damage to the paramedian pontine reticular formation, damage to the frontal eye fields results in an ***ipsilateral* gaze deviation** known as a **gaze preference** in which the eyes deviate *towards* the side of the lesion. You can remember the association between the **F**rontal eye **F**ields, gaze pre**F**erence, and eyes **F**ixated on the side of the lesion by linking the **F** in each of these words.

The **frontal eye fields** are involved in both voluntary and involuntary control of **extraocular muscles**. A lesion here produces an **ipsilateral gaze deviation** known as a **gaze preference** in which the eyes are fixed to the **same side as the lesion**.

Damage to the Frontal eye Fields leads to gaze preFerence in which the eyes Fixate on the side of the lesion.

THE PUPILLARY LIGHT REFLEX

In addition to controlling the movement of the eyes, the body also controls how much light enters them via two pupillary reflexes. The first of these reflexes, the **pupillary light reflex**, determines how much light enters the eye by changing the size of the **pupil**, or the hole through which light enters the eye. In situations of low light, the pupils will **dilate** to allow more light in (a process known as **mydriasis**) which is controlled by the **sympathetic** nervous system. In contrast, when there is too *much* light in the environment, the pupils will **constrict** to reduce the amount of light entering (a process known as **miosis**) which is controlled by the *para*sympathetic nervous system. You can remember the difference between mydriasis and miosis because only my**D**riasis has a **D** in it to allow you to spell **D**ilate.

Miosis   *Mydriasis*

Mydriasis allows **more light** into the eye and is controlled by the **sympathetic** nervous system, while **miosis** allows **less light** into the eye and is controlled by the **parasympathetic** nervous system.

Only myDriasis has enough Ds to allow you to spell Dilation.

Importantly, light entering even *one* eye will cause *both* pupils to constrict. An intact pupillary light reflex relies on both the afferent half (the optic nerves) and the efferent half (the oculomotor nerves) of the reflex to be intact. The reflex arc involves information from the optic nerve traveling to the **midbrain** (specifically an area known as the **pretectal nucleus**) which then sends information to the **Edinger-Westphal nuclei** (also in the midbrain) on *both* the left and the right (this is why light coming into even one eye will cause both eyes to constrict). The

Edinger-Westphal nuclei then sends parasympathetic signals on the oculomotor nerve which then activate the **ciliary sphincter** in the iris of the eye, causing them to contract and thereby reducing the size of the pupils. You can remember the function of the **E**dinger-**W**estphal nuclei by thinking of them looking at something disgusting (like a fly in your coffee) and saying, "**EW**! I don't want to look at that…"

The **Edinger-Westphal nuclei** in the midbrain convert the **afferent signal** of **light entering the eye** into an **efferent signal** to **constrict the pupils.**

*The Edinger-Westphal nuclei says, "**EW!** I don't want to look at that…" and then **constricts the pupils** to block the light from coming in.*

To summarize, the pathway for the pupillary light reflex involves afferent signals coming in on the optic nerve (cranial nerve **2**) and connecting to the ipsilateral **pre**tectal nucleus in the midbrain. Nerves from this nucleus then synapse on the left and right **Ed**inger-Westphal nuclei which send signals in the oculomotor nerve (cranial nerve **3**) to the **cili**ary sphincter, resulting in **pupil**lary constriction. You can remember this pathway by connecting the image of **pupils** with a **religious school** and using the phrase, "**2 pri**ests **ed**ucated **3 cili** (silly) **pupils**."

The **pupillary light reflex** involves both **afferent and efferent nerves** traveling between the **eye** and the **midbrain.**

*2 pri*ests *ed*ucated *3 cili* (silly) *pupils:*
Optic nerve (cranial nerve 2)
*Pre*tectal nucleus
*Ed*inger-Westphal nuclei
Oculomotor nerve (cranial nerve 3)
*Cili*ary sphincter → *pupil*lary constriction

THE ACCOMMODATION REFLEX
The second pupillary reflex, known as **accommodation reflex**, also changes the size of the pupil, but this time the goal is different. Instead of trying to alter the amount of light coming in, this time the pupils are constricting to try and change the shape of the lens so they can better **focus on nearby objects**. This process can be tested clinically by placing a finger or other object close to the space between the patient's eyes and observing for pupillary constriction.

*Changes in the iris during the **accommodation reflex** (indicated by the dotted line).*

Accommodation and the pupillary light reflex involve different processes and pathways, and it is possible for one to be intact while the other is dysfunctional. A particular finding known as **Argyll Robertson pupils** occurs when the pupils constrict in response to a nearby object but do *not* constrict to light. (Argyll Robertson pupils are sometimes called "prostitute's pupils" because they *accommodate but do not react*.) Argyll Robertson pupils have historically been a sign of a **syphilis** infection within the nervous system, although in the age of easy access to antibiotics it is more often a sign of diabetic neuropathy or other types of nerve damage.

> **Argyll Robertson pupils** is a clinical finding in which the pupils **constrict in response to a nearby object** but **not when exposed to light**.
>
> *"Prostitute's pupils"* will *accommodate* but *not react.*

Before we leave vision and move on to hearing, we will touch on one final (and clinically relevant!) note about the oculomotor nerve. Specifically, nerve fibers involved in motor output to the extraocular muscles travels towards the *middle* of the nerve, while parasympathetic nerve fibers responsible for pupillary constriction travel towards the *periphery* of the nerve. On a clinical level, absent extraocular movements with intact pupillary constriction suggests damage to the *middle* of the nerve (for example, in an ischemic stroke, the blood supply can access the outside of the nerve more easily, leaving the inner motor neurons more sensitive to ischemia). In contrast, the opposite set of findings (*intact* extraocular movements with *absent* pupillary

constriction) suggests damage to the *periphery* of the nerve (as could be seen in compression by surrounding structures such as an aneurysm of the nearby posterior communicating artery). You can remember this by thinking **OOMMPP**: the **O**cul**O**motor nerve has **M**otor in the **M**iddle and **P**upils on the **P**eriphery.

> Nerve fibers supplying **extraocular muscles** are found in the **middle** of the **oculomotor nerve** while nerve fibers involved in **pupillary constriction** travel towards the **outside**.
>
> *OOMMPP: The OculOmotor nerve has Motor in the Middle and Pupils on the Periphery.*

> Damage to the **inner nerve fibers** of the **oculomotor nerve** can be caused by **diabetes mellitus** and **ischemia**, while damage to the **outer nerve fibers** can be caused by **compression**.
>
> *Diabetes Mellitus Damages the Middle, and Ischemia gets the Inside. Nearby Objects damage the Outside.*

HEARING

Hearing is the process by which sound waves traveling through the air are converted into neural signals that allow our brain to respond to the environment (such as turning our head to identify the source of a sudden loud noise). The neural pathway by which information about sound travels to the brain is overall quite similar to the visual pathway, but the process is a little simpler given that the ears themselves do not move or respond to the environment nearly as much as the eyes. Sound waves initially travel through the **outer ear** until they hit the **eardrum** (formally known as the **tympanic membrane**). The eardrum then converts these sound waves into vibrations which travel down the three smallest bones in the body: the **malleus**, **incus**, and **stapes**. From there, these vibrations are passed onto the **cochlea**, which is a highly specialized organ with a shape not unlike a snail's shell. The cochlea is filled with specialized sensory receptors known as **hair cells**. As the sonic vibrations travel through the cochlea, they generate action potentials in various parts depending on the pitch of the sound.

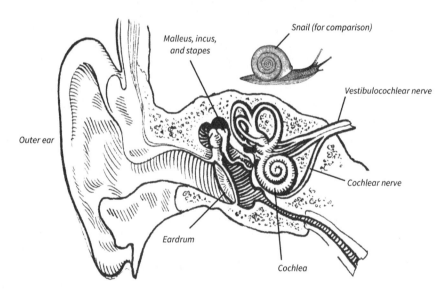

These auditory signals initially travel on the **cochlear nerve** which soon meets up with the **vestibular nerve** to form the **vestibulocochlear nerve** (which you should recognize as the eighth cranial nerve). Auditory signals then travel to the **cochlear nucleus** in the brainstem. From there, they go to the **superior olivary nuclei** (also in the brainstem) before traveling via the **lateral lemniscus** to the **inferior colliculus** in the midbrain. (Just to make sure we have our terms straight, recall that the *medial* lemniscus is part of the pathway carrying epicritic sensation from the body.) From there, the information travels to the **medial geniculate nucleus** of the thalamus (remember **M**aking **G**reat **N**oise?) before finally hitting the primary auditory cortex in the **temporal lobe**. You can remember this long and complicated pathway by thinking about the **sound** of **8 Coc**ky **SON**s **La**ughing **'N M**aking **G**reat **N**oise at the **Te**nt. This should help you recall the vestibulocochlear nerve (cranial nerve **8**), the **Coc**hlear nucleus, the **S**uperior **O**livary **N**uclei, the **La**teral lemniscus, the i**N**ferior colliculus, the **M**edial **G**eniculate **N**ucleus of the thalamus, and the primary auditory cortex of the **Te**mporal lobe.

Medial geniculate nucleus of the thalamus

Inferior colliculus

Lateral lemniscus

Superior olivary nuclei

Cochlear nucleus

The **auditory pathway** carries signals from the **cochlea** to the **temporal lobe**.

8 Cocky SONs Laughing 'N Making Great Noise at the Tent:
Vestibulocochlear nerve (Cranial nerve 8)
Cochlear nucleus
Superior Olivary Nuclei
Lateral lemniscus
iNferior colliculus
Medial Geniculate Nucleus of the thalamus
Primary auditory cortex of the Temporal lobe

TESTS OF HEARING

The auditory pathway can be tested in clinical settings by using two distinctive exam maneuvers. The **Weber test** involves placing a vibrating tuning fork in the middle of the patient's forehead and asking if they hear the sound louder in the right ear, the left ear, or equally on both sides. A normal response is to say that the sound is equal in both ears, while saying that one side is louder than the other indicates that some degree of hearing ability has been lost on one side compared to the other.

However, just using the Weber test won't tell you *which* side has been affected or *what kind* of defect is present. This is where the **Rinne test** comes in. The first step of the Rinne test is to place a vibrating tuning fork directly on the **mastoid bone** to test **bone conduction**. (Recall that the eardrum converts sound waves into vibrations in the three bones of the middle ear. For this reason, *any* vibrations—not just sound—can be picked up by the cochlea. This forms the basis for bone conduction.) When the patient says they can no longer hear the sound, you move the tuning fork in front of the ear to test **air conduction**.
Under normal circumstances, air conduction is louder than bone conduction, so someone should be able to hear the tone again once the fork is moved from the bone to the ear. If bone conduction is greater than air conduction, however, it means that something is blocking sound transmission in the ear, known as **conductive hearing loss**. (You can demonstrate conductive hearing loss on yourself by using a finger to plug your ear and then making a humming at a consistent volume. By doing this, you will see that sound actually becomes *louder* when you plug one ear and quieter when you remove your finger.)

In cases where air conduction is greater than bone conduction but there is clear asymmetry between the right and left ears on the Weber test, the patient likely has a **sensorineural hearing loss** on the quiet side due to damage in the auditory pathway.

To remember the difference between the Weber and Rinne tests, focus on the fact that **W** is a **symmetrical** letter, so doing the **W**eber test tells you about whether hearing ability is symmetrical in both ears. In contrast, **R** is an *a*symmetric letter, so the **R**inne test is used to see which side the hearing loss has affected.

You can combine the results of the Weber and Rinne tests to diagnose what kind of hearing loss is present and where it is located. Under normal circumstances, the Weber test will not lateralize (both ears will hear equally well), and both ears will have stronger air conduction than bone conduction. In conductive hearing loss, the Weber test will lateralize to the *affected* ear, with bone conduction greater than air conduction in that ear (this is the condition you simulated by putting your finger in your ear). In sensorineural hearing loss, the Weber test will lateralize to the *un*affected ear, with air conduction greater than bone conduction in *both* ears.

The **Weber test** is used to test the **symmetry of hearing ability**, while the **Rinne test** compares **air conduction** to **bone conduction**.

*W is a **symmetric** letter, so the Weber test tells you about **symmetry**.*

BALANCE

The sense of **balance** is the other special sense that originates in the inner ear. At its most basic level, balance can be defined as the **sensory information that prevents someone from falling over**. More than simply being a single modality like vision or hearing, balance instead involves a complex integration of various senses, including **visual** information from the eyes, **proprioceptive** information from the dorsal column–medial lemniscus pathway, and signals about **movement, acceleration, and rotation** from the inner ear. We've already talked about vision and proprioception, so we will now turn to the **vestibular system** which, together with the cochlea, forms the inner ear.

The vestibular system is comprised of two components: the **semicircular canals**, which generate information about **rotational** movements, and **otoliths**, which generate information about **linear** accelerations.

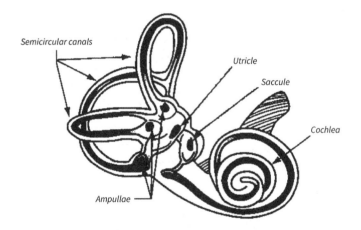

There are three semicircular canals, each of which is able to detect movement in one of the **three rotational axes**, with one detecting rotation in a *vertical* plane (like when a person nods or an acrobat does a somersault), another detecting rotation in a *horizontal* plane (like when a person shakes their head or a ballerina does a pirouette), and the third detecting rotation in a *flat* plane (like when a person touches their head to their shoulder or a gymnast does a cartwheel). These movements are detected by specialized **hair cells** in a sac at the base of each semicircular canal known as an **ampulla**. Together, the three semicircular canals are able to give the brain detailed information about the movement of the head in space.

While the semicircular canals are able to sense movement in each of the three *rotational* axes, there are two additional structures in the inner ear known as **otoliths** that are able to sense *linear* acceleration. The first otolith, the **utricle**, is able to sense movement in a *horizontal* plane (such as someone going from 0 to 60 in a sports car). In contrast, the second otolith, the **saccule**, senses movement in a *vertical* plane (such as someone jumping up and down on a trampoline). You can try to remember the difference between the utricle and the saccule by thinking of the phrase "**drop** it like a **sac**k of potatoes" to associate the **sac**cule and vertical movement.

There are two **otoliths**—the **utricle** and **saccule**—that detect **linear acceleration**, while the **semicircular canals** detect **rotational movements**.

*Say "**drop** it like a **sac**k of potatoes" to associate the **sac**cule and **vertical** movement.*

THE VESTIBULO-OCULAR REFLEX

Together, the three semicircular canals and the two otoliths (combined with visual information from the eyes and proprioceptive information from the body) are able to determine the body's current position in space and use this information to keep itself upright. This information is also used in the **vestibulo-ocular reflex** which helps to keep your eyes focused on a particular object even when your head is moving. When the semicircular canals detect movement, they send signals via the **vestibulocochlear nerve** to the **vestibular nuclei** in the pons and medulla. From there, motor signals are sent to the **abducens nerve** as well as the **oculomotor nerve** via the **medial longitudinal fasciculus** to correct for the movement of the head. This pathway is short and to the point, allowing for very rapid adjustments to the eyes in response to head movement. (In fact, the vestibulo-ocular reflex is among the fastest in the body!)

*The pathways involved in the **vestibulo-ocular reflex**.*

Because the circuit for the vestibulo-ocular reflex travels through the brainstem, it is often used clinically as a test of brainstem function in patients who are comatose. If the eyes move when the head is moved, this suggests that the reflex is intact. However, if the pupils remain fixed in the middle of their eye sockets no matter what direction the head is turned (like a doll's, giving this finding the name "**doll's eyes sign**"), this is highly suggestive of brainstem damage—and a poor prognosis.

VERTIGO

We talked about **vertigo**, or the sense that things are moving when they are not, as one of the cerebellar signs back in Chapter 5. However, vertigo can also result from disruptions in the vestibular system. Cases of vertigo resulting from the cerebellum or brainstem are known as **central vertigo** while those stemming from the inner ear are known as **peripheral vertigo**.

The most common cause of vertigo is a condition known as **benign paroxysmal positional vertigo** (BPPV) in which an otolith breaks off from its usual position and enters the semicircular canals. This "otolith on the lam" then erroneously signals that things are moving when in fact they are not, creating feelings of vertigo (especially when the patient is laying in bed or otherwise changing the position of their head, hence the word "positional" in the name). Benign paroxysmal positional vertigo is a common condition, especially in the elderly. For most people it resolves on its own within a few weeks, although for some it may become recurrent.

Another common cause of vertigo is **Ménière's disease** which occurs as a result of excessive fluid build-up in both the vestibular system and the cochlea. This results in a feeling of "fullness" in the ears accompanied by a classic triad of **vertigo**, **sensorineural hearing loss**, and a ringing in the ears known as **tinnitus**. (Compare this to benign paroxysmal positional vertigo which only involves the vestibular system and therefore does not impact hearing at all.) You can remember the definition of **Ménière's** disease by thinking of someone yelling, "**Mine ears!**" due to their problems in both balance and hearing.

Ménière's disease causes **vertigo** and **hearing problems** as a result of **excessive fluid build-up** in the **inner ear**.

*Think of it as "**Mine ears!**" disease.*

TASTE

Taste is the process by which the nervous system is able to recognize what kinds of chemicals are present in the mouth before swallowing. Certain chemicals (like sugar, which the body needs to function) will generally cause a pleasant taste while other chemicals (like toxins that could potentially harm the body) will instead generate a disagreeable taste, prompting the person to spit out them out rather than risk bringing them further into the body. **Taste buds** on the tongue can detect five basic tastes: **salty** (things containing alkali metals like sodium), **sweet** (things containing carbohydrates like glucose), **sour** (things containing hydrogen ions like an acid), **bitter** (a variety of compounds, some of which are toxic), and **umami** (a Japanese word roughly meaning "savory," "meaty," or "delicious" that is activated by the presence of the amino acid glutamate).

*Taste buds on the surface of the **tongue**.*

Contrary to popular beliefs, different parts of the tongue are not responsible for sensing different tastes. Instead, all types of taste buds are found throughout the tongue. Recall from the previous chapter that sensory information about taste travels to the brain via two different nerves: the **facial nerve**, which covers the anterior two-thirds of the tongue, and the **glossopharyngeal nerve**, which covers the posterior one-third of the tongue. You can remember this by thinking that if a bug makes it to the *anterior* two-thirds of the tongue, you'll probably make a face (as the facial nerve is also responsible for innervating facial muscles), but if that bug makes it to the *posterior* third, you're likely to gag (as the glossopharyngeal nerve is also responsible for the gag reflex).

The **facial nerve** innervates the **anterior two-thirds of the tongue** while the **glossopharyngeal nerve** supplies the **posterior third.**

*If a bug crawls on the **anterior** two-thirds of the tongue you'll probably **make a face**, but if it makes it all the way to the **posterior third** you'll likely **gag.***

Sensory information about taste travels via these two nerves to the **solitary nucleus** in the medulla. (Remember from Chapter 6 that the **sole-lick**-tary nucleus is involved in both taste and the gag reflex.) From the solitary nucleus, information about taste then goes to various parts of the brain including neurons involved in the **parasympathetic nervous system** (which makes sense given its role in "resting and *digesting*"), the **hypothalamus** (which also makes sense since it governs hunger and satiety), and the **thalamus** (where it can then travel to the somatosensory cortex in the parietal lobe to generate the conscious sensation of taste).

SMELL

The last of the special senses we will talk about is **smell**, or the process by which the body can sense and respond to airborne chemicals. Smell is highly complementary to taste, as it allows us to get a sense of whether something is likely to be palatable before we get it anywhere near our mouths. Smells are sensed by the **olfactory system** which begins in the nose. In contrast to the five basic tastes that the tongue can sense, the nose is capable of picking up millions of different smells by responding to distinct combinations of chemicals. When an airborne chemical binds to sensory neurons in the nose, this sets off a process by which an action potential is generated and sent down the first cranial nerve (the **olfactory nerve**).

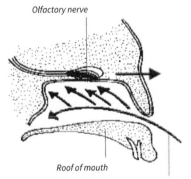

Olfactory nerve

Roof of mouth

Airborne odorants

The olfactory nerve is unique in that it travels *directly* to the olfactory cortex rather than synapsing first in the brainstem or thalamus. The olfactory cortex is strongly connected to parts of the limbic system like the amygdala and hippocampus which explains why our emotional responses to smells are so strong and immediate (you can probably think of times in your life when a distinct smell triggered a vivid memory or when an unpleasant smell immediately ruined your mood). Smell also appears to play a role in mate selection, with humans being able to unconsciously detect when someone's genetics are not sufficiently different from their own and thereby avoid incest. All in all, olfaction is not a complex process, but it is a very important one for survival!

PUTTING IT ALL TOGETHER

On a neurological level, learning about the special senses can help to integrate much of what we have learned already, as their pathways run through many parts of both the central and peripheral nervous systems. For this reason, it is crucial that you have mastered the information found in this chapter, as it will come up again and again (and again and again and again...) as we continue our study of neurologic diseases! Make sure that you have a good grasp on all of the topics we have covered so far, as we have only one more chapter to go before we move on to clinical neurology in earnest!

REVIEW QUESTIONS

1. A 52 y/o M with no significant past medical history is brought to the emergency department following a motor vehicle accident in which he was an unrestrained passenger. He reports significant pain in his face and head as well as difficulty seeing due to double vision. Physical examination reveals bruising around both eyes but no breaks in the skin. A complete neurological exam reveals weakness of sideways gaze in the right eye as seen below:

    The exam is otherwise unremarkable. Which of the following cranial nerves has most likely been affected?
    A. Optic nerve
    B. Oculomotor nerve
    C. Trochlear nerve
    D. Trigeminal nerve
    E. Abducens nerve
    F. Facial nerve

2. A 58 y/o F comes into clinic with a letter from the Department of Motor Vehicles requiring her to undergo a medical evaluation before she can get her driver's license back. She has been pulled over by police twice in the past month after hitting trash cans and mailboxes with her car. She tested negative for alcohol both times. She has no significant past medical history. Her review of systems is negative. Neurological exam is positive only for bitemporal hemianopsia on visual acuity testing. A magnetic resonance imaging scan of the brain is most likely to reveal a tumor compressing which of the following structures?
    A. Retina
    B. Optic nerve
    C. Optic chiasm
    D. Optic tract
    E. Optic radiations
    F. Occipital cortex
    G. Pretectal nucleus
    H. Edinger-Westphal nuclei

3. A 15 y/o F is reading a book on a boat while vacationing overseas. While she is reading, the boat hits some rough waters, causing it to pitch and roll. Despite the movement, the girl is still able to keep her eyes fixed on the line of text that she is reading at that moment. Which of the following structures is *least* involved in the process of maintaining her line of sight while reading in this rough weather?
   A. Semicircular canals
   B. Vestibulocochlear nerve
   C. Midbrain
   D. Pons
   E. Medulla oblongata
   F. Oculomotor nerve
   G. Abducens nerve
   H. Internuclear ophthalmoplegia

4. A 37 y/o F sees her primary care doctor complaining of episodes where "the world is spinning like crazy" on a daily basis for the past week. The episodes of dizziness last only a few minutes at most, but when they occur they are disabling. They are accompanied by a feeling of "fullness" in her right ear. She has also noticed some difficulty hearing out of her right ear during conversations and while watching television which has been worsening over the past few weeks. Which of these additional signs or symptoms is most likely to be reported by this patient?
   A. Transient episodes of blurry vision
   B. "Ringing" sound in her ear
   C. Abnormally low blood pressure
   D. Impaired proprioceptive ability
   E. Lack of taste from the posterior third of the tongue

1. **The best answer is E.** This patient is presenting with inability to abduct his right eye following a traumatic injury. Abduction is controlled by the lateral rectus muscle which is innervated by the abducens nerve. The other extraocular muscles are controlled by the oculomotor and trochlear nerves (answers B and C). The optic nerve is involved in processing sensory information from the eye but does not play a role in eye movements (answer A). The trigeminal nerve provides sensory information from the cornea and the skin around the eyes but does not control extraocular movements (answer D). Finally, the facial nerve controls the muscles of facial expression including blinking but does not control the movement of the eye itself (answer F).

2. **The best answer is C.** Bitemporal hemianopsia is most often related to injury of the optic chiasm through which sensory neurons from the medial retina of both eyes pass. This can occur due to a tumor of the pituitary gland which sits right above the optic chiasm at the base of the brain. Damage to the retina or optic nerve would produce monocular blindness, not bitemporal hemianopsia (answers A and B). Damage to the optic tract or optic radiations would produce a homonymous hemianopia or quadrantanopsia, respectively (answers D and E). Damage to the occipital lobe tends to produce a homonymous hemianopia or quadrantanopsia with macular sparing (answer F). Finally, the pretectal nucleus and Edinger-Westphal nuclei are involved in the pupillary reflex pathway, so damage here generally does not lead to loss of visual fields (answers G and H).

(Answers continued on the next page.)

3. **The best answer is H.** The ability to maintain a stable line of sight despite changes in the position of one's head relies upon an intact vestibulo-ocular reflex. The vestibulo-ocular reflex involves a complex pathway that nevertheless is able to act quickly. Information about head position is sent from the semicircular canals (answer A) in the vestibular system via the vestibulocochlear nerve (answer B) to the vestibular nuclei in the pons and medulla (answers D and E). Some of these pathways connect to the medial longitudinal fasciculus in the midbrain (answer C). Compensatory movements of the eyes are enacted via the cranial nerves controlling the extraocular muscles, including the oculomotor and abducens nerves (answers F and G). Internuclear ophthalmoplegia is not correct, as it is a medical condition involving dysfunction of the medial longitudinal fasciculus, not a neuroanatomical structure in and of itself.

4. **The best answer is B.** This vignette describes a case of Ménière's disease, a disorder characterized by a characteristic triad of vertigo, hearing loss, and tinnitus. While it is not diagnostic of this disease, a sensation of fullness in the ears is often reported as well. Ménière's disease is believed to result from distention of the fluid-filled spaces in the inner ear. While the sense of balance relies upon visual and proprioceptive information in addition to the vestibular system, these are not involved directly in Ménière's disease (answers A and D). Sensory information about taste from the posterior one-third of the tongue is carried on the glossopharyngeal nerve and is not related to the inner ear (answer E). Finally, abnormalities in blood pressure are not commonly seen in Ménière's disease (answer C).

10 THE KITCHEN SINK

At this point in our study of neuroanatomy, you may feel like you've learned just about *everything but the kitchen sink*! And you'd be right! Unfortunately, that still leaves the "kitchen sink." In this final chapter on neuroanatomy, we will cover a few last bits and pieces of the nervous system which didn't fit neatly into any of the other topics we've talked about so far. There is nothing that inherently unites all of these structures other than the fact that they are all *in* the brain but not *made* directly of nervous tissue. Instead, these structures help to **support nervous tissues** in several ways including serving as a protective cushion, filtering out potentially toxic chemicals, and delivering oxygen and other nutrients.

Like the kitchen sink, most of these remaining structures involve fluids and pipes. We will first talk about the **blood supply** of the brain and spinal cord. We will then touch on the **blood-brain barrier** separating the blood coming into the brain from the nervous tissue itself. Next, we will discuss the **meninges**, which are a series of membranes that envelope the brain, as well as the **ventricular system**, which produces and circulates **cerebrospinal fluid**. Finally, we will finish the chapter by talking about the **venous drainage** of the brain that allows all the blood and cerebrospinal fluid flowing around to go somewhere. Despite not being made of nervous tissue themselves, these structures are all incredibly important for maintaining proper functioning of the nervous system, and even small disruptions in these systems can lead to major problems (as we will see shortly)!

CEREBRAL BLOOD SUPPLY

Most of the blood flow to the brain and the upper spinal cord comes from the **carotid arteries** in the neck (which you can easily feel as a bounding pulse when you place a finger on either side of your neck in the soft spot just lateral to the trachea). The carotid arteries divide into the **internal carotid arteries** and the **external carotid arteries**. As the external carotids split off to supply blood to the face and neck, we will instead follow the *internal* carotids which go on to supply the brain.

After traveling up the neck, the internal carotids reach the underside of the brain and join what is known as the **circle of Willis**. Knowing the structure of the circle of Willis is *absolutely crucial* to understanding the effects that bleeds and blockages in various arteries will have on a clinical level, so don't move on from this section until you have this down cold! First, take a look at an unlabeled circle of Willis on the left:

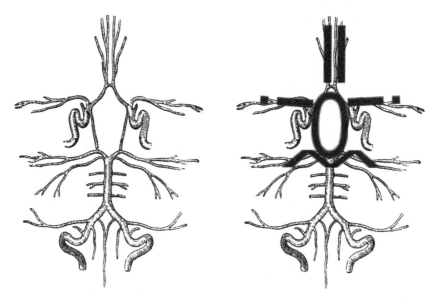

That's no joke, huh? But let's see if we can simplify it down as much as possible and maybe even be able to draw most of it from scratch entirely by memory. Start by focusing on just the *circle* part towards the top (onto which a circle has been drawn in the right image). Then, let's write the word "Willi" going around the circle, starting at the bottom and going clockwise. First draw an upside-down **W** at the bottom, then an **i** in the upper left, two l's together (**ll**) at the top, and another **i** in the upper right. And that's the head of the circle of Willis! Now we just need to label all the parts.

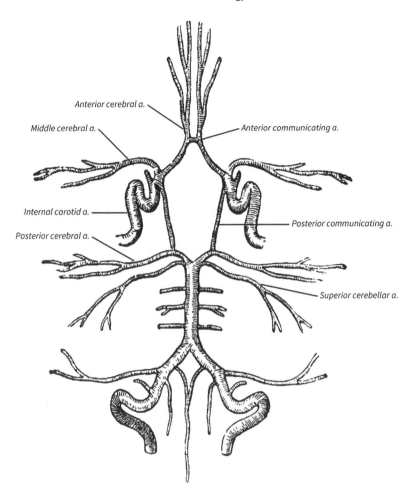

Anterior cerebral a.

Middle cerebral a.

Anterior communicating a.

Internal carotid a.

Posterior communicating a.

Posterior cerebral a.

Superior cerebellar a.

The major components of the circle of Willis are the three pairs of **cerebral arteries**. The upside-down **W** (don't call it an M!) at the bottom represents the two **posterior cerebral arteries**, the **i**'s in the middle represent the **middle cerebral arteries** (which are direct continuations of the **i**nternal carotid artery), and the two **l**'s are the **anterior cerebral arteries**. The circle itself is made up of two communicating arteries: the short **anterior communicating artery** in between the two l's and the longer **posterior communicating arteries** making up the bottom half of the circle. We will discuss what happens when there is a blockage in each of these arteries more in Chapter 12, but for now just know the overall structure.

But wait—didn't we forget the **S** in Willi**S**? Indeed we did. That's because the **S** no longer represents a *cerebral* artery but instead is the first pair of arteries supplying the *cerebellum*: the **Superior cerebellar arteries**. And this leads us to the rest of the arteries supplying the brain and spinal cord! For this, we're basically drawing a stick figure, with the head being the circle that we already drew. Let's name our new stick figure **Willy**.

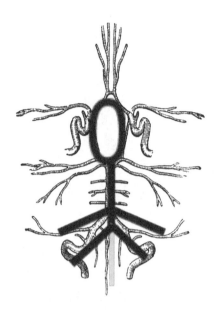

First, draw Willy's neck: this is the **basilar artery** from which many small **pontine arteries** branch off. Next, draw his arms: these are the **anterior inferior cerebellar arteries**. (While there is only a *single* pair of superior cerebellar arteries, there are *two* pairs of inferior cerebellar arteries which are designated as anterior and posterior.) From there, draw Willy's two legs: the **vertebral arteries**. The **posterior inferior cerebellar arteries** form short branches off of the vertebral arteries. Lastly, this particular stick figure has a tail: the **anterior spinal artery** in between his legs.

And that's it! You now know how to draw the circle of Willis and the associated arteries going to the midbrain, cerebellum, and spinal cord. Before we move on, however, there is an important point to note. Despite how it may appear, the vertebral arteries are *not* a continuation of blood flowing *down* from the basilar artery. Instead, they (like the internal carotid arteries) help to bring blood *up* the neck from the heart. In this way, the circle of Willis has two primary blood supplies: the internal carotid arteries in the front and the vertebral arteries in the back. These two sets of arteries effectively form a **bridge** between the anterior circulation (the circle of Willis) and the posterior circulation. This pattern of having multiple redundant connections between blood vessels (known as **anastomoses**) is common in the brain and helps to preserve such a vital organ. If blood supply were to become compromised in any one artery, the other arteries would be able to compensate for this to make sure that all parts of the brain still get the blood they need. For example, if the right internal carotid artery were to become blocked, the left internal carotid artery (as well as blood originating from the vertebral arteries and passing into the anterior circulation by way of the basilar artery) could help to make up the difference. Nevertheless, various situations can create blockages that are severe enough that not even these anastomoses can fully compensate, which can lead to injury and even death of brain tissue (known as a **stroke**, which we will learn about more in Chapter 12).

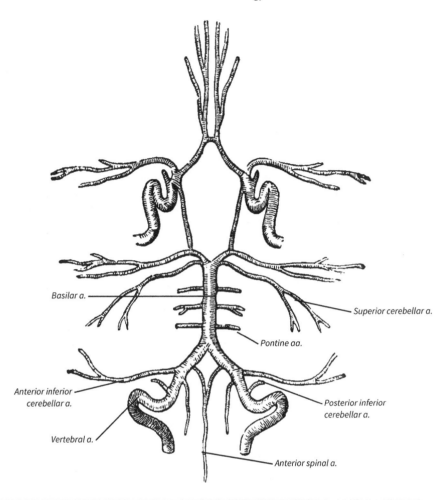

Basilar a.

Superior cerebellar a.

Pontine aa.

Anterior inferior
cerebellar a.

Posterior inferior
cerebellar a.

Vertebral a.

Anterior spinal a.

The **anterior part** of the **cerebral circulation** is supplied by the
two **internal carotid arteries** and helps to perfuse the **cerebrum** via a series of
anastomoses known as the **circle of Willis**.

*Draw the **circle of Willis** by drawing a **circle with the word "Willi" around it**, with the
letters being drawn in a **clockwise rotation** starting at the bottom as seen on page 140.*

The **posterior part** of the **circle of Willis** is supplied by the two **vertebral arteries**
and helps to perfuse the **cerebellum, brainstem**, and **spinal cord**.

*Draw a **stick figure** with the circle of Willis being the **head**, the basilar artery as the
neck, the anterior inferior cerebellar arteries as the **arms**, the vertebral arteries as the
legs, and the anterior spinal artery as the **tail**!*

THE BLOOD-BRAIN BARRIER
Before we move on from discussing the vasculature of the brain, it is worth talking about an important structure known as the **blood–brain barrier**. While the arteries we have discussed help to bring oxygen and other vital nutrients to the central nervous system, the contents of the blood do not go to the nervous tissue directly. Instead, the blood–brain barrier effectively acts as a filter that only permits *some* of what the blood is carrying to come into contact with nervous tissue directly. This helps to prevent potentially toxic chemicals from wreaking havoc on the brain (as damaged nervous tissue cannot easily be replaced). However, from a clinical perspective the blood–brain barrier can also sometimes prevent helpful drugs from reaching where they need to go. In general, **fat soluble** chemicals are much more able to diffuse across the blood–brain barrier than water soluble ones, and this has important implications for any drug that is intended to act on the central nervous system. (Water soluble chemicals that are needed by the brain, such as glucose, are actively transported across the blood–brain barrier by transport proteins.)

"I'm gonna need to see some ID."

THE MENINGES

The next part of the "kitchen sink" we will talk about are the **meninges**, or the membranes that surround the central nervous system. The meninges envelop the brain and spinal cord and serve to protect them from various insults, including mechanical injury. The meninges consist of **three distinct layers**: the **dura mater**, the **arachnoid mater**, and the **pia mater**. (Your brain is "the gift so nice they wrapped it thrice!") In between these layers are additional spaces (like the subarachnoid space within which cerebrospinal fluid flows as part of the ventricular system, which we will discuss in the next section).

Let's "unpeel" the brain to learn about each of these layers in more detail. The first thing we hit when we attempt to lift away the layers surrounding the brain is the **skin**. Peel that away and you have the **skull** (the bony structure encasing the brain) and its associated outer covering known as the **periosteum**. After removing those, you next hit the first layer of the meninges: the **dura mater** (Latin for "tough mother"). The dura mater is appropriately named, as it is a thick and fibrous coating that provides structural support to the brain. Beneath the dura mater lies the **subdural space**, and

immediately beneath that is the next layer of the meninges: the **arachnoid mater** (named for its spider web-like appearance). The arachnoid mater is much thinner than the dura mater but still helps to cushion the central nervous system. Directly beneath the arachnoid mater is the **subarachnoid space** through which cerebrospinal fluid flows. Finally, we reach the innermost layer of the meninges: the **pia mater** (Latin for "tender mother"). The pia mater is a delicate film that wraps the brain quite tightly (even following the brain down into its various folds and wrinkles, in contrast to the dura mater and arachnoid mater which instead form a more sac-like shape). Despite being thin, the pia mater is impermeable to fluid and thereby helps to keep the cerebrospinal fluid flowing in the subarachnoid space separated from the brain itself.

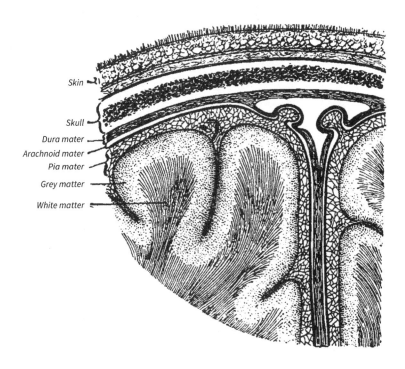

Like most things in the nervous system, the meninges work great—until they don't. The meninges are vulnerable to bruising, bleeding, and tumors in each of the layers we have discussed. We'll go over these conditions in later chapters. For now, just remember the layers of the meninges in order from the inside out by thinking that the brain has a **PAD** made up of the **P**ia mater, **A**rachnoid mater, and **D**ura mater.

The **meninges** consist of three layers (the **dura mater, arachnoid mater,** and **pia mater**) that **envelop the central nervous system** and help to protect it.

*The brain has a **PAD**: **P**ia mater, **A**rachnoid mater, and **D**ura mater.*

The meninges are wrapped tightly to the brain and even make a few unique structures of their own through this process. In particular, *all three* layers of the meninges descend into the longitudinal fissure (which, you will recall from Chapter 2, is the deep "canyon" dividing the left and right hemispheres of the brain). This thick fibrous tissue that physically separates the two hemispheres is known as the **falx cerebri** and creates a sickle-like structure. (An equivalent structure known as the **falx cerebelli** separates the two hemispheres of the cerebellum.)

Falx cerebri

Tentorium cerebelli

Falx cerebelli

While the falx cerebri separates the left and right cerebral hemispheres, another structure known as the **tentorium cerebelli** helps to separate the cerebrum from the cerebellum. The tentorium cerebelli is an extension of the dura mater that forms a "hammock" of sorts that cradles the underside of the cerebrum (around the occipital lobes) and suspends it above the cerebellum sitting beneath it. The tentorium cerebelli thus forms a discrete physical barrier between the "upper" brain and the "lower" brain, and throughout this book you will see occasional references to things being **supratentorial** (above the tentorium) or **infratentorial** (below the tentorium).

THE VENTRICULAR SYSTEM

The **ventricular system** is a series of interconnected holes in the brain that are filled with **cerebrospinal fluid**. (Please make sure not to confuse the *ventricular* system with the *vestibular* system we talked about in the last chapter!) The functions of cerebrospinal fluid include protecting the central nervous system from injury by acting as a **shock absorber**, **facilitating blood flow** by decreasing the amount of fluid pressure, and **removing metabolic waste products** from the brain.

Cerebrospinal fluid is produced by filtering blood in the **choroid plexuses**. (Note that this is *not* the same process as the blood–brain barrier! While the blood–brain barrier also filters blood, it does not produce a distinct fluid in the same way that the choroid plexuses do.) Choroid plexuses are found throughout the four ventricles of the brain. The cerebrospinal fluid they produce then proceeds to circulate in a linear fashion starting from the **lateral ventricles**, the first and largest of the ventricles. Cerebrospinal fluid then flows through the paired **interventricular foramina** (sometimes called the foramina of Monro) into the **third ventricle**. From there, it flows down the **cerebral aqueduct** into the **fourth ventricle**. At this point, the cerebrospinal fluid can go one of two directions: it can either continue into the spinal cord through the **central canal**, or it can pass into the **subarachnoid space** (the area between the arachnoid mater and the pia mater) via several holes. These holes are the two **lateral apertures** (also known as the foramina of Luschka) and a single midline **median aperture** (the foramen of Magendie). Once the cerebrospinal fluid passes into the subarachnoid space, it no longer travels in a linear fashion but instead spreads out to cover the brain and spinal cord all the way down to the sacrum.

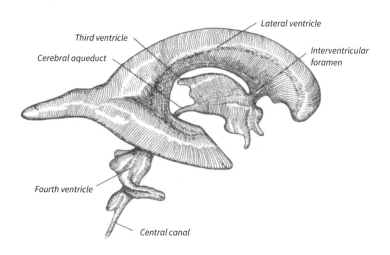

Lateral ventricle

Third ventricle

Interventricular foramen

Cerebral aqueduct

Fourth ventricle

Central canal

To remember the order of the ventricular system, think of how awesome cerebrospinal fluid is, then use some of that new-fangled internet speak to post on social media that "**CSF** is **LIT AF**." This will help you remember that cerebrospinal fluid travels through the **C**horoid plexuses, **L**ateral ventricle, **I**nterventricular foramina, **T**hird ventricle, cerebral **A**queduct, and the **F**ourth ventricle before finally filtering out into either the subarachnoid space or the central canal. (Is this r/fellowkids enough?)

> **Cerebrospinal fluid** is produced in **choroid plexuses**. It then travels through the **ventricular system** in a **linear fashion** before passing into either the spinal cord via the **cerebral canal** or into the **subarachnoid space**.
>
> *CSF is **LIT AF**:*
> *Choroid plexuses*
> *Lateral ventricle*
> *Interventricular foramina*
> *Third ventricle*
> *Cerebral Aqueduct*
> *Fourth ventricle*

On a clinical level, the ventricular system can be the source of various forms of neurologic dysfunction. If part of the ventricular system becomes obstructed, fluid can accumulate in the ventricles and put pressure on other parts of the brain (a condition known as **hydrocephalus** or "water on the brain"). Sometimes this is caused by developmental abnormalities, while in other cases this can be due to things like infection, trauma, or bleeding. We'll cover hydrocephalus more in Chapter 13.

VENOUS DRAINAGE

If more and more blood keeps coming into the brain via the arterial system and more and more cerebrospinal fluid keeps being produced in the ventricular system, where does all this extra fluid *go*? After all, the amount of the fluid in the skull can't keep building up in its enclosed space or else we would end up with a dangerously high intracranial pressure! Luckily, both blood and cerebrospinal fluid are able to exit the brain through a series of **veins** scattered throughout

the central nervous system. Blood enters the venous system immediately after passing through the capillaries. In contrast, cerebrospinal fluid does not enter into the venous system directly but rather is absorbed through **arachnoid granulations**, which are specialized protrusions of the arachnoid mater into the dura mater.

If you've studied anatomy, you'll know that most arteries in the body have an accompanying vein. (For example, the femoral vein in the leg runs directly alongside the femoral artery for most of its course.) However, cerebral veins are an exception to this! It would be a mistake to assume that there is a corresponding vein for each of the arteries supplying the head (there is no "internal carotid vein," for example). This makes learning the venous system of the brain quite complicated, as you need to stuff an entirely new set of information into your brain…

…or *do* you? While it's true that the venous system of the brain can't be easily mapped onto what we have already learned, we may actually be able to get away without memorizing most of it. Why is this? The reason is that, compared to the arterial system, it's not as clinically important to know the precise details of the venous system, as there isn't as direct of a correlation between dysfunction of a particular vein and specific neurologic deficits as there is in the arterial system. Because of this, we can safely try to understand the venous system of the brain using broad strokes rather than fine details.

Okay, so onto broad strokes! There are two general systems of veins in the skull. The first, known as **cerebral veins**, carries blood from the brain itself and runs through the *subarachnoid* space. The second, known as **diploic veins**, instead carries blood from the skull and its overlying skin through the *dura* mater. There are several connecting veins running in the *subdural* space that bridge the gap between these two venous systems which are known, appropriately, as **bridging veins**. (The specific spaces that these arteries and veins run through will become clinically important when we talk about the effects of bleeding into each of these spaces in Chapter 13.)

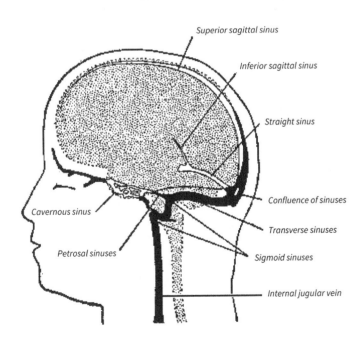

Superior sagittal sinus

Inferior sagittal sinus

Straight sinus

Confluence of sinuses

Cavernous sinus

Transverse sinuses

Petrosal sinuses

Sigmoid sinuses

Internal jugular vein

Cerebral veins are made up of many small veins that, like rivers forming a delta, collectively merge into larger basins known as **dural venous sinuses**. Each dural venous sinus collects blood from broad areas of the brain. The *upper-middle* part of the cerebral cortex is covered by the **superior sagittal sinus** (which runs along the top part of the brain right down the middle like a mohawk), while the *lower-middle* part drains to the **inferior sagittal sinus** (which runs parallel to the superior sagittal sinus but lower down in the brain) which then dumps into the **straight sinus**. The *posterior* aspect of the brain is drained by the **occipital sinus**. These three sinuses (the superior sagittal, straight, and occipital sinuses) themselves merge at a point in the back of the head called the **confluence of sinuses** which lies beneath the occipital protuberance (which you can locate on yourself by placing a hand on the back of your skull and feeling for the small bump right in the middle). The confluence of sinuses then drains via the paired **transverse sinuses** (one going to the left and the other going to the right) which both run anteriorly. Along the way, the transverse sinuses become the **sigmoid sinuses** which pick up blood draining from the *lateral* parts of the brain via the **petrosal sinuses** as well as drainage from the *anterior* aspects of the brain (including the area around the eyes) via the **cavernous sinus**. All of these various drainage basins collect and then drain out of the head via the paired **internal jugular veins**. Make sure to take a few moments to locate each of these structures in the figure on the previous page!

PUTTING IT ALL TOGETHER

Hey, we did it! At this point, we can confidently say that we've covered everything about neuroanatomy *and* the kitchen sink. The arterial supply, meningeal layers, ventricular system, and venous drainage of the brain all work together to support and protect the central nervous system. For this reason, any diseases in these structures can lead directly to dysfunction of the nervous system itself, so an understanding of these systems is crucial for understanding neurology.

From this point forward, we are going to transition from merely *hinting* about what goes wrong in the nervous system to driving head-on into dangerous territory. All those beautiful and intricate neurologic systems we've spent time learning about are going to come crashing down in some surprising and unexpected ways. So buckle up and get ready as we transition away from the foundational anatomy of the nervous system and into a discussion of the diseases and disorders that are seen in clinical settings!

REVIEW QUESTIONS

1. A 60 y/o M comes to the emergency department after feeling dizzy for several hours. He has had two episodes of vomiting during this time. His gait is notably ataxic, and he appears to be increasingly lethargic. An emergent cerebral angiogram is obtained which shows an occlusion in his basilar artery. Which of the following letters best identifies the artery involved?

2. A 23 y/o F is prescribed propranolol, a beta-blocker, to help reduce anxiety related to public speaking. Compared to other beta-blockers, propranolol is believed to have greater effects on the central nervous system due to its ability to easily cross the blood–brain barrier. What property of propranolol likely accounts for this ability?
   A. High bioavailability
   B. Small molecular weight
   C. Tight protein-binding
   D. Low water solubility
   E. Active transport across tight junctions

3. A 33 y/o M is involved in a motor vehicle accident. He initially loses consciousness but then awakens within several minutes. On interview in the emergency department, he complains of nausea and a severe headache. While the doctor is conducting a review of systems, the patient suddenly appears confused and stops responding to questions. Seconds later, he begins having a seizure. A CT

scan is ordered which shows bleeding in the epidural space. Which of the following is the most likely explanation for his seizure?

A. Mechanical compression of brain tissue
B. Dysfunction of grey matter due to direct exposure to blood
C. Tearing of white matter related to the injury
D. Blood mixing with cerebrospinal fluid in the ventricular system
E. Lack of mechanical protection due to loss of cerebrospinal fluid

4. A 10 y/o M is brought to his pediatrician by his parents. Over the past month he has experienced headaches, nausea, and vomiting which have all progressively worsened to the point where he is unable to attend school. His physical exam is notable for bilateral swelling of the optic discs suggestive of increased intracranial pressure. Head imaging is ordered which shows an arteriovenous malformation causing mechanical compression of the cerebral aqueduct. Which of the following areas is *least* likely to show enlargement in size?

A. Third ventricle
B. Fourth ventricle
C. Interventricular foramina
D. Lateral ventricle
E. All of the following are likely to be enlarged

5. A 68 y/o F with no significant medical history is seen in the emergency department for swelling and redness of the left eye. She reports that she first noticed these signs one week ago and that they have been gradually worsening since then. Review of systems is positive for fever, headache, and severe fatigue.

She is diagnosed with a blood clot in the cerebral venous circulation. Given her presenting signs and symptoms, which of the following venous spaces is most likely to show filling defects on neuroimaging?

A. Superior sagittal sinus
B. Inferior sagittal sinus
C. Occipital sinus
D. Transverse sinus
E. Cavernous sinus

1. **The best answer is C.** The basilar artery is an unpaired artery in the posterior circulation of the head. Strokes here can lead to a variety of signs and symptoms, though the cerebellum and brainstem are the regions most often affected leading to signs like ataxia in this case. The posterior cerebral artery (answer A), superior cerebellar artery (answer B), anterior inferior cerebellar artery (answer D), and vertebral artery (answer E) are all paired arteries.

2. **The best answer is D.** Fat-soluble molecules are better able to cross the blood–brain barrier compared to those that are water-soluble. Out of all the beta-blockers, propranolol is unique in that it is by far the most lipophilic (making it also the most hydro*phobic*). Bioavailability refers to the amount of the ingested dose that reaches the bloodstream; however, this has no direct effect on the ability to cross the blood–brain barrier (answer A). A smaller molecular weight is only minimally helpful for allowing a drug to cross the blood–brain barrier (answer B). Protein-bound drugs cannot cross the blood–brain barrier, so a highly bound substance would be *less* able to cross it, not more (answer C). Finally, there is no evidence that propranolol is actively transported across the blood–brain barrier (answer E).

3. **The best answer is A.** Bleeding in the epidural space, known as an epidural hematoma, causes neuronal dysfunction due to compressive forces on the brain tissue itself. When the force is sufficiently strong, it can compress the brainstem, leading to loss of consciousness. The meninges acts to separate the brain from surrounding tissues, so bleeding in the space above the outer layer of the meninges would not lead to blood coming in direct contact with grey matter (answer B), nor would it lead to a tear injury of white matter (answer C). Cerebrospinal fluid flows in the subarachnoid space, not the epidural space (answers D and E).

4. **The best answer is B.** Compression of the cerebral aqueduct is likely to lead to enlargement of areas "upstream" due to build-up of cerebrospinal fluid. Out of the options listed, only the fourth ventricle occurs "downstream" of the cerebral aqueduct and is therefore unlikely to be enlarged. The lateral ventricles (answer D), interventricular foramina (answer C), and third ventricle (answer A) all are found "upstream" of the cerebral aqueduct.

5. **The best answer is E.** Of the listed options, only the cavernous sinus drains venous blood from areas in the front of the head, including the eyes. In contrast, the superior sagittal sinus drains the upper-middle aspect of the cerebral cortex (answer A), the inferior sagittal sinus drains the lower-middle cerebral cortex (answer B), and the occipital sinus drains the posterior aspect of the cerebral cortex (answer C). These three sinuses drain to the confluence of sinuses before continuing on as the transverse sinus (answer D).

11 THE NEUROLOGICAL EXAM

As we transition away from the foundational science of neurology into its actual practice in clinical settings, we're not leaving behind anything that we've learned so far. Instead, all of the knowledge that we've accumulated about the anatomy and physiology of the nervous system is still fair game to pop up for the rest of this book, so feel free to refer back to previous chapters whenever you need a refresher on a particular subject.

The goal of any clinician who is seeing a patient with a neurological complaint is two-fold: first, to find out what is going on (**diagnosis**), and second, to use this information to offer suggestions on how best to help (**treatment**). The starting point for diagnosis in neurology (as it is in any medical field) is to take a detailed **history** and perform a **physical** exam. From there, neurologists will use the **neurological exam** which is a series of systematic tests to assess the function of all aspects of the nervous system across various areas of the body. This exam helps to localize dysfunction to specific parts of the nervous system, making it an invaluable tool for diagnosis.

In modern neurology, however, the neurological exam is just one piece of the puzzle. In many cases, it must be combined with relevant laboratory and imaging data to come to the best diagnosis. For this reason, we will briefly discuss some of the most common tools that are used in neurology to diagnose a patient's condition, including **neuroimaging** modalities such as **computed tomography** (CT) and **magnetic resonance imaging** (MRI) as well as **laboratory analysis** of blood and cerebrospinal fluid samples (the latter obtained using a technique known as a **lumbar puncture**).

THE NEUROLOGICAL EXAM

The neurological exam is a long and complicated procedure, but it kind of has to be, as there is no way to systematically test every major aspect of the nervous system in multiple parts of the body without having to expend some serious time and effort. You'll need a few tools to perform a neurological exam, including a **reflex hammer**, a **tuning fork**, and **vibrating prongs**. When performing a neurological exam, it can be helpful to have a mnemonic to remember each step to make sure you're not skipping any key components. You can use the following rhyme to keep the steps of the neurological exam in mind:

Head and hammer, feet like tots
Bulk and tone, pretend we fought
Stroking, poking, shaking, hot
Touch my finger, stand and walk!

Let's use this rhyme to break down these steps one by one.

MENTAL STATUS AND CRANIAL NERVES ("head")

The starting point for the neurological exam is to assess the patient's **mental status**, which includes their overall **level of consciousness** and **cognitive abilities** such as concentration and memory. Even within the first few seconds of the exam, you can get a sense for whether the patient is fully alert or whether they are sedated, confused, or even comatose. However, if you'd like to assess this more systematically, you can ask the patient basic **orientation questions** including who they are, where they are, what time it is, and the purpose of their visit (person, place, time, and purpose). Additional tests such as simple arithmetic and memory games can provide further clues. In cases where you suspect cognitive impairment, you may consider using a structured test like the Mini–Mental State Examination (MMSE) or Montreal Cognitive Assessment (MoCA) to provide a more detailed picture of the patient's cognitive abilities.

After assessing their mental status, the second part of "head" is to do a cranial nerve examination. Assessing each of the cranial nerves can help to localize specific deficits in the cerebrum or brainstem. (You can use the "Ooh Ooh Ooh To Touch And Feel Very Green Vegetables AH!" mnemonic to remember the order.)

The **olfactory nerve** is difficult to assess unless if you've specifically brought something with you (or haven't bathed in a few days). Some neurologists will carry a small jar of tea, coffee beans, or other objects with a distinct but not unpleasant odor to test that the patient's sense of smell is intact.

The **optic nerve** can be assessed by asking the patient to cover one eye. You can then bring your finger into each of the four quadrants and ask the patient to say where your finger is. You can also test visual acuity by using a chart (such as the **Snellen chart** pictured to the right) at a fixed distance.

The cranial nerves controlling extraocular movements (the **oculomotor**, **trochlear**, and **abducens nerves**) can be tested by asking the patient to follow your finger with their eyes while keeping their head still. Move your finger in an H-shape in

```
        E          1
      F   P         2
     T  O  Z        3
    L  P  E  D       4
   P  E  C  F  D      5
  E D F C Z P         6
  F E L O P Z D       7
  D E F P O T E C     8
```

front of the patient's head to confirm that their eyes are able to move fully in all directions. While doing this, look for **nystagmus**, or the rapid involuntary movements of the eyes which can indicate damage to the cerebellum, inner ear, or other systems involved in balance. Finally, when you are done testing that the eyes move in all directions, move your finger in towards the space between the patient's eyes. This is to test for **accommodation**, meaning that as the patient's eyes cross inwards, the pupils should constrict. Finally, test for the **pupillary light reflex** by shining a light into one eye at a time to ensure that *both* of the patient's pupils constrict in response to this.

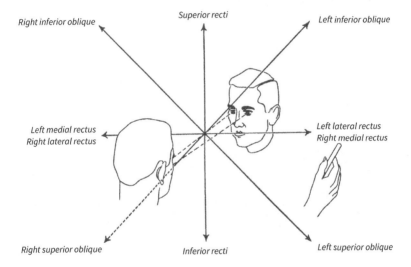

Right inferior oblique

Superior recti

Left inferior oblique

Left medial rectus
Right lateral rectus

Left lateral rectus
Right medial rectus

Right superior oblique

Inferior recti

Left superior oblique

The sensory component of the **trigeminal nerve** can be tested by lightly drawing a soft object like a cotton swab across the forehead, cheek, and jaw on both the left and the right, while the motor component can be tested by asking the patient to clench their jaw as well as open it against resistance ("Open your mouth while I try to hold it shut.").

The **facial nerve** can be tested by asking the patient to perform a variety of actions involving the muscles of the face, including raising their eyebrows, closing their eyes tightly, puffing out their cheeks, and showing their teeth. Look for weakness or asymmetry in any of these actions. You can simultaneously test both the fifth and seventh cranial nerve using the **corneal reflex** in which you try to (gently!) poke the patient's eye with a soft object. The patient should quickly shut their eye to keep out the incoming object. This reflex relies on the ophthalmic branch of the trigeminal nerve for its afferent limb and the facial nerve for its efferent limb.

A quick-and-dirty way to test the auditory component of the **vestibulocochlear nerve** is to rub your fingers together outside of each of the patient's ears and asking if they can hear the sound. If more in-depth testing is required, you can use the Weber and Rinne tests described in Chapter 9.

The **glossopharyngeal** and **vagus nerves** can be tested together, as they both are involved in uvula movement and the gag reflex. (This is the classic "Say ah!" moment when you visit the doctor.) If there is any unilateral weakness of these muscles, the uvula will deviate *away from* the weakness, as the non-affected side is pulling on it stronger than the affected side.

The **accessory nerve** can be quickly tested by asking the patient to shrug their shoulders as well as turn their head from side to side against your resistance.

Finally, the **hypoglossal nerve** is easily tested by asking the patient to stick out their tongue. Any weakness on one side will cause the tongue to deviate, although in contrast to the uvula, this will be *towards* the weakness. You can remember this by thinking, "You lick your wounds."

A lesion of the **hypoglossal nerve** will cause the **tongue to deviate towards the side of lesion**.

*You **lick** your **wounds**.*

DEEP TENDON REFLEXES ("hammer")

The word "hammer" should remind you of a **reflex hammer**, the tool that is commonly used to test **deep tendon reflexes**. As mentioned previously, not all sensory neurons travel all the way to the brain, and not all motor neurons originate in the cortex. Instead, some afferent sensory neurons synapse directly onto efferent motor neurons in the spinal cord to produce an automatic unconscious reaction. The prototype example of this is the **patellar or knee-jerk reflex** (pictured here). When the patellar tendon is tapped, some of the sensory nerve fibers travel directly to the nerve roots of motor neurons in the spinal cord, causing an immediate "kick" of the leg. Decreased or absent reflexes (known as **hyporeflexia** and **areflexia**, respectively) tend to suggest damage in the afferent or efferent nerves involved, while brisk or hyperactive reflexes (known as **hyperreflexia**) tend to suggest involvement of the central nervous system.

There are several other reflex arcs like this in the spinal cord, and they are clinically useful for localizing at what level an injury has occurred. The primary spinal reflexes are the **biceps reflex** (C5-C6), the **triceps reflex** (C6-C7), the **patellar or knee jerk reflex** (L2-L4), and the **Achilles or ankle jerk reflex** (S1-S2). Let's learn a few memory aids to remember the spinal nerves associated with each one. For the biceps and triceps, draw a stick figure but use the numbers **6** and **7** instead of arms as below. The 6 looks like someone flexing their bulging **biceps** while the 7 looks like someone showing off their **triceps**.

For the patellar reflex, draw a stick figure using an **L** for the lower half of the body to show that he is kneeling on two legs or even down on L4s (all fours). This should help you remember that the knee jerk reflex is between L2 and L4.

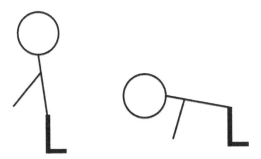

Finally, for the ankle jerk or Achilles reflex, write Achilles as Ach-**I**-**II**-e**S** (using Roman numerals **I** and **II**) to remember that it is between S**1**-S**2**.

The primary spinal reflexes are the **biceps reflex** (C5-C6), the **triceps reflex** (C6-C7), the **patellar reflex** (L2-L4), and the **Achilles reflex** (S1-S2).

*A stick figure with **6**s for arms is showing off its **biceps** (C5-C6).*
*A stick figure with **7**s for arms is showing off its **triceps** (C6-C7).*
*A stick figure with **2 Ls** for legs is either kneeling or down on **L4**s (L2-L4).*
*Ach-**I**-**II**-e**S** reflex (S1-S2).*

PRIMITIVE REFLEXES ("feet like tots")
Next, you will test a set of **primitive reflexes**, which are so-named because they are typically exhibited by infants but not adults. While the underlying reflex circuits are present for people of all ages, as someone gets past one or two years of age, the frontal lobe develops to the point where it is able to automatically *inhibit* these reflexes (it's the part of the brain that says "no"). For this reason, re-appearance of primitive reflexes in an adult is indicative of either **frontal lobe pathology** or of damage to **upper motor neurons** that carry these inhibitory signals down to the body.

By far the most commonly tested primitive reflexes is the **Babinski sign** (also known as the **plantar reflex**). To perform this test, drag an instrument (such as the sharper end of a reflex hammer) on the bottom of the foot on the lateral side from the heel to the toes. In healthy adults, the toes will naturally curve in *towards* the stimulus. In contrast, a positive Babinski sign occurs if the toes instead fan out *away* from the stimulus. This is why testing of primitive reflexes is called "feet like tots": the toes react in the same way that an infant's would. You can remember this by thinking that the **Babi**nski sign is only normal in **Babi**s.

Downgoing Babinski (normal)   *Upgoing Babinski (abnormal)*

Presence of the **plantar reflex** in an adult is indicative of either **frontal lobe pathology** or **upper motor neuron disease**.

*The **Babi**nski sign is only normal in **Babi**s.*

While the Babinski sign is the most commonly tested primitive reflex, a few others exist, including the **rooting reflex** (the baby turns its head if its cheek is touched), the **Moro reflex** (the baby throws its arms out when startled), and the **palmar grasp reflex** (the baby's fingers close around an object placed in the palm). These are used clinically in a similar fashion to the Babinski sign (and by medical professionals who are often unable to resist testing this on their own children!).

Rooting reflex   *Moro* reflex   *Palmar grasp* reflex

THE MOTOR SYSTEM ("bulk and tone, pretend we fought")

Testing the **motor system** involves three components: observing the bulk (or overall size) of various muscles in the body, noting their tone, and testing their strength.

Determining the **bulk** of muscles does not require any sort of sophisticated maneuvers. Instead, you simply observe. Someone with focal wasting or atrophy of specific muscles may have sustained damage to the motor neurons innervating that muscle, as a lack of nerve supply tends to weaken muscles like a flower without water. A generalized atrophy of all muscles in the body may be more suggestive of a disease in the muscle itself (known as a **myopathy**, which we will cover in Chapter 14).

Muscle **tone** can be assessed by asking the patient to completely relax while you perform various movements on their behalf (such as holding their arm in one hand while moving their forearm with the other hand to assess muscle tone around the elbow joint). The tone of one's muscles can suggest different types of pathology. A weak or **flaccid tone** may suggest lower motor neuron damage, especially combined with wasting. In contrast, a **spastic tone** (muscles that are unusually tight, stiff, or jerky) can indicate upper motor neuron damage. A specific finding known as **cogwheel rigidity** (in which manipulating the patient's joints results in a *click-click-click*-like jerking of the joint) is suggestive of a condition known as Parkinsonism (which we will cover further in Chapter 17).

Finally, testing the **strength** of muscles can be done by asking the patient to resist you in performing various actions (hence "pretend we fought"). For example, you can test the muscles of the arm by asking the patient to bend their elbows and try to extend their arms while you push against them. Strength is traditionally graded on a scale between 0 and 5, with 5 being full strength resistance, 4 being some resistance, 3 being resistance against gravity but not the examiner, 2 being some movement but no ability to hold up against gravity, 1 being a flicker or twitching of muscles but no actual limb movement, and 0 being complete paralysis of the muscles.

SENSATION ("stroking, poking, shaking, hot")
Different kinds of sensory information travel along different pathways, so we need to test each kind in order to determine where damage may have occurred. These tests will need to be repeated across various areas of the body. For example, someone may have intact sensation in their upper extremities but not their lower extremities, so if you only tested this in one location, you are likely to miss this finding.

You can test **light touch** by gently pulling something soft against the skin ("stroking"). In contrast, **pain** sensation can be tested by applying a sharp but not dangerous object (such as a toothpick) lightly into the skin ("poking"). You can also consider testing for **discriminative touch** by placing two pins close together on the skin and asking the patient when they can discern that there are two sensations rather than just one. Under normal circumstances, two-point discrimination is much stronger in areas with many sensory nerves (such as the lips or the tips of the finger) and less powerful in insensitive areas such as the back.

Testing **vibration** ("shaking") can be done by applying a vibrating prong against the patient's skin and asking them when they feel it stop vibrating. Make sure to test **proprioception** (which also travels in the dorsal column—medial lemniscus pathway) as well by asking the patient to close their eyes and tell you if you are lifting their fingers or toes up or down (which is kind of like a slow-motion version of "shaking").

Finally, you can test **temperature** ("hot") by applying both a warm and a cold object (such as a heated blanket or a metal stethoscope, respectively) against the skin to ensure that the patient can discriminate between the two temperatures.

COORDINATION ("touch my finger")
Coordination and balance are largely reliant upon the cerebellum. Cerebellar function can be tested in a few ways. The most commonly used test is the **finger-to-nose test** in which you ask the patient to alternate between touching their nose and touching your finger while you move your finger around ("touch my finger"). This requires the

cerebellum to be able to integrate visual information about the position of *your* finger with proprioceptive information about the position of *their* finger. Two other ways to test cerebellar function are the **heel-to-shin test** (in which you ask the patient to place the back of their ankle against the knee of their other leg, then run their ankle down the shin to the foot and back up again) and the **rapid pronation-supination test** (in which you ask the patient to touch the palm of one hand with the front of their other hand then with the back of their other hand and repeat this movement as fast as possible). An inability to perform any of these actions is suggestive of cerebellar dysfunction. There are a few other ways of testing cerebellar function as well, but these three are a good place to start.

THE ROMBERG TEST ("stand")
To perform the **Romberg test**, ask the patient to stand with their feet shoulder-width apart ("stand"). They should then put their arms straight out in front of them palms-up (as if they are holding an invisible platter of food). Ordinarily, someone can do this without falling over by using three senses: their sense of **sight**, their sense of **balance**

from the vestibular system, and their sense of **proprioception**. Even if one of these senses is missing, the patient can still use the other two to compensate and maintain their balance. However, to finish the Romberg test, the patient must close their eyes. By doing this, you are taking sight out of the equation. If they maintain balance even after closing their eyes, you know that both their vestibular system and proprioception are intact. If they fall over after closing their eyes, however, you know that at least one of those functions is absent. (Make sure to stand close to the patient to steady them in case they start falling!) A positive Romberg is indicative of problems with **proprioception** or the **vestibular system**.

GAIT ("walk")
The final step of the neurological exam is to test the patient's **gait** (or their ability to walk). Someone with a normal gait should be able to walk steadily without tripping or falling. They should even be able to walk when given specific conditions, such as walking only on their heels or the tips of their toes. An unsteady or **ataxic** gait can be suggestive of either upper or lower motor neuron damage, cerebellar dysfunction, or various forms of sensory dysfunction.

The **neurological exam** is a **systematic series of tests** of neurological functions.

Head and hammer, feet like tots
Bulk and tone, pretend we fought
Stroking, poking, shaking, hot
Touch my finger, stand and walk!

The best way to learn the neurological exam is to just *do it*! Find someone else who is trying to learn it, then practice with each other until it feels comfortable. You can use the rhyming mnemonic to remind yourself of what steps come next.

NEUROIMAGING

While the neurological exam can net you a wealth of information about the current status of the patient's nervous system, there's something to be said about just *seeing it* with your own eyes. With the advent of neuroimaging techniques, it is now possible to get highly detailed images depicting both the structure and function of the nervous system, allowing for greater diagnostic precision and targeted treatment. There are a few different types of neuroimaging techniques, each of which can be ordered in a variety of configurations depending on the specific clinical situation.

COMPUTED TOMOGRAPHY

Computed tomography scans (also known as **CT** or **CAT scans**) use a series of x-rays to produce an image of the brain. CT scans have the advantage of being **quick** to produce, with images being available within a number of minutes. This makes them ideal for **emergency situations** (like ruling out a brain bleed in a patient who hit their head in an accident). However, this speed comes at a price, as the images that are

produced are often quite a bit muddier looking compared to the highly detailed images you would get from an MRI. In addition, because CT scans use multiple x-rays, they expose the patient to high amounts of potentially harmful **ionizing radiation**. For this reason, it can be helpful to think of **CT** scans as being like a **CaT**: they are quick but can be harmful.

> **CT scans** are **quick to obtain**, but they **lack detail** and expose the patient to **ionizing radiation**.
>
> *CaT scans are like **cats**: they are **quick** but can be **harmful**.*

MAGNETIC RESONANCE IMAGING

Magnetic resonance imaging (or **MRI**) is an advanced neuroimaging technique that uses magnetic fields and radio waves to produce a high-quality image. (Just look at the images on the next page—there's no contest!) MRIs are particularly well-suited for visualizing structures deep in the **posterior fossa** (such as the cerebellum and the brainstem) that x-rays have trouble reaching. Furthermore, because they do not use x-rays, MRIs do not expose the patient to ionizing radiation, making them much **safer** than CTs. So if they're safer and produce better quality images than a CT, why not use them all the time? The main drawback of MRIs is that they are **slow**, with some scans taking an hour or more to produce. Because of this, they are less useful in emergencies where a rapid diagnosis is needed.

> **MRI scans** produce **detailed images** and do not involve ionizing radiation, but they also take **more time to make**.
>
> *MRIs Make Realistic Images but you Must Remain Idle.*

Computed tomography (CT) scan of the head.

Magnetic resonance imaging (MRI) scan of the same patient.

It's worth pointing out that both CT and MRI scans are displayed as though the patient is lying face-up on a table with their toes pointed towards the ceiling. You are standing at the patient's feet looking forward towards their head. For this reason, the patient's *left* brain is actually on the *right* side of the image and vice versa!

Finally, a particular subtype of MRI known as **functional magnetic resonance imaging** (**fMRI**) can differentiate between oxygenated and deoxygenated blood. This makes it useful in situations where you want to look at the *function* of certain areas (as active areas of the brain will use more oxygen than inactive regions). Functional MRI scans are increasingly being used to diagnose strokes and other conditions involving poor blood flow. Because they can pick up ischemia before significant damage has occurred, clinicians can intervene earlier and potentially produce better outcomes.

*An **fMRI** scan with **lighter areas** showing regions of **greater activity***.

POSITRON EMISSION TOMOGRAPHY

Like fMRI, **positron emission tomography** (or PET) scans are able to measure the metabolic activity of specific regions rather than simply showing the structure. For this reason, they are useful for detecting diseases that involve changes in metabolic activity (either too much activity, as in a metabolically hungry brain tumor, or too little, as in certain forms of dementias). Overall, PET scans are quicker while fMRI scans are able to produce more detailed images.

*A **PET scan** showing **normal brain activity**.*   *A **PET scan** in a patient with **Alzheimer's disease**.*

LUMBAR PUNCTURE

Laboratory testing of blood is a common part of the work-up for many conditions in medicine. In neurology, you can take things a step further by also testing a patient's **cerebrospinal fluid** which can reveal things that normal blood testing does not (for example, a localized infection of the meninges that has not spread to the blood). Because cerebrospinal fluid lies deep within the highly protected fortress of the central nervous system, it is not as easy to obtain a sample for testing as it is for a blood test. If you need to test a patient's cerebrospinal fluid, you can use a procedure known as a **lumbar puncture** (also known as a spinal tap) which involves advancing a long needle through the back into the space between the vertebrae.

You can perform a lumbar puncture by asking the patient to bend forward (either in a sitting position or lying on their side) to help open up the intervertebral space as much as possible. Then, feel for the **posterior superior iliac crests** (the highest part of the pelvis that you can feel from the back) and from there bring your fingers medially to the spine. This should place you right about at the intervertebral space between **L3-L4**. Why L3-L4? The spinal cord terminates into the conus medullaris around L1 or L2, so inserting the needle here avoids hitting the spinal cord directly. There are still nerves that travel in this area (the cauda equina), but because they don't form a solid mass like the spinal cord, they easily move out of the way when the needle is inserted. The needle is then used to extract cerebrospinal fluid from this space.

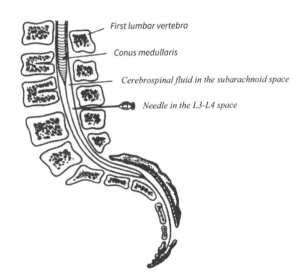

First lumbar vertebra

Conus medullaris

Cerebrospinal fluid in the subarachnoid space

Needle in the L3-L4 space

While a lumbar puncture can be an incredibly helpful procedure for diagnosing diseases of the central nervous system, it is not without risk. In addition to being an uncomfortable or even painful procedure for the patient, inserting a needle into a protected space like the central nervous system introduces the potential for infection, so **sterile technique** must be followed at all times! Finally, there is a risk that removing cerebrospinal fluid from the lower part of the central nervous system can cause the pressure in the spinal cord to drop, thereby creating a vacuum that in some cases can even suck parts of the brain down into the spine (a condition known as **cerebral herniation**). As we will discover in Chapter 13, herniation can compress parts of the brain and can even lead to permanent damage. For most people, the risk of cerebral herniation due to a lumbar puncture is incredibly low. However, if someone has a tumor or other lesion in the brain that is increasing intracranial pressure (and therefore raising the risk of a herniation), you will need to order a CT scan to assess the risk more fully before proceeding with a lumbar puncture. High-risk patients include those with a known history of **C**entral nervous system disease, any **F**ocal neurologic deficits, an **I**mmunocompromised status, evidence of **R**aised intracranial pressure (such as papilledema on eye exam), new-onset or unexplained **S**eizures, and anyone whose **T**hinking is unclear (altered mental status). You can remember these cases by thinking that you have to **C FIRST** before doing a lumbar puncture.

A **lumbar puncture** can be used to obtain a sample of **cerebrospinal fluid** for **diagnosis or treatment**. In certain patients, **brain imaging** is required before performing a lumbar puncture to avoid **cerebral herniation**.

In some patients, you'll want to C (see) FIRST:
Central nervous system disease
Focal neurologic deficits
Immunocompromised
Raised intracranial pressure
Seizures (new-onset or unexplained)
Thinking unclear

PUTTING IT ALL TOGETHER

The number of tools that neurologists and other clinicians have at their disposal for diagnosing and treating disease keeps increasing as medical technology continues to improve. At the end of the day, however, knowing how to take a good history and perform a thorough neurological exam remain vital skills that any clinician needs to have! Keep practicing the neurological exam until you feel completely comfortable doing it. When you meet a patient with a neurological complaint for the first time, you will be glad you did!

REVIEW QUESTIONS

1. A 78 y/o F is brought to the emergency department from her skilled nursing facility after a staff member noticed that she began appearing confused during a meal. In the hospital, a medical student discussing the case with his preceptor says that he believes the patient has had a stroke but wants to get an MRI to determine the exact location. What is the preceptor's most likely response?
    A. "There's no time. We should do a CT instead."
    B. "Let's do a thorough neurological exam first before subjecting the patient to such high doses of radiation."
    C. "An MRI won't produce the kind of images that we would need to localize a stroke for this patient."
    D. "We need a clearer picture of metabolic activity in this patient's brain. Let's do a functional MRI scan instead."
    E. "Before we can do that, we need to do a lumbar puncture."

2. A 38 y/o M is undergoing a thorough neurological exam after he has fallen several times while walking in the past week. On exam, his gait is notably ataxic. As part of the exam, the neurologist asks the patient to stand up and place his feet together. He does this without a problem. When asked to close his eyes, he sways unsteadily for the first 5 seconds. However, he is ultimately able to stay standing upright for a full minute. Based on the results of this test, where is there most likely to be a lesion in this patient?
    A. Cerebellum
    B. Dorsal columns of the spinal cord
    C. Visual pathway
    D. Vestibular apparatus in the inner ear
    E. Vestibulocochlear nerve

3. A 44 y/o M presents to his primary care nurse practitioner complaining of right arm pain. He says the pain goes down his arm and "into my thumb and index finger." X-ray of the neck reveals degenerative bone changes at C5 as below:

After a full history and neurological exam, he is given a presumptive diagnosis of cervical spinal stenosis at the level of C5. The patient is most likely to show an abnormality in which of the following reflexes?

- A.   Biceps
- B.   Triceps
- C.   Patellar
- D.   Ankle jerk
- E.   Plantar

4.   An 18 y/o M is brought to the hospital after he was found lying in the hallway of his dorm appearing sleepy and confused. He is febrile with a temperature of 101.8°F. His dorm has experienced a recent outbreak of meningitis, so a lumbar puncture is ordered. A new intern is called to assist with the lumbar puncture. How should the intern demonstrate where she will place the needle?

- A.   Measuring the length of the back from the shoulders to the waist and inserting the needle halfway down
- B.   Feeling for the bottoms of the ribcage bilaterally and then marking halfway between them
- C.   Feeling for the tops of the pelvis bilaterally and then marking the midpoint between them
- D.   Ordering an x-ray of the spine to determine the location of the cauda equina
- E.   Asking the patient to point to where his back hurts the most

1. **The best answer is A.** Different modalities of neuroimaging each have their advantages and disadvantages. An MRI is better than a CT when it comes to producing detailed images (answer C) and does not involve ionizing radiation (answer B). A specific subtype of MRI known as functional MRI is able to show metabolic processes (answer D). The main disadvantages of an MRI are its cost and the time it takes to produce an image compared to a CT. In an emergency situation like a possible stroke, an MRI would take too long to obtain, making a CT the imaging modality of choice. In cases of suspected stroke, waiting to do a lumbar puncture before performing neuroimaging is likely to harm the patient by allowing ischemic injury to progress (answer E).

2. **The best answer is A.** The Romberg test assesses three things: the patient's sense of proprioception, their vestibular system, and their visual pathways. Under normal conditions, at least two of these three structures must be intact for the patient to remain upright. By asking the patient to close his eyes, the examiner is testing his proprioception and vestibular function. Some degree of swaying is normal and, provided the patient is able to remain upright, actually demonstrates intact functioning of these systems. For this reason, the patient's negative Romberg test is a sign that all three of these systems are working (answers B—E). While it is sometimes mistaken as such, the Romberg test is *not* a test of cerebellar function! Given this, a negative Romberg test suggests that the cause of this patient's ataxia is most likely to be in his cerebellum.

3. **The best answer is A.** The biceps reflex is most often associated with damage to the C5 or C6 spinal nerves or one of their branches. In contrast, the triceps reflex is associated with C6-C7 (answer B), the patellar reflex with L2-4 (answer C), and the ankle jerk or Achilles reflex with S1-S2 (answer D). The plantar reflex, or Babinski sign, is generally a sign of frontal lobe damage and would not be abnormal in a patient with cervical spinal stenosis (answer E).

4. **The best answer is C.** Proper needle placement when performing a lumbar puncture is essential to avoid injuring the spinal cord. The target of the needle is the lumbar cistern, or the cerebrospinal fluid-filled space below the termination of the spinal cord known as the cauda equina. The cauda equina typically occurs around the level of L1 or L2, so needle placement is generally between L3 and L4. The posterior superior iliac crests serve as a useful anatomical landmark to identify this space. The bottom of the ribcage would be too high and would likely result in spinal cord injury (answer B), as would inserting the needle into the midpoint of the back (answer A). A spinal x-ray is not necessary for determining the location of the L3-L4 interspace (answer D), nor are patients' self-reports of back pain relevant to this (answer E).

12 STROKE

A **stroke** (also known as a **cerebrovascular accident** or CVA) is a state of neurologic dysfunction resulting from **interruptions in oxygen supply** to the brain or other nervous tissue. There are two primary forms of stroke. An **ischemic stroke** occurs when blood is unable to get to its destination. This can occur either as a result of a **blockage** (like a tree falling across a river and creating a dam) or due to a **decrease in the amount of blood flow** (like a river drying up as the result of a drought). In contrast, a **hemorrhagic stroke** occurs when blood escapes from its intended path and goes someplace it shouldn't be going (like a pipe bursting, allowing water to flood the surrounding areas). While the mechanism differs between the two forms of stroke, in both cases the effect is the same: the blood does not get to where it needs to go, depriving neurons of needed oxygen and leading to cell death and loss of function. In the case of hemorrhagic stroke, the displaced blood can also cause problems by being in areas that it shouldn't be, as blood can both irritate nervous tissue and lead to increased intracranial pressure.

Ischemic stroke

Hemorrhagic stroke

DIAGNOSIS AND TREATMENT OF STROKES

Because specific arteries supply specific parts of the brain, the signs and symptoms of a stroke are largely dependent upon which areas have been damaged. (For example, a stroke in the frontal lobe will have a completely different presentation than a stroke in the occipital lobe due to the very different functions that each of these lobes perform.) However, a few general signs and symptoms can be seen across multiple types of strokes. These are encapsulated in the mnemonic **BE FAST** which stands for **B**alance issues, **E**ye problems (loss of vision), **F**acial drooping, **A**rm or leg weakness, **S**peech impediments, and **T**ime (a sudden onset). Because the brain requires a constant supply of oxygen to keep running, these signs often begin **suddenly** (within a couple of minutes) as opposed to the slow onset that is seen in other neurologic disorders like an autoimmune disease or a brain tumor.

Despite the wide variation in signs and symptoms, these six signs and symptoms are effective at identifying the majority of patients presenting with a stroke. However, it's important to note that many strokes do not cause any immediate signs or symptoms! These so-called "silent strokes" may not cause obvious damage right away, but they are still associated with permanent neuronal damage and place the patient at higher risk for more strokes in the future.

The most common **signs and symptoms** of a stroke are a **sudden onset** of **facial drooping, extremity weakness, speech difficulty**, and **visual loss**.

*If you recognize a **stroke**, you need to **BE FAST**:*
Balance issues
Eye problems (loss of vision)
Facial drooping
Arm or leg weakness
Speech difficulties
Time (sudden onset)

By definition, any observed neurologic deficits must persist for **at least one day** to be classified as a stroke. (To be clear, there's nothing special about 24 hours—it was arbitrarily chosen as an easy-to-remember cut-off point.) Cases of focal neurologic deficits related to cerebral ischemia that resolve in *less than* 24 hours are classified instead as a **transient ischemic attack** (often abbreviated as TIA and occasionally called a "mini-stroke").

While initial clinical findings (such as those in BE FAST) can help to provide the initial clue that a stroke is happening, neuroimaging is almost always used if available, as this can not only localize the damage in the brain but also distinguish between ischemic and hemorrhagic strokes. Due to its speed, CT is the most widely used imaging modality for strokes, but use of MRI is becoming increasingly common.

*An **MRI** showing an **ischemic stroke** in the territory of the **left middle cerebral artery**.*

Clinical management of a stroke consists of two things: **acute treatment** in the time immediately following a stroke to prevent further damage to the brain, and **long-term prevention** of future stroke episodes. Even with adequate treatment, however, strokes are a deadly disease, with around one-quarter of all patients presenting with a stroke dying within one month.

Immediate treatment of strokes should only be initiated once the type of stroke (ischemic or hemorrhagic) is known. After all, if you go in with a "shoot first, ask questions later" approach, you might end up making things much worse! For *hemorrhagic* strokes, treatment is pretty limited, as once the blood has escaped its confines there is little you can do to put it back. For *ischemic* strokes, however, much more can be done. With an ischemic stroke, the goal is to get rid of the blockage as fast as possible. This is done with either medicine or surgery. A specific medication known as **tissue plasminogen activator** (or tPA) helps to break down blood clots by stimulating key enzymes in the body's fibrinolytic pathway. These medications go by various names that all end in –teplase (such as alteplase or reteplase). When given **within 3 hours** of the stroke, tPA can significantly reduce the amount of brain tissue lost and lead to better functional outcomes in the future. (Unfortunately, the effect of tPA on actual mortality is negligible.) Because it acts to break down blood clots, tPA does carry a risk of *inducing* a hemorrhage. To make some associations here, think of someone who is impatient because they have finished their meal at a restaurant and have been waiting for their server for nearly **three hours**. When another waiter walks by, they grab them and ask, "Hey, where's **te plase te pay**?!" This will help you associate drugs ending in –**teplase**, **tPA**, and the **three hour** time window in which it can be used.

Tissue plasminogen activator (tPA) is used to **treat ischemic strokes** and can **improve functional outcomes** if given **within 3 hours of stroke onset**.

*Think of someone who impatiently grabs a waiter and asks, "Hey, where's **te plase te pay**?!" because they have been waiting to leave for nearly **three hours**.*

Surgical removal of blood clots (known as a **thrombectomy**) is generally only used when an ischemic stroke occurs in a large, easily accessible artery. If initiated within 12 hours of onset, thrombectomy appears to reduce the extent of brain death.

STROKE RISK FACTORS
Given that strokes are disabling and deadly occurrences even *with* treatment, it is imperative not only to treat strokes when they occur but also to prevent them from happening in the first place. This can be done by understanding the specific risk factors that place someone at higher risk of having a stroke. By knowing these risk factors, we can try to modify them as much as possible. Essentially, all stroke risk factors boil down to one (or both) of two mechanisms: either a **narrowing** of blood vessels (which makes blood clots more likely to get trapped in them) or a **weakening** of vessel walls (which makes them more likely to rupture). You can remember the key risk factors using the mnemonic **DASHCAM**:

D is for Diabetes. Diabetes is associated with a higher risk of stroke, as high blood sugars can lead to stiff and weak arterial walls that are prone to clogging or breaking.

A is for Atrial fibrillation. Atrial fibrillation is associated with an increased risk of a **thrombus**, or blood clot, forming in the left atrium. Parts of the blood clot may then break off and travel via the bloodstream to other parts of the body. A thrombus that goes on the lam like this is known as an **embolus**. (To be clear, a "thrombus" and an "embolus" are not the same thing even though you may sometimes hear them used interchangeably. It's more accurate to say that an embolus is a particular *type* of thrombus.) Because the size of the artery tends to narrow the farther into the brain you go, an embolus that was traveling freely in the larger arteries near the heart may become stuck in the narrower passageways in the brain, leading to an ischemic stroke.

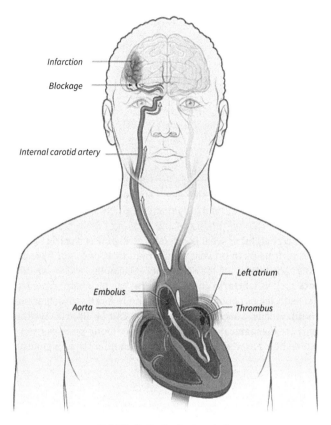

Infarction

Blockage

Internal carotid artery

Left atrium

Embolus

Aorta

Thrombus

Atrial fibrillation *leading to a* **stroke.**

S is for Smoking. Smoking even a single cigarette per day raises one's risk of a stroke significantly by damaging the integrity of arterial walls.

H is for Hypertension. High blood pressure is the **single largest risk factor** for both ischemic and hemorrhagic strokes, as the elevated pressure wears down arterial walls and makes them more likely to rupture and create a *hemorrhagic* stroke. The body then tries to strengthen the arterial walls again, but this tends to make the arteries more brittle and narrow, increasing the risk of an *ischemic* stroke.

C is for Cholesterol. High levels of cholesterol and other lipids increase the risk of forming atherosclerotic plaques that can both weaken and narrow arterial walls.

A is for Age. Old age is a major risk factor for strokes, with almost all strokes occurring in people over the age of 50.

M is for Male. Finally, men are 25% more likely to have a stroke compared to women the same age.

Stroke risk factors include conditions that **narrow or weaken blood vessel walls**.

DASHCAM:
Diabetes
Atrial fibrillation
Smoking
Hypertension
Cholesterol
Age
Male

While some of these factors (like age) cannot be changed, others can, and you should try to modify these as much as possible (such as helping someone to quit smoking, lower their blood pressure, and manage their blood sugar). Specific medications can be helpful as well. For people at high risk, **aspirin** is widely used to prevent strokes as it helps to prevent clot formation. It does not have a huge effect, but it has the advantage of being cheap, available, and easy to take. Oral **anticoagulants** such as **warfarin** and **clopidogrel** can also help to prevent formation of blood clots, especially in people who are prone to clotting (such as someone with atrial fibrillation). Finally, **surgical interventions** can be used as well, with carotid endarterectomy (or mechanical removal of atherosclerotic plaques from the walls of the carotid artery) being used to reduce the risk of another stroke significantly.

CORTICAL STROKES

Okay, now that we have given you a broad overview of how to diagnose and manage strokes, we are going to shift our attention to the process of **stroke localization**, or how to determine the likely location of a stroke based on your clinical exam findings. Everything we've covered so far will come into play here, so don't be afraid to brush up on old topics! To facilitate your learning, the clinical presentations used here are simplified to only show deficits related to a single area at a time. In real life, however, there is no "rule" that only one artery can be affected at a time, so keep that in mind!

Let's start with the three pairs of arteries that supply the cerebral cortex: the **anterior, middle, and posterior cerebral arteries**. Because the cortex is responsible for higher-level functions such as speech, awareness, attention, and vision, strokes in these arteries will produce characteristic deficits including **aphasia** (lack of speech), **agnosia** (lack of recognition), **neglect** (lack of awareness), **apraxia** (inability to plan movements), and **hemianopsia** (blindness in some or all of the visual field). These are known collectively as **cortical signs**. Cortical signs are often associated with specific motor and sensory deficits, as we will see now.

ANTERIOR CEREBRAL ARTERY SYNDROME

In general, occlusions in the early parts of the **anterior cerebral arteries** don't tend to cause much damage due to the presence of collateral circulation through the various communicating arteries. However, occlusions farther down can lead to both **paralysis** and **sensory loss** in the **contralateral lower limbs**. (Why *contra*lateral? Remember that the corticospinal tract and dorsal column—medial lemniscus pathway both cross in the medulla, while the spinothalamic tract crosses in the spinal cord.) There can also be dysfunction of lower body organs such as the bladder, resulting in **urinary incontinence**. Due to damage of the frontal lobe, difficulties in **executive functioning** (including loss of motivation and planning) can occur, and in some cases **primitive reflexes** can re-emerge. Overall, you can remember the association of the **anterior cerebral artery** with the lower extremities and other lower organs by drawing a stick figure where the legs form the letter **A** (for **A**nterior).

MIDDLE CEREBRAL ARTERY SYNDROME

The **middle cerebral artery** is the **most common location** for a cortical stroke. (This is because the middle cerebral artery is the continuation of the internal carotid artery, so a traveling thrombus just needs to go straight to block the middle cerebral artery, as opposed to going left or right to enter the anterior or posterior cerebral arteries.) Damage in the territory of the middle cerebral artery can result in both **paralysis** and **sensory loss** in the **contralateral upper limbs**. The language centers also lie in areas supplied by the middle cerebral artery, so ischemia in the ***dominant* hemisphere** can lead to various forms of **aphasia** depending on what areas have been damaged. You can remember the functions of the **M**iddle **C**erebral **A**rtery by continuing to add to the stick figure, this time using the letter **M** as their arms (as in someone doing the M part of the YMCA dance). This should help you remember the inclusion of the language centers as well, as you can imagine the stick figure **yelling** out "Y! M! C! A!"

"Y! M! C! A!"

Ischemia in the **non-dominant hemisphere** can lead to a condition known as **contralateral hemineglect** in which the patient's awareness of the opposite half of their field of vision is completely ignored. (We talked about this back in Chapter 3, so go back if you need a reminder.) You can remember the association between the **N**on-dominant parietal lobe and hemi**N**eglect by focusing on the **N** in each.

Ischemia in the **middle cerebral artery** of the **dominant** hemisphere can lead to **aphasia**, while ischemia in the **non-dominant hemisphere** can lead to **hemineglect**.

Picture a person **yelling** *out "Y! M! C! A!"*
The **N**on-dominant parietal lobe leads to hemi**N**eglect.

POSTERIOR CEREBRAL ARTERY SYNDROME

Ischemic damage in the territory of the **posterior cerebral artery** is associated with various defects in the visual pathway. The most typical pattern seen is **contralateral homonymous hemianopsia** with macular sparing. (It's worth noting that, while part of the visual fields may be missing, visual information from the macula often remains intact. This **macular sparing** occurs because the parts of the cerebral cortex that process information from the macula actually have a *dual* blood supply from not only the posterior cerebral artery but also the middle cerebral artery.) In cases of severe damage, complete **cortical blindness** can result. You can remember the association of the posterior cerebral artery with the visual cortex by drawing two **P**s like sunglasses on our stick figure.

The **anterior cerebral arteries** supply parts of the brain responsible for the **lower limbs** and **bladder**; the **middle cerebral arteries** are involved in the **upper limbs**, the **face**, and **language**; and the **posterior cerebral arteries** are involved in the **visual cortex**.

Draw a stick figure with an **A** *as the* **legs**, *an* **M** *as the* **arms**, *and two* **P**s *as sunglasses over the* **eyes**.

A stroke in the *left* posterior cerebral artery specifically can cause a finding known as **alexia without agraphia** in which someone is unable to read (owing to damage of both the visual cortex and a part of the corpus callosum) but can still engage in other forms of language including writing, speaking, and understanding speech. You can remember the association of this syndrome with the left **post**erior cerebral artery by thinking of someone who **cannot read letters** because the workers at the **post** office have **left** for the day.

A **left posterior cerebral artery stroke** can lead to **alexia without agraphia** in which someone is **unable to read** but can still **write, speak, and listen**.

*Someone **cannot read letters** if the **post** office workers have **left** for the day.*

Finally, because the posterior cerebral artery lies near the arteries going to parts of the midbrain (such as the basilar artery and pontine arteries), a blockage here can produce various deficits that overlap with those seen in subcortical and midbrain strokes, which we will discuss in the next sections.

LACUNAR STROKES

A **lacunar stroke** is one that occurs in the **subcortex** rather than the cortex. ("Lacunar" here comes from the Latin word for "lakes" or "empty spaces," a name that makes more sense when you consider that strokes in these areas have a tendency to leave *literal holes* in brain tissue!) Patients with lacunar strokes often present with **motor deficits** and **loss of sensation**, but the **lack of cortical signs** helps to

place us firmly in the region of the subcortex rather than the cortex. These subcortical regions are supplied by small branches off of the main cerebral arteries, and the narrow width of these arteries makes them particularly vulnerable to blockage (in fact, lacunar strokes are even more common than cortical strokes!). There are three main forms of lacunar strokes, which we will go over now.

PURE MOTOR STROKE
As its name implies, a **pure motor stroke** results in **hemiparesis of the contralateral face, arm, and leg** *without* any sensory deficits or associated cortical signs. This often results from ischemic damage to the **posterior limb of the internal capsule** which carries the corticospinal and corticobulbar tracts (remember the **PoLICe**-man). A pure motor stroke is the most common form of small vessel stroke.

PURE SENSORY STROKE

A **pure sensory stroke** is also pretty straightforward and features **numbness of the contralateral face, arm, and leg** *without* any motor deficits or associated cortical signs. As you might guess, a pure sensory stroke often results from ischemic damage to the **thalamus** (since the **th**alamus processes **th**e**nth**ory information).

SENSORIMOTOR STROKE

Because the posterior limb of the internal capsule and thalamus are adjacent to each other, occasionally a stroke will produce ischemic damage in both of these regions at once, leading to **both hemiparesis and numbness** of the **contralateral face and extremities**. As with any lacunar stroke, cortical signs will be absent.

BRAINSTEM STROKES

As we move down from the subcortex to the brainstem, localization starts to become a bit more complicated. But before we get into these specifics, first things first: how do we even know that we're dealing with a brainstem stroke in the first place? The pattern that should immediately make you think "It's in the brainstem!" is the presence of **crossed findings** where deficits in the *face* are on the *opposite* side as deficits in the *body*. Take a few moments to repeat this to

yourself: "**Crossed findings = brainstem stroke.**" (Note that this is different than Brown-Séquard syndrome which instead involves different types of deficits on the *right* side of the body compared to the *left*. This should instead have you thinking of a unilateral *spinal cord* lesion.)

Once you have a sense that the lesion is in the brainstem, your job then becomes to figure out exactly where. This is where things get more complicated. It's no longer enough to simply say *which* part of the brain has been affected. Instead, with brainstem strokes there are three questions to answer:

1. *What part* of the brainstem is the lesion in (midbrain, pons, or medulla)?
2. Is it more *medial or lateral* in this region?
3. Is the lesion on the *right or left* side?

To answer the first question, we'll need to use what we know about the **cranial nerves** in each region. Recall the Rule of 4's which states that the first 4 cranial nerves exit from the brain and midbrain, the middle 4 exit from the pons, and the last 4 exit from the medulla. The presence or absence of dysfunction in these nerves serves as a helpful "map" of sorts to tell you what part of the brainstem has been affected on a **vertical** plane (the "latitude" of the lesion). For example, if someone presents with an oculomotor nerve palsy, the lesion is likely to be at the level of the midbrain. In contrast, someone presenting with facial nerve paralysis is likely to have a lesion at the level of the pons, while a third patient presenting with an absent gag reflex is more likely to have a stroke in the medulla.

To answer the second question (whether the lesion is more medial or more lateral), it can be helpful to think about which structures are found medially in the brainstem and which are found laterally. There are 4 main **M**edial structures to think of, and luckily they all begin with the letter **M**: the **M**otor pathway going to the body (the corticospinal tract); the **M**edial lemniscus carrying fine touch, vibration, and proprioception; the **M**edial longitudinal fasciculus that controls movements

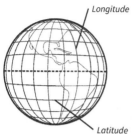

of the eyes; and the **M**otor component of some (*but not all!*) cranial nerves, including the three nerves controlling extraocular movements and the hypoglossal nerve controlling the tongue. In contrast, there are 4 main structures that are found to the **S**ide that each begin with the letter **S**: the **S**pinocerebellar pathway which connects to the cerebellum; the **S**pinothalamic tract carrying crude touch, temperature, and pain; the **S**ympathetic pathway traveling to the face; and the nuclei for several **S**ensory neurons coming from the face via the trigeminal nerve. The presence or absence of any of these functions can help you figure out the coordinates of the lesion on a **horizontal** plane (the "longitude" of the lesion).

Finally, to answer the third question (which side the lesion is on), in general you can expect that deficits in the face will be *ipsilateral* to the side of the lesion while deficits in the body will be *contralateral* to the side of the lesion. This is because the cranial nerves exit from the brainstem and innervate structures on the same side, while motor and sensory pathways traveling to the body all cross further down (at the very tail end of the medulla for the corticospinal tract and dorsal column—medial lemniscus pathway, and in the spinal cord for the spinothalamic tract).

Brainstem strokes present with **crossed findings** of **ipsilateral facial deficits** and **contralateral body deficits**. The **cranial nerves** involved can help to localize the stroke to the **midbrain, pons, or medulla**.

Cranial nerves exit in groups of 4: the first 4 from the brain and midbrain, the next 4 from the pons, and the last 4 from the medulla.

There are 4 Medial structures: the Motor pathway, Medial lemniscus, Medial longitudinal fasciculus, and Motor component of several cranial nerves.

There are 4 Side structures: the Spinocerebellar pathway, Spinothalamic tract, Sympathetic pathway, and Sensory nuclei of the trigeminal nerve.

You are now equipped to localize lesions in the brainstem! Let's walk through a few cases together, starting with the medulla at the bottom and working our way up.

MEDIAL MEDULLARY SYNDROME

As its name suggests, medial medullary syndrome involves a lesion in the **medial medulla**. This manifests through **contralateral hemiparesis** of the body (but not the face!), **contralateral** loss of **epicritic sensation**, and **ipsilateral tongue weakness**. Notably, protopathic sensation is *intact*. How could we have predicted the location of this lesion based on the clinical findings?

First, we know we are in the brainstem because of the presence of crossed findings (contralateral hemiparesis in the *body* but not the *face*). Next, we can figure out the "latitude" of the lesion by determining what cranial nerves are involved. Given that tongue movement maps to the twelfth cranial nerve, we can feel confident saying that this lesion is localized to the medulla. (The sparing of the face also confirms that the lesion is *not* in the pons where the trigeminal and facial nerves are located.) The tongue weakness will be ipsilateral (remember that "you lick your wounds"). To determine the "longitude" of the lesion, consider that the **M**otor pathway, **M**otor function of the hypoglossal nerve, and the epicritic nerves traveling in the **M**edial lemniscus are all involved, while **S**ide structures such as the **S**pinothalamic tract are not. Based on this information, we can determine that the lesion is in the **M**edial medulla.

Medial medullary syndrome is caused by a stroke in the **anterior spinal artery**. You can remember the association of **M**edial **M**edullary syndrome, **tongue weakness**, and the **A**nterior **S**pinal **A**rtery by thinking of licking some açaí (**ASA**-i) berries with your **tongue**. They're so tasty you say, "**MM** that's good!"

> **Medial medullary syndrome** involves **contralateral hemiparesis**, **contralateral epicritic numbness**, and **ipsilateral tongue weakness**. It is caused by a stroke in the **anterior spinal artery**.
>
> *"**MM**! These açaí (**ASA**-i) berries are so tasty I want to **lick** them!"*

LATERAL MEDULLARY SYNDROME

Lateral medullary syndrome (also known as **Wallenberg's syndrome**) involves loss of **protopathic sensation** *contralaterally* in the extremities and *ipsilaterally* in the face, ipsilateral **Horner's syndrome** (remember "H**O** h**O** h**O**!" for pt**O**sis, mi**O**sis, and anhydr**O**sis), problems with **balance** (including ataxia, vertigo, and nystagmus), and difficulty with both **speaking** (dysarthria) and **swallowing** (dysphagia). We can figure out that this is in the brainstem by the crossed findings, then determine the "latitude" by looking at the cranial nerves involved. The presence of dysphagia and dysarthria strongly suggests involvement of the **glossopharyngeal and vagus nerves**, which as the ninth and tenth cranial nerves exit from the medulla. (You may also remember that the nucleus ambiguus is located in the medulla.) To determine the "longitude," let's look at whether the structures involved are found **M**edially or to the **S**ide. Given that there appears to be involvement of the **S**pinothalamic tract (contralateral body numbness), the **S**ympathetic nervous system (ipsilateral Horner's syndrome), the **S**pinocerebellar pathway (ataxia, vertigo, and nystagmus), and **S**ensory information from the trigeminal nerve (ipsilateral facial numbness), we can conclude that this involves the **S**ide of the medulla. Lateral medullary syndrome is associated with a stroke in the **posterior inferior cerebellar artery**. You can remember this by thinking of the word **PICA-chew** to help you associate a stroke in the **P**osterior **I**nferior **C**erebellar **A**rtery with some of its most specific findings (in this case, difficulty with **chew**ing and speaking).

> **Lateral medullary syndrome** involves loss of **protopathic sensation** in the **contralateral extremities** and **ipsilateral face**, **ipsilateral Horner's syndrome**, **cerebellar signs, dysarthria**, and **dysphagia**. It is caused by a stroke in the **posterior inferior cerebellar artery**.

*PICA-chew: A **P**osterior **I**nferior **C**erebellar **A**rtery stroke makes it so you can't chew.*

LATERAL PONTINE SYNDROME

Lateral pontine syndrome is in many ways quite similar to lateral medullary syndrome. This is because the "longitude" of the lesion is the same, so many of the same findings (loss of protopathic sensation contralaterally in the extremities and ipsilaterally in the face, ipsilateral Horner's syndrome, and ipsilateral cerebellar deficits) will still be present. Instead, only the "latitude" of the lesion has changed, meaning that different cranial nerves are going to be involved. Specifically, now that we are in the pons, we have to worry about the **facial nerve**. (Of note, the facial nerve is *not* one of the 4 motor cranial nerves with its nuclei in the *medial* brainstem!) Lateral pontine syndrome presents with exactly what you would

expect with damage to the facial nerve, including **facial asymmetry** and loss of **taste sensation** from the anterior two-thirds of the tongue. In addition, involvement of the **vestibulocochlear nerve** can result in partial or complete **deafness**. (In fact, lateral pontine syndrome is the only stroke-related syndrome that produces hearing loss!) The vestibular part of the vestibulocochlear nerve can be involved as well, causing nausea, vomiting, nystagmus, and vertigo.

Lateral pontine syndrome is associated with a stroke in the **anterior inferior cerebellar artery**. Just as we can use **PICA-chew** to remember some of the more specific findings of lateral medullary syndrome, we can think of the **A**nterior **I**nferior **C**erebellar **A**rtery as causing problems in the f**AICA**l nerve.

> **Lateral pontine syndrome** is similar to lateral medullary syndrome but also involves **facial nerve paralysis** and **hearing loss**. It is caused by a stroke in the **anterior inferior cerebellar artery**.

*A stroke in the **A**nterior **I**nferior **C**erebellar **A**rtery messes up the f**AICA**l nerve.*

MEDIAL PONTINE SYNDROME
Just as lateral pontine syndrome is very similar to lateral medullary syndrome, so too is **medial pontine syndrome** similar to medial medullary syndrome. As before, the main distinction has to do with the cranial nerves involved! The motor component of cranial nerves 5 through 8 involve facial muscles and extraocular eye movements, so medial pontine syndrome can also lead to **facial asymmetry** and **horizontal gaze palsy**. (While the facial nerve was already involved in a *lateral* pontine lesion, it is still involved in a *medial* pontine lesion as well, as the nerve runs medially after exiting the pons.) However, there is also another Medial structure we need to account for in the pons that wasn't in the medulla: the Medial longitudinal fasciculus. This means that

medial pontine syndrome can produce **internuclear ophthalmoplegia** (flip back to Chapter 9 if you need a refresher on what this would look like). Medial pontine syndrome is associated with occlusion of a branch off of the **basilar artery**. You can remember this association by thinking of an u**MP**ire playing **base**ball.

Medial pontine syndrome resembles **medial medullary syndrome** but features **facial nerve palsy, horizontal gaze palsy**, and **internuclear ophthalmoplegia**. It is caused by a stroke in the **basilar artery**.

To link Medial Pontine syndrome and the base-ilar artery, think of an uMPire playing baseball.

WEBER'S SYNDROME
Like all brainstem strokes we have talked about so far, midbrain strokes will produce crossed findings. However, because only two cranial nerves exit from the midbrain (the **oculomotor nerve** and **trochlear nerve**), the crossed findings will tend to be more subtle, involving only eye movements rather than a more dramatic presentation like facial asymmetry. However, the rule of crossed findings still exists! It just involves less nerves than before.

Your primary clue to a midbrain stroke will be an **oculomotor nerve palsy** (manifesting in ptosis, mydriasis, and a "down and out" position of the pupil) in addition to some form of **motor findings**. Depending on the exact areas impacted, the motor findings can present in a variety of different ways. The condition most classically associated with a medial midbrain stroke is called **Weber's syndrome**. Weber's syndrome involves the combination of an **ipsilateral oculomotor nerve palsy** and a **contralateral hemiplegia** (there are those crossed findings so that you know it's in the brainstem!). How can we remember Weber's syndrome? Think about what happens when you're walking and suddenly get a spider **web** in your **eye**. You immediately try to close your eye (looking like ptosis) and you will likely try to use your *ipsilateral* arm to swat the spider web away, meaning that your *contralateral* side stays still (almost as if it's paralyzed!). Weber's syndrome results from a stroke in the **posterior cerebral artery** or the upper portion of the **basilar arteries**.

Weber's syndrome results from a **midbrain stroke** and presents as a combination of **ipsilateral oculomotor nerve palsy** and **contralateral hemiplegia**. It is caused by a stroke in either the **posterior cerebral artery** or the **basilar artery**.

*When you get a spider **web** in your **eye**, your eyelid will shut (like **ptosis**) and your will use your ipsilateral hand to swat it away (leaving your **contralateral extremities still**).*

LOCKED-IN SYNDROME
The **basilar artery** forms a bridge of sorts between blood from the circle of Willis (which is brought up via the internal carotid arteries) and blood from vertebrobasilar system (which is brought up via the vertebral arteries). As seen in the drawing below, the basilar artery runs along the underside of the pons and medulla and sends off branches to the midbrain. Because it supplies all three parts of the brainstem, a stroke in the basilar artery can have wide-reaching and severe consequences. One possible manifestation of a basilar artery stroke is known as **locked-in syndrome**, a tragic condition in which someone is almost completely paralyzed due to damage of the corticospinal tract as well as most of the cranial nerves. However, because cortical functions remain intact, the person is usually fully aware of their situation. Depending on the extent of the damage, higher cranial nerves may be spared, so someone with this condition may at times be taught to communicate using eye movements and blinks. Overall, locked-in syndrome is a devastating reminder of just how important the brainstem is for our ability to function.

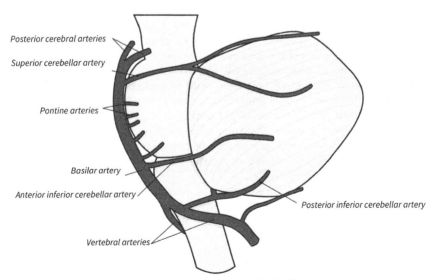

Posterior cerebral arteries

Superior cerebellar artery

Pontine arteries

Basilar artery

Anterior inferior cerebellar artery

Posterior inferior cerebellar artery

Vertebral arteries

Blood supply to the brainstem and cerebellum.

CEREBELLAR STROKES

There are a few misconceptions about **cerebellar strokes** to clear up right off the bat. First, as you can see in the drawing on the previous page, arteries with "cerebellar" in the name do *not* necessarily affect the cerebellum! (Think of the anterior inferior cerebellar artery and lateral pontine syndrome, or the posterior inferior cerebellar artery and lateral medullary syndrome.) Second, the presence of cerebellar signs (such as vertigo, ataxia, nystagmus, and the rest of the "**dizzy ANT** trying to **balance 3 dys'es**" mnemonic from Chapter 5) is not automatically indicative of a stroke in the *cerebellum* itself! Because cerebellar pathways travel in the cerebrum, brainstem, and spinal cord, lesions throughout the central nervous system can produce these signs. (Recall that cerebellar signs can be seen in lateral brainstem syndromes due to involvement of the spinocerebellar pathway.)

While significantly less common than cerebral or brainstem strokes, cerebellar strokes can occur. When they do, the presence of the aforementioned cerebellar signs are key for picking up on them, especially if they are sudden in onset (although due to the fact that the arteries supplying the cerebellum also supply the brainstem, there will often be overlapping features with some of the syndromes we have talked about so far). Remember from Chapter 5 that the *cerebellum* is a dirty **double crosser**! This means that a stroke in the cerebellum will lead to deficits that are *ipsilateral* to the lesion (rather than contralateral as is seen in cortical strokes).

SPINAL CORD STROKES

While most people associate strokes with the brain, strokes can and do occur in the spinal cord as well. Depending on the parts of the spinal cord that are involved, a variety of presentations can occur. By far the most common is an **anterior cord stroke** which, as you might guess, presents clinically as an anterior cord syndrome (including loss of motor function as well as crude touch, temperature, and pain sensation below the level of the lesion, with sparing of fine touch, pressure, and proprioception). Ischemia in the anterior spinal artery occurs most commonly in the **thoracic cord**, as the anterior spinal artery receives collateral supply from additional arteries that come off of the aorta. These "booster" arteries are most pronounced in the cervical and lumbar cord, making the thoracic cord a **watershed area** that is particularly vulnerable to ischemia.

In contrast, **posterior cord strokes** are quite rare. This is because the posterior cord is supplied by the *two* **posterior spinal arteries** (as opposed to the single anterior spinal artery), making ischemia less likely. If a posterior cord stroke does occur, it tends to present as a posterior cord syndrome involving loss of fine touch, vibration, and proprioception in affected areas.

PUTTING IT ALL TOGETHER

Strokes are among the most devastating neurologic diseases, as they can occur with little warning and leave a trail of destruction in their wake. Because of the potential for irreversible neurologic deficits and even death, the ability to rapidly recognize and treat a stroke is crucial. The **BE FAST** mnemonic can help you to recognize the overall pattern of a stroke, while your neurological exam can assist in identifying the specific areas involved. Neuroimaging with CT or MRI is almost always used as well.

When it comes to stroke localization, being as systematic as possible with conducting your neurological exam and interpreting its findings is the key. Broadly, the presence of **cortical signs** should have you thinking of a stroke in the cerebral cortex, while the *absence* of cortical signs is more consistent with stroke lower down in the subcortex or brainstem. If you see **crossed findings** (facial deficits on one side and limb deficits on the other), you can be pretty sure you are working with a stroke in the brainstem. From there, look at the specific muscle groups and sensory modalities involved which should help you to pinpoint *where* in this area they are occurring. By using what we have already learned about the vascular supply of the central nervous system, you will likely be able to identify even the specific artery involved when asked (and you *will* be asked). Use the practice questions on the next few pages to get comfortable with the process of stroke localization!

REVIEW QUESTIONS

1. A 61 y/o right-handed F with a history of diabetes mellitus, atrial fibrillation, hypertension, hyperlipidemia, and tobacco use is brought to the emergency department after she awoke and noticed that she could not move her left arm. Vital signs are HR 104, BP 184/108, RR 20, and T 98.8°F. The doctor reviewing her medical record notices that one year ago she underwent MRI angiography which showed narrowing in her cerebral circulation as seen below:

   Which of the following is most likely to be found on exam?
   A. Numbness to pain and temperature in the right arm
   B. Weakness of the left leg
   C. Not responding to activity in her left visual field
   D. Difficulty understanding what is being said
   E. Being able to only speak one or two words at a time with extreme difficulty

2. (Continued from previous question.) Which of the following is most likely to have prevented this outcome?
   A. Aggressive management of her blood pressure
   B. Anticoagulant medication
   C. Smoking cessation
   D. Use of a cholesterol-lowering medication
   E. Tight glycemic control

3. (Continued from previous question.) The doctor asks the patient how much time has passed since she last had full use of her left arm. She replies by saying that she went to bed around 10:30 last night. It is currently 11:00 in the morning. What is the most likely reason why the doctor asked this question?

    A.   To localize the lesion more precisely
    B.   To determine whether the stroke is ischemic or hemorrhagic
    C.   To decide on the most appropriate medications to prescribe
    D.   To assess her prognosis for functional recovery of her left arm
    E.   To estimate her chance of mortality within the next 24 hours

4.   An 83 y/o M comes to the hospital after noticing the sudden onset of weakness in his left face, left arm, and left leg. On exam, there is significant facial asymmetry. He has a widely dilated right pupil, with the right eye pointed inferiorly and laterally compared to the left eye as seen below:

Hearing is intact bilaterally. The gag reflex is present. There is no tongue deviation. Pain, temperature, vibration, and proprioception sensation are intact throughout. Which part of the midbrain has most likely sustained damage in this patient?

    A.   Left medial midbrain
    B.   Right medial midbrain
    C.   Left lateral midbrain
    D.   Right lateral midbrain
    E.   Left medial pons
    F.   Right medial pons
    G.   Left lateral pons
    H.   Right lateral pons
    I.   Left medial medulla
    J.   Right medial medulla
    K.   Left lateral medulla
    L.   Right lateral medulla

5.   A 64 y/o M presents to the emergency department reporting a sudden onset of headache, dizziness, and difficulty walking. On exam, extraocular movements are intact, but the left pupil is significantly smaller than the right. There is drooping of the left eyelid, though all other muscles of facial expression are intact. There is numbness to pain and temperature on the left face as well as the right arm and leg, drooping of the left eyelid, and difficulty with heel-to-shin and finger-to-nose testing on the left side. His speech is mumbling and difficult to understand. Oral examination reveals the soft palate being pulled to the right side as seen below:

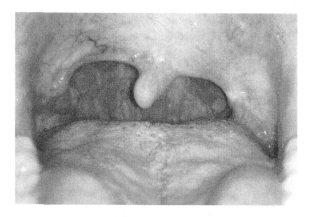

Vital signs are HR 78, BP 146/78, RR 18, and T 98.8°F. Neuroimaging is most likely to reveal an occlusion of which of the following arteries?

A. Left anterior cerebral artery
B. Right anterior cerebral artery
C. Left middle cerebral artery
D. Right middle cerebral artery
E. Left posterior cerebral artery
F. Right posterior cerebral artery
G. Left anterior inferior cerebellar artery
H. Right anterior inferior cerebellar artery
I. Left posterior inferior cerebellar artery
J. Right posterior inferior cerebellar artery
K. Anterior spinal artery

6. (Continued from previous question.) Which of the following is this patient at particularly high risk for?

A. Swallowing food into his airway while eating
B. Progressive hearing loss
C. Double vision related to weakness of extraocular muscles
D. Requiring a ventilator due to weakness of the diaphragm
E. Urinary incontinence

1. **The best answer is C.** The patient's presentation and medical history are both highly consistent with a stroke in the region of the right middle cerebral artery, and the available imaging shows significant stenosis in this region. As the patient is right-handed, we can be fairly certain that she has a left-dominant hemisphere. Therefore, a stroke in the non-dominant territory of her right middle cerebral artery is likely to lead to hemineglect, which would present as her ignoring things occurring to her left. A stroke in her non-dominant hemisphere is likely unlikely to lead to aphasia, as the language centers are most often found in the dominant hemisphere (answers D and E). Sensory deficits would be found on the contralateral arm, not the ipsilateral arm (answer A). Finally, weakness of the left leg would be expected in a right anterior cerebral artery stroke, not a middle cerebral artery stroke (answer B).

2. **The best answer is A.** All of the patient's comorbid conditions place her at higher risk for a stroke. However, in almost all cases, hypertension is the single largest risk factor, making aggressive management of elevated blood pressure a key step in stroke prevention.

3. **The best answer is C.** Knowing how long it has been since the onset of the stroke is crucial for determining whether tissue plasminogen activator can be given. Tissue plasminogen activator helps to improve functional outcomes but only when given within 3 hours of symptom onset. In cases where it has been longer than 3 hours since symptom onset, the risks of this treatment often outweigh the benefits. Knowing the amount of time that has passed since symptom onset may help to provide an estimate of functional and mortality prognosis, but this is not as immediate of a decision as whether or not to administer tissue plasminogen activator (answers D and E). Knowing time of symptom onset does not help to localize a stroke or determine its likely etiology (answers A and B).

4. **The best answer is B.** The combination of an oculomotor nerve palsy with contralateral weakness is known as Weber syndrome, which localizes to the medial midbrain. Weakness of the face and body is caused by involvement of the corticospinal and corticobulbar tracts, respectively, while the oculomotor nerve exits the brainstem at the level of the midbrain. In Weber syndrome, the oculomotor nerve palsy is ipsilateral while the weakness is contralateral, placing this on the right, not left (answer A). The involvement of the motor pathways places this medially in the midbrain, not laterally where deficits in pain and temperature sensation would be more likely (answers C and D). A lesion in the medial pons would likely involve the abducens nerve, not the oculomotor nerve (answers E and F). Further, intact hearing argues against lateral pontine syndrome (answers G and H), an intact gag reflex argues against lateral medullary syndrome (answers K and L), and lack of tongue deviation argues against medial medullary syndrome (answers I and J).

5. **The best answer is I.** Crossed findings (in this case, numbness on the left face and right extremities) are highly suggestive of a brainstem lesion rather than a stroke in the anterior, middle, or posterior cerebral arteries (answers A—F). To determine which part of the brainstem has been damaged, consider which cranial nerves are involved. The presence of palatal asymmetry and dysarthria both are suggestive of the 9th and 10th cranial nerves being involved, which localizes this to the medulla. To determine whether it is medial or lateral, consider that the spinothalamic tract (numbness to pain and temperature), sympathetic nervous system (Horner's syndrome), and spinocerebellar tracts (vertigo and ataxia) are involved, all of which travel laterally in the brainstem. Lateral medullary syndrome is often related to a stroke in the posterior inferior cerebellar artery. Facial deficits are ipsilateral while deficits in the extremities are contralateral, which localizes this to the left, not the right (answer J). Anterior inferior cerebellar artery strokes are more associated with lateral pontine syndrome which would present with facial weakness and/or asymmetry (answers G and H). A stroke in the anterior spinal artery is associated with medial medullary syndrome which would involve the corticospinal tract and the medial lemniscus, neither of which appear to be involved here (answer K).

6. **The best answer is A.** A stroke in the lateral medulla is likely to affect the nucleus ambiguus which is responsible for swallowing and speech. This patient already shows signs of dysarthria, so it is likely that his swallowing muscles may be impaired as well. Weakness of the glossopharyngeal and vagus nerves will also impair his gag reflex, putting him at even higher risk of aspiration. For this reason, care must be taken to prevent aspiration in patients admitted with lateral medullary syndrome. Extraocular muscles are controlled by cranial nerves exiting from the midbrain and pons, not the medulla (answer C). Hearing is controlled by the vestibulocochlear nerve which attaches to the brainstem at the level of the pons (answer B). The diaphragm is controlled at the level of the C3-C5 spinal nerves (answer D). Finally, urinary incontinence is more likely to be seen with an anterior cerebral artery stroke (answer E).

13 INTRACRANIAL PRESSURE

Gently knock on your head a few times with your fist. Pretty hard right? It's not at all like the soft, squishy texture that we normally associate with the brain. This is because the brain is kept safe within the hard and inflexible bones of the **skull**. For the most part, this is a good thing, as the skull helps to protect the brain from injury. However, in some cases the enclosed nature of the skull can actually be a liability. Because the skull cannot expand, any increase in the amount of matter inside the skull (whether that is **blood, cerebrospinal fluid**, or **nervous tissue** itself) must necessarily be accompanied by an increase in pressure, as there is no wiggle room for the volume of the intracranial space to increase. Therefore, a significant expansion of any of these components will lead to a state of **intracranial hypertension** (not to be confused with the high *blood* pressure that is often called simply "hypertension"). Intracranial hypertension can be damaging or even deadly to the brain, as it not only compresses the nervous tissue directly but also can impinge upon the arteries in the area, cutting off the supply of oxygen and vital nutrients.

Intracranial hypertension can result in various forms of dysfunction depending on the specific brain regions affected, although its most common manifestations include **headaches, nausea, vomiting, changes in mental status** (such as sleepiness or loss of cognitive abilities), **focal neurologic signs** (including changes in vision and motor strength), and **seizures**. Increased intracranial pressure can also lead to a particularly high-yield sign known as **papilledema**, or swelling of the optic disc (as seen in the image on the next page). If left untreated, this pressure on the optic disc can even lead to progressive visual loss, often starting at the periphery of vision and working inwards.

*Swelling of the optic disc known as **papilledema**, which is a sign of **increased intracranial pressure**.*

On an autonomic level, a sudden increase in intracranial pressure can lead to a trio of signs known as **Cushing's triad** which consists of irregular breathing, a slow heart rate, and increased blood pressure. You can link Cushing's triad to increased IntraCranial Pressure using the letters **ICP**: **I**nspirations, **C**ardiac, and **P**ressure.

A **sudden increase in intracranial pressure** can lead to **Cushing's triad** of **irregular breathing, bradycardia**, and **hypertension**.

Increased IntraCranial Pressure leads to Irregular Inspirations, a Crawling Cardiac rate, and Pushed up blood Pressure.

There are many possible causes of intracranial hypertension. In this chapter, we will focus on three main forms in particular: **intracranial bleeds, hydrocephalus**, and **idiopathic intracranial hypertension** (also known as pseudotumor cerebri). We will also discuss a dreaded complication of intracranial hypertension known as **brain herniation** in which the increased pressure pushes parts of the brain into places they don't belong. (It should be noted that this chapter should not be seen as an exhaustive list of all the potential causes of intracranial hypertension! We will talk about a few other types of neurologic diseases that can also raise intracranial pressure, such as brain tumors or infections, in later chapters.)

INTRACRANIAL BLEEDS

The first major cause of increased intracranial pressure that we will talk about is **intracranial bleeding**. In contrast to strokes (where most of the problems are caused by the *absence* of blood in places that it *should* be), with intracranial bleeding most of the problems are related to the *presence* of blood in places that it *shouldn't* be.

There are four main types of intracranial bleeding depending on the location of bleeding in the skull: **epidural hematomas, subdural hematomas, subarachnoid hemorrhages**, and **intracerebral hemorrhages**. (The words "hemorrhage" and "hematoma" both refer to bleeds, with "hematoma" used to describe a *localized* collection of blood while "hemorrhage" is generally used to describe a *diffuse* bleed.) While all of these will result in the characteristic signs and symptoms of increased intracranial pressure, the specifics of the patient's history and clinical presentation will vary between these four, making it possible for a diligent clinician to make a diagnosis based on what they are seeing.

Intracranial bleeding can have several possible causes. **Mechanical head trauma** is by far the most common cause of most intracranial bleeds. However, as with strokes, **high blood pressure** is also a major risk factor. Uncontrolled hypertension also increases the risk of developing an **aneurysm**, or a ballooning of an arterial wall. Aneurysms create a weak point in the artery, significantly increasing the risk of future rupture and subsequent hemorrhage. Prior to rupturing, aneurysms may cause focal neurologic deficits by compressing nearby structures. For example, an aneurysm of the **anterior communicating artery** can compress the optic chiasm, while an aneurysm of the **posterior communicating artery** can disrupt the **oculomotor nerve**. (In fact, aneurysms of the posterior communicating artery are so common that an acute oculomotor nerve palsy with ipsilateral pupil dilation should be considered to be a posterior communicating artery aneurysm until proven otherwise!)

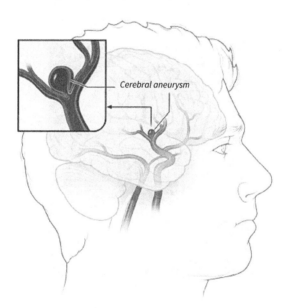

Cerebral aneurysm

For the next few pages, we will talk in more detail about each of the four types of intracranial bleeds. While learning about these, pay close attention to the differences in the clinical history, as this will often allow you to guess at what type of bleeding is present even before seeing the brain scan!

EPIDURAL HEMATOMA

An **epidural hematoma** arises from bleeding in the space between the dura mater and the skull. It is frequently caused by **blunt head trauma** (such as being hit in the head during a mixed martial arts match). Typically, this trauma causes a brief **loss of consciousness** after which the patient will regain consciousness and may even say they are totally fine, with no significant symptoms or neurologic deficits (this is known as a **lucid period**). However, during this time the bleeding continues, leading to a swelling of blood that gets larger and larger. As the hematoma grows, it begins to compress other structures in the brain, leading to the re-emergence of neurologic deficits. As the intracranial pressure rises, compression of the brainstem can again lead to unconsciousness and loss of function. If not treated, death can quickly follow.

An epidural hematoma is diagnosed on the basis of a characteristic history involving blunt head trauma, a lucid period, and re-emergence of neurologic signs and symptoms. A CT scan of the head can confirm the presence of blood in the epidural space. Because the dura mater is attached to the skull in various places, the expansion of blood is limited, leading to a characteristic **bulge-like appearance** on CT:

Treatment of an epidural involves **surgical removal of the blood** through a burr hole to reduce intracranial pressure.

In most cases, an epidural hematoma is caused by bleeding from the **middle meningeal artery** (which supplies the dura mater and the upper part of the skull). You can remember the association between an **epi**dural hematoma, **head trauma**, a **lucid** period, and the **M**iddle **M**eningeal **A**rtery by thinking of someone who passes out after getting punched during an **epi**c **M**ixed **M**artial **A**rts (**MMA**) match. If they get knocked out like this, they probably wouldn't win the match—they would **lose it** (lucid).

An **epidural hematoma** is typically caused by **head trauma** which leads to bleeding of the **middle meningeal artery**. Patients often **lose consciousness**, briefly regain it during a **lucid period**, and then become **unconscious again** after a few hours.

*Think of someone getting **knocked out** during an **epi**c (epidural) Mixed Martial Arts (Middle Meningeal Artery) match. They probably wouldn't win the match—they would **lose it** (lucid)!*

SUBDURAL HEMATOMA

While an epidural hematoma results from bleeding in the space *above* the dura mater, a **subdural hematoma** results from bleeding in the space *below* it (between the dura mater and arachnoid mater). Like epidural hematomas, subdural hematomas are often related to head trauma and can cause an increase in intracranial pressure. However, in contrast to epidural hematomas, subdural hematomas generally take **longer to develop** and are less likely to progress to coma and death (in fact, some people can live with a subdural hematoma for months or years before it is discovered).

Why is this? A key part of the reason is because subdural hematomas result from injuries of the **bridging veins** that cross the subdural space. Because venous pressure is significantly lower than arterial pressure, the build-up of blood tends to happen much more slowly. For this reason, the classic clinical presentation associated with a subdural hematoma involves a **gradually increasing headache with confusion** (as opposed to the sudden loss, regaining, and re-loss of consciousness seen with an epidural hematoma). Because the walls of veins are often quite weaker than those of arteries, the force required to break them is often less, making subdural hematomas more common than epidural hematomas.

Diagnosis is based on the classic history of (even minor) head trauma with a gradual build-up of symptoms. A head CT will show a characteristic **crescent shape** in the area of the bleed as seen below:

This crescent shape occurs because, unlike in the epidural space, there are no barriers to prevent the blood from spreading out as far as it damn well pleases, leading to a wider but flatter appearance.

In cases of a small or chronic hematoma, no treatment may be required. For larger or more acute cases, however, neurosurgical intervention may be needed to control the bleeding and reduce intracranial pressure.

You can remember the association of a **sub**dural hematoma with **bridging** veins by picturing a **sub**marine going under the **bridge** at night under a **crescent** moon. Think about how **slowly** the submarine is going. However, because the sub **sneaks up** on you, it can still be **deadly**!

A **subdural hematoma** involves bleeding from the **bridging veins** after **head trauma**. It often presents with **gradually increasing headache and confusion**.

*Picture a **sub**marine (**sub**dural) going under a **bridge** (**bridging** veins) at night under a* *crescent moon (its shape on CT) to **slowly sneak up** on its target.*

SUBARACHNOID HEMORRHAGE

A **subarachnoid hemorrhage** involves bleeding into the subarachnoid space between the arachnoid mater and the pia mater. The classic presentation of a subarachnoid hemorrhage is a **thunderclap headache**, or a severe headache with a sudden onset that is often described as "the worst headache of my life." Other signs such as nausea, vomiting, changes in consciousness, and **neck stiffness or pain** (due to irritation of the meninges in the spinal cord) are common. As the intracranial pressure grows, various neurologic deficits may develop, including **seizures**. A head CT will show blood localized to the subarachnoid cisterns, or the small pockets filled with cerebrospinal fluid in specific parts of the brain (often radiating out from around the ventricles in an almost **spider-like shape**):

Because the subarachnoid space is where cerebrospinal fluid flows, a lumbar puncture may reveal an elevated number of **red blood cells**. In cases of suspected subarachnoid hemorrhage when a head CT is negative, a lumbar puncture is required.

A subarachnoid hemorrhage is no joke, with a one-month mortality rate around 50%. (Many patients don't even reach the hospital.) For this reason, it is important to keep this condition on your radar whenever someone presents with a sudden onset headache. While a sudden headache is associated with a subarachnoid hemorrhage, it is only a very small minority of patients with headaches who actually have a subarachnoid hemorrhage and would require head imaging to rule this in or out. You can remember the factors that increase someone's risk of needing brain imaging when presenting with a headache using the convenient mnemonic **CT HEAD** which stands for **C**onsciousness loss, a **T**hunderclap quality to the headache, **H**urt neck, **E**xertional onset (many subarachnoid hemorrhages are brought about by physical exertion), patient **A**ge above 40 years, and **D**ecreased flexion of the neck.

A **subarachnoid hemorrhage** is a type of **hemorrhagic stroke** that is associated with a severe, sudden-onset **thunderclap headache**.

*Consider a **CT HEAD** to rule out a subarachnoid hemorrhage when there is:*
Consciousness loss
Thunderclap headache
Hurt neck
Exertional onset
Age 40 years or older
Decreased neck flexion

As with epidural and subdural hematomas, most cases of subarachnoid hemorrhage are associated with a history of trauma. Unlike epidural and subdural hematomas, however, a subarachnoid hemorrhage is not reliably associated with a break in any *particular* artery. Instead, because many arteries pass through the subarachnoid space, any of them can be affected by mechanical trauma. Spontaneous cases of subarachnoid hemorrhage (those not related to trauma) most often occur due to a **ruptured aneurysm**, typically in the circle of Willis.

INTRACEREBRAL HEMORRHAGE

While epidural hematomas, subdural hematomas, and subarachnoid hemorrhages all can cause problems in the brain due to compressive damage, it's important to remember that the site of bleeding is not actually in the *brain tissue itself* but rather in the meningeal pad *around* the brain. In contrast, cases of **intracerebral hemorrhage** *do* involve bleeding within the brain itself, allowing the blood to run amok and wreak havoc on nerves directly. Because intracerebral hemorrhages occur in the deepest part of the skull, they are by far the most difficult to treat. Intracerebral hemorrhages can occur in either the nervous tissue (known as an **intraparenchymal hemorrhage**) or in the ventricular system (known as an **intraventricular hemorrhage**).

The presentation of an intracerebral hemorrhage can resemble a subarachnoid hemorrhage, including a sudden onset of headache and other symptoms such as nausea and vomiting. Because intracerebral hemorrhages not only lead to ischemia but can also increase intracranial pressure, a wide variety of additional signs and symptoms can be seen depending on the specific areas involved. For example, putaminal hemorrhages (the most common type) often present with exclusively **mo**tor deficits (remember to "**put an M** for **putamen!**") while **th**alamic hemorrhages (the second most common type) involve **th**en**th**ory deficits. **P**ontine hemorrhages often present with **p**in**p**oint **p**up**i**ls and an abrupt loss of consciousness, with a high associated mortality rate.

Pontine hemorrhages are associated with **bilateral pupillary constriction**.

Pontine hemorrhages present with pinpoint pupils.

Due to this heterogeneity in presentation, an intracerebral hemorrhage is more often diagnosed by head imaging than by a neurological exam. An intraparenchymal hemorrhage will show focal areas of bleeding (called a "**spot sign**" as seen in the left image below) while an intraventricular hemorrhage will have signs of bleeding in the ventricular system (as seen on the right).

*CT imaging of an **intraparenchymal hemorrhage** (left) and an **intraventricular hemorrhage** (right).*

Like a subarachnoid hemorrhage, an intracerebral hemorrhage is a serious condition, with nearly half of patients dying within one month. Patients generally need to be managed on an intensive care unit. Treatment depends on the nature and size of the bleed, with medications, neurosurgical intervention, and life support measures often being required.

HYDROCEPHALUS

While intracranial bleeds contribute to increased intracranial pressure by bringing too much *blood* into the enclosed space of the skull, you can also increase intracranial pressure by bringing in more *cerebrospinal fluid* into the ventricular system. This is known as **hydrocephalus**. (The third mechanism—increasing the volume of the brain tissue directly—will be covered more in Chapter 19 when we talk about brain tumors.)

*A CT scan of a patient with enlarged ventricles due to **hydrocephalus** (left) compared to a **normal** scan (right).*

When hydrocephalus occurs in a developing fetus or infant, it may lead to growth in the size of the skull (as the bones are not yet set).

Compressed brain tissue
Enlarged head size
Enlarged ventricles

*A **normally developing** infant (left) compared to an infant with **hydrocephalus** (right).*

Hydrocephalus falls into four main categories. The first two forms (obstructive and communicating) are more common in **children** and *are* associated with increased intracranial pressure, while the second two forms (normal pressure hydrocephalus and hydrocephalus *ex vacuo*) are more common in **adults** and are *not* associated with increased intracranial pressure. We'll go over each of these four forms now.

OBSTRUCTIVE HYDROCEPHALUS

Obstructive (or non-communicating) hydrocephalus is caused by a **blockage in the flow** of cerebrospinal fluid anywhere along its path through the ventricular system. This tends to happen most often in the narrow foramina, aqueducts, and canals compared to the larger ventricles. These obstructions lead to the build-up of fluid in any ventricles "upstream." For example, narrowing of the cerebral aqueduct (known as **aqueductal stenosis**) leads to enlargement of both the lateral and third ventricles while obstruction of the interventricular foramina would lead to obstruction of only the lateral ventricles. This is why it's so important to know the order in which cerebrospinal fluid travels through the ventricular system (remember "**CSF** is **LIT AF**" from Chapter 10!) so that you can determine the likely location of any obstruction.

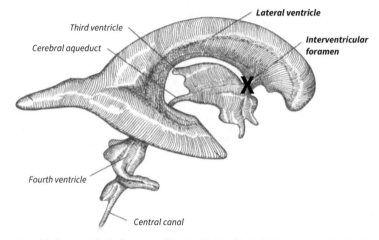

*Obstruction of the **interventricular foramen** will lead to dilation of the bolded structures in this drawing...*

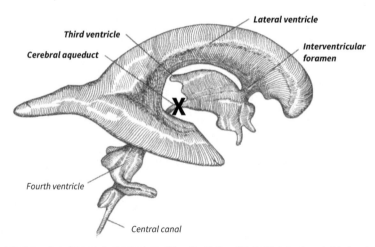

*... while obstruction of the **cerebral aqueduct** will lead to dilation of the bolded structures in this drawing.*

Obstructive hydrocephalus can also be caused by intracranial tumors, with **ependymomas** (tumors of cerebrospinal fluid-producing ependymal cells) being a particularly common cause.

COMMUNICATING HYDROCEPHALUS
Communicating (or non-obstructive) hydrocephalus involves **impaired absorption** of cerebrospinal fluid due to dysfunction of the **arachnoid granulations**. Given that the function of the arachnoid granulations is to absorb cerebrospinal fluid back into the bloodstream, any damage here will cause an outflow obstruction, leading to build-up of cerebrospinal fluid in *all* of the ventricles as well as in the subarachnoid space. The underlying causes of communicating hydrocephalus include any condition that causes inflammation of or damage to the arachnoid granulations, with **meningitis** (or inflammation of the meninges, which we will talk about more in Chapter 20) being a particularly common cause.

NORMAL PRESSURE HYDROCEPHALUS
Normal pressure hydrocephalus (or NPH) sets itself apart from the first two forms of hydrocephalus in that it does *not* always result in increased intracranial pressure (even though the pressure can be intermittently elevated). Instead, an **imbalance** between the amount of cerebrospinal fluid *produced* to the amount that is *absorbed* leads to dilated ventricles. Notably, the typical signs and symptoms of increased intracranial pressure (like headache or nausea) are often absent! Instead, cases of normal pressure hydrocephalus are characterized by a triad including **D**ementia, **I**ncontinence, and **G**ait instability (which you can remember using the mnemonic **DIG** or the phrase "wet, wobbly, and wacky"). Of the three, gait instability tends to present first, with cognitive impairment and incontinence coming later. Normal pressure hydrocephalus is a treatable condition, with the first-line intervention being placement of a shunt that allows cerebrospinal fluid to drain into the abdomen.

> **Normal pressure hydrocephalus** involves **dilation of the ventricular system** without necessarily increasing intracranial pressure, leading to **gait instability, cognitive impairment**, and **urinary incontinence**.

> *DIG: Dementia, Incontinence, and Gait instability (or "wet, wobbly, and wacky").*

HYDROCEPHALUS EX VACUO
Hydrocephalus *ex vacuo* is not a true form of hydrocephalus. Instead, it occurs when a generalized death of neurons in the brain (such as you might see in various forms of dementia or due to recurrent strokes) leads to loss of brain volume. The vacuum created by this atrophy leads to enlargement of the ventricles on brain imaging, giving the appearance of hydrocephalus without the actual increase in intracranial pressure. You can pick up on cases of hydrocephalus *ex vacuo* by looking at the brain tissue itself, as the overall volume will be decreased, giving it a shriveled or sunken appearance.

IDIOPATHIC INTRACRANIAL HYPERTENSION

The final cause of increase intracranial pressure that we will talk about in this chapter is **idiopathic intracranial hypertension** which involves increased pressure within the skull ("intracranial hypertension") with no known cause ("idiopathic"). Like other causes of increased intracranial pressure, headache is a common presenting symptom, with **papilledema** often being seen on exam. (An older term for this disease—**pseudotumor cerebri**—was used because the clinical presentation strongly resembled a brain tumor which is another cause of intracranial hypertension, although in these cases no actual tumor could be found.)

By definition, idiopathic intracranial hypertension is a **diagnosis of exclusion** because it assumes that all other causes have been ruled out (it wouldn't be "idiopathic" otherwise). Imaging of the brain typically should be ordered to rule out any intracranial lesions (like an actual tumor!). There should also be no other focal neurologic deficits, with the only exception to this rule being that the increased pressure can sometimes lead to dysfunction of specific **cranial nerves** (most often those involved in extraocular muscles but occasionally the facial nerve as well).

Idiopathic intracranial hypertension tends to be diagnosed primarily in three groups: the **young** (typically patients in their 20s and 30s), the **overweight** (with the incidence going up drastically as the patient's weight increases), and **women** (who are diagnosed over 5 times as often as men). Use of certain drugs, including hormonal contraceptives and vitamin A derivatives (like those used to treat acne) increase the risk as well.

Immediate treatment of idiopathic intracranial hypertension involves a **lumbar puncture** to drain cerebrospinal fluid and relieve some of the pressure. This helps to reduce the risk of developing long-term complications of uncontrolled intracranial hypertension, including permanent visual loss and cranial nerve damage. A medication known as **acetazolamide** can be used to reduce cerebrospinal fluid production as well. Over the long-term, weight loss can help to reduce the severity of the condition. In severe cases where other efforts have failed, **venous sinus stenting** and other neurosurgical techniques can help to reduce intracranial pressure.

You can remember the typical case presentation for idiopathic intracranial hypertension using the mnemonic **HAPY NOW** which stands for Headaches And Papilledema in a Young, Normal, Obese Woman (with normal referring to the normal mental state and negative neurological exam, imaging findings, and lab results seen in this condition). You can connect this mnemonic to this condition by thinking that someone will be relieved when they are told that their recurrent headaches are *not* in fact a sign of brain cancer.

Idiopathic intracranial hypertension presents as **headaches** and **papilledema**, typically in **young obese women**.

HAPY NOW: *Headaches **A**nd **P**apilledema in a **Y**oung, **N**ormal, **O**bese **W**oman.*

BRAIN HERNIATION

While the first three disease categories we've talked about in this chapter all *cause* increases in intracranial pressure, in this last section we will talk about a potential *consequence* of intracranial hypertension known as **brain herniation**. When intracranial pressure gets high enough, parts of the brain may get forced through various holes leading into, out of, or between various compartments of the skull. (It's kind of like squeezing a water balloon with your hand: with enough pressure, the contents will squeeze out of whatever holes are available to them.)

Because herniation affects large parts of the brain at once, it tends to present in a dramatic way, often with **sudden loss of consciousness**. In cases of severe damage, the patient may show one of two forms of involuntary posturing. When upper parts of the brain such as the cerebral cortex and subcortex have been affected, the patient may display **decorticate posturing** which involves holding the arms inward towards the chest, almost like a mummy. In contrast, when vital structures in the brainstem have been affected, the patient may show **decerebrate posturing** which involves extension of the arms out to the side with generalized rigidity across the body. (Other functions of the brain, such as sensory processing and hormone production, are often compromised as well, although these tend to be forgotten as they are not as immediately life-threatening as the other effects of central herniation.)

Decorticate *posturing*　　　　　　***Decerebrate*** *posturing*

There are a few types of brain herniations to be aware of which are illustrated visually in the drawing below. We will talk about each one as well.

207

SUBFALCINE HERNIATION

The falx cerebri is the meningeal barrier separating the left and right cerebral hemispheres. With enough pressure on either side, the cerebrum can be forced under the falx cerebri into the other hemisphere, creating a **subfalcine herniation**. The particular part of the brain that is most often affected is the cingulate cortex of the **frontal lobe**. The **anterior cerebral artery** supplying this part of the brain may also get dragged in, creating an anterior cerebral artery stroke. Due to the involvement of these two brain regions, a subfalcine herniation tends to cause **leg weakness** and **gait instability** from compression of the motor cortex deep within the longitudinal fissure.

Falx cerebri

Tentorium cerebelli

Subfalcine herniations are the most common form of brain herniation, as less pressure is generally needed to force brain tissue below the falx cerebri compared with the smaller holes we will discuss next. They also tend to be less damaging than the other types (although in severe cases loss of consciousness and coma can occur). However, subfalcine herniations can also be a "canary in a coal mine" by being the first herniation to occur when a source of increased intracranial pressure (such as a bleed or tumor) is present. For this reason, subfalcine herniations still require prompt attention to determine the cause of the increased intracranial pressure and to fix it. You can remember the association of a canary and subfalcine herniations by thinking

of them as **sub-falcon** herniations, as a canary is generally agreed to be a lesser bird than a falcon (a "sub-falcon" bird, if you will). The word "**CAN**-ary" can also help to remind you of the involvement of the **C**ingulate cortex and **AN**terior cerebral artery strokes in cases of subfalcine herniation.

A **subfalcine herniation** involves the **cingulate cortex** being pushed under the **falx cerebri** and potentially compressing the **anterior cerebral artery**.

A **sub-falcon herniation** is like a **CAN**-ary in a coal mine and is associated with compression of the **C**ingulate cortex and the **AN**terior cerebral artery.

TRANSTENTORIAL HERNIATION

A **transtentorial herniation** involves displacement of the brain down past the tentorium cerebelli, or the extension of the dura mater that separates the "upper" cerebrum from the "lower" cerebellum. The most common region that is involved here is the **uncus**, a part of the temporal lobe that sits on the innermost portion of the cerebrum right above the tentorium cerebelli. For this reason, the uncus is extra vulnerable to slipping through the tentorium if enough pressure is applied to it.

When it slips down past the tentorium, the herniated uncus has a tendency to compress the **midbrain** and other nearby structures. In particular, dysfunction of the ipsilateral cranial nerves coming out of the midbrain are a reliable sign of this condition (with the **oculomotor nerves** being affected to a greater degree than the trochlear nerves). Damage to the oculomotor nerve first manifests through a **dilated pupil** followed by weakness of the extraocular muscles innervated by the oculomotor nerve leading to a "**down and out**" deviation of the eye due to the combined action of the remaining extraocular muscles. (The fact that pupillary dilation happens first makes sense if you remember **OOMMPP**: the **O**cul**O**motor nerve has **M**otor in the **M**iddle and **P**upils on the **P**eriphery, so compression will affect the pupils first.)

Transtentorial herniation can also produce *ipsilateral* motor weakness in the body due to compression of the motor tracts running in the **cerebral peduncles** (remember the two "ears" of the midbrain's bear-like face!). Wait a minute… why are the motor deficits *ipsilateral* to the lesion? Shouldn't they be *contralateral* because the pyramidal decussation hasn't occurred yet? That's a good catch, and the kind of thinking that will get you far in neurology! The reason that motor deficits are ipsilateral in an uncal herniation is because of a phenomenon known as **Kernohan-Woltman syndrome**. Essentially, what happens here is that if there is increased intracranial pressure and a resultant uncal hernia on *one* side of the brain, this can cause the cerebral peduncle on the *opposite* side to be pressed up into the tentorium there, causing an indentation (or "notch") that compresses and ultimately causes dysfunction of the motor neurons traveling in the corticospinal tract. By causing dysfunction of the cerebral peduncles on the *opposite* side (which then crosses over in the medulla), an uncal herniation can result in *ipsilateral* paralysis. Because this phenomenon has a tendency to get clinicians to "call it" for the wrong side, it is sometimes called a **false localizing sign**. To avoid getting confused, keep in mind that the side of the dilated pupil is the affected side in over 90% of cases!

Transtentorial herniation also has a tendency to compress the nearby posterior cerebral artery, leading to occipital lobe infarction and its associated visual field deficits (**contralateral homonymous hemianopsia with macular sparing**). Finally, all of this pressure onto the midbrain can itself cause bleeding, a finding known as **Duret hemorrhages**. To remember all of the features associated with an uncal herniation, think of your dear **Uncle CHIP the Third**. This should help you associate an uncal herniation with **C**ontralateral **H**emianopsia, **I**psilateral **P**aralysis (due to Kernohan's notch), and a palsy of the **Third** cranial nerve.

Uncal herniation involves the innermost part of the **temporal lobe** moving past the tentorium cerebelli and putting pressure on the **midbrain**.

Uncle CHIP, the Third:
Uncal *herniation*
Contralateral ***H****emianopsia*
I*psilateral* ***P****aralysis*
Third *nerve palsy*

Subfalcine and transtentorial herniation related to a brain tumor.

CENTRAL HERNIATION

Central herniation is similar in some ways to an uncal herniation, as it involves medial parts of the brain (including the inner aspect of the temporal lobes) being displaced downward through the tentorium cerebelli. However, in central herniation lower parts of the cerebral **subcortex** such as the **thalamus, epithalamus**, and **hypothalamus** are all involved as well. The involvement of the hypothalamus leads to hormone deficiencies, while involvement of the epithalamus leads to a weakness of upward eye movements with resultant downward displacement of the eyes (as in Parinaud's syndrome). This finding is sometimes called **"sunset eyes"** as the eyes cross the eyelids like a sun setting past the horizon.

Because central herniation also puts direct pressure on the critically important areas of the brainstem (including those associated with consciousness, respiration, and heart beat), the clinical presentation often includes a significant alteration in consciousness and breathing patterns. Decorticate or even decerebrate posturing may be seen as well, both of which portend a poor prognosis.

UPWARD HERNIATION

Upward herniation is the opposite of central herniation. Instead of the cerebrum coming *down* through the tentorium cerebelli, the cerebellum goes *up*. (Technically speaking, central herniation can also involve upwards movement of the cerebellum and midbrain up into the upper brain, but this is much less common than downward herniation.)

TONSILLAR HERNIATION

Tonsillar herniation involves parts of the **cerebellum** being pushed through the **foramen magnum**, or the large hole at the bottom of the skull through which the medulla travels right before becoming the spinal cord. Accordingly, tonsillar herniation tends to affect the **medulla** (including the cardiorespiratory centers) and can be **life-threatening**. The upper cervical spinal cord is often affected as well. The primary signs and symptoms of a tonsillar herniation include headache, neck stiffness, a decreased level of consciousness, and flaccid paralysis throughout the body.

Foramen magnum

TRANSCALVARIAL HERNIATION

Finally, **transcalvarial herniation** is a rare form of brain herniation in which the brain is forced out through a hole in the **skull** itself. Under normal conditions, the skull is hard enough that a soft, squishy substance like the brain isn't able to force its way out. For this reason, transcalvarial herniation is really only a problem when the skull has been compromised somehow, whether that is a skull fracture related to a motor vehicle accident or a hole intentionally being made in the skull during certain neurosurgical procedures.

PUTTING IT ALL TOGETHER

In this chapter, we've covered several different causes of intracranial hypertension, including **intracranial bleeds, hydrocephalus**, and the disease known as **idiopathic intracranial hypertension**. We've also talked about **brain herniation** as a particular manifestation of increased intracranial pressure. In general if you understand the idea that the skull is a fixed space and the concept that compression is damaging to nervous tissue, the presentations of these diseases shouldn't come as too much of a surprise. Pay close attention to the particular way that each of these presents clinically to help you sleuth out which one of these devastating conditions may be occurring!

REVIEW QUESTIONS

1. A 55 y/o F undergoes a cerebral angiogram which shows an aneurysm in her right anterior communicating artery as seen below:

Which of the following conditions is she most at risk of developing first?
A. Intracerebral hemorrhage
B. Epidural hematoma
C. Subarachnoid hemorrhage
D. Subdural hematoma
E. Subfalcine herniation
F. Uncal herniation
G. Central herniation
H. Transcalvarial herniation
I. Upward herniation
J. Tonsillar herniation
K. Idiopathic intracranial hypertension

2. (Continued from previous question.) If this aneurysm were to rupture, what is the most likely clinical presentation?
   A. An abrupt onset of motor and sensory deficits in the face, arms, and legs
   B. A brief loss of consciousness followed by regaining consciousness and then losing it again
   C. A slow onset of headache and confusion over weeks or months
   D. A sudden onset of "the worst headache of my life" with neck stiffness and pain
   E. Involuntary extension of the arms and legs with downward displacement of the eyes

3. A 25 y/o M is pitching in a baseball game without wearing a helmet. After one pitch, the batter accidentally loses his grip on the bat and sends it flying into the air, hitting the pitcher in the head. He loses consciousness for around 5 minutes but then awakens. He reports feeling dazed but, despite encouragement, does not go to the hospital for evaluation. Several hours later, he suddenly experiences a severe headache with nausea and vomiting. Alarmed, his wife calls 911. On the way to the hospital, he becomes increasingly lethargic and confused, and he is unconscious by the time of arrival. Which of the following is the most likely blood vessel that has been injured?
   A. Anterior cerebral artery
   B. Anterior communicating artery
   C. Posterior communicating artery
   D. Middle meningeal artery
   E. Bridging veins

4. (Continued from previous question.) In the emergency department, the patient is noted to have a dilated left pupil and a "down and out" positioning of the left eye. Visual exam is notable for a right homonymous hemianopsia. There is complete motor weakness on his left side. Knowing that damage to the brain produces motor deficits on the opposite side, the clinical team diagnoses him with a right-sided hematoma and rushes him to the operating room for a craniotomy, a surgical procedure intended to control bleeding in the intracranial space. When the surgical team makes a hole in the right side, however, they find no bleeding. Surprised, they drill again on the left side and find a hematoma. Which of the following mechanisms most likely accounts for the unexpected findings in this patient?
   A. Developmental abnormality resulting in an absent decussation of the corticospinal tract in the medulla
   B. Damage to the cerebellum rather than the cerebrum
   C. Diagnosis of situs inversus, or a congenital condition in which all major organs are reversed on their left-right axis
   D. Sufficient compressive force to injure the opposite side of the brain
   E. Medical error on the part of the medical team accidentally confusing left for right

1. **The best answer is C.** While trauma is the most common cause of subarachnoid hemorrhage, a close second is the rupture of a cerebral aneurysm due to their propensity to bleed into the subarachnoid space. Intracerebral hemorrhage, epidural hematomas, and subdural hematomas are all associated with a history of head trauma as well, although they do not have the same link to cerebral aneurysms that a subarachnoid hemorrhage does (answers A, B, and D). On its own, an unruptured aneurysm is unlikely to increase intracranial pressure sufficiently to cause any form of herniation (answers E—J). Idiopathic intracranial hypertension is not associated with a cerebral aneurysm (answer K).

2. **The best answer is D.** The typical presentation of a subarachnoid hemorrhage involves a sudden onset "thunderclap" headache with neck stiffness and pain due to irritation of the meninges. Motor and sensory deficits in the face, arms, and legs are more consistent with a stroke in the region of the anterior or middle cerebral artery (answer A). The specific pattern of losing, regaining, and then losing consciousness again is more associated with an epidural hematoma (answer B), while a slow onset of headache and confusion is seen more often in a subdural hematoma (answer C). Finally, decerebrate posturing and "sunset eyes" are more often seen in central herniation.

3. **The best answer is D.** This case describes an epidural hematoma which is strongly associated with head trauma. The classic presentation is an initial loss of consciousness followed by a lucid period and a later lapse back into unconsciousness. Rupture of the middle meningeal artery, which supplies the dura mater, is a common cause of an epidural hematoma. Rupture of bridging veins is associated with a subdural hematoma (answer E), while a stroke in the anterior cerebral artery is associated with a subfalcine herniation (answer A). The anterior and posterior communicating arteries are both common sites of aneurysm formation in the circle of Willis which may then rupture and lead to a subarachnoid hemorrhage (answers B and C).

4. **The best answer is D.** As an epidural hematoma grows, it can increase intracranial pressure to the point of causing a transtentorial herniation. When there is sufficient compressive force, brain tissue on the *opposite* side of the bleeding can be compressed, a phenomenon known as Kernohan's notch. This can lead to motor weakness on the side *ipsilateral* to the bleeding. For this reason, in potential cases of uncal herniation, it is important to rely upon neuroimaging rather than observed motor deficits to localize the lesion. (The dilated pupil will also be ipsilateral to the lesion in the vast majority of all cases, which is another helpful clue.) The medical team mistaking the patient's left for his right would not account for the accurate representation of his ocular findings (answer E). Damage to the cerebellum would cause ataxia and other cerebellar signs but not the frank motor weakness observed in this case (answer B). Situs inversus does exist, but it would not account for the fact that the muscle weakness is generally contralateral to the side of the bleeding regardless of the positioning of the organs (answer C). Finally, there are no known cases of people being born without a pyramidal decussation (answer A).

14 MYOPATHY

Starting here and continuing on for the next few chapters, we will pivot away from talking about the pathology of the central nervous system and begin a tour through diseases affecting the **motor system**. The term **neuromuscular disease** is used to refer broadly to the various forms of pathology that can all affect muscle function. These disorders can happen at any step along the way, including the **muscle itself** (as in myopathies like muscular dystrophy), the **nerves** supplying the muscles (as in motor neuron diseases such as amyotrophic lateral sclerosis), the **neuromuscular junction** connecting the two (as in neuromuscular junction diseases like myasthenia gravis), or in the regions of the **brain** controlling movement (as in movement disorders like Parkinson's disease). We will attempt to group these disorders by the location where the pathology is occurring.

In this chapter, we will focus on a group of diseases known as **myopathies** which all involve dysfunction of the muscles themselves (rather than stemming from any step upstream like the neuromuscular junction, motor neuron, or central nervous system). Despite their power, muscles are one of the simpler organs in the body, as they have one primary goal: to contract. Nevertheless, a variety of insults can cause dysfunction in the muscle. These processes include inflammation of the muscles, degeneration of muscle tissues, and environmental insults. We'll go over a few key diseases in each of these categories.

MUSCULAR DYSTROPHIES

Muscular dystrophy refers to the loss, destruction, or degeneration of muscle in the body due to a **genetic condition**. While there are many possible causes of muscular dystrophy, we will focus on just three: **Duchenne muscular dystrophy** (which is the most common childhood-onset form of muscular dystrophy), its related condition **Becker's muscular dystrophy**, and **myotonic muscular dystrophy** (which is the most common adult-onset form).

DUCHENNE MUSCULAR DYSTROPHY
Duchenne muscular dystrophy is an **X-linked recessive** genetic disorder in which muscle tissue is progressively destroyed, leading to muscle atrophy and weakness. Duchenne muscular dystrophy affects **boys** more than girls. The telltale pattern of muscle weakness generally appears around the **age of 4**, although some signs (such as delayed motor milestones) may be apparent as early as the first two years. The first muscles affected are generally those in **proximal** groups like the **hips and upper legs**, with more distal muscles like the calves generally spared. This leads to a characteristic way of getting up from the floor known as **Gower's sign** in which weakness of the hip and upper leg muscles leads to an overreliance on the calves and arms to move one's body off the ground, as seen below.

While wasting and atrophy of the affected muscles is often seen, hypertrophy of more distal muscles (like the calves) often occurs due to the compensatory overuse of these muscles. You can remember this by thinking that someone with **Duchenne** muscular dystrophy will "**do shins**" more than most, leading to **hypertrophic calves**.

Duchenne muscular dystrophy is an **X-linked recessive disorder** that presents as **proximal weakness**, leading to overuse and hypertrophy of more distal muscles.

*If you always **do shins** (Duchenne's) in the gym, your **calves** will get **hypertrophic**.*

While the muscle weakness *begins* proximally, it often spreads distally as the disease progresses, and many people with this condition are unable to walk by adolescence. Life expectancy is often greatly reduced, and most patients die in their 20s or 30s (largely due to respiratory or cardiac failure, as the disease can progress to the point where the muscles of the heart and lungs are involved as well).

Duchenne muscular dystrophy is caused by a mutation in the **dystrophin** gene which produces a protein responsible for stabilizing the cytoskeleton of muscle cells. Without dystrophin, the cell membrane becomes weak, leading to mitochondrial dysfunction and the eventual death of the cell. For this reason, laboratory markers of muscle damage such as **creatine kinase** (CK) are almost always high in patients with this condition.

BECKER'S MUSCULAR DYSTROPHY

Becker's muscular dystrophy is a related condition that is similar to Duchenne muscular dystrophy in almost every way. The major difference is that Becker's often has a better prognosis, with a longer life expectancy and a better quality of life.

MYOTONIC DYSTROPHY

While Duchenne muscular dystrophy is the most common muscular dystrophy of *childhood*, **myotonic dystrophy** is the most common in *adults* (although it can begin during childhood as well). The term "myotonic" here refers to an **inability to relax a muscle once it has contracted**. (If it helps, you can remember the association between myotonic dystrophy and an inability to relax a muscle by thinking of someone saying, "It's <u>my</u> otonic dystrophy!" and imagining that they *can't let go*.) This inability to relax is also combined with a generalized **muscle weakness**.

Myotonic dystrophy is not a single disease but rather a pair of diseases (type 1 and type 2). For this reason, it has considerable variation in its presentation, with some people having only mild disability while others are severely disabled. Both forms of myotonic dystrophy feature prominent weakness of **distal muscles** such as the hands and feet, although type 2 can involve proximal weakness as well. Both forms of myotonic dystrophy are associated with an increased risk of developing specific other medical conditions including cataracts, insulin resistance, intellectual disability, and cardiac conduction abnormalities.

Both forms of myotonic dystrophy are **autosomal dominant** genetic disorders involving an expansion of the **trinucleotide repeat CTG**. While it typically does not appear until someone is in their adult years, in rare cases it may be present from birth. While there is no cure for myotonic dystrophy, physical therapy can help to improve the patient's quality of life.

Myotonic dystrophy is an **autosomal dominant genetic disorder** that presents as **distal weakness** and an **inability to relax muscles once contracted**.

*"It's **my** otonic dystrophy!" (This person is having trouble **letting go**.)*

INFLAMMATORY MYOPATHIES

Inflammation is a complex process in which the body attempts to respond to harmful or noxious stimuli by unleashing the power of the immune system, leading to the classic combination of **calor** (heat or warmth), **dolor** (pain), **rubor** (redness), and **tumor** (swelling). Inflammation is generally an uncomfortable state but, provided that it is helping to fight off infections and other threats to health, it can be functional. However, there are also times when inflammation occurs in the absence of an external threat or to such a great extent that it becomes maladaptive. When the immune system decides to attack muscle in particular, it leads to a state of muscle weakness and pain known as an **inflammatory myopathy** (or a **myositis**). Inflammatory myopathies come in a few different forms, three of which we will cover now.

POLYMYOSITIS

Polymyositis is an inflammatory myopathy in which **cytotoxic T cells** invade muscle tissues. This often presents as a slow onset of muscle weakness and atrophy over months or years. The clinical hallmark of polymyositis is **bilateral proximal weakness**, with the **hip extensors** often being affected first. This leads to difficulties in specific actions such as **rising from a chair**, which in many cases is the initial complaint that ultimately leads to a diagnosis of polymyositis. There is often **muscle pain** as well (remember "dolor!"). The extent and severity of muscle dysfunction increases as inflammation continues, making polymyositis a **progressive condition**. For unknown reasons, **women** are affected more often than men. The widespread inflammation seen in polymyositis can also cause problems in other organ systems as well, leading to heart failure, lung disease, and an increased risk of various forms of cancer.

A diagnosis of polymyositis is based on a characteristic history and neurological exam findings of proximal muscle weakness and atrophy. However, to definitively diagnose this disease, you must order a muscle biopsy which will show the invasion of T cells *within* the muscle fibers, as seen below. (Compare this to dermatomyositis, discussed next, in which the T cells are mostly found *outside* of the muscle fibers.)

Treatment of polymyositis involves **corticosteroids** to rapidly reduce the state of immune system hyperactivation. Steroids are highly effective treatments for this condition, and most patients improve dramatically. Interventions such as physical therapy are a key component of helping patients to regain functional ability as well.

To remember the details of **poly**myositis, imagine a situation where **Polly** (an **adult woman**) wants a cracker but **can't get up from her chair** to get one. For this reason, she is stuck **inside**. This will help you remember the most common initial presenting complaint for polymyositis, its greater frequency in adults and females (as opposed to children or males), and the fact that the T cells are found *inside* of the muscle fibers on biopsy.

> **Polymyositis** is an **inflammatory myopathy** characterized by **progressive bilateral proximal weakness**. It most often affects **adult women**. Muscle biopsy will show T cells **within muscle fibers**.
>
> *Polly wants a cracker but **can't get up from her chair**, so she is stuck **inside**.*

DERMATOMYOSITIS

Dermatomyositis is another inflammatory myopathy that is similar in many ways to polymyositis. Both present with **progressive bilateral proximal weakness** affecting the thighs and upper arms, leading to similar presenting complaints (difficulty getting up from a chair, climbing stairs, or lifting something above the head). Both tend to begin in later adulthood (around 40 or 50 years old), are more common in women than men, and are associated with inflammatory changes in other parts of the body such as the heart and lungs. As with polymyositis, dermatomyositis can be effectively treated with **steroids**.

Where dermatomyositis differentiates itself, however, is with its involvement of the **skin**, as this condition is associated with **rashes** in various parts of the body. These rashes are generally red in color, are very sensitive to sunlight, and may be itchy or painful. An example of a dermatomyositis-associated rash on the elbow is seen below.

Dermatomyositis also differentiates itself from polymyositis in its findings on muscle biopsy. While invasion of the muscle tissues by immune cells is seen in both, in dermatomyositis these cells are seen primarily around the *outside* of the muscle fibers (in contrast with polymyositis in which they are stuck *inside*). Compare the image below with the one from the previous page.

Just as you should associate polymyositis with the word *inside*, try to associate derm-**out**-omyositis with the word **out**-side. This should remind you of the rashes found on the *outside* of one's body (the skin) and the presence of immune cells *outside* the muscle fibers.

Dermatomyositis is an **inflammatory myopathy** that is similar to polymyositis but also involves **skin rashes**. Muscle biopsy will show white blood cells in the space **surrounding muscle fibers**.

*Derm-**out**-omyositis is found **out**side:*
***out**side the body (on the skin) and **out**side the muscle fibers (on a biopsy).*

INCLUSION BODY MYOSITIS

The last of the inflammatory myopathies we will talk about is **inclusion body myositis**. Out of the three, inclusion body myositis is the odd one out. While it shares with polymyositis and dermatomyositis a tendency towards slowly progressive muscle weakness, it stands out in a few other ways. First, inclusion body myositis tends to affect **proximal and distal muscles** equally (including **finger flexors**, which aren't affected very often in polymyositis and dermatomyositis). Second, it often progresses **asymmetrically** (as opposed to bilaterally in the other two). Third, it primarily affects **elderly** adults, with **men** being affected more often than women. Fourth, it is not responsive to most forms of treatment (whereas both polymyositis and dermatomyositis respond well to immunosuppressive treatments such as steroids). In fact, the lack of a good response to treatment with steroids is sometimes used diagnostically to differentiate between inclusion body myositis and the other two inflammatory myopathies.

You can use the abbreviation **IBM** to remember the features of **I**nclusion **B**ody **M**yositis. The term IBM was often used synonymously with "computer" back in the 1980s and 1990s. This will help you remember the involvement of distal muscles like **finger flexors** (since you use your fingers for typing). Also, because use of the term "IBM" as a generic word for computer is not very common anymore, you will likely only hear **old men** say it.

Inclusion body myositis is an **inflammatory myopathy** that involves **asymmetric weakness of both proximal and distal muscles**. It primarily affects **older men** and is **not responsive to immunosuppressive treatment**.

*Think of an **older man** typing at an **IBM** using his **finger flexors**.*

IATROGENIC MYOPATHIES

The term **iatrogenic** (Greek for "inflicted by the healer") refers to any harm that comes as an intended or unintended effect of medical treatment. A variety of medications can cause myopathies. However, the most common form (and the one you should know cold) is a **statin-induced myopathy**, or one caused by the cholesterol-reducing medications known as **HMG-CoA reductase inhibitors** (or simply "statins" as many of their names end in –statin such as atorvastatin, lovastatin, and simvastatin). Statins are among the highest selling drugs of all time, which combined with the relatively high frequency of muscle injury as a side effect (around 10 to 15% of people taking the drug) makes statin-induced myopathy a particularly common clinical phenomenon. The most common manifestation of statin-induced myopathy is **myalgias**, or persistent muscle aches. Muscle weakness occurs in around one-quarter of cases as well, but it is generally less pronounced than in other myopathies. When it does occur, weakness tends to affect proximal muscles more than distal ones. As in other forms of myopathy, creatine kinase levels may be elevated. Most patients can continue taking a statin by switching to a different type or by adjusting their dosage.

PUTTING IT ALL TOGETHER

Myopathies are the first step along the way to understanding neuromuscular diseases, so make sure to learn them well by reviewing the mnemonics from this chapter! Remember that "**do shins**" muscular dystrophy results in hypertrophic calves while *my*-otonic dystrophy results in someone having trouble letting go. Polymyositis makes it so that **Polly** is stuck **inside**, while derm-**out**-omyositis leads to rashes on the **out**side of the body. Finally, you need finger flexors and other **distal muscles** to type on your **IBM**, so these are the muscles that can be affected in **I**nclusion **B**ody **M**yositis!

REVIEW QUESTIONS

1. A 28 y/o F has been seeing her neurologist since the age of 21. She was first seen in the clinic with concerns about her muscles tiring easily. She also noted at that time that her hand would "get stuck" on a door handle after opening it. During her initial evaluation, she had decreased motor strength in her hands and feet, with difficulty unclenching muscles once they had contracted. The patient was adopted and does not know her family's genetic history. She struggled with academics in her childhood but performed well enough to graduate from high school. She currently works as a grocery store bagger. At her visit today, the neurologist notes that when he shook her hand, she did not release his hand for several seconds. Her exam is notable for atrophy of several muscles in the face, decreased motor strength in all extremities, hypoactive reflexes in the arms, and absent reflexes in the legs. The patient informs the neurologist that she and her husband have been discussing the idea of having children. However, she is concerned about passing her disease on to her children. Her husband has no personal or family history of this disease. What is the most accurate response for the neurologist to give?
   A. "There is no chance of you passing this disease to your children."
   B. "There is a small chance of your children inheriting this disease, but it is remote enough that it shouldn't influence your decision making."
   C. "It is a definite possibility that you will pass it to your children, but it is still more unlikely than likely."
   D. "There is a very good chance you will pass it to your children, especially if you have more than one child."
   E. "It is completely assured that your children will inherit this disease."

2. A 35 y/o M sees a neurologist with a chief complaint of increasing muscle weakness. On exam, there is marked weakness of muscles of the wrist extensors, finger flexors, hip abductors, and calves. Which of the following is the most likely diagnosis at this time?
   A. Duchenne muscular dystrophy
   B. Inclusion body myositis
   C. Polymyositis
   D. Dermatomyositis
   E. All of the above are equally likely

3. A 6 y/o M is seen by a pediatrician for an initial evaluation. His family immigrated to the United States recently, and due to prior societal instability he has not been in medical care for several years. His parents note that over the past year he has had difficulty engaging in physical activities at school and in the park. He sometimes trips while running, and after falling he often takes several moments to lift himself up by his hands. He has difficulty climbing the stairs up to his apartment. A picture of his legs is below:

Which of the following is most likely to be seen on further evaluation?
A. Clouding of the lenses in the eyes
B. High levels of muscle breakdown products in the blood
C. A red itchy rash that is sensitive to sunlight
D. Invasion of immune cells within muscle fibers
E. Increased fasting glucose levels due to insulin resistance

4. A 39 y/o F presents to the emergency department reporting difficulty breathing. She has no history of asthma or any other medical condition. On interview, she reports severe "aching" pain in her neck, shoulders, and thighs over the past 2 months along with difficulty rising from a chair or walking, especially for long distances or up a flight of stairs. On exam, motor strength is decreased in her shoulders and hips but intact in her hands and feet. Deep tendon reflexes are intact throughout. Labs are notable for increased creatine kinase levels. Which of the following is the most accurate statement about the patient's condition?
A. "This condition is generally treatable with medication."
B. "This condition is generally treatable with surgery."
C. "There is no treatment for this condition, although physical therapy can help preserve function for longer."
D. "There is no need for treatment, as this will likely get better on its own."
E. "This is probably related to a medication you started recently. Once you stop the medication, you should get better quickly."

1. **The best answer is D.** This patient has myotonic dystrophy as evidenced by her motor weakness accompanied by action myotonia, or delayed relaxation of muscles following voluntary contraction. Myotonic dystrophy is an autosomal dominant disease, meaning that there is a 50% chance of her child inheriting this condition. While the chance remains 50% for each individual child, her chance of having at least one child with the disorder goes up with every subsequent birth. Despite the high likelihood of passing this disease to her children, it is not completely assured that it will happen (answer E). However, the risk is still high enough that she should not be told that it is a small or unlikely risk (answers A—C).

2. **The best answer is B.** This patient is presenting with weakness involving both proximal and distal muscle groups. Notably, all of the other conditions listed present primarily with weakness of proximal muscles such as the hips and upper legs in Duchenne muscular dystrophy (answer A), hip extensors in polymyositis (answer C), and thighs and upper arms in dermatomyositis (answer D). Duchenne muscular dystrophy is also unlikely to present for the first time in adulthood.

3. **The best answer is B.** The most likely diagnosis in this case is Duchenne muscular dystrophy given the onset of proximal muscle weakness during childhood, presence of calf hypertrophy, and positive Gower's sign. Duchenne muscular dystrophy is associated with high levels of creatine kinase, a muscle breakdown product, in the blood. Cataracts and insulin resistance are more characteristic of myotonic dystrophy (answers A and E). A red itchy rash is more often seen in dermatomyositis (answer C), while invasion of T cells within muscle fibers is characteristic of polymyositis (answer D).

4. **The best answer is A.** The most likely diagnosis in this case is polymyositis given the patient's age, female sex, and clinical presentation including proximal muscle weakness with preservation of distal motor function. Polymyositis is generally treated with medications, with corticosteroids being the first-line option. It is not appropriate to say that there is no treatment for the condition (answer C) even if physical therapy can be helpful as well. Surgery plays no role in management of polymyositis (answer B). Polymyositis is unlikely to resolve on its own, and with the presence of her breathing difficulties, neglecting to provide treatment is an unwise option (answer D). Finally, there is no evidence that the patient is taking a medication like a statin that could induce a myopathy. Further, statin-induced myopathy tends to present primarily with muscle pain rather than the severe weakness seen in this case (answer E).

15 NEUROMUSCULAR JUNCTION DISEASE

In the last chapter, we covered disorders involving the muscle itself. In this chapter, we will begin to work backwards and talk about diseases involving the connection between the muscle and the nerve supplying it: the neuromuscular junction. **Neuromuscular junction diseases** are a group of conditions that are united only by the fact that they all have an adverse effect on the transmission of a signal from the motor nerve to the muscle itself. However, within that loose framework lies an incredibly diverse group of diseases, each of which helps to illustrate the function of the neuromuscular junction itself!

For this reason, it can be helpful to briefly review exactly what happens at the neuromuscular junction before we begin. The primary function of the neuromuscular junction is to take an action potential traveling on the axon of a motor neuron and translate it into a contraction of the muscle itself. When an action potential arrives at the end of an axon, it activates voltage-dependent calcium channels which allow calcium ions to enter the neuron. This influx of calcium activates a group of protein complexes known as **SNARE proteins** which then help synaptic vesicles to fuse with the cell membrane, releasing the **acetylcholine** inside. The released acetylcholine then diffuses across the neuromuscular junction and activates **nicotinic receptors** on the muscle cell. Binding of acetylcholine to the nicotinic receptors depolarizes the muscle cell and begins a cascade of events that results in muscle contraction. Neuromuscular junction diseases can disrupt this process at various steps along the way, as we will see now. We will focus on four diseases in particular: **myasthenia gravis**, **Lambert-Eaton syndrome**, **botulism**, and **tetanus**.

MYASTHENIA GRAVIS

Myasthenia gravis is an **autoimmune disease** in which the immune system creates antibodies against the body itself. In myasthenia gravis, these antibodies specifically target **nicotinic acetylcholine receptors** by competing with acetylcholine and preventing it from activating these receptors on the muscle. This has the effect of blocking the transmission of the motor signal across the neuromuscular junction. (Note that these antibodies are only directed against *nicotinic* acetylcholine receptors! For this reason, parasympathetic effects and other functions that rely on *muscarinic* acetylcholine receptors are unaffected.)

This disruption in signal transmission across the neuromuscular junction leads to muscle weakness in multiple areas of the body. Weakness is often first noted in the **eyes** (including both extraocular movements, resulting in double vision or **diplopia**, and the eyelids, resulting in **ptosis** as seen in the picture below). The weakness then spreads to other parts of the body, with the muscles used for speech and swallowing often affected early on while those in the arms and legs are not affected until later in the disease.

On a clinical level, you can look at the electrical activity of muscles using a technique known as **electromyography** (or EMG). In patients with myasthenia gravis, the electrical signal coming from the muscle is often strongest at the beginning but then slowly weakens with repeated stimulation of the muscle, a pattern known as **"fatiguing weakness."** This correlates with what is seen clinically, with muscle weakness usually getting worse *after* activity and then improving following a period of rest. Fatiguing weakness also accumulates throughout the day such that patients are strongest in the morning but generally get weaker as the day progresses, with the **greatest weakness in the evening**.

A medication known as **edrophonium** (brand name Tensilon) was previously used to differentiate between myasthenia gravis and other conditions that may present similarly. Edrophonium acts as an **inhibitor of acetylcholinesterase**, which is the enzyme that breaks down acetylcholine in the neuromuscular junction. By inhibiting the enzyme that breaks down acetylcholine, edrophonium acts to *increase* the amount of this neurotransmitter that is active and available in the synapse, essentially giving the acetylcholine "army" more troops to fight the antibodies in the battle for nicotinic receptors. If someone's fatiguing weakness *improves* after administering edrophonium, a diagnosis of myasthenia gravis is more likely. (You may hear this referred to as a "Tensilon test.")

So if antibodies against the nicotinic acetylcholine receptor are the problem here, where exactly did these errant antibodies come from in the first place? While the exact pathophysiology is not known, there does appear to be an association with abnormalities in the **thymus**, an organ in the immune system that "teaches" white blood cells how to recognize invading pathogens. Evidence for an association between myasthenia gravis and the thymus comes from the fact that over 10% of people with the condition will have a **thymoma**, or a tumor of the thymus that often must be surgically removed.

Treatment of myasthenia gravis often involves use of an **acetylcholinesterase inhibitor**. Given the association of myasthenia gravis with a thymoma, screening for this form of cancer should be done, with surgical removal of the thymus performed if cancer is found (although a thymectomy does not necessarily improve the symptoms of myasthenia gravis itself). In cases where myasthenia gravis has progressed to the point where the muscles of respiration are involved (known as a **myasthenic crisis**), hospitalization with ventilator support may be necessary, with rapid removal of the offending antibodies from the bloodstream via **plasmapheresis** (in which the patient's blood is removed, filtered, and returned) or **intravenous immunoglobulins** (a mixture of antibodies donated by healthy people, often abbreviated IVIG).

Overall, you can remember the important associations to make with myasthenia **gravis** by thinking of it as myasthenia **gravi-TTT**, with the three Ts representing the faTiguing nature of weakness, the edrophonium (or Tensilon) test, and the association with a Thymoma. The world "gravity" can also remind you of the image of **falling** eyelids that get worse when the sun **falls**.

> **Myasthenia gravis** is an **autoimmune disease** in which the body produces antibodies against **nicotinic acetylcholine receptors**, resulting in a pattern of **fatiguing weakness**. It is associated with a **tumor in the thymus**.
>
> *Myasthenia gravi-TTT:*
> *FaTiguing pattern*
> *Tensilon test*
> *Thymoma*
>
> *Gravity "falls": falling eyelids when the sun falls.*

LAMBERT-EATON SYNDROME

Like myasthenia gravis, **Lambert-Eaton syndrome** is an **autoimmune disease** in which antibodies attack the neuromuscular junction and prevent signal transmission. *Unlike* myasthenia gravis (in which the antibodies are attacking nicotinic acetylcholine receptors on the *post*-synaptic membrane), in Lambert-Eaton syndrome the auto-antibodies are directed against **voltage-gated calcium channels** on the *pre*-synaptic membrane, thus preventing the *release* of acetylcholine rather than its binding. (Recall from Chapter 2 that **call**-cium acts as the battle **call** to send neurotransmitters like acetylcholine marching out into the synapse.) For this reason, administering an acetylcholinesterase inhibitor (as in the edrophonium test) will *not* improve muscle weakness in Lambert-Eaton syndrome, as the problem isn't that there isn't enough acetylcholine to compete with antibodies on the post-synaptic membrane—it's that acetylcholine isn't even being released into the synapse in the first place! Because Lambert-Eaton syndrome interferes with the release of acetylcholine throughout the body, **both nicotinic and muscarinic** receptors will be affected, resulting in not just muscle weakness but also autonomic dysfunction including constipation, dry mouth, and abnormal blood pressure.

EMG findings in Lambert-Eaton syndrome are characterized by an **incremental response** in which repeated stimulation of the nerve causes a stronger contraction of the muscle, as more acetylcholine will be released. (Compare this to the fatiguing pattern seen in myasthenia gravis in which repeated stimulation of the nerve will cause *less*, not more, muscle activity.) Like myasthenia gravis and thymoma, there is an association between Lambert-Eaton syndrome and cancer, in this case a type of lung cancer known as **small-cell lung cancer**. You can remember the association between **Lambert-Eaton** syndrome, **pre**-synaptic antibodies, and **small**-cell lung cancer by thinking of someone named **Lambert** who's always **eatin' small, dry pre**tzels (the kind they have at bars, *not* the large fresh kind they have at baseball games). This should remind you of **small**-cell lung cancer, **dry** mouth and other anticholinergic effects, and the **pre**-synaptic membrane.

> **Lambert-Eaton syndrome** is an **autoimmune disease** in which antibodies against **pre-synaptic voltage-gated calcium channels** cause **muscle weakness** and **anticholinergic signs and symptoms**. It is associated with **small-cell lung cancer**.
>
> *Lambert's always **eatin' pre**tzels (the **small** kind) which gives him a **dry** mouth.*

BOTULISM

Botulism is a disease in which exposure to the **botulinum toxin** produced by the bacterium *Clostridium botulinum* leads to muscle weakness. Similar to Lambert-Eaton syndrome, the botulinum toxin interferes with the release of acetylcholine, resulting in a lack of stimulation of both nicotinic and muscarinic receptors. This presents clinically as both **muscle weakness** (with the same **incremental response** as seen in Lambert-Eaton syndrome, which makes sense as they are both *pre*-synaptic problems) as well as **anticholinergic** signs and symptoms like constipation. In contrast to both myasthenia gravis and Lambert-Eaton syndrome, however, botulism generally has an **acute onset** rather than the slow, insidious onset seen with auto-immune diseases.

So how exactly is the botulinum toxin preventing the release of acetylcholine? Botulinum toxin interferes with the process of exocytosis by **damaging SNARE proteins**, thus preventing the vesicles from releasing their acetylcholine into the neuromuscular junction.

Exposure to botulinum toxin is classically associated with a few specific clinical scenarios. First, botulism can develop in **infants given honey**, as *C. botulinum* toxins are commonly found in this food product. While older children and adults can eat honey without a problem, infants haven't yet developed the protective mechanisms against these spores, leading them to be at risk of widespread muscle paralysis if they ingest honey. In adults with a functioning immune system, botulism generally develops after one of two things: either eating **improperly canned foods** or using certain **intravenous drugs**. Because *C. botulinum* is an anaerobic organism that thrives in the absence of oxygen, improperly canned foods are a perfect medium for their growth. *C. botulinum* also loves to grow in open wounds like the kinds that are created with recurrent injection of drugs like heroin.

Botulinum isn't all bad news! The fact that this toxin causes muscle weakness and paralysis is actually used to positive effect in treating spasticity and other kinds of muscle overactivity. In addition, it can be used cosmetically to reduce facial wrinkles (known as Botox). So botulinum isn't necessarily your enemy as long as it's used in the right place, at the right time, and in the right amount!

TETANUS

Like botulism, **tetanus** occurs when a spore-forming bacterium produces a toxin that interferes with signal transmission across the neuromuscular junction. In this case, the bacterium is *Clostridium tetani*, and the toxin it produces is known as **tetanospasmin**. Unlike all of the diseases we have discussed so far, tetanus does not result in muscle *weakness*. Instead, the opposite happens: muscles begin contracting *too much*, often becoming so tight that they begin to spasm throughout the body. This tends to start at the top of the body (with **lockjaw** being one of the earliest manifestations) and slowly spread downward. In this way, tetanus does the *opposite* of botulism and turns all the muscles in the body "**on**" as seen below:

Like botulinum toxin, tetanospasmin interferes with the function of SNARE proteins, preventing vesicles from releasing their contents. While botulism prevents vesicles filled with *acetylcholine* from being released, tetanus interferes with vesicles containing two other neurotransmitters: **glycine** and **GABA** (short for gamma-aminobutyric acid). Both of these are **inhibitory** neurotransmitters that make neurons less likely to "fire." By *inhibiting* the release of *inhibitory* neurotransmitters, tetanus leads to the **widespread activation of muscles** that is characteristic of this disease.

While *C. tetani* is commonly found in soil, it can produce problems when it enters the body. The classic clinical scenario for tetanus is when someone steps on a rusty nail while working out in the yard, as breaking the skin allows this normally benign bacterium to bypass the body's defenses and wreak havoc in the wound. However, tetanus can be contracted in other ways as well, including during childbirth.

Treatment generally involves infusing an antibody against the tetanus toxin to remove it from the body. Supportive measures, such as giving benzodiazepines and muscle relaxants, can be used as well. Antibiotics are sometimes used to treat the *C. tetani* infection, although the evidence that this helps is not clear. Ultimately, the most effective treatment is prevention by **vaccination.**

To remember that both **B**otulism and **T**etanus block the release of neurotransmitters from vesicles in the neuromuscular junction by interfering with **SNARE** proteins, think of a **snare drum** on which someone is playing a **BeaT**, with tetanus on the **on beat** (since it turns all muscles "on") and botulism on the **off beat** (since it turns all muscles "off").

Both **botulism** and **tetanus** block **neurotransmitter release** by interfering with **SNARE proteins**. Botulism blocks the release of **acetylcholine**, leading to **weakness**. Tetanus blocks the release of **glycine** and **GABA**, leading to **spasms**.

Play a BeaT (Botulism and Tetanus) on a SNARE drum,
*with tetanus on the **on beat** and botulism on the **off beat**.*

PUTTING IT ALL TOGETHER

While the four diseases in this chapter all disrupt signaling at the neuromuscular junction, they each do so in different ways that allow us to understand the process better. **Myasthenia gravis** results in the release of auto-antibodies that compete with acetylcholine for receptors on the muscle, **Lambert-Eaton syndrome** interferes with neurotransmitter release from the pre-synaptic neuron by blocking voltage-gated calcium channels, and **botulism** prevents exocytosis of acetylcholine from the pre-synaptic neuron, all of which lead to muscle weakness. In contrast, **tetanus** blocks the release of inhibitory neurotransmitters, leading to muscle spasms and sustained involuntary contractions. Do your best to memorize the mechanisms at play here to enhance your understanding of the neuromuscular junction!

REVIEW QUESTIONS

1. A 66 y/o M sees his primary care doctor complaining of progressive weakness of his arms and legs. He first noticed weakness in his legs a few months ago, with arm weakness following around one month later. His legs are now weak to the point where he needs to walk with a cane. He denies any daily pattern to his muscle weakness, saying, "It's basically always there." Review of systems is positive for dry mouth and constipation, with his last bowel movement occurring three days ago. Exam is notable for decreased motor strength in proximal muscles and absent deep tendon reflexes in all extremities. Which of the following tests is most likely to reveal an abnormality?
   A. Radiographic imaging of the chest
   B. Edrophonium test
   C. Needle biopsy of the thymus
   D. Urine drug screen
   E. Physical exam for puncture wounds

2. A 55 y/o F schedules an intake appointment with a dermatologist after she is encouraged to go by a friend who says that this dermatologist made her look "decades younger." After a brief consultation, the dermatologist proceeds to inject a neurotoxin into various sites in her forehead, cheeks, and around her eyes as seen below:

Within several hours, she notices fewer wrinkles on her face. Which of the following mechanisms explains the effect of this neurotoxin?
   A. Demyelination of the pre-synaptic neuron
   B. Interference with acetylcholine binding with nicotinic receptors
   C. Inhibition of voltage-gated calcium channels
   D. Prevention of synaptic vesicle binding to the cell membrane
   E. Impedance of inhibitory neuron exocytosis

3. A 45 y/o F sees a neurologist saying, "It feels like my body is falling apart." She reports that around one year ago she began having episodes of double vision. She notices this the most when using her phone in bed at night, saying, "The letters on the screen get blurry and then separate." Around six months ago, she noticed that it felt like food was "getting stuck in my throat." She has had particular difficulty with hard foods such as apples and carrots, as she feels she "cannot chew them enough." These problems are particularly noticeable when eating dinner, as she says that breakfast usually doesn't cause her the same problems. She has lost 15 pounds over the past 3 months. During the interview, the neurologist notices that her speech is soft and difficult to understand at times. Vital signs are HR 88, BP 122/80, RR 16, and T 98.9°F. On exam, she is alert and oriented. There is drooping of her eyelid on the right as seen below:

Her right eye shows weakness of lateral gaze. Her motor strength is decreased in both proximal and distal muscle groups in all four extremities, with greater levels of weakness the longer that the testing continues. The neurologist prescribes her an acetylcholinesterase inhibitor and sends her to radiology for a CT scan of the chest which shows no abnormalities. On a follow-up appointment several weeks later, he examines her eyes again and sees the following:

Which of the following is the best next step?
   A. Stopping the acetylcholinesterase inhibitor as it is used for diagnostic purposes only
   B. Continuing the acetylcholinesterase inhibitor
   C. Surgical removal of the thymus
   D. Mechanical filtration of the blood
   E. Administration of donated antibodies

1. **The best answer is A.** The presence of muscle weakness with a gradual onset and anticholinergic signs and symptoms such as dry mouth and constipation is highly concerning for Lambert-Eaton syndrome. Lambert-Eaton syndrome is frequently related to the presence of a small-cell lung cancer, so ordering chest imaging is a high priority. Botulism can present similarly to Lambert-Eaton syndrome but tends to involve a much more rapid onset; it can be associated with use of certain intravenous drugs which would be picked up on a urine drug screen (answer D). An edrophonium test does not improve muscle weakness in Lambert-Eaton syndrome and is more specific for myasthenia gravis (answer B) which is associated with a thymoma (answer C). Myasthenia gravis is unlikely in this patient as his presentation lacks a fatiguing pattern but does include anticholinergic symptoms, which are absent in myasthenia gravis. Puncture wounds are more likely to be seen in cases of tetanus, though this would present with widespread muscle spasms, not weakness (answer E).

2. **The best answer is D.** Botulinum toxin can be dangerous under certain conditions, but when injected locally it can have beneficial effects by reducing muscle contraction. For this reason, it can be used cosmetically to reduce facial wrinkling. The mechanism by which botulinum toxin prevents muscle contraction is by interfering with SNARE proteins in the pre-synaptic neuron, preventing vesicular exocytosis and the release of acetylcholine into the synaptic cleft. Tetanospasmin also interferes with SNARE proteins, but it instead prevents the release of inhibitory neurotransmitters, thereby increasing muscle excitation (answer E). Interference with acetylcholine binding to nicotinic receptors describes myasthenia gravis (answer B), while inhibition of voltage-gated calcium channels describes Lambert-Eaton syndrome (answer C). Botulinum toxin does not affect the myelin sheath (answer A).

3. **The best answer is B.** Acetylcholinesterase inhibitors are the mainstay of treatment for myasthenia gravis and often help people achieve better functioning than they would without medications. While acetylcholinesterase inhibitors can be helpful diagnostically, they are used for long-term treatment as well (answer A). Surgical removal of the thymus should be pursued if there is evidence of a thymoma, but in this case the chest CT did not show evidence of cancer (answer C). Plasmapheresis (answer D) and intravenous immunoglobulins (answer E) are expensive and logistically complicated, so they are generally only used in cases of myasthenic crisis requiring admission to the hospital.

16 MOTOR NEURON DISEASE

Let's continue our study of neuromuscular diseases by continuing to move up the neuronal "chain to the brain." We started with the muscle itself and then touched on the neuromuscular junction, and we will now direct our attention to diseases involving the **motor neurons** that connect muscles to the central nervous system. Motor neurons can be damaged by a variety of pathological processes, including various forms of peripheral neuropathy (which we will discuss further in Chapter 22). For the purposes of clarity, however, in this chapter we will limit our discussion to specifically those diseases that *only* affect motor neurons (while leaving other peripheral nerves, such as those responsible for transmitting sensory information, intact).

When learning about motor neuron diseases, it is crucial to understand the distinction between upper and lower motor neurons. Recall that there are **three neurons** between brain and muscle: the neuron connecting the brain to the anterior horn of the spinal cord, the interneuron in the anterior horn, and the peripheral nerve exiting out of the anterior horn and traveling to the muscle. In this way, the anterior horn acts as a "line in the sand" separating upper and lower motor neurons, as seen in the image on the next page. Lesions in the *first* neuron create **upper motor neuron signs** while lesions in the *third* neuron create **lower motor neuron signs**. (It's worth pointing out that upper and lower motor neuron signs can occur simultaneously in the same person at the same time. For example, someone who sustains damage to their cervical spinal cord could develop a *lower* motor neuron syndrome in their *upper* extremities while showing signs of *upper* motor neuron syndrome in their *lower* extremities.)

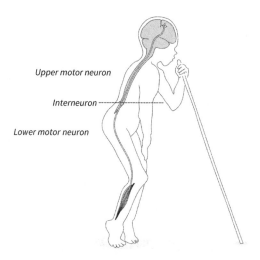

Each type of neuron produces a completely different set of signs when it is injured. In cases of *lower* motor neuron damage, the lack of innervation causes the muscle to wither and wilt (like a f*lower* deprived of sunlight), producing a state of **flaccid paralysis**. This causes the muscle to *lower* its output, producing weak or absent reflexes, poor muscle tone, diminished power, decreased bulk, and a downgoing Babinski response. When using electromyography to assess the muscle, a specific pattern called **fibrillations** (or many small motor signals that are not coordinated and therefore are unable to actually produce an effective movement) can be seen. Fasciculations, or sudden twitches, are also seen as well.

In contrast to lower motor neuron damage, *upper* motor neuron damage generally produces a pattern where everything seems to go *up*: the muscle tone becomes jerky and spastic, reflex strength is increased, and the Babinski reflex is upgoing. The reason this occurs is because upper motor neurons are responsible not just for *initiating* movements but *inhibiting* them also. When the upper motor neuron is damaged, this inhibition is lost, leading the lower motor neurons in the spinal circuits to become too strong. So why is this a bad thing? What's the downside of stronger muscles? The key is that upper motor neuron damage doesn't make you buffer. Instead, it leads to a tightly-wound muscle that is ready to fly off the handle at any moment. Upper motor neuron damage also produces an inability to engage in *fine* movements requiring a high level of dexterity (like playing the piano), with muscles only being able to engage in *broad coarse* movements (like swinging the entire arm).

Lower motor neuron injuries lead to a state of **flaccid paralysis**, while **upper motor neuron injuries** lead to a state of **spastic weakness**.

Lower motor neuron damage **lowers** muscle output, while **upper** motor neuron damage **ups** muscle output.

Not all kinds of damage to the motor system will produce upper or lower motor neuron findings. For example, the neuromuscular junction disorders we discussed in the last chapter do not present with lower motor neuron findings because the dysfunction does not lie in the lower motor neuron itself—it's the junction between the neuron and the muscle that is messed up. In addition, damage to the cerebellum does not cause upper or lower motor neuron findings, instead producing cerebellar signs (remember the **dizzy ANT** failing to **balance 3 dys'es** from Chapter 5!). Finally, damage to the basal ganglia does not cause either upper or lower motor neuron signs but rather results in movement disorders (which we will discuss in the next chapter).

With these basic principles in mind, let's talk about some of the most high-yield motor neuron diseases to know!

MOTOR NEURON DISEASES

The most common motor neuron disease, and the one that we will spend the most time discussing, is **amyotrophic lateral sclerosis**. In fact, the term "motor neuron disease" is sometimes used synonymously with amyotrophic lateral sclerosis despite the fact that there are other diseases that also fall under this banner.

AMYOTROPHIC LATERAL SCLEROSIS

Amyotrophic lateral sclerosis (which also goes by the acronym ALS or "Lou Gehrig's disease" after the baseball player who was famously diagnosed with this disease in the 1930s) is a condition in which degeneration of motor neurons leads to **progressive muscle weakness and atrophy**. Notably, amyotrophic lateral sclerosis affects **both upper and lower motor neurons** (in contrast to most other motor neuron diseases which tend to affect only one or the other). You can remember this by thinking that **A**myotrophic Latera**L** sclerosis wreaks havoc **ALL** over the place (both upper and lower motor neurons).

> Amyotrophic lateral sclerosis is a **progressive neurodegenerative disease** that affects **both upper and lower motor neurons**.
>
> *Amyotrophic LateraL sclerosis wreaks havoc **ALL** over the place.*

Signs and symptoms of amyotrophic lateral sclerosis generally begin in **middle age** (between 40 and 60 years old). Muscle weakness and atrophy are usually **bilateral** (which helps to distinguish them from dysfunction in any one peripheral nerve). Unlike some of the other motor neuron diseases we will talk about later in this chapter, amyotrophic lateral sclerosis doesn't have a preference for beginning in one part of the body or another. Instead, **any muscles** can be affected, including the arms and legs (although certain muscles, including those responsible for bowel function, bladder contraction, and eye movement are often preserved until late in the disease). In some cases, the muscles of the mouth and throat are affected due to death of neurons in the medulla; these cases are said to have **bulbar** involvement.

Consistent with the idea that amyotrophic lateral sclerosis involves all motor neurons, signs of *both* upper motor neuron damage (including spasticity, hyperreflexia, and re-emergence of primitive reflexes) *and* lower motor neuron damage (such as atrophy, poor muscle tone, hyporeflexia, and fibrillations) are present. **Fasciculations** in particular are a key sign, although they are not specific to this condition. Weakness is often subtle at first but becomes more pronounced as the disease progresses. In later stages, the diaphragm begins to fail, and most people with amyotrophic lateral sclerosis die from respiratory complications within 5 years of the initial diagnosis. While it was long thought that dementia was rare in this condition, some people with amyotrophic lateral sclerosis will exhibit cognitive impairment.

Most cases of amyotrophic lateral sclerosis are **sporadic** (occurring "out of the blue" with no known genetic or environmental triggers). However, inherited forms of the disease do exist. These tend to involve defects in the **superoxide dismutase 1** (SOD1) gene. You can remember this association by thinking of a baseball player (like Lou Gehrig) playing out on the **SOD** (or grass).

Most cases of **amyotrophic lateral sclerosis** are **sporadic**. Inherited versions of the disease tend to involve the **superoxide dismutase 1** (SOD1) gene.

*Think of **Lou Gehrig**, a baseball player who developed ALS, out on the **SOD** (grass).*

There is no cure for amyotrophic lateral sclerosis, and available treatments are often quite limited. Use of **physical and occupational therapy** can help to promote movement and independence, while **speech therapy** can be useful for cases with bulbar involvement. In patients with respiratory failure, **non-invasive ventilation** with a face or nose mask has been shown to improve quality of life and prolong survival, particularly in people with normal bulbar function. Two medications have been shown to have beneficial effects in amyotrophic lateral sclerosis, although the mechanisms by which they work in this condition are poorly understood. The first, **riluzole**, decreases release of the neurotransmitter glutamate and can prolong life by around 2 or 3 months. The second, **edaravone**, can slow the rate of functional loss; however, it is very expensive and requires daily intravenous infusions, making it difficult to access. When the diaphragm becomes paralyzed, ventilator support is often required. Overall, amyotrophic lateral sclerosis is a tragic and deadly disease, although research efforts are ongoing to identify better treatments or even a cure.

PRIMARY LATERAL SCLEROSIS

The next two conditions we will talk about are similar to amyotrophic lateral sclerosis in many ways, and some have even argued that they should be seen as *variants* of amyotrophic lateral sclerosis rather than separate diseases. For the sake of clarity, we will treat them as separate conditions even though there is a significant degree of overlap between them and amyotrophic lateral sclerosis.

Primary lateral sclerosis is a progressive disease that exclusively damages **upper motor neurons**, resulting in muscle spasticity, hyperreflexia, and primitive reflexes. Notably, lower motor neuron signs will be *absent*! Signs of weakness tend to first be seen in the lower half of the body, with the disease affecting the legs before **moving up** into the trunk, the arms, and eventually the face. Compared to amyotrophic lateral sclerosis, primary lateral sclerosis has a **slower progression**, and many people with the condition have a **normal life span**. You can remember the key features of **P**rimary **L**atera**L** sclerosis by thinking of someone doing a Pu**LL**-up, with the **up** reminding you of the presence of **upper** motor neuron signs and the fact that it often begins in the legs and moves **up**.

Primary lateral sclerosis is a neurodegenerative disease that only involves **upper motor neurons**. It has a **better prognosis** than amyotrophic lateral sclerosis.

*Primary LateraL sclerosis = PuLL-up (**up**per motor neuron, moves **up** the body).*

PROGRESSIVE MUSCULAR ATROPHY
Progressive muscular atrophy is the yin to primary lateral sclerosis's yang. Both are very similar to amyotrophic lateral sclerosis, but in **progressive muscular atrophy** only **lower motor neurons** are involved. This means that upper motor neuron signs are conspicuously *absent* compared to the other two conditions! Like primary lateral sclerosis, progressive muscular atrophy is associated with a **better prognosis** than "textbook" amyotrophic lateral sclerosis. You can remember the association of **progressive** muscular atrophy with **lower motor** neurons by thinking of the insurance company **Progressive** which tries to offer **lower** rates on **motor** vehicle insurance. (Please note that this book has neither been sponsored nor endorsed by The Progressive Corporation!)

Progressive muscular atrophy is similar to amyotrophic lateral sclerosis except that it only involves **lower motor neurons** and has a **better prognosis**.

*Progressive muscular atrophy only affects **lower** motor neurons, just like the Progressive insurance company tries to offer **lower** rates on car insurance.*

BULBAR PALSY AND PSEUDOBULBAR PALSY
If you remember that the term "bulbar" when used in neurology generally refers to the brainstem, it makes sense that **bulbar palsy** is a *lower* motor neuron disease that primarily affects the **brainstem** (in particular the medulla). Muscles responsible for speaking, chewing, swallowing, and moving the tongue are most often affected (remember that the nucleus ambig-"uh uh's" is located in the medulla!). This leads to

difficulty with speech as well as an increased risk of choking. Neurological exam will often reveal tongue atrophy, fasciculations, and an absent gag reflex consistent with lower motor neuron damage. There may also be motor deficits in the arms and legs as well, although these tend to be affected to a much lesser degree.

Another condition known as **pseudobulbar palsy** is similar to bulbar palsy in some ways, as both involve dysarthria and dysphagia. However, pseudobulbar palsy is specifically an *upper* motor neuron disease and tends to present with specific signs (including spasticity of the tongue as well as exaggerated gag and jaw jerk reflexes) that aren't found in bulbar palsy. Pseudobulbar palsy also tends to produce a state known as **pseudobulbar affect** in which the "shuffle" button has been pressed on someone's emotions, leading to rapid switching between laughing, crying, and other emotional extremes that do not correlate with how the person is actually feeling (which is why pseudobulbar affect is sometimes referred to as "emotional incontinence"). You can remember these two distinctions by thinking that the **EU** of ps**EU**dobulbar adds the **E**motional incontinence and the **U**pper motor neuron involvement.

> **Bulbar palsy** involves damage to **lower motor neurons** in the **lower half of the brainstem**, leading to **dysarthria** and **dysphagia**. **Pseudobulbar palsy** affects **upper motor neurons** in the same area and can lead to **emotional incontinence**.
>
> *The **EU** of ps**EU**dobulbar adds **E**motional incontinence and **U**pper motor neurons.*

Both bulbar and pseudobulbar palsy can occur on their own, although they tend to occur more often as a result of a stroke in the brainstem or as a manifestation of another neurodegenerative disease. Most people with the condition are older (in their 70s or 80s), with men being affected more than women. Treatment primarily involves **speech therapy**, with medications to target individual symptoms (such as muscle relaxants to lower spasticity or anticholinergic drugs to reduce drooling).

POST-POLIO SYNDROME

Polio is a viral illness that specifically targets the neurons in the **anterior horn** of the spinal cord, leading to muscle weakness. In the modern day, the availability of a polio vaccine has led to drastic reductions in the prevalence of this infection. However, someone who was infected with polio as a child may develop **post-polio syndrome** later in life (even decades after the initial illness!). Post-polio syndrome is like "polio's revenge," as the motor neurons in the anterior horn are attacked a second time, leading to diffuse muscle weakness. You can remember the association of polio with motor weakness by thinking that someone with **pole**-io can't **pole** vault.

Polio infection in the anterior horn.

Polio is a **viral infection** that targets the **anterior horn** of the spinal cord, leading to muscle weakness. **Post-polio syndrome** may develop later in life.

*Someone with **pole-io** can't **pole** vault.*

SPINAL MUSCULAR ATROPHY
Spinal muscular atrophy is a motor neuron disease affecting **lower motor neurons** exclusively (so upper motor neuron signs should be absent). There is a wide range of severity in this disease, although all but the most mild forms of the disorder will begin in **infancy and childhood**. This is because spinal muscular atrophy is an **autosomal recessive genetic disorder** in *all* cases (rather than only in some as with amyotrophic lateral sclerosis). You can remember these two key facts by adding two L's to the end of **S**pinal **M**uscular **A**trophy to form the word **SMALL**, with the L's standing for **L**ower motor neurons and **L**ittle ones (infants and children).

Spinal muscular atrophy is an **autosomal recessive** genetic disorder in which **lower motor neuron damage** leads to muscle weakness and wasting.

SMALL: Spinal Muscular Atrophy affects Lower motor neurons in Little ones.

The most severe form of the disorder, known as **Werdnig-Hoffmann disease** or "floppy baby syndrome," is the one you are most likely to be tested on. This tends to present within the first few months of life as a **sudden onset of complete muscle paralysis** with areflexia and poor muscle tone (the "floppiness" mentioned earlier). It is rapidly progressive, and many infants die within the first year even with adequate treatment. You can remember the association between Werdnig-H**off**mann disease and floppy baby syndrome by thinking of one person asking another, "Hey, doesn't that baby look a little floppy to you?" and the other person responding, "Yeah, it looks like someone turned that baby **off, man**."

The **most severe form of spinal muscular atrophy** is known as **Werdnig-Hoffmann disease** and is **fatal in most cases**.

"Yeah, it looks like someone turned that baby off, man."

An initial diagnosis of spinal muscular atrophy is based on the characteristic history of muscular weakness in an infant. However, genetic testing is required for a definitive diagnosis. The specific gene involved is **SMN1** which codes for the **SMN** (or **S**urvival of **M**otor **N**euron) protein. As its name implies, SMN protein is essential for the survival of motor neurons. When there is a defect in this gene, motor neurons become damaged and eventually die, leading directly to the loss of lower motor neurons that

defines this condition. Interestingly, there is another gene (known as SMN2) which codes for the exact same protein, functionally acting as a "back-up" copy. People differ in the number of SMN2 gene copies that they have, and it is this variation that accounts at least in part for the wide range of severity seen in spinal muscular atrophy. People who develop a severe form of the condition as infants (Werdnig-Hoffmann disease) tend to have only 1 or 2 copies of the SMN2 gene, while those who don't develop the disease until adulthood often have 4 or more of these back-up copies. These additional copies of the SMN2 gene help to delay the onset of the disease and give it a better prognosis.

As with other forms of motor neuron disease, there is **no cure**. Treatment is primarily focused on improving quality of life through various forms of therapy, including **physical, occupational, speech, and nutritional therapy**. Assistive devices such as orthotics can be helpful as well. Pharmacologically, a medication known as **nusinersen** has been shown to halt progression of the disease when injected directly into the cerebrospinal fluid (known as an **intrathecal injection**). Nusinersen acts by modifying the SMN2 gene in such a way that it is functionally converted into the SMN1 gene, effectively increasing the level of SMN protein in the central nervous system. While it has been shown to be effective, this medication is not without risk, including some pretty severe side effects. For this reason, a full exploration of the risks and benefits of treatment should be undertaken before beginning treatment with nusinersen. (It is also, as of the time of this book's publication, one of the most expensive drugs in the world, with the first year of treatment costing up to $750,000.)

PUTTING IT ALL TOGETHER

Motor neuron diseases are a diverse group of conditions that are unified by the fact that they all attack motor neurons preferentially over other types of nerve tissue. However, within that framework there is wide variation in what type of motor neurons are affected (upper, lower, or both) and in what parts of the body. **A**myotrophic Latera**L** sclerosis is the prototype motor neuron disease and attacks motor neurons **ALL** over the body. **Primary lateral sclerosis** and **progressive muscular atrophy** are two less severe variants of amyotrophic lateral sclerosis that affect exclusively upper and lower motor neurons, respectively (remember **PuLL-up** and **Progressive** trying to sell you **lower** rates on auto insurance!). **Bulbar palsy** and **pseudobulbar palsy** each involve damage to the motor tracts of the medulla, with bulbar palsy affecting lower motor neuron and ps**EU**dobulbar palsy hitting **U**pper motor neurons (as well as causing **E**motional incontinence). While **polio** is rare today due to vaccines, you may still encounter post-polio syndrome in people who had the infection earlier in life (in which case they wouldn't be able to **pole** vault). Finally, **S**pinal **M**uscular **A**trophy is a genetic disorder that tends to affect **L**ower motor neurons in **L**ittle ones (remember **SMALL!**) and with varying degree of severity.

REVIEW QUESTIONS

1. A 48 y/o F living in Manhattan notices that over the past year she is having increasing difficulty walking up the stairs to her apartment, so she decides to see her primary care nurse practitioner. In the meantime, she notices increasing difficulty with some everyday activities including squeezing shampoo out of the bottle and scooping ice cream out of the carton. On exam, she appears alert with no cognitive deficits. Her cranial nerves are intact. No sensory deficits are noted in any modality. Motor strength is decreased to 4/5 in all extremities, with particular difficulties in raising her arms past her shoulders. Deep tendon reflexes are intact throughout. Her gait is slowed but otherwise normal. Her Romberg sign is negative. On a follow-up visit several months later, her weakness has progressed to the point where she is unable to walk without assistance. There are signs of muscle atrophy in both arms and legs. Her deep tendon reflexes are exaggerated in her right arm and left leg but are absent in her left arm and right leg. The Babinski sign is positive bilaterally. An MRI is ordered which shows the following:

The patient wants to know about treatment. Which of the following is the most accurate statement?
    A. "No treatment is needed. This will get better on its own."
    B. "This is a treatable condition. As long as you stay on the medication you will likely make a full recovery."
    C. "Our goal is to help you live as long as possible, and only medications can help with that."
    D. "Medication can help with some of the symptoms, but really our focus should be on physical and speech therapy."
    E. "I'm very sorry, but there is no treatment for this disease."
    F. None of the above

2. (Continued from previous question.) The patient's disease continues to progress, and she passes away less than a year later. Which of the following is the most likely cause of death for this patient?
   A. Mechanical fall resulting in head trauma
   B. Aspiration of food into the airway
   C. Congestive heart failure
   D. Respiratory failure
   E. Systemic infection
   F. Malignancy

3. A 65 y/o F with no past medical history sees a neurologist out of concern that her arms are getting weaker. Exam reveals 4/5 weakness of the upper extremities bilaterally but full strength in the lower extremities. At a follow-up visit one month later, her arm strength has decreased to 3/5, and she now shows 4/5 weakness in both legs. Electromyography reveals fibrillations with occasional fasciculations. Over the course of the next several years, her muscle strength continued to deteriorate. A repeat exam 2 years later shows significant wasting of muscle tissues. Which of the following is most likely to be seen?
   A. Extension of the toes in response to stroking of the foot on exam
   B. Detectable mutation on genetic testing
   C. Neuronal loss in the anterior horns of the spinal cord on autopsy
   D. Degeneration of the corticospinal tract on autopsy
   E. Atrophy of the motor cortex on autopsy

4. A 4 m/o F is brought to the emergency department after 2 days of cough, fever, and difficulty breathing. Her mother notes that over the past month the patient has been less active than before, and for the past week she would go limp in her arms "like a doll" when picked up. On exam, the infant is in clear respiratory distress but shows little movement of intercostal muscles. There is generalized hypotonia throughout her body. Saliva is seen running down out of the corner of her mouth. The patient is admitted to the hospital but passes away from aspiration pneumonia several days later. Which of the following mechanisms explains the patient's presentation?
   A. Autosomal dominant mutation resulting in upper motor neuron damage
   B. Autosomal dominant mutation resulting in lower motor neuron damage
   C. Autosomal recessive mutation resulting in upper motor neuron damage
   D. Autosomal recessive mutation resulting in lower motor neuron damage
   E. Sporadic disease resulting in upper motor neuron damage
   F. Sporadic disease resulting in lower motor neuron damage

1. **The best answer is F.** The presence of both upper and lower motor neuron signs in this case are highly suggestive of amyotrophic lateral sclerosis, as is the rapidly progressive nature of the disease. The MRI shows abnormalities in both the motor cortex and basal ganglia which is consistent with upper motor neuron involvement. Amyotrophic lateral sclerosis is not curable, but treatment can be beneficial (answer E). In particular, a medication called riluzole can be helpful, with most guidelines suggesting that this medication should be started as soon as possible after an initial diagnosis. However, medications are not the only option that can prolong life, with non-invasive ventilation also being effective for this outcome (answer C). While physical and speech therapy is an important cornerstone of amyotrophic lateral sclerosis management and should be included as part of the treatment plan, it is not accurate to say that medication only helps with symptoms, as riluzole has been shown to prolong survival by several months (answer D). However, the benefits of the medication should not be oversold, as it will not enable patients to make a full recovery (answer B). Amyotrophic lateral sclerosis is not a self-limiting condition, and with or without treatment most patients will die from this disease (answer A). For these reasons, none of the listed statements would be appropriate at this time.

2. **The best answer is D.** The most common cause of death in amyotrophic lateral sclerosis is respiratory failure. While the diaphragm is often spared early in the disease, as amyotrophic lateral sclerosis progresses it often begins to involve respiratory muscles as well, necessitating respiratory support. Aspiration pneumonia can occur in amyotrophic lateral sclerosis as well, but it is not the most common cause of death (answer B).

3. **The best answer is C.** This vignette describes a case of progressive muscular atrophy, a motor neuron disease that primarily affects lower motor neurons. Due to sparing of upper motor neurons, the Babinski sign should be absent (answer A), and degeneration of upper motor neurons in regions including the motor cortex (answer E) and corticospinal tract (answer D) should not be observed. Instead, the primary areas of neuronal loss should be observed in peripheral motor nerves which have their cell bodies in the anterior horn of the spinal cord. Progressive muscular atrophy has not been shown to have a genetic component in the same way that some cases of amyotrophic lateral sclerosis do (answer B).

4. **The best answer is D.** This describes a case of spinal muscular atrophy type I (also known as Werdnig-Hoffman disease) which presents with a sudden onset of generalized hypotonia and other lower motor neuron signs in an infant. Upper motor neurons are not involved in spinal muscular atrophy (answers A and C). Spinal muscular atrophy is an autosomal recessive disease, not an autosomal dominant disease (answers A and B) or a sporadic disease (answers E and F).

17 MOVEMENT DISORDERS

We've looked at diseases of the muscle, the neuromuscular junction, and the motor neuron. Now, we finally arrive at the upper-most part of the motor pathway: the **brain** itself. As we have learned in our initial study of neuroanatomy, the part of the brain that is most involved in movement is the **basal ganglia**, and indeed many of the conditions we will talk about in this chapter involve one or more parts of the basal ganglia directly.

Movement disorders are a **highly heterogeneous** group of conditions, and at first there can seem to be few unifying principles connecting one movement disorder to another. However, at their core all movement disorders boil down to one of two problems: either they involve **difficulty initiating movement** (resulting in *hypo*kinetic movement disorders) or they present as **trouble with stopping movement** (leading to *hyper*kinetic movement disorders). We will start off by discussing hypokinetic movement disorders, the prototype of which is **Parkinson's disease**. From there, we will move on to hyperkinetic movement disorders, including both broad categories (such as various forms of **tremors** and **dystonias**) as well as specific conditions such as **Huntington's disease**, **Wilson's disease**, and **hemiballismus**. (There are a few other diseases that are sometimes classified as movement disorders, including tic disorders and restless legs syndrome, that are not covered here. Refer to the relevant chapters of *Memorable Psychiatry* for an overview of these!)

PARKINSON'S DISEASE

Any discussion of hypokinetic movement disorders needs to start with **Parkinson's disease**, as it is the prototypical disorder involving difficulty initiating movement (and the one you will need to know best both on boards and for wards!). However, there are also several other conditions that feature many of the same signs and symptoms of Parkinson's disease but add their own unique twists. We will cover three of these **Parkinson-plus syndromes** after learning about "textbook" Parkinson's disease.

PARKINSON'S DISEASE

Parkinson's disease is a **neurodegenerative disorder** that primarily affects the motor system. Specifically, Parkinson's disease involves the death of dopaminergic neurons in the **substantia nigra**, leading to a general **dopamine deficit** in the brain. (Recall from Chapter 6 that the substantia nigra is located in the midbrain and is a major site of dopamine production.) A subregion of the substantia nigra known as the **pars compacta** appears to be hit the hardest in Parkinson's disease.

Dopamine plays an interesting role in movement. It doesn't *cause* motion per se (remember that it is the neurotransmitter acetylcholine that directly activates muscle cells at the neuromuscular junction). Rather, dopamine makes motion *more likely to happen* (similar to grease or WD40). When dopamine-producing cells begin to die, it is as if all the joints in the body lose their grease, and movements start to become difficult to initiate. You can remember the role of dopamine in this condition by thinking that **Pa**rkinson's **D**isease is what happens when do**Pa**mine is **D**epleted.

> **Parkinson's disease** involves the death of **dopamine-producing neurons** in the **substantia nigra**, particularly **the pars compacta**.
>
> *Parkinson's Disease is what happens when doPamine is Depleted.*

Dopamine depletion manifests in the slowed movements that are the hallmark of hypokinetic movement disorders. More than just slowing movements in general, loss of dopamine results in a specific combination of signs and symptoms known as **Parkinsonism**. There are four cardinal signs of Parkinsonism: **slowed or absent movement** (known as bradykinesia and akinesia, respectively), **tremor**, **rigidity**, and **postural instability**. You can remember these using the word **TRAP** which you can visualize as someone who has been **TRAP**ped inside of a statue.

T is for Tremor. Hold on, hold on, hold on... aren't we talking about movement disorders that are defined by too *little* movement? Then what is tremor doing here? This is our first clue that the pathophysiology of Parkinson's disease is much more complex than it appears at first, as the tremor seen in this condition does not appear to result directly from dopamine depletion. Regardless of the mechanism behind it, **tremor** is a common finding in this disease, and it is often one of the first signs to appear. A classic Parkinson's disease tremor has a few distinctive characteristics. First, it is typically a **resting tremor**, meaning that it is there most of the time but will disappear when someone initiates a voluntary movement. Second, it is a **slow tremor** (around 5 shakes per second). Third, it is often described as a "**pill-rolling**" tremor, as it almost looks as if the patient is continuously rolling a pill between their thumb and index finger.

R is for Rigidity. Someone with Parkinson's disease looks, well, *stiff*. Not only is movement slowed, but the disease seems to give the appearance of *actively resisting* movement due to the presence of increased muscle tone at rest. When you ask a patient to relax and then try to move their arms for them, you will often be met with some degree of resistance, either in a sustained way known as **lead-pipe rigidity** or in a ratchety *click-click-click* manner known as **cogwheel rigidity** (as it resembles the clicking of cogwheels or gears). Rigidity is often progressive in Parkinson's disease, being localized to just a few areas at first and then slowly taking over more of the body, almost as if the body is becoming **TRAP**ped in a statue. Rigidity also encompasses the muscles of the face, leading to a "frozen" or "mask-like" face that is devoid of emotional expression (as seen in the image below):

*Mask-like face in **Parkinson's disease**.*

A is for Akinesia and bradykinesia. Bradykinesia, or slowness of movement, is the hallmark sign of Parkinson's disease and is found in every case. The slowness involves all stages of a movement, including planning it, starting it, and completing it. When slowness becomes particularly severe, it can even lead to a total lack of movement known as **akinesia**. Slowness is particularly noticeable in the distinctive way that people with the disease walk, as they tend to walk slowly with their body flexed forward, barely bringing their feet off of the ground. Turning is often done slowly in small increments, almost like a heavy statue being turned through much effort. All of this gives a "shuffling" appearance to the patient's walk which is known as a **Parkinsonian gait** or **festination**. Notably, **arm swinging** is generally absent in one arm, almost as if the patient is walking around with one hand in an invisible pocket. Decreased arm swing is generally **unilateral** and **asymmetrical** at the beginning of the disease (although it may progress to being bilateral as the disease advances).

*A **Parkinsonian gait** with forward flexion of the body.*

P is for Postural instability. The final cardinal sign of Parkinson's disease is a distinct **lack of balance** which tends to emerge late in the disease. Indeed, the number of falls that someone experiences is often a marker of how severe their condition is.

> The **four cardinal signs of Parkinson's disease** are **bradykinesia, tremor, rigidity,** and **postural instability.**
>
> Someone with **Parkinson's disease** becomes **TRAP**ped inside of a statue:
> **T**remor
> **R**igidity
> **A**kinesia and bradykinesia
> **P**ostural instability

Outside of the four cardinal signs, Parkinson's disease can also present with a variety of **neuropsychiatric phenomena**. These include **cognitive changes** ranging from mild impairment to outright dementia; a high rate of comorbid psychiatric symptoms such as **depression** and **anxiety**; **psychotic symptoms** including paranoid delusions and auditory hallucinations; and **sleep changes** such as fatigue and insomnia. While it was long thought that Parkinson's disease primarily affected only the *somatic* aspect of the efferent nervous system, some patients with the disease can develop **autonomic instability** as well, including changes in blood pressure, gastrointestinal motility, bladder function, and sweat production.

Parkinson's disease tends to affect **older people**, with an average age at diagnosis of over 60 years. While it is known that Parkinson's disease results from the death of dopaminergic neurons in the substantia nigra, what *isn't* known is why these neurons start dying in the first place (although a history of head injury or exposure to specific chemicals does appear to raise the risk of developing the disease slightly). Diagnosis is typically made on the basis of clinical signs and symptoms, although head imaging can help to support the diagnosis.

MRI showing degeneration of the **substantia nigra** *in a patient with* **Parkinson's disease**.

There is **no cure** for Parkinson's disease, so treatment is targeted towards reducing the symptom severity and increasing one's quality of life. Exercise as well as **physical, occupational, and speech therapy** all can have beneficial effects. The most widely used medication for treating Parkinson's disease is a combination drug known as **carbidopa-levodopa**. Levodopa is a precursor to dopamine which is able to cross the blood-brain barrier and be converted into dopamine, effectively helping to replace some of the dopamine that has been lost in the brain. (Dopamine itself is available as a drug; however, because it cannot cross the blood-brain barrier, it is not effective for treating Parkinson's disease.) Carbidopa, which makes up the other half of the drug, does not turn into dopamine itself but instead plays a supporting role by inhibiting the conversion of levodopa into dopamine in places *outside* the central nervous system. This not only helps more of the levodopa get to the brain but also prevents excess dopamine from causing unpleasant side effects (like severe nausea and vomiting) in the rest of the body. You can remember the function of each component of carbidopa-levodopa by thinking that **car**bidopa is the **car** that drives levodopa to its destination.

Carbidopa-levodopa is used to treat **Parkinson's disease**. **Levodopa** is the **active ingredient** while **carbidopa** helps to **prevent peripheral conversion** of levodopa.

Carbidopa is the car that drives levodopa to its destination (the brain).

Even with carbidopa around, carbidopa-levodopa can still cause some pretty obnoxious side effects. For this reason, a different class of drugs known as **dopamine agonists** (which are less effective than carbidopa-levodopa but also tend to cause less severe side effects) can be preferred in some cases, especially early on in the disease when symptoms are not as severe. In rare cases, a **deep brain stimulator** may be surgically implanted into the basal ganglia to help improve symptoms. Even with treatment, however, Parkinson's disease remains a stubbornly progressive disease, with more dopaminergic neurons being lost as time passes, leading to increasingly severe symptoms and greater functional impairment. Many patients end up entirely dependent upon others, and life expectancy is significantly reduced.

MULTISYSTEM ATROPHY

The first of the **Parkinson-plus syndromes** we will talk about is **multisystem atrophy** (also known as Shy-Drager syndrome). Essentially, multisystem atrophy can be described as "Parkinson's *plus* autonomic and cerebellar dysfunction." It presents similarly to Parkinson's disease, including the four cardinal signs of Parkinsonism. In contrast to Parkinson's disease (where autonomic dysfunction is either absent or plays a small role), multisystem atrophy prominently features signs and symptoms of **autonomic nervous system dysfunction** such as abnormal blood pressure, loss of sexual function, excessive sweating, dry mouth, and lack of bladder control. Ataxia and other **cerebellar signs** are often present as well.

PROGRESSIVE SUPRANUCLEAR PALSY

Progressive supranuclear palsy is another Parkinson-plus syndrome. This time, it can be thought of as "Parkinson's *plus* abnormal eye movements." It shares with "textbook" Parkinson's disease both motor deficits (including abnormal gait, loss of balance, and frequently bumping into other people or objects) and dementia-like deficits in memory and cognition. However, progressive supranuclear palsy uniquely involves a **downward gaze palsy** or an inability for the extraocular muscles to point

the eyes down. To remember the association of **P**rogressive **S**upranuclear **P**alsy with a downward gaze palsy, think of someone who is asked to **P**lease **S**top **P**eering. What is the first thing they do? Try to avert their gaze by looking down.

Progressive supranuclear palsy is a Parkinson-plus syndrome resulting in **movement deficits, cognitive impairment**, and **downward gaze palsy**.

*Someone who is asked to **P**lease **S**top **P**eering immediately tries to **look down**.*

CORTICOBASAL DEGENERATION

The final Parkinson-plus syndrome we will talk about is **corticobasal degeneration** which, like progressive supranuclear palsy, features both **motor and cognitive deficits** including slow movements, difficulty walking, memory loss, and trouble speaking. One sign that is quite specific for corticobasal degeneration is **alien hand syndrome** which occurs in around 60% of people with this disorder. People with alien hand syndrome will fail to spontaneously move one of their hands due to a sensation that their limbs are foreign to them. Notably, this is often unilateral, affecting only one hand.

Overall, you should consider one of these Parkinson-plus syndrome when many of the core signs of Parkinson's disease are there *plus* a few that don't quite match (whether that is autonomic dysfunction and cerebellar signs in multisystem atrophy, downward gaze palsy in progressive supranuclear palsy, or alien hand syndrome in corticobasal degeneration). Compared to people with "textbook" Parkinson's disease, patients with Parkinson-plus syndromes tend to have a more **rapidly progressive course** and receive less benefit from treatments like carbidopa-levodopa.

CHOREA

For the rest of this chapter, we will shift our focus from *hypo*kinetic movement disorders like Parkinson's disease towards *hyper*kinetic movement disorders. These conditions are all unified by the presence of too much movement, whether that takes the form of large dance-like movements as in **chorea**, involuntary shaking as in **tremors**, or a sustained muscle contraction as in **dystonias**. We'll focus on chorea first, the prototype of which is seen in Huntington's disease.

HUNTINGTON'S DISEASE

Huntington's disease is a movement disorder that presents clinically as progressively worsening **movement and behavioral problems**. The hallmark movement abnormality seen in Huntington's disease is **chorea**, or a series of quick, jerky, flailing movements that resembles dancing (in fact, the word is Greek for "dance," as in "*chore*ography"). The movements of chorea are not under voluntary control, and they occur without any effort on the part of the patient.

While chorea is the hallmark sign of Huntington's disease, the disorder can also cause changes in motor abilities, cognition, behavior, and personality. Indeed, it is these latter changes that are often *most* disabling to the patient and distressing to their families. Chorea is typically the first sign to appear, but soon other **motor deficits** (such as difficulty walking, talking, chewing, and swallowing) become noticeable as well. This will often progress to the point where the patient becomes incapable of coordinated movement. **Cognitive disabilities**, including memory loss and difficulty planning, begin to appear and slowly become more prominent so that, by the time of death, most patients meet criteria for clinical dementia. On a behavioral level, both **impulsive and compulsive behaviors** can emerge, including aggression, substance abuse, gambling, and uninhibited sexual behavior.

> The **hallmark sign of Huntington's disease** is a dance-like movement known as **chorea**, although other **motor and neuropsychiatric deficits** are seen as well.
>
> Think *"chorea"* like in *"choreography,"* or the art of designing a dance.

The first signs of the disorder often begin in **adulthood** between the ages of 30 and 50, with most patients dying within 20 years of diagnosis (often due to aspiration pneumonia, as the ability to swallow becomes increasingly impaired). However, up to a quarter of patients attempt suicide, making this one of the largest causes of death in this group and reinforcing the severity of the psychiatric dimension of this disease.

Huntington's disease is an **autosomal dominant genetic disorder** involving mutations in the **huntingtin gene** on **chromosome 4**. A significant portion of this gene is made up of the **trinucleotide repeat CAG**. It is normal to have some amount of this repeat sequence. However, in people who have too many CAG repeats (more than 35), the gene becomes affected and begins to produce a mutant version of the huntingtin protein that damages the brain and leads to neuronal death, particularly in the **caudate** and other parts of the striatum. The number of CAG repeats is directly correlated with the severity of the disease, with people who have 36 to 39 copies often showing a later onset and slower progression than people with more than 40 (who may show signs of the disease as early as age 20, with subsequent rapid progression). However, when passing the gene on to one's offspring, the number of CAG repeats may spontaneously increase. This means that people with few or no symptoms (who may have less than 36 copies) can still end up passing a more severe version of the disease on to their children if the number of CAG repeats increases. This steady increase in the number of repeats resulting in greater disease severity over successive generations is known as **anticipation**. It is more likely for CAG repeats to increase during spermatogenesis than oogenesis, so fathers are more likely to pass on a mutated version of the gene to their children than mothers.

These concepts are crucial to understanding Huntington's disease, so let's try to link them all together. Imagine a young man who sees a beautiful girl on the first day of school and develops a crush. A few days later, he tells one of his new friends about his love interest. His friend reacts with a horrified expression and says, "You **caun't date** Huntington's **daughter**! Her **father** is very **dominant**. If he finds out, he'll hunt **4** you and put you in a **CAG**e." This mnemonic ties together the primary location of cell damage (the **caudate**), the concept of anticipation (with **fathers** being more likely to pass a more severe version of their disease on to their children), the autosomal **dominant** pattern of inheritance, and the location of the **CAG** repeats on chromosome **4**.

> **Huntington's disease** involves a **CAG trinucleotide repeat** on **chromosome 4**, leading to a **mutated huntingtin protein** that damages neurons in the **caudate**.
>
> *"You* ***caun't date*** *(caudate)* ***Huntington's daughter****! Her* ***father*** *is very (autosomal)* ***dominant****. He'll hunt* ***4*** *you and put you in a* ***CAG****e (CAG repeat on chromosome 4)."*

As with most movement disorders, there is **no cure** for Huntington's disease. Treatment is directed towards improving the patient's quality of life and level of functional ability using **physical and occupational therapy** (such as preparing foods to be easier to swallow). A medication known as **tetrabenazine** can be prescribed to reduce the severity of chorea, although the mechanism by which it does this is unknown. Genetic counseling can be offered to people with the disease who are considering having children, although because the first signs of the disease often do not appear until after the age of 30, some may have had children already.

HEMIBALLISMUS
We've talked about hemiballismus before when we first introduced the **Su**bthalamic **N**ucleus in Chapter 4 (remember the throwing arm movements like on **Su**nday **N**ight football?), but it's worth briefly mentioning it in the context of movement disorders. While we didn't know the term back then, these ballistic movements are essentially a severe form of chorea, with the small movements seen in Huntington's disease turning into large, dramatic swinging motions. Hemiballismus occurs most often as a result of an injury to the brain (such as a stroke or a traumatic head injury).

TREMOR

The word **tremor** refers to an **involuntary rhythmic shaking** of the hands or other body parts. A tremor is not always a sign of pathology. For example, most people will shiver when they are cold, which is essentially an adaptive form of tremor. In other cases, tremor can be a manifestation of anxiety, agitation, or other emotional states. Certain substances, including both prescription and recreational drugs, can cause tremor (like drinking too much caffeine in a single sitting). However, in other cases tremor can be a sign of a specific disease process, like in Parkinson's disease. When it occurs on its own to a severe extent, tremor can also be considered a hyperkinetic movement disorder all by itself.

Because of the many possible causes of tremors, it can be helpful to break them down into a few distinct categories. There are four main forms of tremor that we will cove here: physiologic tremor, resting tremor, action tremor, and intention tremor.

PHYSIOLOGIC TREMOR

Many people have some degree of tremor that is barely noticeable and generally doesn't lead to any distress or disability. This is known as a **physiologic tremor**. A physiologic tremor tends to occur most when a particular body part is held upright against gravity for a prolonged period of time (such as a child raising their hand to go to the bathroom). In many cases, the tremor is so slight as to be barely noticeable. You can see your own tremor better by taking a piece of paper in your hand and holding your arm straight out in front of you. You should be able to see small twitches in the paper, especially if you hold it long enough.

RESTING TREMOR

A **resting tremor** (also known as a Parkinsonian tremor) occurs when the body is not actively moving. We've talked about a resting tremor previously in the context of Parkinson's disease, and while there are other possible causes of a resting tremor, as a general rule of thumb the presence of a resting tremor should make you immediately think of Parkinson's disease, especially if it is accompanied by other signs such as muscle rigidity or bradykinesia. Other causes of Parkinsonism (such as certain dopamine-blocking medications) can lead to a resting tremor as well.

ACTION TREMOR

An **action tremor** is one that worsens when you try to use that particular part of the body. For example, you can place a pencil in someone's hand and it will remain still, but as soon as they try to write with the pencil their hand will begin to shake. (Knowing this, ask yourself who you would rather have operating on you: a surgeon with Parkinson's disease, whose tremor disappears with voluntary movement, or a surgeon with essential tremor?)

The most common cause of an action tremor is an idiopathic condition known as an **essential tremor**. Essential tremor is the **most common movement disorder**, with up to 5% of the population having it. It generally affects the hands and upper extremities, although less often it can affect other parts of the body as well. There is no known cause, although genes appear to be involved in around half of all cases, with transmission generally following an **autosomal dominant** pattern.

Essential tremor is a progressive condition, with most cases being mild at the initial onset but then progressing to become more and more severe as time passes. Because an essential tremor interferes with one's ability to carry out intentional actions such as writing, it can be quite disabling in severe forms. Consider the image below of someone who attempted to draw the figure on the left:

Treatment of essential tremor generally involves use of **beta-blockers** such as propranolol which are effective at reducing the severity of the tremor, with few side effects. Interestingly, **alcohol** is quite effective at reducing tremors as well, and a patient's report that their tremor improves after a few drinks is highly diagnostic of an essential tremor. However, alcohol is not an appropriate form of long-term treatment for essential tremor due to the brief duration of action, rebound effects, and risk of alcohol addiction!

INTENTION TREMOR

Finally, an **intention tremor** (also known as a **cerebellar tremor**) is one that tends to occur at the *end* of an intentional action. For example, if someone is reaching their hand out to press a button, the beginning of this action may be smooth, but by the end (with their arm completely outstretched) a tremor may appear. (This is in contrast to an action tremor in which the tremor would be present *throughout* the duration of the action, including its beginning). An intention tremor is closely associated with damage to the **cerebellum** and is commonly associated with other cerebellar signs, including ataxia, nystagmus, and difficulty speaking.

DYSTONIA

Dystonias are **sustained muscle contractions** that lead the patient to adopt a specific posture, as seen below. If you've ever experienced a dead leg or Charley horse, then you know that sustained involuntary muscle contractions can be quite painful! Like tremors, dystonias can either be a manifestation of another pathological process, a side effect of particular substances, or a diagnosis in and of itself. For that reason, the presence of a dystonia often requires further evaluation.

When a dystonia happens recurrently without any clear cause, it is known as a **primary focal dystonia** ("primary" for the fact that they are not happening secondary to another cause and "focal" because they tend to affect one part of the body in particular). These are generally named by their location, such as **blepharospasm** (dystonia of the eyelids), **cervical dystonia** (dystonia of the neck), **writer's cramp** (dystonia of the hand), and **spasmodic dysphonia** (dystonia of the vocal cords). Dystonias can be incredibly impairing, and many people have been unable to continue careers as musicians, engineers, or other occupations due to the onset of a dystonia. Local injections of **botulinum toxin** can help to relax the muscle and effectively treat the dystonia, although the effect is not permanent, so the injections must be repeated periodically. Medications that block acetylcholine can be used as well.

WILSON'S DISEASE

The final movement disorder we will talk about is **Wilson's disease**, or an inherited **defect of copper metabolism** that results in copper deposits progressively accruing throughout the body. A certain amount of copper in the body is normal. However, when copper collects in excessive amounts, it can damage organs. The **liver** is particularly sensitive to copper, and a variety of liver-related conditions (including cirrhosis, ascites, asterixis, esophageal varices, and hepatic encephalopathy) are common in people who have Wilson's disease. The **brain** is also quite sensitive, with the putamen and basal ganglia being particularly affected. For this reason, movement abnormalities including **ataxia, bradykinesia, chorea, dysarthria,** and **tremor** are all commonly seen in Wilson's disease. Given that both types of abnormal movement can be seen, Wilson's disease resists easy classification as either a hypokinetic or hyperkinetic movement disorder.

On a clinical level, your primary clue that Wilson's disease is occurring is when a **young patient** presents with signs of a movement disorder (as the disease tends to begin in childhood or adolescence). Given that most movement disorders primarily affect *older* adults, any movement disorder in a *young* individual should put Wilson's disease high on the differential!

Laboratory testing can often reveal evidence of abnormal copper metabolism, including **increased serum copper** and **decreased ceruloplasmin** (which is the major copper-carrying protein in the blood). When levels of copper become high enough, it can deposit into various tissues in a way that is even visible to the naked eye. In particular, copper has a tendency to deposit in the cornea of the eye, leading to the appearance of **Kayser-Fleischer rings** that are *pathognomonic* for Wilson's disease (meaning that if you see these, you can be 100% confident in your diagnosis of Wilson's disease).

*Kayser-Fleischer rings in a patient with **Wilson's disease**.*

Wilson's disease is an **autosomal recessive genetic disorder** in which the ATP7B gene, which codes for an enzyme that transports copper into bile, becomes mutated and produces a defective enzyme. The affected gene is on **chromosome 13** (write WI, turn the W 90° to the left, switch it with the I, and you have 13).

There is no cure for Wilson's disease. However, people with the disease can lead relatively normal lives by adhering to a **low-copper diet**. Medication treatments include **penicillamine** which binds copper in the blood and causes it to be excreted in the urine, thus reducing copper levels in the body. **Zinc acetate** can also be used to maintain low copper levels by preventing the absorption of copper in the gastrointestinal tract. As with other movement disorders, physical and occupational therapy can be helpful for managing the neurologic effects.

To summarize, **Wilson's disease** is an Inherited error of copper metabolism leading to Liver disease, Serum abnormalities (including increased copper and decreased ceruloplasmin), Ocular findings (Kayser-Fleischer rings), and movement-related Neurologic signs including ataxia, bradykinesia, chorea, dysarthria, and tremor. You can remember this by thinking of a **cop** named **WILSON** who is holding his hand out, like the flapping hands of a patient with asterixis due to liver failure.

Wilson's disease is an **autosomal recessive genetic disorder** resulting in **defective copper metabolism** which manifests as **liver failure** and **abnormal movement**.

*Think of **WILSON the Cop** holding his hand out:*
Wilson's disease
Inherited (autosomal recessive)
Liver disease
Serum abnormalities (↑ copper, ↓ ceruloplasmin)
Ocular findings (Kayser-Fleischer rings)
Neurologic signs (movement disorders)
Copper's the culprit!

PUTTING IT ALL TOGETHER

When evaluating a movement disorder, your first priority should be to determine whether the movement disorder is *hypo*kinetic or *hyper*kinetic. There is really only one major form of hypokinetic movement disorder to know (**Parkinson's disease** and its related conditions), while there are a few hyperkinetic movement disorders you may encounter (**chorea, tremors**, and **dystonias**). Wilson's disease straddles both worlds and may present with either hypokinetic signs, hyperkinetic signs, or both.

When diagnosing a hyperkinetic movement disorder, look at what kind of movement is in excess. Is it a constant shaking? A sudden sustained contraction? A wild swinging of the arms? While all these would be united under the banner of "hyperkinetic movement disorders," on a clinical level they will present quite differently. As with any neurologic condition, use the neurologic exam to conduct a structured assessment, then combine your findings with what you know about the patient's history to come up with a clinical diagnosis.

REVIEW QUESTIONS

1. A 30 y/o F comes to see her neurologist for a follow-up visit. One year ago she began having abnormal movements of the arms and face that she describes as "jerky" and "writhing." These movements began in a mild form but have progressively worsened over time. During the interview, she is seen constantly moving her head and hands in fluid motions with no detectable purpose to an outside observer. When asked, she is unable to stop these movements and stay completely still. Her speech is slurred and difficult to understand at times. She is currently married and has two children aged 3 and 5. Her husband accompanies her to the visit, although they are currently separated. The husband says that she is "a totally different person now" and wonders if she has "bipolar" because of her "constant mood swings." Which of the following is *least* likely to be present?
   A. Positive family history of the disease
   B. Deficits in executive functioning on cognitive testing
   C. Motor weakness in the limbs and arms
   D. Difficulty completing heel-to-toe walking
   E. Atrophy in the region of the basal ganglia on MRI
   F. All of the above are likely to be present

2. (Continued from previous question.) Which of the following is most predictive of her prognosis?
   A. Number of trinucleotide repeats on genetic testing
   B. Extent of atrophy seen on neuroimaging
   C. Number of affected family members
   D. Severity of motor weakness in the limbs
   E. Age of onset at 29 years
   F. None of the above are predictive of prognosis for this disease

3. A 61 y/o M is brought to the doctor by his wife who reports that he "looks depressed." He previously worked as an elementary school teacher and won several awards for his work with children. However, over the past 6 months his wife reports that "it's like he's stopped existing." During the interview, he rarely responds with more than one or two words at a time, saying he feels "fine" and that he "dunno" why he is here. He is diagnosed with major depressive disorder and started on an antidepressant. When he returns for a follow-up visit one month later, his presentation is largely unchanged. His wife says, "The drugs you prescribed didn't do much. If anything, they made things worse." The patient now rarely takes care of himself and will only eat if food is put in front of him. On exam, the patient has a tremor in his right hand that goes away when the doctor asks him to shake hands. There is positive cogwheel rigidity in the right arm. Rapid alternating movements are intact but slowed. When asked to walk, his gait is slow and unsteady, with a forward-leaning posture as seen below:

Which of the following regions is most likely affected?
A.   Motor cortex
B.   Caudate nuclei
C.   Internal capsule
D.   Substantia nigra
E.   Red nuclei
F.   Periaqueductal grey

4.   (Continued from previous question.) The patient is started on pramipexole, a dopamine agonist. However, after several months with little benefit from this drug, he is switched to carbidopa-levodopa. What is the function of carbidopa?
A.   Stimulating dopamine receptors in the central nervous system
B.   Stimulating the release of dopamine in the central nervous system
C.   Inhibiting dopamine receptors in the central nervous system
D.   Stimulating peripheral conversion of levodopa to dopamine
E.   Inhibiting peripheral conversion of levodopa to dopamine
F.   Inhibiting dopamine receptors in the peripheral nervous system
G.   Inhibiting the release of dopamine in the peripheral nervous system
H.   None of the above

1. **The best answer is C.** This patient likely has Huntington's disease as evidenced by the presence of chorea and other characteristic signs and symptoms including mood changes. While chorea is often the initial and most noticeable sign of the disorder, Huntington's disease does not only affect movement but can also cause cognitive impairment (answer B) and unsteady gait (answer D). As an autosomal dominant disease, there is often a positive family history (answer A). Atrophy of the caudate nuclei occurs and can be seen on MRI (answer E). While Huntington's disease affects movement, it does not necessarily affect motor strength, and many patients with this disorder have intact strength on exam, even if they are unable to stop their chorea while doing so.

2. **The best answer is A.** The number of CAG repeats in the huntingtin gene on chromosome 4 is directly correlated with the severity of Huntington's disease, as people who have more than 40 repeats are often more severely affected than those with 36 or fewer repeats. The extent of brain atrophy and the age at onset are best seen as manifestations, rather than predictors, of a more severe disease (answers B and E). The number of affected family members is driven more by genetics and chance than disease severity (answer C). As in the previous question, motor weakness is not a core feature of this disease (answer D).

3. **The best answer is D.** This vignette describes a classic presentation of Parkinson's disease including bradykinesia, muscle rigidity, a resting tremor, a mask-like face, and a festinating gait. Parkinson's disease is associated with loss of dopaminergic neurons in the substantia nigra of the midbrain. Disorders related to the motor cortex or the internal capsule would instead present with motor weakness (answers A and C). Damage to the caudate nuclei is seen in Huntington's disease (answer B). The red nuclei is also found in the midbrain but plays a relatively small role in movement in humans (answer E). The periaqueductal grey, another resident of the midbrain, is largely involved in pain perception (answer F).

4. **The best answer is E.** Levodopa is the active ingredient in carbidopa-levodopa. It crosses the blood–brain barrier and is converted to dopamine which helps to offset the loss of dopaminergic neurons. However, levodopa is also converted to dopamine in the rest of the body as well where it can cause side effects including nausea and vomiting. Carbidopa acts as an inhibitor of peripheral conversion to dopamine and thereby helps to reduce these side effects. Stimulating peripheral conversion to dopamine would have the opposite effect and would likely *increase* side effect burden (answer D). Carbidopa does not act in the central nervous system (answers A—C), nor does it act on peripheral dopamine release or on receptors directly (answers F and G).

18 SEIZURES

A **seizure** (also known as a convulsion or a fit) is a period of **excessive neuronal activity in the brain,** like an "explosion" of neurons all firing in unison. Seizures can have dramatic effects throughout the body, including muscle contractions and changes in consciousness. They can occur as a result of specific stresses on the body (such as a fever, infection, or electrolyte imbalance), be caused by the effects of particular substances (such as alcohol withdrawal), or occur completely on their own. When seizures occur repeatedly with no clear cause, they are diagnosed as **epilepsy.**

Seizures can occur in a variety of different "flavors," and the key to correctly diagnosing and treating epilepsy is to be able to distinguish between the various forms that you will see. For this reason, our first priority will be to learn some new vocabulary so that we can communicate clearly about what we are observing when a patient presents with a seizure. We can then use these differences in presentation to come to a more specific diagnosis and be able to match that to the best treatment. It's worth pointing out that the vocabulary used to describe seizures has changed over time, so you may see different words used to describe the same thing (for example, a "complex partial" seizure is now called a "focal-onset impaired-awareness" seizure). In this book, we will try to adhere to the updated terminology whenever possible. However, there's no denying that the older terms are simpler to use and understand, so you are likely to still encounter them on a regular basis.

Similar to a stroke, a seizure can take on many forms depending on which parts of the brain are affected. A **generalized seizure** is one that encompasses both the left *and* right hemispheres of the brain. On a clinical level, the key sign that a seizure has become generalized is when the patient develops *loss of consciousness* (as the entire brain is seizing and is unable to normally process conscious information). In contrast, seizures that affect only particular parts of the brain are known as **focal** or **focal-onset seizures** (previously called "partial" seizures). Because a focal seizure is localized to a *single* hemisphere, the patient generally remains conscious throughout the episode.

It's important to know that focal seizures can turn into generalized ones, like a small fire that blazes out of control and begins spreading throughout the entire forest. This is known as a **focal to bilateral seizure** (or formerly a "secondarily generalized" seizure). In fact, focal to bilateral seizures are the rule rather than the exception, as around two-thirds of generalized seizures begin as focal seizures and then secondarily generalize.

The majority of seizures are **convulsive seizures**, meaning that they affect the motor system and lead to uncontrollable muscle contractions. Convulsive seizures themselves come in a few types, including **tonic, clonic**, and **myoclonic** (each of which we will talk about soon). In contrast, **non-convulsive** seizures spare the muscles but can cause abnormalities in other areas such as **sensation** or **attention**.

All seizures consist of a period of excessive neuronal activity known as the **ictal phase**. The ictal phase generally lasts anywhere from a few seconds to a few minutes. Seizure activity lasting for more than 5 minutes is known as **status epilepticus** and can represent a life-threatening emergency. Following certain forms of seizures, some people enter into a **postictal state** characterized by drowsiness, confusion, and disorientation. The postictal state usually lasts between 10 and 15 minutes.

Seizures can be either **provoked** (occurring as the direct result of a particular physiologic stress) or **unprovoked** (striking "out of the blue" with no clear cause). People who *only* have seizures in response to specific stimuli (for example, seeing flashing lights or hearing specific sounds) are said to have **reflex seizures**.

Some people experience certain phenomena that clue them into the fact that a seizure is about to occur. This is known as an **aura** and is more common with focal seizures than generalized ones. The specific clues that make up an aura vary from person to person. For some, it may take the form of seeing bright lights; for others, it may involve a distinct odor; for still others, an aura isn't a specific thing but rather a vague premonition (like a "Spidey sense") that a seizure is about to occur.

Okay! That's a lot of new words. Now that we have a vocabulary with which to describe seizures, let's talk about the most common forms of seizures that you will encounter in clinical practice, beginning with generalized seizures.

GENERALIZED SEIZURES

Generalized seizures, or those that involve a **complete loss of consciousness**, come in a variety of forms. These can be hard to keep straight, as many of the words sound similar even if they refer to completely different things. To keep clear in your mind the different ways that generalized seizures can present, think of a man named **General McTATA** whose name stands for all the forms that a **General**-ized seizure can take: **M**yoclonic, **T**onic-clonic, **A**tonic, **T**onic, and **A**bsence. We will go over each one of them now (though not necessarily in mnemonic order).

The **primary forms of generalized seizures** are **tonic-clonic, tonic, atonic, myoclonic**, and **absence seizures.**

General McTATA:
Myoclonic
Tonic-clonic
Atonic
Tonic
Absence

TONIC-CLONIC SEIZURES

The most common and severe form of a generalized seizure is known as a **tonic-clonic seizure** (formerly known as a "grand mal" seizure). This form of seizure begins with a change in consciousness and evolves into a widespread sustained contraction of muscles (the **tonic phase**) that causes the body to contort into odd or seemingly uncomfortable positions, as seen below:

The tonic phase of the seizure is short, lasting only 10 or 20 seconds, and may cause the patient to fall if they are standing up. The rest of the seizure is the **clonic phase** which is characterized by rapid alternation between contraction and relaxation across the entire body. (This is the characteristic **shaking** that most people think about when they hear the word "seizure.") The clonic phase is longer than the tonic phase, often lasting 1 to 2 minutes. To remember the difference between the tonic and clonic phases, think of them as the "town-ic" and "clown-ic" phases. In the "town-ic" phase, the body is completely *rigid* like the brick buildings of an old medieval town, whereas in the "clown-ic" phase it is *shaking* like a hyperactive clown.

Tonic

Clonic

Town-ic

Clown-ic

A **generalized tonic-clonic seizure** involves an initial **loss of consciousness** accompanied by **widespread sustained contraction** (the **tonic phase**) followed by **rapid alternation between contraction and relaxation** (the **clonic phase**).

*During the **town**-ic phase the body is **stiff and rigid** like the walls of a town, while in the **clown**-ic phase the body is **shaking** like a hyperactive clown.*

Since generalized seizures cause excessive neuronal activity in all areas of the brain, muscles throughout the body are activated which can lead to injury (such as biting of the tongue related to muscle contraction in the jaw). Urinary and fecal incontinence may also occur. Given how the entirety of both the brain and body are involved, generalized tonic-clonic seizures are almost always followed by a profound **postictal state**. Some people may develop neurologic deficits following a seizure, including weakness or paralysis in the arms, legs, vocal cords, or eyes. This is known as **postictal paresis** (or Todd's paresis) and occurs in over 10% of seizure cases. These deficits are transient, lasting only a day or two at most.

TONIC SEIZURES

Some people have seizures involving only the tonic phase *without* an accompanying clonic phase. These are known as **tonic seizures**. (Interestingly, while *tonic* seizures without a *clonic* phase exist, *clonic* seizures without a *tonic* phase are exceedingly rare and are not considered to be a subtype of generalized seizures.) Tonic seizures are generally shorter than a tonic-clonic seizure (lasting less than 20 seconds), and there is not always a postictal period. However, due to the sudden widespread muscle contraction and loss of consciousness, patients may still injure themselves if they fall.

MYOCLONIC SEIZURES

A **myoclonic seizure** involves a series of **repeated and uncontrollable jerks** in specific muscles. Two common examples of myoclonus are hiccups and the "sleep starts" that some people get right before falling asleep. To avoid confusion, it's worth pointing out that myoclonus is *not* the same thing as clonus! *Clonus* is a repetitive *rhythmic* series of contractions alternating with relaxation that leads to shaking, while *myo*clonus is an *irregular* contraction of a muscle that appears as a jerk or a spasm. To remember the definition of a myoclonic seizure, think of them as "my-old-clinic seizures." Why did you leave your old clinic and find a new one? Because the people there were a **bunch of jerks**.

A **myoclonic seizure** involves a **series of uncontrollable jerks** in specific muscles.

*I left **my-old-clinic** because the people there were a **bunch of jerks**.*

ATONIC SEIZURES

In contrast to tonic, tonic-clonic, and myoclonic seizures (all of which involve *too much* muscle contraction), **atonic seizures** result in a sudden *loss* of muscle tone, leading the patient to pass out and fall (they are sometimes called "**drop attacks**" for this reason). Drop attacks are usually brief (lasting no more than a few seconds), but because they can occur without warning while someone is doing other things, they can result in injuries to the head, neck, back, and the vital organs contained within. Atonic seizures can easily be confused for a syncopal episode. To remember the meaning of **ate**-onic seizures, think of the phrase "**ate** it" which is used to describe someone who fell (as in, "Dude, that guy totally **ate** it!")

An **atonic seizure** involves a **sudden loss of muscle tone** which can lead to a fall.

*The phrase "**ate** it" describes someone who fell, so **ate**-onic seizures refer to the same.*

ABSENCE SEIZURES

Finally, the last type of generalized seizure we will talk about is an **absence seizure** (formerly called a "petit mal" seizure). Like any generalized seizure, absence seizures involve a **sudden loss of consciousness**. However, unlike the other seizure types we have talked about so far, they are generally *not* associated with significant motor abnormalities. Instead, the only outward sign of an absence seizure may be a sudden (though not necessarily dramatic) change in the patient's level of consciousness. This may appear to others as a **blank stare**, a sudden break in the activity that they are doing, and/or a lack of responding to stimuli. Notably, absence seizures are also *not* associated with a postictal period. Really, absence seizures are **all about absence**: *absence* of mind, *absence* of a motor component, and *absence* of postictal period.

> An **absence seizure** involves a **sudden loss of consciousness** with **no corresponding changes in muscle tone.**
>
> *Absence* seizures are *all about absence*: Absence of *mind*, absence of *motor component*, and absence of *postictal period*.

FOCAL SEIZURES

Focal (or focal-onset) seizures involve excessive activity in the brain leading to motor and other abnormalities. Unlike generalized seizures, however, they do *not* involve a loss of consciousness. While significantly less dramatic to witness, **focal seizures** are actually more common than generalized seizures, accounting for around 80% of seizures in people with epilepsy.

While focal seizures do not result in a total loss of consciousness, that is not to say that consciousness remains fully intact during an episode. This is because focal seizures can result in an *alteration* in consciousness even if they do not involve a *complete* loss of consciousness as in a generalized seizure. Seizures in which consciousness is altered but not completely lost are known as **focal-onset impaired-awareness seizures** (or "complex partial" seizures) and tend to manifest as a momentary loss of memory or awareness. In contrast, seizures that do not result in *any* change in consciousness are known as **focal-onset aware seizures** (or "simple partial" seizures). We'll now go over both of these in more detail.

FOCAL-ONSET AWARE SEIZURES (SIMPLE PARTIAL)

During a focal-onset aware seizure, the patient remains fully awake and aware of what is happening to them. Compared to generalized seizures, focal-onset aware seizures are much more variable in their presentation. This is because the specific location of the seizure activity in the brain can differ from person to person and even from seizure to seizure. For example, a seizure in the parietal lobe may cause sensory abnormalities such as numbness or tingling, while a seizure in the occipital lobe may instead lead to visual warping or hallucinations. When seizure activity occurs in the motor strip, it can cause movements ranging from slight twitching all the way to full-on muscle contractions. Even during a single seizure episode, the site of excessive activity can move within the brain. Abnormal movements often begin in one's extremities and then make their way up the arm and into the neck and face. This is known as a **Jacksonian march** (named after the neurologist who discovered them) and reflects the spreading wave of seizure activity in the brain. Unlike generalized tonic-clonic seizures, there is **no postictal period**, and the person typically has complete awareness and memory of the event.

FOCAL-ONSET IMPAIRED-AWARENESS SEIZURES (COMPLEX PARTIAL)

While "focal-onset impaired-awareness seizure" is a mouthful to say, it really does describe what is going on during this type of seizure (although the older, and much easier to say, terminology of "complex partial seizure" is still used frequently as well). Like focal-onset aware seizures, focal-onset impaired-awareness seizures only involve a part of the brain, and the presenting signs are often quite similar. Where focal-onset impaired-awareness seizures differentiate themselves is that they *impair* one's consciousness *without fully eliminating it*. The borderland between awareness and unconsciousness can be difficult to describe, but the patient often appears awake but does not respond to stimuli or engage in purposeful activities. Instead, their behavior often involves **automatisms**, or pre-set motor "tasks" such as eye rolling, teeth clenching, lip smacking, or chewing that are more elaborate than a simple twitching or contraction of a single muscle but still fall short of fully purposeful behavior.

*Automatisms as seen during a **focal-onset impaired-awareness seizure**.*

Focal-onset impaired-awareness seizures tend to be **brief**, lasting only a minute or two. Because the behaviors involved appear normal (even if they are a bit odd for the situation, such as someone engaging in a chewing automatism with no food in their mouth), these seizures are often misdiagnosed as a psychiatric condition, especially when the patient appears confused during or after these events.

DIAGNOSIS AND TREATMENT OF SEIZURES

Now that we have built up a sizeable vocabulary with which we can describe seizures, we are ready to learn about how to diagnose and treat them. Seizures are **common**, with around 10% of people having had a seizure at some point in their lifetime. For those who have had at least one seizure, the chance of having another seizure increases to around 50%. Seizures are not necessarily a disease in and of themselves, as the vast majority of seizures occur as the result of another condition. These are known as **symptomatic seizures**, and they do not necessarily require long-term treatment. (For example, most infants who have seizures as the result of a fever—known as febrile seizures—are not at risk of worse health outcomes, and treatment of the seizures themselves is generally not recommended.) The full list of medical conditions that can cause seizures is extensive and could likely fill a book of its own, but it includes everything from brain tumors and infections to drug intoxication and dietary deficiencies. (We'll cover a few of these in later chapters.)

Around a quarter of all people who have recurrent seizures appear to experience them with no clear cause. These people are said to have **epilepsy**. Someone with epilepsy can have multiple different seizure types or even switch from one to another over time. (For example, someone who initially presents with focal-onset aware seizures may later develop generalized tonic-clonic seizures.) An initial diagnosis of epilepsy is often based on the clinical history, with a particular focus on ruling out potential causes such as infections or tumors that could provide an alternative explanation. A **seizure calendar** can be used to systematically track the timing and location of seizures. An **electroencephalogram** (EEG) is often performed to provide an objective measure of brain activity, which can help to distinguish between different seizure types.

*Someone undergoing **electroencephalography** (left) with **normal resting state activity** seen (right).*

Treatment of epilepsy involves not only **acute management** of seizure activity but also **long-term prevention** of future episodes. Because most seizures are self-limited (lasting only a few minutes), immediate management of a seizure mostly involves simple safety measures such as placing the patient on their side to prevent aspiration. In cases of status epilepticus (where seizure activity continues for more than 5 minutes), pharmacologic interventions may be needed as well. The first-line treatment for status epilepticus is a **benzodiazepine**, a class of central nervous system depressants that helps to rapidly abort a seizure episode.

For long-term prevention of seizures, a class of drugs known as **anticonvulsants** is used. Many anticonvulsants work by either directly or indirectly inhibiting the ion channels that help neurons to fire, reducing their ability to generate and transmit an electrical signal (kind of like throwing water on dry brush to make it less likely to catch fire). Anticonvulsants are generally effective, with around 70% of people becoming seizure-free provided they stay on the medication. There are many anticonvulsant medications available, with some of the most common being valproate, levetiracetam, carbamazepine, oxcarbazepine, lamotrigine, phenytoin, ethosuximide, lacosamide, gabapentin, pregabalin, topiramate, and zonisamide. Choosing between these drugs depends on a lot of factors, including which types of seizures are present. As a general rule, **valproate** is the most broad-spectrum anticonvulsant available, so if you are unsure of what to pick, this is a reasonable guess! (A major exception to this is if the patient is pregnant, as valproate is a known teratogen and can cause spinal cord defects in the fetus.)

Outside of medications, make sure to consider **psychosocial interventions** as well, including stress reduction, sleep hygiene, and both psychological and behavioral therapies. In addition, consider whether someone who has had an unexplained seizure should be engaging in driving or other activities where a sudden loss of consciousness could lead to harm.

EPILEPSY SYNDROMES

Once the pattern of seizure activity is clear, the next step in diagnosing epilepsy is to determine whether the recurrent seizures fit any known patterns that might help to differentiate them from other forms of epilepsy. Cases of epilepsy that involve specific combinations of signs and symptoms are known as **epilepsy syndromes**, and diagnosing an epilepsy syndrome has important implications for both prognosis and treatment response. While there are dozens of epilepsy syndromes, we will limit our discussion to the most high-yield ones that you are most likely to encounter on boards and on wards. Most epilepsy syndromes begin in childhood, although we will cover some that begin in adulthood as well.

TEMPORAL LOBE EPILEPSY
The most common syndrome leading to recurrent focal seizures is **temporal lobe epilepsy**. Of note, the *medial* temporal lobe (near the amygdala, hippocampus, and other parts of limbic system) is most often affected, with only 20% of cases involving the outer cortex. For this reason, seizures in the temporal lobe often present as **memory or mood changes**, including amnesia, sudden feelings of fear, rapid swings in emotion, flashbacks to old memories, and/or feelings of *déjà vu*. Hallucinations can occur, although they are rarely auditory (which makes sense as hearing takes place in the *outer* cortex while temporal lobe epilepsy involves more *medial* structures). Instead, hallucinations generally take the form of distinct odors and smells (known as **olfactory hallucinations**). Because the motor strip in the frontal lobe is not involved,

there is no tonic-clonic component unless if the seizure secondarily generalizes. For those with onset of temporal lobe seizures in childhood, many will stop having them by adulthood. However, people with continued temporal lobe seizures may have **mesial temporal sclerosis**, or damage in their temporal lobe that is identifiable on neuroimaging as seen below:

*MRI showing **mesial temporal sclerosis**.*

FRONTAL LOBE EPILEPSY

The frontal lobe is the second most common site of recurrent focal seizures. Because you know the function of this lobe already, you can predict what sorts of signs and symptoms you might see. Due to the location of the motor cortex in the frontal lobe, frontal lobe seizures tend to involve **abnormal movements** including twisting, turning, grimacing, tics, body posturing, rocking, and even pedaling (as if the patient were riding an invisible bicycle). In around one-third of cases, a tumor in the frontal lobe is the culprit.

*A **brain tumor** is a common cause of **frontal lobe epilepsy**.*

BENIGN ROLANDIC EPILEPSY

Benign Rolandic epilepsy is the most common epilepsy syndrome in **childhood**, affecting 15% of all children with epilepsy. Benign Rolandic epilepsy is characterized by infrequent **focal aware seizures** that manifest as a wide variety of experiences, including tingling sensations, grunting noises, and impaired speech. These seizures tend to last only a minute or two at most, although they may at times generalize to a full tonic-clonic seizure. Seizures typically occur at night without interrupting the child's ability to function (as suggested by the "benign" in the name). EEG will show

centrotemporal spikes which are characteristic of this syndrome. Due to the infrequent and non-impairing nature of these seizures, treatment is often not necessary, and many children will outgrow it by adolescence. You can remember benign **Roll**-andic epilepsy by thinking of the acronym **FAST ROLL** which stands for **F**ocal **A**ware **S**eizures **T**hat **R**arely **O**utlast **L**ater **L**ife. The **Roll** of **Roll**-andic can also help you to remember the centrotempo-**Roll** spikes that are seen on EEG.

Benign Rolandic epilepsy is the most common form of epilepsy in **childhood**. It involves **focal aware seizures** and generally **does not require treatment**.

FAST ROLL: Focal Aware Seizures That Rarely Outlast Later Life.

Benign Roll-andic epilepsy should remind you of centrotempo-Roll spikes on EEG.

CHILDHOOD ABSENCE EPILEPSY

Childhood absence epilepsy is another common form of epilepsy (accounting for around 10% of childhood epilepsy cases) that is characterized by the presence of **recurrent absence seizures**. Absence seizures can occur several or even dozens of times per day. However, because the sudden losses of consciousness come and go so quickly, it is often diagnosed as mere inattention or even attention deficit hyperactivity disorder (ADHD). For this reason, thorough history taking is key for correctly identifying this condition. Absence seizures can often be provoked through **hyperventilation**, which can be a useful diagnostic test. Another key finding supporting a diagnosis of absence seizures is the presence of a fast (3 Hz) **spike-and-wave** pattern on EEG. You can remember this by thinking of some students who decide to skip school (resulting in their **absence**) and go to the beach to play volleyball ("**Spike!**") and surf the **waves**.

Generalized 3 Hz spike-and-wave discharges on EEG related to childhood absence epilepsy.

Childhood absence epilepsy presents as **recurrent brief losses of consciousness.** EEG will show a **3 Hz spike-and-wave** pattern.

*Think of some students who decide to be **absent** from school so they can go to the beach to play volleyball ("**Spike!**") and surf the **waves**.*

A specific anticonvulsant known as **ethosuximide** is very effective for treating absence seizures (although unfortunately not other kinds of seizures). You can remember the association of absence seizures with ethosuximide by thinking of it as etho-**sucks-the-mind**, as an absence seizure *sucks* thoughts out of the mind like a vacuum, leading to the blank mind and blank stare that are characteristic of these episodes. With etho-**sucks-the-mind**, absence seizures can't do that anymore. In cases where someone has both absence *and* other forms of seizures, you could consider a more broad-spectrum anticonvulsant like valproate.

Absence seizures can be treated with **ethosuximide** or **valproate**.

*With etho-**sucks-the-mind**, absence seizures won't **suck the mind** anymore.*

JUVENILE MYOCLONIC EPILEPSY
Juvenile myoclonic epilepsy is another common epilepsy syndrome that involves **sudden involuntary irregular muscle contractions** (remember that "my-old-clinic was a bunch of jerks") beginning in late childhood or adolescence. These contractions tend to involve the arms and occur in the transition between sleep and wakefulness, although other triggers may include flashing lights or loud sounds. Many people who have juvenile myoclonic epilepsy also have other seizure forms as well, including

absence seizures and generalized tonic-clonic seizures. **Valproate** is the most commonly used medication treatment (remember: if you're ever unsure about which anticonvulsant to pick, valproate may be your best bet!).

LENNOX-GASTAUT SYNDROME

Lennox-Gastaut syndrome is a rare but severe form of epilepsy that is characterized by a triad of **seizures, intellectual disability**, and **specific EEG findings**. Almost all cases of Lennox-Gastaut syndrome begin in **early childhood** (before the age of 5), although the vast majority of patients continue to have seizures into adulthood. Most cases occur as a direct result of damage to the brain (such as brain infections, tumors, and trauma), although one-third occur with no known trigger.

Seizures in Lennox-Gastaut syndrome take many different forms, with the most common being **tonic-only seizures** (which are normally quite rare). These seizures often occur on a daily basis and are incredibly difficult to treat, with anticonvulsants being much less effective than in other forms of epilepsy. In addition, patients with Lennox-Gastaut syndrome also have intellectual disabilities which can limit their ability to function. EEG will show characteristic **spike-and-wave discharges**. (Remember that spike-and-wave discharges are also seen in absence seizures! While the pattern is the same, it tends to be slower in Lennox-Gastaut syndrome, typically less than 3 Hz.) You can remember the core triad of **Le**nnox-**G**astaut **S**yndrome by thinking of its acronym as **LeGS** which should then make you think of **ARMS**, which stands for **A**ll types of seizures, **R**esistant to treatment, **M**ental disabilities, and **S**low spike-and-wave discharges on EEG.

> **Lennox-Gastaut syndrome** is a rare form of epilepsy characterized by **multiple seizure types, intellectual disability**, and **slow spike-and-wave discharges** on EEG.
>
> *LeGS (Lennox-Gastaut Syndrome) should make you think of ARMS:*
> *All types of seizures*
> *Resistant to treatment*
> *Mental disabilities*
> *Slow (<3 Hz) spike-and-wave discharges on EEG*

PSYCHOGENIC NON-EPILEPTIC SEIZURES

Not everything that looks like a seizure is actually epilepsy. In fact, it is estimated that up to 20% of all patients who come to clinics reporting seizures do not have epilepsy. Many of these patients will have **psychogenic non-epileptic seizures**, or seizure-like episodes that are not clearly linked to any abnormal electrical activity in the brain. The name "psychogenic" underscores that many of these cases occur in the context of severe life stress, maladaptive behavioral patterns, and other findings that suggest a psychological origin to the behavior.

Knowing what *is* and *is not* a common clinical finding in epilepsy is the key to picking up this diagnosis. A few signs are very common in psychogenic non-epileptic seizures but very *un*common in generalized tonic-clonic seizures and are therefore high-yield to know! You can remember these features using the mnemonic **2 minute RAGES**, as psychogenic non-epileptic seizures tend to last more than **2 minutes** (which is rare for epileptic seizures). In addition, people experiencing a psychogenic non-epileptic seizure are more likely to show **R**ecall of events that occurred during the episode, **A**synchronous movements, a **G**radual (rather than sudden) onset of seizure activity, **E**yes that are closed or crying, and **S**ide-to-side shaking of the head (all of which are incredibly unusual for an epileptic seizure).

> **Psychogenic non-epileptic seizures** are episodes of shaking that are related to **psychosocial factors** rather than excessive electrical activity in the brain.
>
> *2 minute RAGES:*
> *2 minutes or greater in duration*
> *Recall of events during the episode*
> *Asynchronous movements*
> *Gradual onset of seizure activity*
> *Eyes that are closed or crying*
> *Side-to-side shaking of the head*

It is important to note that most patients with this condition do not intentionally or purposefully produce psychogenic non-epileptic seizures and may even be unaware that these episodes are non-epileptic. If you suspect that a patient is experiencing psychogenic non-epileptic seizures, take their impairment and distress seriously while trying to avoid anticonvulsants (many of which are associated with some pretty major side effects). Instead, consider a referral to more helpful forms of treatment including **psychological and behavioral therapies**.

PUTTING IT ALL TOGETHER

Even for an experienced clinician, seizures can be complicated to diagnose and treat, as they come in such a wide variety of different types and combinations. Let's briefly review the terms that can help us to arrive at an accurate diagnosis. The difference between generalized and focal seizures forms the first point of separation (although even this boundary is blurry, as focal seizures can become generalized). From there, each type of seizure can be broken down into additional subtypes. **Generalized seizures** include those in the **General McTATA** mnemonic, with **M**yoclonic, **T**onic-clonic, **A**tonic, **T**onic, and **A**bsence seizures being seen. **Focal seizures** involve both **focal-onset aware** (or "simple partial") seizures and **focal-onset impaired-awareness** (or "complex partial") seizures. These seizures can either occur entirely on their own or as the result of another medical condition like a brain tumor or infection. When they do occur on their own, they are known as **epilepsy**. To make matters even more complicated, epilepsy itself can come in a few different varieties (known as **epilepsy syndromes**) that each require additional memorization.

Rather than get lost in the complexity, it can be helpful to have a structured way of evaluating seizures that you can use both on tests and when seeing patients in a clinical setting. The mnemonic **CAPELLA** can help to clue you in to the right diagnosis:

C is for Consciousness. Whether the patient loses consciousness, has impaired consciousness, or retains full consciousness helps to distinguish between generalized, focal-onset impaired-awareness, and focal-onset aware seizures, respectively.

A is for Activity. The specific kinds of motor activity present (whether tonic, clonic, myoclonic, and/or atonic) should be assessed. If motor activity is not involved, an absence or focal seizure is more likely.

P is for Postictal state. Most generalized tonic-clonic seizures are followed by a postictal state. If there is no postictal period, it may suggest a different etiology (such as an absence, focal, or psychogenic non-epileptic seizure).

P is for Provoked. Whether the seizure was provoked by a related medical condition, is related to a known trigger (such as loud sounds or flashing lights), or came entirely out of the blue matters for the final diagnosis.

E is for EEG findings. Specific findings on EEG are suggestive of specific types of seizures (such as 3 Hz spike-and-wave patterns being suggestive of an absence seizure or centrotemporal spikes being characteristic of Benign Rolandic epilepsy).

L is for Localizing symptoms. Specific symptoms that occur around the time of a seizure can help to localize the precise location of seizure activity in the brain (like olfactory hallucinations suggesting temporal lobe epilepsy).

A is for Age of onset. Most epilepsy syndromes have their onset in childhood, so any new-onset seizures in adulthood are more likely to be related to a secondary source like an infection or brain tumor.

Being **systematic** when evaluating **seizures** can lead to a more accurate diagnosis.

CAPELLA:
Consciousness
Activity
Postictal state
Provoked
EEG findings
Localizing symptoms
Age of onset

REVIEW QUESTIONS

1. An 18 y/o M is brought to the emergency department after falling in a grocery store. His mother reports that while they were out shopping, he suddenly began to "look distant." She then saw his eyes roll back in his head before he fell to the ground. Initially his back was arched, with outward rolling of his wrists. However, within several seconds he began shaking across his entire body. His mother called 911, and an ambulance arrived 5 minutes later. At the time of arrival to the hospital, he continues to convulse. Vital signs are HR 138, BP 132/88, RR 24, and T 100.1°F. His oxygen saturation is 97%. Which of the following is the best next step in management?
   - A. Ordering a 24-hour electroencephalography
   - B. Ordering a CT scan of the brain
   - C. Ordering an MRI of the brain
   - D. Administering valproate, an anticonvulsant
   - E. Administering lorazepam, a benzodiazepine
   - F. Immediate endotracheal intubation

2. A 23 y/o M presents to a neurology clinic for "staring spells" that have gradually worsened over the past few months. He describes these episodes as "blacking out" with no memory of what happens during the spell. Friends who have observed these episodes report that he will smack his lips and pull at his shirt repeatedly. Prior to each episode he experiences a "rising feeling" along with an "odd smell, kind of like burnt rubber." He also describes having a sense of *déjà vu* before each episode, saying, "I get this overwhelming feeling that this has all somehow happened before. I can't explain it any better than that." Following these episodes he typically is "confused and out of it" for up to half an hour. Seizure activity is most likely to be localized to which of the following structures?

3. A 7 y/o F is brought to a child psychiatrist for evaluation of possible attention deficit hyperactivity disorder. Over the past 6 months, she has been struggling at school, and her teacher has requested that she undergo a full psychiatric evaluation. Her teacher's report notes that she regularly "spaces out" during class and has difficulty paying attention to the subject matter. These episodes last for around 10 seconds at a time and happen "dozens of times a day." There is no loss of consciousness or abnormal movements observed before, during, or after these episodes. Electroencephalography demonstrates generalized spike-and-wave discharges at 3 Hz. Which of the following is the best next step in management?

    A. Starting methylphenidate, a stimulant used to treat ADHD
    B. Starting amphetamine salts, a stimulant used to treat ADHD
    C. Starting clonazepam, a benzodiazepine used to treat seizures
    D. Starting lamotrigine, an anticonvulsant used to treat seizures
    E. Starting ethosuximide, an anticonvulsant used to treat seizures
    F. None of the above

4. A 22 y/o F is brought to the hospital after a seizure that was witnessed by her husband. She has a history of epilepsy beginning in her teenage years for which she is taking valproate. Since starting this medication 5 years ago, she has not had any further seizures until today. Upon arriving to the emergency department, she has another seizure lasting for 10 minutes. During this time, her body is seen shaking. Her fists are clenched, and her toes are curled. Her eyes are shut tight, and she is shaking her head back and forth. After the episode ends, she is unresponsive to questions for 90 minutes, though she does withdraw from deep pressure applied to her fingernail beds. Physical exam reveals no injuries to the inside of her mouth or evidence of incontinence. Laboratory analysis is unrevealing except for a positive urine pregnancy test. A 24-hour EEG shows no abnormal activity. Which of the following is the best next step?

    A. Stopping valproate
    B. Adding a second anticonvulsant
    C. Adding a benzodiazepine
    D. Discharging the patient immediately
    E. Increasing the dose of valproate

1. **The best answer is E.** This patient is in a state of status epilepticus, as he has been having continuous seizure activity for more than 5 minutes. The first-line treatment for status epilepticus is use of a benzodiazepine, as these medications are effective at rapidly lowering neuronal activity and quickly aborting a seizure. Valproate may be indicated in the future for prevention of additional seizures but does not have a role in immediate management of status epilepticus (answer D). Additional diagnostic studies such as electroencephalography or neuroimaging are important but do not take precedence over treating status epilepticus, which is a medical emergency (answers A—C). Endotracheal intubation is needed in some cases of status epilepticus, but this patient's intact oxygenation level shows good circulatory function at this time (answer F).

2. **The best answer is D.** This vignette describes a prototypical case of temporal lobe seizures with automatisms and olfactory hallucinations. The presence of *déjà vu* also suggests involvement of the hippocampus, which is located on the inner aspect of the temporal lobe. Less than 20% of temporal lobe seizures involve the cerebral cortex, so outer structures are less likely to be involved (answers A, B, and E). The lateral ventricles are not made of nervous tissue and therefore cannot be the origin of abnormal electrical activity (answer C).

3. **The best answer is E.** Absence seizures are characterized by the absence of several features that are commonly seen in tonic-clonic seizures such as noticeable convulsions or a postictal period. They are instead defined by recurrent brief episodes of lapsed consciousness and a characteristic spike-and-wave pattern on electroencephalography. The primary treatment for absence seizures is an anticonvulsant that has efficacy at T-type calcium channels, including ethosuximide and valproate. Other anticonvulsants, such as lamotrigine, that do not interact with this type of calcium channel will not be effective (answer D). Benzodiazepines are primarily used for treating an ongoing seizure rather than as prophylaxis (answer C). Starting a stimulant when there is no clear evidence of attention deficit hyperactivity disorder is unlikely to help (answers A and B).

4. **The best answer is A.** Several features of this patient's presentation are highly suggestive of psychogenic non-epileptic seizures, including a seizure duration greater than 2 minutes, head shaking, and lack of incontinence or unintentional injury. While she may have a history of epileptic seizures as well, it is not uncommon for someone presenting with psychogenic non-epileptic seizures to also have a history of epileptic seizures. The first priority should be stopping valproate given valproate's teratogenic effects, not increasing the dose (answer E). Adding another medication in the absence of clear seizure activity is not indicated (answers B and C). In cases of suspected psychogenic non-epileptic seizures, arranging for immediate discharge of a patient is not helpful (answer D). Instead, a discussion should be had regarding the diagnosis and the reasons why the treatment team feels that other forms of treatment such as psychological or behaviorally therapy may be more necessary at this time.

19 NEOPLASMS

A **neoplasm** refers to any abnormal and excessive growth of tissue, including various forms of **cancer**. Neoplasms can occur in organs all across the body, and the nervous system is no exception. While a tumor in any organ can be frightening, when one grows in such a vital organ as the brain, it can be particularly devastating. Much of this comes from the fact that cancers of the nervous system are often difficult to treat, as it much harder to remove cancerous tissue from the brain than it is to remove it from a more peripheral organ.

When discussing neoplasms of the nervous system, it is helpful to make a few key distinctions. First, most central nervous system cancers present as a **tumor**, or a focal area of unregulated cell growth. However, it's important to point out that not all tumors are necessarily cancerous! Some tumors are **benign**, meaning that they are growing only within a localized area and have not invaded surrounding tissues. In contrast, **malignant** tumors have begun to spread outside of their initial area and are now invading nearby tissues. Only malignant tumors are considered to be cancer (a benign tumor would not be referred to as cancer). A malignant tumor that spreads to another distal location (such as a liver tumor that spreads to the brain) is said to have **metastasized**.

Second, just because a tumor is *in* the brain doesn't mean it's *from* the brain! Tumors in the nervous system can either be **primary** (a tumor originating from nervous tissue) or **secondary** (a metastasis from a tumor originating in a different organ). In fact, secondary tumors make up around 50% of all tumors in the brain, so they are far from a rare entity. Inversely, primary brain tumors themselves rarely metastasize to other organs.

Third, different cancers tend to strike children compared to older adults. As a general rule, brain tumors in children are often **infratentorial** (meaning that they grow *below* the cerebellar tentorium, or the extension of the dura mater that separates the cerebellum from the cerebral cortex) while brain tumors in adults tend to be **supratentorial**. This is not a hard and fast rule, but it is accurate enough to serve as a helpful rule of thumb. To remember this distinction, think about what would happen if a storm struck while a family was out camping. The adults will try to protect the children by getting them *under* the tent (*infra*-**tent**-orial) while bravely staying outside of the tent themselves to set up a rain cover *above* it (*supra*-**tent**-orial).

As a general rule, **brain tumors** in **adults** tend to be **supratentorial** while those in **children** tend to be **infratentorial**.

*If a storm hits while a family is out camping, the adults will try to protect the **children** by getting them **under the tent** (infra-**tent**-orial).*

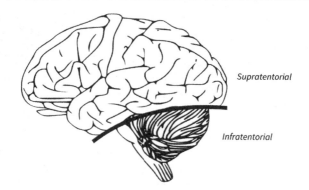

Supratentorial

Infratentorial

The specific clinical manifestations of a brain tumor are usually related to its **mass effect**, or the specific functions that are impaired when the tumor grows large enough to impinge upon or compress nearby structures. This means that the tumor will not necessarily cause any signs or symptoms until it reaches a certain size. In addition, because mass effect is independent of the tissue, the signs and symptoms are often the same regardless of whether it is a primary or secondary tumor!

Remember from Chapter 13 that there are three ways to increase intracranial pressure: increasing the amount of blood, the amount of cerebrospinal fluid, or the amount of nervous tissue. A tumor in the brain does the third thing, so signs and symptoms of **intracranial hypertension** are often seen. **Headaches** are probably the most common presenting symptom (although, contrary to what certain online websites will suggest, not all headaches are evidence of a brain tumor!). **Seizures** are the initial presenting sign in around 20% of all cases, especially supratentorial tumors, so a sudden seizure without a clear origin should prompt an investigation for a brain tumor, especially in an older adult who has never had a seizure before. **Papilledema** can often be seen on exam as well. Aside from these more general signs and symptoms, there may be more specific effects depending on the precise areas of the brain involved. For example, a tumor in the frontal lobe may cause disinhibited behavior, a tumor in the parietal lobe may cause sensory abnormalities, a tumor in the occipital lobe may lead to changes in vision, and so on. Use your knowledge of neuroanatomy to guide you here.

Mass effect caused by a tumor in the posterior fossa.

However, even with a full understanding of neuroanatomy, diagnosing a brain tumor can rarely be done by neurological exam alone. Instead, a definitive diagnosis generally relies upon **neuroimaging** to demonstrate the presence of a tumor. In fact, in some cases brain tumors do not cause signs and symptoms at all, so the only way they get diagnosed is as an incidental finding when imaging is ordered for another reason (such as someone who is in a car accident and gets a CT scan done which reveals a previously undiscovered brain tumor).

Once the presence of a tumor has been established, a **biopsy** (or a sample of brain tissue that has been surgically removed for examination under a microscope) is needed to determine if the tumor is primary or secondary, benign or malignant, and other characteristics which have important implications for prognosis and treatment.

As with other forms of cancer, there is no single "correct" treatment for a brain tumor. The three mainstays of cancer treatment are **surgery**, **radiation**, and/or **chemotherapy**. The decision on which type (or types) of treatment to use is informed by the specific kind of neoplasm present and whether it is localized or metastasized (with surgery often being more effective when the tumor has not yet metastasized).

With these principles in mind, we are ready to look at the specific types of tumors that can occur in the brain. We will first talk about adult-onset tumors before moving on to discuss childhood-onset tumors. To keep our focus on what is most high-yield, we will limit our discussion to the **five most common tumors** in each category, so there will be rarer tumor types that aren't covered here.

ADULT-ONSET BRAIN TUMORS

In this section, we will cover five adult-onset brain tumors in order from most common to least common. As a reminder, most adult-onset brain tumors are found in the cerebrum *above* the tentorium cerebelli. As we go through this section (and the next), pay attention to specific **buzzwords** that you would do well to associate with each tumor type in as Pavlovian of a way as possible!

GLIOBLASTOMA MULTIFORME

Glioblastoma multiforme (often abbreviated GBM) is the **most common** primary brain tumor in adults, making up 15% of all brain tumors. As with most brain tumors, there are no signs or symptoms that are specific to glioblastoma multiforme. Instead, many patients present with non-specific symptoms like headaches, nausea, seizures, unexplained focal neurologic deficits, or even no symptoms at all. Once symptoms do appear, they tend to progress quickly in severity, as glioblastoma multiforme is a very **fast-growing cancer**. Accordingly, the **prognosis is often poor**, and most patients diagnosed with glioblastoma multiforme will live only around one year. You can remember the rapidly-growing nature of glio**blast**oma multiforme by thinking of a speedy rocket **blast**ing off into space.

Glioblastoma multiforme is a **rapidly-growing tumor** with a **poor prognosis**.

*Glio**blast**oma is fast like a rocket **blast**ing off into space.*

Glioblastoma multiforme is diagnosed more often in **men** than women, with an average age at diagnosis of 65 years. Cases of glioblastoma multiforme can either appear "out of the blue" (known as **primary** glioblastoma) or can grow from a pre-cancerous lesion (a **secondary** glioblastoma). Primary and secondary glioblastomas have very different prognoses and treatment responses, so making this distinction via biopsy is important.

To recognize glioblastoma multiforme on test questions, you should be on the lookout for a few key words. First, serum levels of a specific protein known as **G**lial **F**ibrillary **A**cidic **P**rotein or **GFAP** are elevated in people with glioblastoma multiforme, making this a diagnostic marker for the condition with very high specificity. Second, when looked at under a microscope, glioblastoma multiforme appears as areas of **pseudopalisading necrosis** in which tumor cells surround central areas of necrosis. Finally, if the tumor grows large enough that it crosses the corpus callosum, it can have a symmetrical butterfly-like appearance on brain imaging (sometimes called a "**butterfly glioma**"). To associate **G**lio**B**lastoma **M**ultiforme with elevated serum levels of **G**FAP, a **B**utterfly glioma appearance on neuroimaging, and a predilection for older **M**en, pack those three ideas into the initials **GBM** themselves!

Glioblastoma multiforme is diagnosed most often in **older men**. Serum levels of **GFAP** are typically **elevated**. Neuroimaging can show a "**butterfly glioma**" pattern.

GlioBlastoma Multiforme = GFAP + Butterfly glioma + Male predominance.

MENINGIOMA

A **meningioma** is a tumor that arises from the **meninges** wrapping around the brain. It is the second most common form of brain tumor in adults. They often grow either in the central falx cerebri or along the surface the brain between the brain and the skull. On imaging, the tumor is usually **well circumscribed** with clearly demarcated borders as in the image below:

In contrast to the aggressive nature of glioblastoma multiforme, meningiomas are often **benign** and **slow-growing**. In fact, most cases don't even need to be treated unless if they become symptomatic. Meningiomas that grow large enough to be bothersome can be effectively treated with **surgery**, as they are considered to be a highly **resectable** tumor with a low recurrence rate. While most meningiomas are relatively benign, a small percentage (roughly 10%) are more invasive and aggressive.

As with glioblastoma multiforme, there are a few words you will need to associate with meningiomas. First, meningiomas often have a **whorled appearance** when viewed under a microscope (as seen below).

Meningiomas also have a tendency to calcify and form **psammoma bodies**, or rounded collections of calcified tissue (as seen below). Unlike GFAP and glioblastoma multiforme, psammoma bodies are *not* specific to meningiomas and are found in a variety of other conditions as well.

Many meningiomas also express **estrogen receptors**. The higher levels of circulating estrogen in women make them more prone to developing meningiomas, with about twice the rate as men. You can remember this association by thinking that **Psam** (Sam) is a good name for both **men**(ingiomas) and **women** (due to estrogen).

Meningiomas are **slow-growing tumors** of the **meninges** with a relatively **good prognosis**. Due to **estrogen sensitivity**, they are more common in **women** than men. A **whorled pattern** and **psammoma bodies** are often seen microscopically.

*Psam (Sam) is a good name for both **men**(ingiomas) and **women** (higher rates).*

SCHWANNOMA

Schwannomas are neoplasms of **Schwann cells**, or the support cells that myelinate peripheral nerves. Schwannomas are generally **slow-growing** and **benign**, with only 1% becoming malignant. However, they can still cause problems in the nerve that is being myelinated. The most common location is in the **vestibulocochlear nerve** where a schwannoma can cause unilateral **sensorineural hearing loss**, tinnitus, poor balance, and vertigo. As the tumor grows, it may begin to impact the adjacent **facial and trigeminal nerves** (causing loss of motor function and/or sensation in the face) as well as the **cerebellum** (resulting in ipsilateral ataxia).

Schwannomas are **highly resectable**, and surgery is generally quite successful at removing the tumor (as schwannomas tend to "stay in their lane" rather than messily mixing with surrounding tissues, making surgical removal relatively simple— well, as simple as brain surgery can be, anyway).

Time for some more buzzwords! Schwannomas produce **S-100 proteins** which are found in multiple cell types derived from the neural crest, meaning that they are found in all cases of schwannomas (making them very sensitive) even if they are found in other tumors as well (they are not specific). You can remember this by expanding our mnemonic from earlier: **Schw-one cells** (which myelinate only **one** neuron at a time) are **Schw-one-hundred positive**.

> **Schwannomas** are **slow-growing tumors** of **Schwann cells**. They most commonly occur in the **vestibulocochlear nerve**. **S-100 protein** is a very sensitive marker.
>
> *Schw-one cells are Schw-one-hundred (S-100) positive.*

As a final note, schwannomas tend to occur sporadically on one side of the brain or the other. However, if a patient has *bilateral* schwannomas, this is highly suggestive of a genetic disease known as **neurofibromatosis type II** (which we will cover in more detail in Chapter 24).

OLIGODENDROGLIOMA

The fourth most common type of adult-onset brain tumor is an **oligodendroglioma** which is a neoplasm of oligodendrocytes (or the support cells that myelinate neurons in the central nervous system). Oligodendrogliomas are **slow-growing** tumors with a **good prognosis**. However, because they tend to set up shop in the **frontal lobe**, they can be bothersome to patients, causing **headaches** (due to increased intracranial pressure) and **seizures** (which are often the first sign of the disease).

Like most brain tumors, an initial clinical diagnosis can be supported by head imaging, although definitive diagnosis generally requires a biopsy. There is no cure for oligodendrogliomas, but many people with the disease live for years or even decades following the diagnosis due to its slow-growing nature.

We learned earlier on in Chapter 2 that ol-egg-odendrocytes have a **"fried egg"** appearance under the microscope, and it is this very feature that can help us to identify this tumor on biopsy. A proliferation of fried egg cells surrounded by branching blood vessels (sometimes described as **"chicken wire"** capillaries) is the characteristic finding on microscopic examination, as seen below. Thinking of **chickens** and **eggs** is the easiest way to remember the buzzwords for an ol-**egg**-odendroglioma: the **fried egg** cells, the **chicken wire** capillaries, and the **fried brain** (seizures) that can result from an oligodendroglioma in the frontal lobe.

Oligodendrogliomas are **slow-growing tumors** of **oligodendrocytes**. They often grow in the **frontal lobe** where they can cause **seizures**.

Think of chickens and eggs: ol-egg-odendrocytes, fried egg cells, chicken wire capillaries, and fried brain (seizures).

PITUITARY ADENOMA

The last adult-onset brain tumor we will talk about is a **pituitary adenoma,** or a tumor of the pituitary gland. Most pituitary adenomas are benign—so benign, in fact, that most people with pituitary adenomas never become symptomatic, and their tumors are only ever found incidentally when imaging the brain for other reasons. These **incidentalomas** are common, with up to a quarter of the population having one. In contrast, *clinically significant* pituitary adenomas are more rare. The specific signs and symptoms of a pituitary adenoma relate both to its **anatomical location** in the brain as well as its **specific physiologic functions**. Let's look at each part separately.

Anatomically, the pituitary gland sits right above the optic chiasm, so a tumor here can compress this part of the visual tract, leading to **bitemporal hemianopsia**.

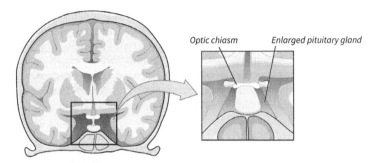

Optic chiasm   Enlarged pituitary gland

On a functional level, the anterior pituitary gland is responsible for releasing the six hormones as in the **FLAT PiG** mnemonic, so an adenoma can result either in too many of these hormones being released *or* too few. (Recall that the hormones released by the *posterior* pituitary gland are actually produced in the *hypothalamus*, so a pituitary adenoma wouldn't necessarily change production of either vasopressin or oxytocin.) Around 75% of all pituitary adenomas tend to "specialize" in secreting excessive amounts of a single hormone, with the most common being adenomas that secrete either **prolactin** or **growth hormone** (around 15 to 30% of all cases). ACTH- and FSH-producing adenomas are less common (5 to 10%), while TSH- and LH-producing adenomas are the most rare (around 1% or less). In contrast, the remaining quarter of pituitary adenomas are **non-secreting**, meaning that they produce no hormones or can even lead to *hypo*pituitarism. Each hormone is variably sensitive to mass effect, with some (like growth hormone) being lost very quickly and others (like prolactin) going missing only in severe cases. You can remember the order of sensitivity using the phrase "**Go Look For The Adenoma Please**" to remind yourself that hormones tend to be lost in this order: **G**rowth hormone, **L**uteinizing hormone, **F**ollicle stimulating hormone, **T**hyroid stimulating hormone, **A**drenocorticotropin hormone, and **P**rolactin.

Non-secreting pituitary adenomas reduce hormone secretion by **mass effect**, with release of some hormones being affected more than others.

Go Look For The Adenoma Please:
GH > LH > FSH > TSH > ACTH > Prolactin.

PEDIATRIC BRAIN TUMORS

We now move onto brain tumors that typically have their onset in childhood and adolescence. Recall that most of these will be *infra*tentorial (in contrast to the supratentorial location of most adult-onset brain tumors). As with adult-onset tumors, pay attention the buzzwords for each!

PILOCYTIC ASTROCYTOMA
Pilocytic astrocytomas are the most common type of brain tumor in people under the age of 20, accounting for almost half of all cases. Astrocytomas are tumors of **astrocytes**, or the support cells of the central nervous system. While astrocytes are found throughout the brain, astrocytomas tend to arise near the cerebellum, brainstem, hypothalamus, and other infratentorial regions. Luckily, pilocytic astrocytomas are generally **slow-growing** and have a **good prognosis**.

The main signs and symptoms of a pilocytic astrocytoma include headache, nausea, visual abnormalities, and poor balance. Head imaging will reveal a **well-circumscribed** mass in the lower part of the brain, as in the image below.

Given how well-defined the tumor is, **surgical resection** is often the treatment of choice. However, because the tumors are located deep in the brain, resection is not always possible. In these cases, chemotherapy and/or radiation are considered.

As with other brain tumors, definitive diagnosis can only be accomplished by looking at the tissue under a microscope. When looking at a pilocytic astrocytoma, long thin hair-like processes are often observed (giving this neoplasm its name, as "pilocytic" means that the cells look like fibers). These fibers are **GFAP positive** (see if you can remember which type of adult-onset brain tumor is GFAP positive as well). In addition, thick worm-like bundles known as **Rosenthal fibers** are often seen as well, as in the next image. You can remember the association of a pilocytic astrocytoma and Rosenthal fibers by thinking that a **pile o' roses enthralls children** (**pilo**cytic astrocytoma, **Rosenthal** fibers, and most common brain tumor in **children**).

Pilocytic astrocytomas are the **most common pediatric brain tumor**. They are **slow-growing** with a **good prognosis**. Biopsy will reveal **GFAP-positive processes** and **Rosenthal fibers**.

*Think of how much a **pile o' roses enthralls children** to associate **pilo**cytic astrocytoma, **Rosenthal** fibers, and **pediatric** brain tumors.*

MEDULLOBLASTOMA

A **medulloblastoma** is a tumor of **cerebellar stem cells** that arises near the fourth ventricle between the brainstem and the cerebellum. It is the second most common pediatric brain tumor (accounting for about 25% of all cases) and tends to occur in the first decade of life. They are usually **well-circumscribed**, with a stone-like appearance on head imaging (as seen below).

Because medulloblastomas are typically located around the brainstem and cerebellum, as they grow they can compress the fourth ventricle, leading to **increased intracranial pressure** and **obstructive hydrocephalus**. This causes the distressing (but ultimately non-specific) signs and symptoms that are so classic of brain tumors, including fatigue, headache, vomiting, and papilledema. If the tumor continues to grow, **cerebellar signs** may appear as well, including ataxia and frequent falling.

Unlike slow-growing pilocytic astrocytomas, medulloblastomas are often **highly malignant**, growing rapidly and even (unlike most brain tumors) metastasizing into other areas of the central nervous system. (The term "drop metastasis" is used to describe cases that travel all the way down to the cauda equina.) Because of their aggressive nature, medulloblastomas have a **high mortality rate**, with less than half of patients surviving 10 years after the diagnosis.

Treatment generally involves **surgery** aimed at removing as much of the tumor as quickly as possible. However, given their rapidly spreading nature, radiation and/or chemotherapy must often be used as well to target areas away from the initial tumor.

Under a microscope, the cells of a medulloblastoma are usually solid and well-circumscribed. They are often said to form **rosettes**, or a pattern of cells surrounding an empty central hub (like the rose windows found on many gothic cathedrals).

Apparently these resemble each other?

How to remember all of this? When you hear "**medu**lloblastoma," think of **Medusa**, the mythological Greek monster with living snakes for hair. Medusa had the ability to turn humans to **stone**, just as a **Medusa**-blastoma has the ability to put a "stone" in someone's head (the well-circumscribed solid mass). Stones are heavy and want to drop down to the lowest part of the brain (the posterior fossa) or even all the way down into the cauda equina of the spinal cord (as in a "drop metastasis"). Like Medusa, Medusa-blastoma is a **highly deadly** monster that should be cut open as soon as possible (with a sword in ancient Greece, and a scalpel in modern medicine).

Medulloblastomas are **aggressive tumors** that often grow
near the fourth ventricle in the **posterior fossa.**

*Medusa-blastoma can create a **stone** in the brain (a **solid tumor** that falls to the lowest*
*part of the brain or even the spinal cord) and should be **cut open quickly.***

EPENDYMOMA

An **ependymoma** is a tumor of ependymal cells which, as you'll recall from Chapter 2, form a lining on the inside of the ventricular system and are responsible for producing, circulating, and absorbing cerebrospinal fluid. While an ependymoma can theoretically form anywhere in the ventricular system, it has a tendency to form most often in the **fourth ventricle** where it can lead to **obstructive hydrocephalus**. Signs and symptoms of increased intracranial pressure are common, including headaches, papilledema, visual changes, nausea, poor balance, and altered mental status.

An ependymoma is a **fast-growing** tumor with a **poor prognosis**. Treatment generally consists of **surgical removal** of the tumor followed by radiation. In general, chemotherapy is not very helpful for treating ependymomas.

It may seem like every brain tumor has its own buzzword, and ependymomas are no exception! The word you are looking for is **perivascular pseudorosettes** (or just "pseudorosettes") which are collections of cells surrounding an inner blood vessel as seen below. Perivascular pseudorosettes are found in almost all cases of ependymoma, making them very sensitive markers of this condition. To remember the association of ependymomas and pseudorosettes, take the visual image you have of an ependyma (an e-**pen**-dyma dipped in cerebrospinal **fluid**) and then tape some fake flowers to the pen (just like they always seem to do in certain restaurants). They're not real flowers, they're *fake* flowers… like *pseudo*-rosettes.

Ependymomas are **fast-growing tumors** of the cells lining the **ventricular system**. They show **perivascular pseudorosettes** when examined under the microscope.

Think of fake flowers tied to a pen to associate e-pen-dymomas with pseudorosettes.

HEMANGIOBLASTOMA

Hemangioblastomas are brain tumors that originate not from the nervous tissue of the brain but from the vascular system supplying it. Their classification as a pediatric brain tumor is somewhat dubious, as they are actually more common in adults! However, for patients with a specific genetic disorder known as **von Hippel-Lindau disease** (which we will talk about in Chapter 24), they may show up in childhood.

Hemangioblastomas are often found in the posterior fossa and in particular seem to enjoy popping up in the **cerebellum**. They are typically **slow-growing** and can often be successfully removed with **surgery**, with an overall **good prognosis** when they arise on their own. (However, people who develop hemangioblastomas as a result of von Hippel-Lindau disease often have multiple tumors and therefore have a worse prognosis.)

A unique feature of hemangioblastomas is that they can produce **erythropoietin**, the hormone that stimulates production of red blood cells. This can cause a secondary **polycythemia**, or an excessive amount of red blood cells in the bloodstream. This will not necessarily present with any signs or symptoms on a clinical level, although it may be picked up when doing lab tests. To make this association, think of this tumor as a **He-Man**(glioblastoma) and form a mental image of a buff dude who considers himself a **red-blooded** male.

Hemangioblastomas are brain tumors derived from the **vascular supply of the brain**. They can produce **erythropoietin** and cause a **secondary polycythemia**.

*A **He-Man**(glioblastoma) is a burly dude who considers himself a **red-blooded** male.*

CRANIOPHARYNGIOMA

Finally, the fifth most common pediatric brain tumor is a **craniopharyngioma**, or a tumor of embryonic cells in the **pituitary gland**. (Of note, craniopharyngiomas are the only one of the five pediatric brain tumors we will discuss that are *supra*tentorial!) A commonly tested point is that craniopharyngiomas are derived from remnants of **Rathke's pouch**, an embryonic structure that gives rise to the anterior pituitary. This means that, while they are found in the pituitary, they are not made of pituitary tissue, so these tumors don't result in hypersecretion of hormones. In fact, due to mass effect they may even *suppress* hormone secretion. Due to their overlap in location, craniopharyngiomas are often confused with pituitary tumors, as both are located near the optic chiasm and can cause **bitemporal hemianopsia**. Interestingly, because craniopharyngiomas arise from the same embryonic cells that form teeth, they have a tendency to **calcify**, leading to a bright appearance on head imaging as seen below:

It kind of looks like a face...

Craniopharyngiomas are often slow-growing and **benign**. Nevertheless, because they have the ability to turn malignant in rare cases, it is generally worth pursuing **surgical removal** with additional radiation and/or chemotherapy.

You can remember the important associations for a craniopharyngioma by thinking of a **child standing on a chair to get away from a rat**. This should help you think of **children** (the population most affected by craniopharyngiomas), the **supra**tentorial nature of this tumor (as the child is standing **above** the chair), **Rat**hke's pouch (from which a craniopharyngioma derives), the **calcified** nature of both rat teeth and craniopharyngiomas, and a **bite**-temporal hemianopsia (which is caused compression of the optic chiasm). In addition, if you use your imagination, the calcified tumor almost looks like the mouth of an evil rat! Rat bites, while painful, are **rarely deadly**, reflecting the benign nature of this tumor.

Craniopharyngiomas are **benign brain tumors** derived from **Rathke's pouch**,
They can compress the optic chiasm and lead to **bitemporal hemianopsia**.

*Think of a **child afraid of a rat bite** to associate this with **children**, **Rat**hke's pouch, **bite**-temporal hemianopsia, **calcified** teeth, and a **rarely deadly** prognosis.*

BRAIN METASTASES

As pointed out earlier, just because a tumor is *in* the brain doesn't mean it's *from* the brain. In fact, secondary brain tumors are actually *more* common than primary brain tumors! These **brain metastases** often set up shop in multiple locations and can therefore present with diffuse neurologic findings (in contrast to a primary brain tumor which is more often localized to a single area). However, this pattern is not consistent enough to rely on, so diagnosis ultimately relies on head imaging and a brain biopsy. As a general rule, any patient with a known history of cancer who presents **with new-onset neurological or behavioral changes** should be evaluated immediately for possible brain metastases.

Different forms of cancer have varying tendencies for metastasizing to the brain. **Lung cancer** is far and away the most common, accounting for nearly half of all cases. However, **breast cancer** is not far behind. Rounding out the top five are **melanoma**, **colon cancer**, and **kidney cancer**. You can remember these using the phrase "Lotsa Bad Stuff Can Kill" which stands for **L**ung, **B**reast, **S**kin, **C**olon, and **K**idney.

*Multifocal **brain metastases** from a primary **breast cancer**.*

The **most common types of cancer** that **metastasize to the brain** are **lung** and **breast** followed by **melanoma, colon**, and **kidney**.

Lotsa Bad Stuff Can Kill: Lung > Breast > Skin > Colon > Kidney.

The presence of a brain metastasis often involves a **poor prognosis**, as it shows just how aggressive the cancer is (as it has not only escaped from its original location but has managed to breach one of the hardest-to-reach parts of the body). For this reason, treatment generally tends to be **palliative** rather than curative, although patients who are younger or who have only a single site of metastasis may benefit from more aggressive treatment. All in all, though, brain metastases are generally nothing but bad news.

PUTTING IT ALL TOGETHER

Brain tumors can be difficult to diagnose, as they often present with **variable signs and symptoms** depending on the specific parts of the brain involved. They also tend to come on very **slowly** (reflecting the slow but steady growth of the tumor itself) which is often less dramatic and noticeable compared to the sudden-onset nature of, say, a stroke. Accordingly, you should always keep brain tumors on your differential, especially when the clinical presentation is unusual in any regard! For example, someone with a known history of headaches who presents with another headache is unlikely to need brain imaging to rule out a tumor. In contrast, someone who has no history of prior headaches who now presents with a severe headache that awakens them from sleep at night and is associated with dizziness and confusion would absolutely warrant an immediate investigation for a brain tumor. Keep an eye out for any atypical patterns, especially when they appear to have come on slowly in a patient with no prior history.

When diagnosing brain tumors, the first helpful distinction to make is between *supra*tentorial tumors (which are more common in adults) and *infra*tentorial tumors (which are more common in children). Use the image of adults ushering the children **under the tent** when it is raining to make this association. From there, be familiar with the most common types of tumors in both children and adults. All of these tumors come with various **buzzwords** that should immediately make you think of them (such as psammoma bodies in meningiomas, S-100 in schwannomas, and so on). For whatever reason, many of the childhood-onset brain tumors have buzzwords related to "roses" (such as **Rose**nthal fibers in pilocytic astrocytomas, pseudo**rose**ttes in medulloblastomas, and perivascular pseudo**rose**ttes in ependymomas), but don't let this confuse you! Do your best to keep these straight in your mind using the provided mnemonics.

REVIEW QUESTIONS

1. A 48 y/o M makes an appointment with a primary care doctor. He is wary of seeking medical care and has not seen a health care provider in over 20 years. However, he decided to make an appointment after experiencing increasingly severe headaches with nausea and occasional vomiting over the past 3 months. A full physical and neurological exam reveals no significant abnormalities. His vital signs are within normal limits. A CT scan reveals a lesion in his right temporal lobe with surrounding edema and compression of the right lateral ventricle. A tissue biopsy confirms the diagnosis. When discussing the case with the patient, the doctor says, "This is a very difficult condition to treat, and while we should never lose hope, it is important to prepare for all possible outcomes." Which of the following is the most likely diagnosis?
   A. Pilocytic astrocytoma
   B. Glioblastoma multiforme
   C. Oligodendroglioma
   D. Hemangioblastoma
   E. Meningioma
   F. Schwannoma

2. A 6 y/o F is brought to the pediatrician for refusing to eat for the past several days, with vomiting this morning. The patient is visibly upset and refuses to answer the doctor's questions. However, when asked if she is having any pain, she points to the back of her head. Neurological exam reveals bilateral papilledema and an unsteady gait. She is unable to name the animal when shown a picture of a dog. MRI reveals a cystic tumor in the right cerebellum. She is diagnosed with the most common primary brain tumor in children and is scheduled for surgery. During the surgery, a sample of the tumor is sent for microscopic analysis. Which of the following is most likely to be seen?
   A. Rosenthal fibers
   B. Rosettes
   C. Perivascular pseudorosettes
   D. Pseudopalisading necrosis
   E. None of the above

3. A 3 y/o M with a history of delayed motor development is seen by his pediatrician after he becomes increasingly irritable over the past month, with frequent crying. His mother notes that she has seen him falling while walking several times in the past week. He had previously been toilet trained, but he has had several episodes of both bowel and bladder incontinence in the past 3 days. On exam, his cranial nerves are intact including pupillary response and extraocular muscles, though some nystagmus is appreciated. Moderate papilledema is seen bilaterally. His upper extremities are at full motor strength, but there is significantly decreased strength in his lower extremities bilaterally, with absent patellar and ankle jerk reflexes. Anal sphincter tone is absent. Which of the following is the most likely explanation for these findings?

A. Supratentorial tumor in the cerebellar cortex
B. Infratentorial tumor in the cerebellum
C. Spinal cord tumor in the cervical cord
D. Spinal cord tumor in the thoracic cord
E. Spinal cord tumor in the lumbar cord
F. Spinal cord tumor in the cauda equina
G. More than one of the above
H. None of the above

4. A 45 y/o M is brought to the hospital by his wife after he appeared drowsy and confused this morning. On exam, he is stuporous and does not respond to questions, though he does flinch when painful stimuli is applied. His wife reports that he has been complaining of increasingly severe headaches for the past 2 weeks, with vomiting over the past 3 days. While the doctor is talking with his wife, the nurse runs out of the room and yells, "He's having a seizure!" The doctor observes a generalized tonic-clonic seizure lasting approximately 90 seconds. A CT scan is obtained which shows a space-occupying lesion in the right frontal lobe. Surgical excision is scheduled. Biopsy of the tumor is diagnostic for oligodendroglioma. Which of the following images is most likely to be seen by the pathologist examining the excised tissue?

A   B   C

D   E   F

1. **The best answer is B.** Of the listed brain tumors, glioblastoma multiforme is the one with the worst prognosis, and many patients do not live more than one or two years after their initial diagnosis. Oligodendrogliomas, meningiomas, and schwannomas are all slow-growing or highly resectable (answers C, E, and F). Pilocytic astrocytomas and hemangioblastomas are both diagnosed more often in children than adults and are each associated with a good prognosis (answers A and D).

2. **The best answer is A.** The most common primary brain tumor in children is a pilocytic astrocytoma, accounting for about half of all cases. Microscopic analysis of the tumor will often reveal Rosenthal fibers as well as characteristic cells with long hair-like GFAP-positive processes. Rosettes are seen in medulloblastomas (answer B), perivascular pseudorosettes are seen in ependymomas (answer C), and pseudopalisading necrosis is seen in glioblastoma multiforme (answer D).

3. **The best answer is G.** This vignette describes a case of medulloblastoma with a drop metastasis causing a cauda equina syndrome. A cerebellar lesion on its own could explain the presence of ataxia and nystagmus. However, it could not also explain the additional presence of motor weakness limited to the lower extremities as well as the presence of bowel and bladder dysfunction (answer B). These findings strongly suggest the involvement of the spinal cord, and in particular the cauda equina given the reduced anal sphincter tone (answers C–F). However, a tumor in just the cauda equina would not explain the ataxia and nystagmus, so it is most likely that there is both a primary tumor in the cerebellum and a secondary "drop metastasis" in the cauda equina (answer F). Supratentorial tumors are rare in children and would not explain these findings (answer A).

4. **The best answer is B.** Oligodendrocytes have a characteristic "fried egg" appearance when examined under a microscope, so it should not come as a surprise that oligodendrogliomas have this feature this as well. Whorling (answer A) and psammoma bodies (answer C) are seen in meningiomas, Rosenthal fibers (answer D) are seen in pilocytic astrocytomas, rosettes (answer E) are seen in medulloblastomas, and perivascular pseudorosettes (answer F) are seen in ependymomas.

20 INFECTIONS

A variety of **infectious diseases** can all target neurons, resulting in various forms of dysfunction in one or more parts of the nervous system. Infectious diseases are often accompanied by **inflammation**, which is the process by which the body uses the immune system to fight off potentially harmful threats from the environment (remember "calor, dolor, rubor, and tumor" from Chapter 14). Inflammation is not inherently bad, but at times the body's inflammatory response can cause just as many problems as the infectious disease itself.

In this chapter, we will focus on infectious diseases that have a particular tendency to attack the nervous system and cause various forms of neurologic dysfunction. There are two ways to "slice the bread" here. We can either divide up the diseases by the **specific parts of the nervous system** that they affect (either the brain, spinal cord, meninges, and/or peripheral nerves), or we can group the diseases based on their **causative agents** (the specific viral, bacterial, and fungal organisms creating the mess in the first place). As with the rest of this book, we will opt for the approach that is most clinically relevant by focusing on how patients present with infections in various parts of the nervous system (while deferring a full discussion of the specific infectious diseases involved to your nearest microbiology textbook). The main forms of neurologic infection we will discuss are **meningitis** (inflammation of the meninges), **encephalitis** (inflammation of the brain), **myelitis** (inflammation of the spinal cord), and **peripheral neuritis** (inflammation of the peripheral nervous system, although you may hear this referred to as simply a "peripheral neuropathy" which includes non-infectious forms of peripheral nerve dysfunction as well).

MENINGITIS

While it may seem strange to start off this chapter by talking about infections of the meninges (rather than of the brain or other nervous tissues themselves), **meningitis** is a critically important disease to understand, as it is not only **common** but also incredibly deadly. Indeed, meningitis is considered to be a **clinical emergency**, and rapid diagnosis and treatment are essential. The classic triad of symptoms involves **fever, headache**, and **neck stiffness** resulting in an inability to flex the neck forward (you can refer to this as "nuchal rigidity" if you're feeling fancy). Additional clinical signs including confusion, headache, nausea, seizures, and photophobia (or extreme discomfort or pain from looking at lights) can occur as well. Like most infectious illnesses, these symptoms often come on over several hours or days.

On a clinical level, an initial diagnosis of meningitis is made by taking a history and doing a physical exam. There are two exam maneuvers in particular that can help to support the diagnosis. The first is to bend both the hip and the knee to a 90° angle (as seen in the image below). If the patient shows signs of severe pain when you try to extend the knee back out, there is likely to be inflammation of the meninges. This is known as **Kernig's sign**.

The second exam maneuver you can do is to have the patient lie flat on their back while you gently flex their neck by raising their head up with your hand. If they reflexively draw in their legs towards their chest due to pain, this is also consistent with meningitis. This finding is known as **Brudzinski's sign**. You can remember the difference between Kernig's sign and Brudzinski's sign by thinking that **Ker**nig involves extending the **Kn**ee while **B**rudzinski involves **B**owing the head.

Kernig's sign and **Brudzinski's sign** are two exam maneuvers that suggest **infection or irritation of the meninges.**

Kernig involves extending the Knee while Brudzinski involves Bowing the head.

While clinical evaluation can help to support an initial suspicion of meningitis, deciding on the correct treatment involves pinpointing exactly *what* is causing the meningitis. In most cases, this will be related to an infection, although cases of non-infectious meningitis related to drugs or other medical conditions do exist. **Viral meningitis** (also called **aseptic meningitis** due to the lack of living organisms in the meninges) is the most common infectious cause, although it is thankfully also the least debilitating and deadly. **Bacterial meningitis** is less common but can be quite deadly. **Fungal meningitis** can be lethal as well, although this form of meningitis is less common, as it primarily affects those who are immunocompromised.

Determining the primary cause of a meningeal infection almost always requires doing a **lumbar puncture**, as viral, bacterial, and fungal forms of meningitis each present with a distinct pattern of cerebrospinal fluid findings which are summarized in the table below:

	Viral	**Bacterial**	**Fungal**
Appearance	Clear	Cloudy	Cloudy
Pressure	Normal or slightly ↑	↑	↑
Glucose	Normal	↓	↓
Protein	Normal	↑	↑
Cells	Lymphocytes	Neutrophils	Lymphocytes

What patterns can we take away from this table? First, notice that findings in viral meningitis are all pretty normal, while those in bacterial and fungal meningitis are distinctly *abnormal*. Second, notice that the abnormal findings in bacterial and fungal meningitis are pretty much the same, with a cloudy appearance, high opening pressure, low glucose, and high protein. Given that both bacterial and fungal cases of meningitis are incredibly **strong** (high protein) infections, it makes sense that this is a **high pressure situation** (increased opening pressure) that is **not sweet** (low glucose) in any way. However, you'll also notice when looking at this general pattern that there is *one major difference* between bacterial and fungal meningitis: the type of cells present! Fungal meningitis causes an increase in *lymphocytes*, while bacterial meningitis causes an increase in *neutrophils*. This is how you're going to tell bacterial and fungal infections apart based on lumbar puncture findings, as they are otherwise quite similar!

Bacterial and fungal meningitis show specific findings on lumbar puncture, including a **high opening pressure**, **low glucose**, and **high protein.**

*Both are **strong** (high protein) infections, so it makes sense that this is a **high pressure situation** (increased opening pressure) that is **not sweet** (low glucose) in any way.*

While a lumbar puncture is helpful for confirming the causative organisms, because meningitis is a clinical emergency, you often cannot wait for the results of testing to return before starting treatment! Particularly in cases of suspected bacterial meningitis, time is so much of the essence that you should not wait for the lab results to return and should instead *start empiric treatment right away.* Even with prompt treatment, the mortality rate for bacterial meningitis is high (around 10%). Patients who survive are typically left with no lasting repercussions, although some will have chronic problems related to meningitis, including recurrent seizures, cognitive dulling, focal neurologic deficits, ataxia, and hearing loss.

On the whole, *Streptococcus pneumonia* and *Neisseria meningitidis* are the two most common causes of bacterial meningitis in adults, and basically all meningitis treatment regimens include a **cephalosporin** that not only is effective against both of these bugs but also is able to get into the central nervous system by crossing the blood–brain barrier. You can associate **cephalo**sporins with meningitis treatment by focusing on the **cephalo-** part (which is Greek for "head"). While cephalosporins are great, unfortunately they don't cover all possible causes of meningitis. This is really **LAME**! Actually, you can use the word **LAME** to remember the organisms against which cephalosporins do not have activity, including *Listeria*, **A**typicals organisms like *Mycoplasma* and *Chlamydia*, **M**ethicillin-resistant *Staphylococcus aureus*, and *Enterococci*. Because these bugs would escape unharmed if a cephalosporin was the only antibiotic used, additional drugs (like ampicillin or vancomycin) should be added for complete coverage.

Cephalosporins are effective against the **two most common causes of meningitis**, although **additional antibiotics** are often needed for **complete coverage**.

*It's really **LAME** that cephalosporins do not cover all possible causes of meningitis!*
Listeria
Atypicals organisms
Methicillin-resistant Staphylococcus aureus
Enterococci

Fungal meningitis should be treated with **antifungals** such as amphotericin or fluconazole. In contrast to both bacterial and fungal meningitis, most cases of viral meningitis require no specific treatment at all.

Because meningitis requires you to take a "**shoot first and ask questions later**" approach, deciding on a course of treatment often relies upon making assumptions about what the most likely causative organisms will be. This is generally done by knowing the most common infectious agents in each **age group**, allowing you to use the patient's demographics to choose the antibiotics that are most likely to be effective. For this reason, we will spend the next few sections going over not only how meningitis presents in each age group but also the causative organisms that are most commonly found.

INFANT MENINGITIS
Compared to cases of meningitis in children and adults, meningitis in infants requires some unique considerations. First, infants are not able to report their symptoms, so you may need to rely on some additional clinical signs that can be suggestive of meningitis, including **inconsolable crying**, **bulging of the fontanelles** (or the soft openings in the skull where the bones have not yet fused), and an arched back and neck known as the **opisthotonus position**:

*An infant with **bulging fontanelles** (left) and in the **opisthotonus position** (right).*

The causative organisms in infant meningitis are very different from those seen in children and adults. You can remember the three bugs that cause infant meningitis using the acronym **GEL** which stands for **G**roup B streptococcus, **E**. coli, and **L**isteria.

Group B streptococcus is a Gram-positive coccus that is the **most common cause** of meningitis in **neonates**. It is often picked up from the mother's vaginal canal during childbirth, as it is a common part of normal vaginal flora. Most newborns will pick up this bacteria and, like their mother, proceed to live with it in peace. In some cases, however, this bacteria can overwhelm the infant's protective mechanisms and cause meningitis. Group B streptococcal meningitis is particularly difficult to diagnose because the classic meningitis signs are either not present or the patient does not yet have the language skills report to report them. For this reason, meningitis must be on the differential for **all infants presenting with a high fever**! Some guidelines also suggest routine screening of all expectant mothers to prevent transmission, although other guidelines argue that this is unnecessary. You can remember the association of **G**roup **B S**treptococcus with neonatal meningitis by thinking of it as the mother **G**iving **B**aby a(n unpleasant) **S**urprise.

Group B streptococcus is the most common cause of meningitis in **neonates**. It is picked up from the mother's vaginal canal during childbirth.

Group B Streptococcus Gives Baby a(n unpleasant) Surprise.

Escherichia coli (almost always referred to by its shorter name *E. coli*) is a Gram-negative rod that is the second most common cause of meningitis in **neonates**. Like Group B streptococcus, it is often picked up from the mother during childbirth. While *E. coli* is associated with infections in various parts of the body such as gastrointestinal and urinary tract infections, strains of *E. coli* that have the **K1 capsular antigen** appear to be particularly able to infect the meninges. You can remember this by thinking of **K-one heads** (as *E. coli* with K1 are more likely to go to the head).

Escherichia coli is a common cause of meningitis in **neonates**. *E. coli* possessing the **K1 capsular antigen** are most likely to result in meningitis.

K-one heads: E. coli *with* **K-one** *are more likely to go to the head.*

Finally, *Listeria monocytogenes* is a Gram-positive rod that is a common cause of meningitis in newborns (as well as the **elderly** and other people with **compromised immune systems**, including those with AIDS, severe diabetes, or conditions that require them to take steroids).

The most common causes of **infant meningitis** are **Group B streptococcus**, *E. coli*, and *Listeria*.

Bulging fontanelles (a sign of infant meningitis) are filled with GEL: Group B streptococcus, **E.** coli, *and* Listeria.

MENINGITIS IN CHILDREN AND ADULTS

Cases of meningitis in children and adults involve a different set of organisms compared to infants. The most common bugs in this age group are *Streptococcus pneumoniae*, *Neisseria meningitidis*, and **enteroviruses**. *Haemophilus influenza* is common in children between the age of 1 and 6, while **herpes simplex virus** is common in teenagers and adults. You can think of these using the mnemonic **HENS** (as **hens** are **grown-up** chickens, they're no longer young chicks).

Neisseria meningitidis (sometimes referred to as meningococcus) is a Gram-negative diplococci that is the most common cause of bacterial meningitis among **children and teenagers** between the ages of 2 and 18. There are a few key points to know about meningococcal meningitis. First, it is often accompanied by a **purpuric rash** that is **non-blanching** (meaning that it does not lose its color when pressure is applied). The combination of any classic meningitis symptoms plus a non-blanching rash should immediately have you thinking of meningococcus, although it's important to note that some patients may develop the rash without showing any of the classic signs of meningitis!

Second, *N. meningitidis* often spreads among people living in **close quarters** such as college students or military recruits. For this reason, once a case is identified, treatment involves not only treating the patient but also close contacts around them to prevent the spread of infection.

Third, meningococcal meningitis is associated with a deadly complication known as **Waterhouse-Friderichsen syndrome** in which bleeding into the adrenal glands occurs, leading to **adrenal insufficiency**. Waterhouse-Friderichsen syndrome must be identified rapidly when it occurs. For this reason, a patient presenting with any combination of meningitis symptoms, petechial rash, and/or sudden-onset hypotension and tachycardia should have you thinking of Waterhouse-Friderichsen syndrome! To remember this, think of your kidneys as **waterhouses** (organs that produce fluid) that get **fried** in meningococcal disease, leading to **Waterhouse-Fride**richsen syndrome. Treatment involves use of a cephalosporin, although the best way to combat this disease is to prevent people from getting it in the first place by giving the meningococcal vaccine.

Waterhouse-Friderichsen syndrome is a severe complication of meningococcal disease that leads to **adrenal insufficiency**.

*Your body's **waterhouses** (kidneys) get **fried** in **Waterhouse-Fride**richsen syndrome.*

Streptococcus pneumonia is a Gram-positive diplococcus that is the single **most common cause of bacterial meningitis in children and adults** over the age of 18. Part of the reason it is so common is because it is a resident of most people's upper respiratory tract, where it generally lives in peace with its host. However, under certain conditions, it can grow out of control and lead to infection. Treatment involves a cephalosporin, though prevention via immunization is the best option.

Finally, *Haemophilus influenzae* is a Gram-negative rod that causes meningitis primarily in children under the age of 5. Like *S. pneumoniae*, it is a common resident in the sinuses of children and can either spread to the meninges directly or via seeping into the bloodstream. Treatment consists of a cephalosporin. Even with treatment, up to a third of all patients are left with permanent damage, including deafness in some cases. In recent years, the availability of a vaccine has decreased rates significantly.

> The most common causes of **meningitis in children and adults** are *Streptococcus pneumoniae*, *Neisseria meningitidis*, and **enteroviruses**. *Haemophilus influenzae* is common in children, while **herpes simplex virus** is common in teenagers and adults.

> *HENS* are ***grown-up*** *chickens that can get these causes of **hen***-*ingitis:*
> *H. influenzae and **H**erpes simplex*
> ***E**nteroviruses*
> ***N**eisseria meningitides*
> ***S**treptococcus pneumoniae*

FUNGAL MENINGITIS

Fungal infections are a rare cause of meningitis, although they are more common in patients who are **immunocompromised**. Fungal meningitis presents with similar signs and symptoms as bacterial meningitis but tends to have a poor prognosis and high mortality rates. There are a few species of fungus that are able to infect the central nervous system, with most of these also being able to cause other types of infections as well (such as pneumonia). Each of these species is found in specific **geographic distributions** which are commonly included as clues on test questions.

Cryptococcus neoformans is the most common cause of fungal meningitis and is found **worldwide**. It has a tendency to be found in soil that has been fouled (or should we say *fowled?*) by droppings from pigeons and other birds. You can remember this association by thinking of it as *Crypto-**caca** neoformans* to associate it with pigeon poop. Use of a special stain known as **India ink** is helpful for visualizing this fungus under a microscope.

> *Cryptococcus neoformans* is the **most common cause of fungal meningitis** worldwide and is associated with **bird dropping infested soil**. An **India ink** stain is used to visualize it in cerebrospinal fluid.

> *Crypto-**caca** neoformans is found in pigeon **poop**.*

Coccidioides immitis is another potential cause of fungal meningitis that is found in the **southwestern United States** as well as parts of Central and South America. It most often is associated with a **lung infection** producing flu-like symptoms (known as "Valley fever" for the Central Valley of California), but in some cases it may develop into meningitis.

Histoplasma is a genus of fungus that can infect the central nervous system and cause meningitis. It is found worldwide but is particularly prevalent in the **Midwest United States** near the Ohio and Mississippi Rivers in places like the insides of caves that have been contaminated by bird or bat droppings. You can remember this association by sticking an **O** in front of it to make *OHIstOplasma*.

> *Histoplasma* is a potential cause of **fungal meningitis** that is endemic to the **Midwestern United States**. It is associated with **bird and bat droppings**.
>
> *OHIstOplasma is found in **OHIO** and nearby places.*

The last potential cause of fungal meningitis we will talk about is *Blastomyces dermatitidis*. Like *Histoplasma*, *Blastomyces* is found predominantly in the **midwestern United States** east of the Mississippi River. This time, however, it is associated with **wet and damp places** such as near lakes and rivers or in moldy wood.

VIRAL MENINGITIS

Finally, viruses are a common cause of meningitis in adults and may even represent a majority of cases in the United States. **Enteroviruses** are the most common cause, although **herpes simplex** often occurs as well. Compared to bacterial meningitis, viral meningitis is generally more benign, with less severe symptoms, a slower progression, and a more rapid resolution (patients generally feel better within a week). Most cases of viral meningitis do not require specific treatment outside of supportive care, although if herpes simplex meningitis is suspected an antiviral medication known as **acyclovir** can be used.

CENTRAL NERVOUS SYSTEM INFECTIONS

While meningitis involves inflammation of the layers covering the brain, **encephalitis** refers to a state of inflammation in the brain itself. This can occur as the result of an infection, an autoimmune reaction (where the immune system attacks its own body), or without a clear cause (known as an idiopathic encephalitis). To stay true to our theme, in this chapter we will focus specifically on *infectious* causes of encephalitis (saving other causes for later chapters).

As with meningitis, a wide range of infectious diseases can lead to encephalitis, including viruses, bacteria, fungi, and parasites. Many of these will present clinically with **non-specific symptoms** including fever, altered mental status, headache, drowsiness, nausea, hallucinations, and seizures, although some infectious diseases (such as rabies or syphilis) will have more specific signs, as we will discover soon. Depending on the areas involved, encephalitis can present with **focal neurologic deficits** (this helps to distinguish it from meningitis, which usually doesn't). However, the boundary between meningitis and encephalitis is blurry, especially when the infection spreads to involve both at the same time, known as **meningoencephalitis**.

Evaluation of these patients typically involves a complete history and physical, neuroimaging, and lab testing of both blood and cerebrospinal fluid. If an infectious cause is found, treatment should be provided (such as **antibiotics** for a bacterial encephalitis or **antivirals** for a viral encephalitis). **Steroids** can be used to reduce swelling in the brain, while other medications can be used to increase the patient's comfort (like using NSAIDs for fever or sedatives for restlessness).

With that broad overview under our belts, we will now look at some of the most high-yield specific organisms with a tendency to infect the central nervous system.

HERPESVIRAL ENCEPHALITIS

Viruses are the most common cause of encephalitis, with bacterial and fungal causes of encephalitis being less common (even if they are often more severe). **Herpes simplex** is the most commonly identified cause of viral encephalitis, with HSV-1 (the form of the virus that causes oral herpes or "cold sores") being much more common than HSV-2 (the form that causes genital herpes). Herpes simplex has a particular affinity for the **temporal lobe**, including the hippocampus and other parts of the limbic system. Inflammation in these areas can even show up on neuroimaging (as in the MRI below).

Involvement of the temporal lobe can be seen clinically, with **temporal lobe seizures** being common. Other classic signs and symptoms of encephalitis including fever, headache, and altered mental status are seen as well. Treatment involves the antiviral medication **acyclovir** which should be administered quickly and at high doses. Without treatment, herpes simplex encephalitis is almost uniformly fatal. Even with treatment, there is a high mortality rate. People who survive are often left with long-term neurologic deficits including memory loss and amnesia (which makes sense considering that the hippocampus is often affected). You can remember the predilection of herpes for the hippocampus and other areas in the temporal lobe by thinking of it as the **herpe**-campus.

Herpes simplex is the most common cause of **viral encephalitis**. It has a particular affinity for the **temporal lobe** and can cause **seizures**.

*Herpes tends to hit the **herpe-campus** and other parts of the temporal lobe.*

ARBOVIRUS ENCEPHALITIS

Arboviruses are carried by arthropods which includes insects like **mosquitos**. (In fact, the name arbovirus is a direct nod to this: **ar**thropod-**bo**rne **virus**.) Arboviruses are another leading cause of encephalitis, spanning a wide array of different syndromes that include such fanciful names as eastern equine encephalitis, western equine encephalitis, St. Louis encephalitis, and West Nile fever. The severity of these infections can vary significantly, with some cases producing only minimal symptoms and others resulting in life-threatening illness. The prevalence of arboviral encephalitis varies from region to region and even from season to season, with late summer (the period of highest mosquito activity, naturally) being the highest risk.

RABIES

Rabies is an infection of the central nervous system involving various *lyssaviruses*. It is most often caused by a bite from an infected animal. While dog bites are the most frequent source of rabies worldwide, in the United States **bat bites** are the most common. Most people do not show symptoms of rabies right away. Instead, between the time of the bite and the disease presenting clinically is an **incubation period** lasting 1 to 3 months. During this time, the virus replicates and, once it has gathered sufficient numbers, marches up along motor neurons towards the central nervous system (essentially using the "streets" of the peripheral nervous system and the "highway" of the spinal cord to reach the "headquarters" of the brain in a process known as **retrograde transport**). Once there, it continues to replicate in the brain before sending additional viruses back out into the peripheral nervous system, with a plan to set up shop in the **salivary glands**.

Once an infection has outgrown its incubation period, the initial signs and symptoms of rabies are highly suggestive of generalized infection of the brain and/or meninges, including fever, headache, confusion, irritability, anxiety, and behavioral changes. One particularly notable sign that is specific for rabies is **hydrophobia** (or "fear of water") which is found in the vast majority of cases. Someone infected with rabies may give a panicked response when presented with water even though they are extremely thirsty, and attempting to drink water will induce incredibly painful spasms of muscles in the throat. Hydrophobia is likely due to the tendency of the rabies virus to thrive in the salivary glands, as preventing water ingestion helps the virus to self-preserve and thereby increase its chances of transmission through a bite. A diagnosis of rabies can be confirmed on autopsy, with a particular microscopic finding known as **Negri bodies** being found in motor neurons.

Rabies is almost always a **fatal** disease, and without treatment most people will die within a week of presentation. Indeed, by the time a patient is showing symptoms, it is already too late, as treatment is almost never effective at this stage. Instead, the cornerstone of treatment is trying to prevent symptoms from happening in the first place using **post-exposure prophylaxis**. This involves giving the rabies vaccine to anyone with a known or suspected bite from a rabid animal. Provided the vaccine is given within 10 days, it is 100% effective for preventing progression to rabies.

To put all of the important points about rabies together, use the phrase **FINISH** to remember that it is Fatal without Immunization and is associated with Negri bodies on autopsy, an Incubation period, the Salivary glands, and Hydrophobia.

*Note the **bat** wings, large **salivary glands**, and gaze away from the bowl of **water** in front of him.*

Rabies is a **viral disease** that infects the **central nervous system** after an **incubation period**, leading to **hydrophobia** and signs of **meningoencephalitis**.

FINISH:
Fatal without Immunization
Negri bodies
Incubation period
Salivary glands
Hydrophobia

SUBACUTE SCLEROSING PANENCEPHALITIS

Subacute sclerosing panencephalitis (or SSPE) is a rare but often fatal condition that is characterized by **widespread inflammation in the brain** related to the **measles virus**. It is unique among the forms of infectious encephalitis we have talked about so far in that it does *not* occur at the time of an acute infection. Instead, it can develop *years* after the patient has recovered from the initial illness.

While the vast majority of people who get measles will recover completely, a minority (0.01%) will go on to develop subacute sclerosing panencephalitis, with an average delay of 7 years. During this initial period, the person is completely asymptomatic. However, over time some concerning signs and symptoms begin to emerge, including changes in personality, cognitive deficits, muscle spasms, visual changes, and seizures. These abnormalities progressively accumulate to the point where vital functions such as breathing and heart rate are compromised, leading to death. Unfortunately, there is **no cure** for subacute sclerosing panencephalitis, so management is largely directed towards preventing infection with measles in the first place by use of a **vaccine**. You can remember the typical course of SSPE by thinking of it as a comic book-like onomatopoeia for the sound of a bomb fuse slowly burning (SSsssssssssss) and then, after a long build-up, exploding (PppppEeeeeeee!).

S
S
S
S
S
S
S
PppppppppppppppppppEeeeeeeeeeee!

Subacute sclerosing panencephalitis (SSPE) is a disease involving **widespread inflammation in the brain** that occurs years after an initial **measles viral infection.**

*Think of **SSPE** as an onomatopoeia for a **bomb fuse** slowing burning (**SS**sssssss...) and then exploding (**P**pppppp**E**eeeeee!) after a long build-up.*

BRAIN ABSCESSES

Infections of the central nervous system can sometimes create an **abscess**, or a localized collection of **pus**. Pus consists of exudates from an infection that includes dead white blood cells from the immune response. Brain abscesses tend to produce similar signs and symptoms to encephalitis, although because they are localized they can produce more **focal signs and symptoms** as well. In this way, brain abscesses can sometimes present similarly to brain tumors, although abscesses tend to come on faster and present with other signs of infection (such as fever and leukocytosis). Neuroimaging is almost always indicated if a brain abscess is suspected, where it can appear as a hole or "bubble" if it gets large enough (as seen below). A lumbar puncture is generally not helpful as abscesses are by definition localized, meaning that organisms won't be found in the cerebrospinal fluid.

Most brain abscesses are due to the spread of bacteria from the sinuses following a sinus infection, although a minority of cases are due to spread across the blood–brain barrier. Commonly identified organisms include *Streptococcus*, anaerobic organisms (such as *Bacteroides*), and *Staphylococcus aureus*. Treatment involves **antibiotics** tailored to the organisms present, with **surgery** being used if the abscess is sufficiently large or close enough to ventricular system where it could potentially spread to other areas.

TOXOPLASMOSIS

Unlike with meningitis (where most cases can be attributed to either viruses, bacteria, or fungi), with encephalitis some cases are caused by **parasites** as well. One potential cause of parasitic encephalitis is *Toxoplasma gondii*, a single-celled protozoan parasite that is most often picked up from **cat feces** or handling **undercooked meat**. Infection by toxoplasmosis is common, with up to half of the world's population carrying this parasite around. Almost all carriers of toxoplasmosis are completely asymptomatic.

However, two groups in particular are at high risk for a clinically significant toxoplasmosis infection: **newborns** and **immunocompromised adults**.

An infected mother can pass this parasite onto her fetus across the placenta, whose immune system is not able to fight it off as effectively. Babies with **congenital toxoplasmosis** are often born with the classic triad of **chorioretinitis** (inflammation of the eyes), **hydrocephalus**, and **intracranial atherosclerosis**, though they are also at risk of developing additional problems such as deafness, cognitive delays, and seizures. For this reason, pregnant women should not change cat litter!

In adults, the majority of people with active toxoplasmosis are those with compromised immune systems, with **HIV/AIDS** being the most common cause. Cases of toxoplasmosis involving the central nervous system can be identified by the classic signs and symptoms of encephalitis. CT scans of the head will reveal **abscesses** in a particular pattern known as **ring-enhancing lesions** as seen in the image below. This combination (multiple ring-enhancing lesions in a patient with HIV/AIDS) is so highly suggestive of toxoplasmosis that treatment is often started even before the diagnosis can be confirmed. You can remember the link between cats, multiple ring-enhancing lesions, and toxoplasmosis by focusing on the **OXO** of t**OXO**plasmosis. Imagine the two **O**'s as the multiple ring-enhancing lesions surrounding an X superimposed on top of a brain (to suggest that its function has been wiped out).

Toxoplasma gondii is a **protozoal parasite** that can lead to **encephalitis** in **newborns** and **immunocompromised adults** (particularly those with **HIV/AIDS**).

Think of the **OXO** in t**OXO**plamosis as multiple **ring-enhancing lesions** in the brain.

PRIMARY CNS LYMPHOMA

Wait a minute, isn't a lymphoma a type of neoplasm? Then why are we studying it in this chapter and not Chapter 19? The reason is that cases of primary CNS lymphoma are almost always associated with infection by the **Epstein-Barr virus**, making it one of a few kinds of cancer that have a direct relationship to a viral infection. There is a great deal of overlap between central nervous system toxoplasmosis and primary CNS lymphoma, as both occur almost exclusively in **immunosuppressed** patients and can present with **ring-enhancing lesions**. While this combination should always make you think of toxoplasmosis *first*, in cases where a patient is not getting better after adequate treatment of toxoplasmosis, consider primary CNS lymphoma.

NEUROCYSTICERCOSIS

Cysticercosis is an infection with *Taenia solium*, a **parasitic tapeworm** found in **pigs**. When its larvae attack the central nervous system, it can lead to **neurocysticercosis**, with signs and symptoms including headaches, confusion, blindness, and seizures. The "cysts" of neuro-"cyst"-icercosis refer to the cavitary lesions that occur in this condition, which can be picked up on neuroimaging (as seen below). Due to its prevalence, neurocysticercosis is one of the leading causes of seizures worldwide, especially in parts of the world with poor sanitation. Treatment involves use of an **antiparasitic** medication such as albendazole or praziquantel as well as an **anticonvulsant** to help control seizures.

SYPHILIS

Syphilis is a sexually transmitted infection caused by *Treponema pallidum*, a corkscrew-shaped bacterium. Before the advent of antibiotics, syphilis was a highly feared disease. (In fact, throughout history people have had a tendency to blame it on anyone but themselves, with Italians calling it "French disease," the French calling it "Italian disease," the Portuguese calling it "Spanish disease," and so on.) Syphilis is notorious for causing a wide variety of symptoms affecting every part of the body, making it one of the "great imitators" of medicine. However, it is particularly known for affecting the nervous system in later stages of the disease, often 5 to 10 years after the initial infection. Collectively, the neurologic manifestations of late-stage infection are called **neurosyphilis** (or **tertiary syphilis**).

Neurosyphilis can take several different forms depending on where the infection is. When syphilis affects the brain, it produces a syndrome known as **general paresis** which involves a variety of **psychiatric phenomena**. Most prominent among these is a state of **dementia** related to atrophy of the brain (particularly in the frontal and temporal lobes) combined with loss of memory, personality changes, and mood instability. One finding in general paresis is that the pupils will constrict in response to a nearby object but do *not* constrict to light (these are the **Argyll Robertson pupils**, or "prostitute's pupils," that we talked about back in Chapter 9).

While general paresis results from a syphilis infection in the brain, syphilis can also attack the spinal cord as well, leading to a particular syndrome known as **tabes dorsalis** (also known as syphilitic myelopathy). Tabes *dorsalis* involves demyelination of the *dorsal* columns of the spinal cord, leading to loss of **F**ine touch, **V**ibration, and **P**roprioception (from the **F**eeling **V**ery **P**atient mnemonic back in Chapter 7) with preservation of crude touch, pain, and temperature.

*Cross-section of the spinal cord showing **dorsal column demyelination** related to **tabes dorsalis**.*

Neurosyphilis is relatively rare in the age of easy access to antibiotics. When it occurs, it can be quickly treated using **penicillin** (although any neuronal damage that has already taken place can usually not be reversed).

CAVERNOUS SINUS THROMBOSIS

Cavernous sinus thrombosis occurs when a blood clot gets trapped within the **cavernous sinus**, which you'll remember as one of the dural venous sinuses that drains blood from the anterior part of the brain. The reason we are discussing cavernous sinus thrombosis in this chapter is because it is frequently caused by an infection, with *Staphylococcus aureus* being the most common pathogen found.

Ordinarily a clot in any area of the venous drainage from the head isn't a big deal (in contrast to the arterial system where a clot can be a *very* big deal indeed) due to the extensive system of anastomoses that provide alternative routes for blood to leave the brain and return to the body. However, in the case of the cavernous sinus, a clot has the potential to cause clinically significant problems due to the sheer number of other structures that pass through the cavernous sinus. You can remember these structures using the mnemonic **TOM COAT** which stands for the **T**rigeminal nerve (specifically its **O**phthalmic and **M**axillary divisions), the internal **C**arotid artery, the **O**culomotor nerve, the **A**bducens nerve, and finally the **T**rochlear nerve. In total, four different cranial nerves pass through here as well as part of a major artery supplying the brain, making a clot in the cavernous sinus a potentially dangerous situation!

The specific signs and symptoms you would observe in a patient with cavernous sinus thrombosis include **swelling or bulging of the eyes** (due to a blockage in fluid drainage from the eyes), changes in vision (due to the close proximity of the cavernous sinus to the eyes), paralysis of extraocular muscles (due to the involvement of the oculomotor, trochlear, and abducens nerves), and numbness of the upper two-thirds of the face (which are covered by the ophthalmic and maxillary divisions of the trigeminal nerve). By knowing the structures that course through the cavernous sinus, these signs and symptoms should not come as too much of a surprise.

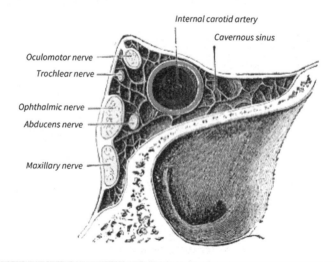

Cavernous sinus thrombosis involves a **blood clot** blocking venous drainage from the **cavernous sinus** around the eyes.

TOM COAT:
Trigeminal nerve (Ophthalmic and Maxillary divisions)
Internal Carotid artery
Oculomotor nerve
Abducens nerve
Trochlear nerve

Diagnosis is based on the presence of specific signs and symptoms as well as neuroimaging, with an **MRI with flow venogram** being the modality of choice. Treatment consists of **antibiotics**, with broad-spectrum agents used until the specific pathogen can be determined. Cavernous sinus thrombosis is a serious condition, with a high mortality rate (up to 100% without treatment and even as high as 20% with treatment), so keep it on your radar.

PRION DISEASE

Prions are an unusual form of central nervous system infection in which the causative "organisms" are not organisms at all. Instead, prion diseases are characterized by the presence of **misfolded proteins** that are toxic to neurons (the word prion itself being short for "**pr**otein **infecti**on"). These proteins cause other nearby proteins to misfold as well, setting off a cascade of neurotoxicity that punches microscopic holes into nervous tissue, giving it a "spongy" appearance as seen below:

The prion that sets off this chain of events can either be picked up from the environment (often by eating infected animal products), inherited, or acquired sporadically. The initial presenting signs and symptoms are highly variable but tend to include memory problems, changes in behavior, and poor coordination. Unfortunately, once this process has started, it **progresses rapidly**. While certain medications may help slow the progress, there are currently no treatments that have been shown to stop or reverse the progress. Sadly, most people die within one year of diagnosis. In humans, there are a few specific prion diseases that have been recognized, including **Creutzfeldt–Jakob disease**, **kuru**, and **fatal familial insomnia**.

Prions are **misfolded proteins** that are **toxic to neurons** and induce nearby proteins to misfold, resulting in **rapidly progressive neurodegenerative diseases**.

Prions are protein infections.

PERIPHERAL NERVOUS SYSTEM INFECTIONS

Finally, we will talk about infections that attack the peripheral nervous system (either exclusively or in addition to the central nervous system).

SHINGLES

Shingles is a **painful blistering rash** that occurs as a result of infection by the **varicella zoster virus** (the same virus that causes **chickenpox**). After an infection with chickenpox, the virus is not cleared from the body but instead lays dormant in the **dorsal root ganglion** of specific spinal nerves. The virus can then reactivate years or even decades later, at which point it travels down the axons of the spinal nerve to the skin where it causes inflammation, including the characteristic rash (as seen below). This rash occurs in a **dermatomal distribution** depending on the specific spinal nerve involved, so make sure to know your dermatomal landmarks!

This rash typically lasts several weeks before the virus returns to a latent state. However, in some people the nerve damage caused by shingles can lead to lasting pain even after the infection has gone back to being dormant (known as **postherpetic neuralgia**). Treatment with acyclovir can help to shorten the duration of the rash. However, rather than treating after the fact, the best strategy is to prevent shingles from occurring in the first place through **vaccination**.

LYME DISEASE

Lyme disease is a tick-borne illness caused by the bacterium ***Borrelia burgdorferi***. The hallmark sign of early infection is a characteristic "bull's eye" rash known as **erythema migrans** (as seen in the following image) which is often accompanied by flu-like symptoms. Following this initial local infection, *Borrelia* can travel through the bloodstream and cause problems in other areas of the body, causing pain in various joints in the body (arthritis) and abnormal heart rhythms (cardiac conduction abnormalities). When it infects the nervous system, it causes a syndrome known as **neuroborreliosis**.

Neuroborreliosis can disrupt various parts of the nervous system, including both the central and peripheral nervous system. Central nervous system involvement can present as **encephalitis** (including confusion, mood changes, and cognitive deficits) as well as the possibility of developing **meningitis**. However, Lyme disease is perhaps best known for its peripheral nerve manifestations, as it can lead to a generalized **peripheral neuropathy** (including shooting pains and sensory abnormalities) as well as **Bell's palsy** (or a paralysis of the facial nerve as seen below).

You can remember all of these features of **Lyme** disease by thinking of limes. What do you do with a bunch of **Lymes**? Why, **BAKE 'EM** into a **Key Lyme pie** of course! The phrase **BAKE 'EM** can help you remember the key associations of Lyme disease with **B**ell's palsy and other peripheral neuropathies, **A**rthritis, abnormalities on E**K**G, **E**rythema migrans (the "bull's eye" rash), **E**ncephalitis, and **M**eningitis.

Lyme disease is a **tick-borne disease** that causes **flu-like symptoms** and a **bull's eye rash** in its initial stages, followed by various **neurologic, rheumatologic,** and **cardiac** manifestations.

*What do you do with a bunch of **Lymes**? Why, **BAKE 'EM** into a Key Lyme pie of course!*
B*ell's palsy and other peripheral neuropathies*
A*rthritis*
E*KG abnormalities*
E*rythema migrans*
E*ncephalitis*
M*eningitis*

Treatment of Lyme disease involves **antibiotics** such as doxycycline that can target the *Borrelia* bacteria. As with other infections, prevention is the most important step here, which in this case involves **avoidance of ticks** (either by staying out of areas known to have ticks, wearing long-sleeve clothing, or using insect repellents).

PUTTING IT ALL TOGETHER

The number of infectious diseases that can affect the nervous system is vast, and there is no way to cover them all in just a single chapter. Instead, we have focused on those diseases that are the most **common** (the ones most likely to appear in patients and on tests), the most **devastating** (the ones that must be recognized and treated promptly to avoid a poor outcome), or the most **educational** (the ones that reinforce what we have learned about the anatomy and physiology of the nervous system by illustrating what happens when one aspect of it becomes dysfunctional).

A good starting point for recognizing an infection of the nervous system is to decide whether it is affecting the brain, the meninges, or the peripheral nerves. "**Head symptoms**" such as headache, confusion, and focal neurologic signs are suggestive of encephalitis, while "**neck symptoms**" such as nuchal rigidity, Kernig's sign, and Brudzinski's sign are suggestive of meningitis. Other infectious symptoms such as fever or nausea are not specific to either and can be found in both.

Ultimately a lot of what we've covered can feel like trivia ("Which type of fungal meningitis is bats and which one is pigeons?"). However, in high-stress clinical situations, this sort of information suddenly becomes relevant for helping to figure out what might be the cause of the patient's disease. Use the mnemonics here to try and remember as much information as you can. You never know when it will pop back into your head!

REVIEW QUESTIONS

1. A 19 y/o M college student comes to the emergency department complaining of chills and a worsening headache over the past 3 days. He continued to go to class on the first day, but since then he has been in his room unable to get up or attend to his studies. Vital signs are HR 112, BP 118/78, RR 20, and T 101.3°F. On exam, there is significant pain when asked to bend his neck forward. He is unable to tolerate a test of his pupillary light reflexes and yells when a penlight is used. Lumbar puncture is performed and shows a dusty appearance of the cerebrospinal fluid, with an elevated opening pressure, increased protein, decreased glucose, and high polymorphonuclear neutrophils. Which of the following is the best next step in management?
    A. Ordering a CT of the head
    B. Ordering an MRI of the head
    C. Administering an antibiotic drug
    D. Administering an antiviral drug
    E. Administering an antifungal drug
    F. Providing immunizations to the patient
    G. Providing immunizations to the patient's close contacts
    H. Discharging with ibuprofen and a follow-up appointment in 1 week
    I. None of the above

2. (Continued from previous question.) The remainder of the exam is notable for several patches of punctate red dots over the abdomen and chest as seen below:

These patches do not lose their color when pressure is applied. Several hours after his initial presentation to the hospital, the patient begins to appear lethargic and has trouble answering questions. Repeat vital signs are HR 144, BP 70/32, RR 6, and T 101.8°F. He is seen coughing up blood, and his hands have turned a blue tint. Repeat labs are notable for hypoglycemia, hyponatremia, hyperkalemia, and thrombocytopenia. Which of the following is the most likely causative organism?

A. *Escherichia coli*
B. *Listeria monocytogenes*
C. *Streptococcus pneumonia*
D. *Neisseria meningitidis*
E. *Haemophilus influenza*
F. Herpes simplex
G. Herpes zoster
H. *Cryptococcus neoformans*
I. *Coccidioides immitis*
J. *Histoplasma*
K. *Blastomyces dermatitidis*

3. A 42 y/o M sees his nurse practitioner after developing right ear pain, headache, and fever over the past 2 days. He is diagnosed as having an infection of the middle ear and is prescribed antibiotics. Within several hours of taking the medication, he feels better. However, 3 days later, he begins feeling feverish and confused. His husband rushes him to the hospital after he is unable to say his own name. Vital signs in the emergency department are HR 108, BP 142/84, RR 20, and T 102.9°F. His exam is notable for a bulging left eye as seen below:

There are unilateral deficits in visual acuity and pupillary response on the left. A CT scan with contrast reveals irregular vascular filling within the cavernous sinus with engorgement of several nearby veins. Which of the following findings is *least* likely to be seen on exam?
   A. Inability to move the left eye towards the nose
   B. Inability to move the left eye towards the ear
   C. Inability to move the left eye towards the forehead
   D. Inability to move the left eye towards the chin
   E. Sensory loss over the forehead
   F. Sensory loss over the cheeks
   G. Sensory loss over the jaw
   H. All of the above are likely to be seen

4. A 45 y/o F is out walking in the woods with her dog when she notices a tick on her leg. She quickly brushes it off of her leg. Three weeks later, she presents to an urgent care clinic reporting a severe headache, fevers, and excessive thirst. Vital signs are normal except for a temperature of 102.7°F. During the exam, a rash is discovered on her leg as seen below:

All of the following are likely to be found in patients with this condition *except*:
    A. Severe joint pain in multiple joints
    B. Cardiac conduction abnormalities on EKG
    C. Pain with neck flexion
    D. "Electrical" pain running down her legs
    E. Lopsided weakness of the muscles of facial expression
    F. All of the above are likely to be found

1. **The best answer is C.** The patient's clinical presentation of headache, fever, nuchal rigidity, and photophobia is highly suggestive of meningitis, and his cerebrospinal fluid analysis makes bacterial infection the most likely cause. For this reason, administering an antibiotic should be the highest priority. His cerebrospinal fluid findings do not support a diagnosis of viral meningitis which would either be treated with antivirals or supportive care (answers D and H). Fungal meningitis would present with a predominance of lymphocytes, not neutrophils (answer E). Given the classic presentation of meningitis, there is no need for urgently ordering head imaging, especially if this would delay starting an antibiotic (answers A and B). Immunizing the patient would be of little benefit now (answer F). Depending on the specific organism causing the infection, immunizing close contacts should be done, but this is not the highest priority compared with treating the patient (answer G).

2. **The best answer is D.** The presence of a petechial rash as well as the patient's age range should both put *Neisseria meningitidis* high on your differential at this point. However, the strongest evidence is the development of Waterhouse–Friderichsen syndrome, or acute adrenal failure related to bleeding into the adrenal glands. Waterhouse–Friderichsen syndrome is strongly associated with meningococcal meningitis and is considered to be one of the most tragic outcomes, with a high mortality rate even with treatment. *Escherichia coli* and *Listeria monocytogenes* are both more common in infants than a young adult (answers A and B). The patient is in the correct age range for meningitis from *Streptococcus pneumonia* and *Haemophilus influenza*, though the presence of petechial rash and Waterhouse–Friderichsen syndrome make these much less likely (answers C and E). There is little evidence of viral meningitis (answers F and G) or fungal meningitis (answers H—K).

3. **The best answer is G.** The cavernous sinuses contain veins that drain blood from the eyes and other anterior parts of the head. However, they also contain several important structures including the internal carotid artery and all three of the cranial nerves responsible for extraocular movements. When the cavernous sinus becomes thrombosed, these structures can be injured, leading to loss of extraocular movements in all directions (answers A—D). The ophthalmic and maxillary divisions of the trigeminal nerve, which supply the upper and middle face respectively, also pass through the cavernous sinus (answers E and F). Notably, the mandibular division of the trigeminal nerve does not, so sensation to the jaw and lower face would likely be preserved.

4. **The best answer is F.** Lyme disease is a tick-borne infectious disease involving the bacterium *Borrelia burgdorferi*. A characteristic "bull's eye" rash known as erythema migrans is highly suggestive of the disease. Lyme disease affects both the central and peripheral nervous systems and is a potential cause of peripheral neuropathy (answer D), Bell's palsy (answer E), and meningitis (answer C). However, it can affect other organ systems as well, including the heart (answer B) and joints (answer A).

21 DEMYELINATING DISEASES

The **myelin sheath** covering many neurons in both the central and peripheral nervous system is essential for rapid transmission of signals, particularly in neurons carrying motor impulses and proprioceptive information where lightning-fast communication is absolutely essential. Because the body relies on this speed, any disease that damages the myelin sheath is likely to result in noticeable deficits in a variety of processes including decreased motor strength, impaired coordination, and loss of sensation.

These **demyelinating diseases** come in a variety of forms, including environmental exposures, nutrient deficiencies, infectious diseases (like tabes dorsalis in syphilis), and even some genetic diseases. However, a surprisingly large proportion of demyelinating diseases are **autoimmune diseases**, or those in which the patient's immune system becomes confused and attacks its own body in the same way it would attack an invading pathogen. As we talk about these diseases, keep in mind which neurons are myelinated and which are not, as this will help to identify when a demyelinating disease is present (for example, if someone presents with loss of motor strength and fine touch, vibration, and proprioception but has intact crude touch, pain, and temperature sensation). In addition, try to focus on whether the damage is occurring in the central nervous system, the peripheral nervous system, or both, as this forms a line of separation between **central demyelinating diseases** and **peripheral demyelinating diseases**. The prototype of a central demyelinating autoimmune disease is **multiple sclerosis**, which we will spend the most time talking about. However, there are a few others to know as well, including **neuromyelitis optica**, **acute disseminated encephalomyelitis**, and **progressive multifocal leukoencephalopathy**. We will wrap up by talking about **Guillain–Barré syndrome** which is the prototype of a peripheral demyelinating disease.

CENTRAL DEMYELINATING DISEASES

Central demyelinating diseases specifically target myelin in the central nervous system. We will start our discussion with multiple sclerosis.

MULTIPLE SCLEROSIS

The name **multiple sclerosis** essentially means "many scars," and this helps to illustrate that the autoimmune attack on myelin is occurring in *multiple* locations across the central nervous system. For this reason, the associated neurologic deficits are quite variable from person to person. In fact, people with multiple sclerosis can present with basically **any neurologic sign or symptom**, including muscle weakness (sometimes with upper motor neuron findings), cerebellar signs (including nystagmus and trouble with balance and coordination), problems with autonomic function (such as urinary incontinence), changes in sensation (including numbness, tingling, and neuropathic pain), and neuropsychiatric phenomena (such as mood changes and poor cognition). Visual changes are particularly common in multiple sclerosis, including a sudden loss of vision due to **optic neuritis** (or inflammation of the optic nerve which leads to demyelination and subsequent vision loss). **Internuclear ophthalmoplegia** is common as well, as the medial longitudinal fasciculus is quite heavily myelinated.

Multiple sclerosis cannot be diagnosed on the basis of any one neurologic sign or symptom on its own (even though, in most cases, this is how the disease begins). Instead, demyelinating episodes in multiple sclerosis must be both **disseminated in space** (meaning that more than one area of the central nervous system has been affected) and **disseminated in time** (meaning that there has been more than one attack). Dissemination in time is more easily established, as dissemination in space often requires repeat neuroimaging showing migration of the characteristic scars (as seen in the following images).

For the majority of people with the disease, multiple sclerosis follows a **relapsing-remitting course** in which the deficits wax and wane seemingly at random. In between exacerbations, function is often restored due to remyelination of affected neurons. For this reason, misdiagnosis of multiple sclerosis is quite common, especially in the initial parts of the illness. (In places where there is a wait time for medical care, someone with multiple sclerosis may find that their neurologic problems have all resolved by the time they actually get an appointment and end up canceling the visit, only to find that their symptoms have returned a few weeks later.) It can be helpful to think of multiple sclerosis as **multi-pool sclerosis**, with each "pool" being a different neurologic deficit. People with this disease may be in one pool for a time, then be outside the pool (without symptoms) for a few months, then find themselves in a different pool.

Multiple sclerosis is an **autoimmune disease** involving **demyelination in the central nervous system**. It can present with **any neurologic sign or symptom**. Attacks must be **disseminated in both time and space**.

Multi-pool sclerosis involves getting in and out of different "pools."

*Serial MRIs in a patient with **multiple sclerosis** showing dissemination of lesions in both time and space.*

While many cases *begin* with a relapsing-remitting course, over time the disease often shifts to a progressive course, with slowly accumulating deficits even between episodes (this is known as "**secondary progressive multiple sclerosis**").

Diagnosis of multiple sclerosis is based on a characteristic clinical history, neurological exam findings, and imaging results demonstrating demyelinating attacks that are disseminated in both time and space. Lumbar puncture can also reveal the presence of **oligoclonal bands**, which is a sign that a wider-than-normal range of antibodies are present in the cerebrospinal fluid. In fact, the *absence* of oligoclonal bands strongly argues *against* a diagnosis of multiple sclerosis, as almost all patients with multiple sclerosis will have oligoclonal bands. You can remember this association by thinking of multiple sclerosis as a disease of **oligo**clonal bands attacking the **oligo**dendrocytes that make myelin in the central nervous system.

Oligoclonal bands in cerebrospinal fluid are diagnostic for **multiple sclerosis**.

*Oligoclonal bands destroy **oligo**dendrocytes in the central nervous system.*

As with most autoimmune diseases, multiple sclerosis is more common in **women** than men. It tends to begin in one's 20s or 30s. (For this reason, you should think of multiple sclerosis in **any young person presenting with upper motor neuron signs or sudden visual changes**— findings that are more often seen in older adults!) For unclear reasons, the incidence of multiple sclerosis seems to go up the farther away you go from the equator, with a low incidence in tropical areas like Central America and Southeast Asia and a higher incidence in cooler climates like Europe and North America. To remember this, think of how much worse it is to get into multiple **pool**s in **frigid climates** (as opposed to in a hot tropical climate near the equator where getting into a pool is fun).

The **incidence of multiple sclerosis** is higher in people living in **temperate climates** compared to **tropical areas**.

*Being in **multiple pools** is worse the farther away from the equator you go.*

There is **no definitive cure** for multiple sclerosis. Instead, treatment is aimed at managing acute attacks as well as preventing future episodes. Acute treatment involves **steroids** which act to quickly calm an overactive immune system. However, steroids cannot be used for long-term treatment due to their side effects, so chronic treatment instead involves **disease-modifying drugs** aimed at *preventing* attacks. The first-line treatment is either **glatiramer acetate** or a class of drugs known as **interferons**. Glatiramer acetate is a mixture of proteins that resembles **myelin basic protein** (the antigen found in myelin) which can serve as a "decoy" of sorts for the body's immune system. In contrast, interferons are **cytokines** (or compounds that are involved in signaling between different cells of the immune system) that help to regulate the immune response. Both glatiramer acetate and interferons have been

shown to reduce the rate of relapses in multiple sclerosis by about 30%. Other drugs such as **natalizumab** (an antibody targeting a specific protein on white blood cells) are even more effective at preventing relapses, but due to their harsher side effects they are generally not the first drugs used. To remember the association of g-**ladder**-amer acetate with multi-**pool** sclerosis, think of someone needing a **ladder** to get out of a **pool**.

> **Glatiramer acetate** and **interferons** can both be used as a **first-line treatment** for **multiple sclerosis**.
>
> *Use g-**ladder**-amer acetate to get out of multi-**pool** sclerosis.*

Despite the availability of treatment, most people with multiple sclerosis will develop increasing levels of disability with time. Life expectancy is reduced by around 5 or 10 years, with most patients passing away in their 60s or 70s.

NEUROMYELITIS OPTICA

Neuromyelitis optica (also known as NMO or **Devic's disease**) is an autoimmune central demyelinating disease involving inflammation of both the spinal cord (known as **transverse myelitis**) and the optic nerve (**optic neuritis**). Specifically, antibodies are generated that target the **astrocytes** supporting neurons in both of these regions. Because neuromyelitis optica targets these two areas of the central nervous system preferentially, the signs and symptoms can often be traced to both of these structures, with optic neuritis leading to **visual loss** and transverse myelitis leading to **weakness and numbness** of the extremities as well as **bowel and bladder dysfunction**.

There is ongoing debate as to whether neuromyelitis optica is simply a variant of multiple sclerosis or an entirely different disease. Like multiple sclerosis, the majority of cases are characterized by a **relapsing-remitting course**. Unlike multiple sclerosis, however, the regions affected are pretty narrow (the optic nerve and spinal cord only), and in some cases the presence of **antibodies against aquaporin-4** (which are not present in multiple sclerosis) can be demonstrated on specialized lab testing. Further, treatment for neuromyelitis optica involves **steroids** and/or **plasmapheresis** (rather than the immune-modulating drugs used in multiple sclerosis). Whether it ends up ultimately being classified as a different disease or not, on a clinical level it can help to differentiate between them so you know the correct treatment. To differentiate between the focused attack of neuromyelitis optica versus the widespread destruction seen in multiple sclerosis, think of it as **narrow**-myelitis optica.

> **Neuromyelitis optica** is a **demyelinating autoimmune disease** involving both **optic neuritis** and **transverse myelitis**.
>
> ***Narrow**-myelitis optica is like multiple sclerosis but more **narrow** in its scope.*

ACUTE DISSEMINATED ENCEPHALOMYELITIS

Acute disseminated encephalomyelitis (or ADEM) is a rare autoimmune disease involving widespread inflammatory demyelination throughout the central nervous system. Wait, central nervous system demyelination? Didn't we just learn about this with multiple sclerosis? Indeed, both ADEM and multiple sclerosis share the pathologic feature of demyelination in the central nervous system, but they differ in a few key ways. First, ADEM tends to hit **children** while multiple sclerosis affects adults. Second, ADEM is generally a **one-time event** as opposed to the relapsing-remitting course that characterizes multiple sclerosis. Third, ADEM is much more likely to be

fatal than multiple sclerosis (which shortens lifespan only a little, if at all).

Okay, moving on! Acute disseminated encephalomyelitis often occurs following exposure to an antibody-generating infection like the **measles virus**... *just like subacute sclerosing panencephalitis!* (It sure seems at times like ADEM is having trouble carving out a unique identity for itself.) It's important to differentiate ADEM from SSPE, as both occur following exposure to measles (which is easy to get tripped up on during tests). Despite having this in common, these two diseases are otherwise quite different, with a different presentation (central nervous system *demyelination* in ADEM versus *inflammation* in SSPE) and time of onset (occurring *weeks* after the measles infection in ADEM versus *years* in SSPE). Treatment involves high-dose **steroids** and other measures aimed at reducing immune system activity. The prognosis is often quite good, with survival and recovery occurring in the vast majority of cases (which is another point of comparison with SSPE, as SSPE is fatal much more often than ADEM).

*MRI showing the **widespread lesions** characteristic of **acute disseminated encephalomyelitis**.*

 You can put these core features of **A**cute **D**isseminated **E**ncephalo**M**yelitis into a mnemonic by thinking of **ADEM**'s **APPLE**, which stands for **A**utoimmune **P**ost-infectious **P**ediatric (more common in children) **L**imited-time **E**vent (that doesn't recur in most cases).

Acute disseminated encephalomyelitis is an **autoimmune disease** leading to **central nervous system demyelination** following exposure to **measles**.

*Think of ADEM's **APPLE**:*
*A**utoimmune*
*P**ost-infectious*
*P**ediatric*
*L**imited-time*
*E**vent*

PROGRESSIVE MULTIFOCAL LEUKOENCEPHALOPATHY

Finally, **progressive multifocal leukoencephalopathy** (or PML) is a central demyelinating disease characterized by **destruction of oligodendrocytes**. As you might expect, it tends to present similarly to multiple sclerosis, although the progression is often much faster. You can remember the aggressive nature of Progressive **M**ultifocal **L**eukoencephalopathy by linking it to the word **PuMmeL** (meaning "to beat with fists"). Progressive multifocal leukoencephalopathy is related to **JC virus** (short for John **C**unningham virus, after a patient who contracted the disease). It's not unusual for someone infected with JC virus to be completely healthy and asymptomatic. However, in cases where someone is **immunocompromised** (such as with **HIV/AIDS**), the virus can grow in strength and wreak havoc. There is no treatment available for the virus *itself*, so management consists of trying to bolster the patient's immune system (such as by treating HIV or stopping any immunosuppressant medications that may be interfering). Even with treatment, the disease has a **poor prognosis**, with up to half of all patients dying within several months due to its rapidly progressive nature.

> **Progressive multifocal leukoencephalopathy** is a **central demyelinating disease** related to infection with **JC virus** in an **immunocompromised patient**.

> *Progressive Multifocal Leukoencephalopathy will PuMmeL you (poor prognosis).*

PERIPHERAL DEMYELINATING DISEASES

While central demyelinating diseases strip the myelin sheath off of neurons in the *central* nervous system, peripheral demyelinating diseases do the same for *peripheral* nerves. Here, the prototype disease is **Guillain-Barré syndrome** as well as its longer-lasting version **chronic inflammatory demyelinating polyneuropathy** (CIDP).

GUILLAIN-BARRÉ SYNDROME

Guillain-Barré syndrome is the peripheral nervous system's counterpart to multiple sclerosis. Both are **autoimmune** diseases in which the myelin sheath is attacked by the immune system in various places, leading to motor deficits (including weakness or paralysis) and sensory changes (such as numbness and tingling). You can remember the demyelinating nature of this disease by thinking that Guillain–**Bare**-é leaves your peripheral nerves **bare**.

> **Guillain-Barré syndrome** is a **demyelinating disease** involving **autoimmune destruction** of **peripheral nerves**.

> *Guillain–**Bare**-e leaves your peripheral nerves **bare**.*

The motor deficits in Guillain–Barré syndrome tend to occur in an **ascending and symmetric** fashion, beginning in the limbs and then traveling towards the trunk and face over several weeks. Of note, the neurological exam will reveal only *lower* motor neuron signs (not upper motor neuron signs as would be seen in multiple sclerosis). Worryingly, this ascending paralysis will end up hitting the diaphragm in around 25% of people with this disease, leading to **respiratory failure** and death without medical treatment. The autonomic nervous system is also affected in most patients with this condition, leading to an irregular heart beat, unstable blood pressure, and/or absent pupillary responses.

Interestingly, many cases of Guillain–Barré syndrome are preceded by exposure to an infectious disease, with **Campylobacter jejuni** being the culprit in around a third of all cases. It is believed that this infection induces the immune system to make antibodies against these pathogens. However, on a molecular level these bugs bear a

 striking resemblance to gangliosides, or the fatty molecules found in the myelin of peripheral nerves. Because of this **molecular mimicry**, these newly created antibodies attack not only the pathogens but also the gangliosides present on peripheral nerve cells, leading to demyelination. You can remember the association of Guillain-**Berry** syndrome with **Camp**ylobacter je**juni** by thinking of going **camp**ing in **Jun**e which is when **berries** are most ripe.

Guillain–Barré syndrome is often preceded by a **Campylobacter jejuni** infection.

*You go **camp**ing in **Jun**e (**Camp**ylobacter ju**jun**i) when the **berries** (Guillain-**Berry** syndrome) are most ripe.*

Diagnosis is based on the patient's history, physical findings, and lab test results. Lumbar puncture will often show **albuminocytologic dissociation**, or an increased protein level combined with a normal cell count, in the cerebrospinal fluid. Imaging can help to rule *out* other conditions that may resemble the findings in Guillain–Barré syndrome (such as compression of the spinal cord by a tumor) but is not necessarily helpful for ruling this *in*. Other findings include slowed conduction on EMG (which makes sense, as the main function of myelin is to speed up neuronal transmission).

Treatment is aimed at removing the autoantibodies out of the bloodstream. This is done by either **plasmapheresis** or by administering **intravenous immunoglobulins** (both of which we discussed back in Chapter 15 in the context of autoimmune neuromuscular junction diseases). These treatments are equally effective, with neither being superior to the other. With treatment, there is usually a **good prognosis**, with most patients recovering lost functions within a few weeks and surviving without long-term complications.

CHRONIC INFLAMMATORY DEMYELINATING POLYNEUROPATHY

Chronic inflammatory demyelinating polyneuropathy (or CIDP) is best thought of as the **chronic counterpart** to Guillain–Barré syndrome, as it involves many of the same signs and symptoms with a similar pathophysiology. This time, however, the disease does not simply go away on its own but instead lingers for months or even years. Some people with CIDP have persistent deficits while others experience a relapsing-remitting course similar to multiple sclerosis. Treatment is the same as for Guillain–Barré syndrome.

PUTTING IT ALL TOGETHER

Demyelination is a feature of many neurologic diseases, and you will see the characteristic pattern (impaired motor strength and epicritic sensation with intact protopathic sensation) pop up again and again. In this chapter, we have primarily focused on those diseases that feature demyelination as the core pathology. Multi-**pool** sclerosis will present with lesions that are disseminated in both time and space (like getting into and out of various "**pools**" of neurologic deficits), **narrow**-myelitis optic is like multiple sclerosis but more **narrow** in its scope (only affecting the optic nerve and spinal cord), acute disseminated encephalomyelitis is an **A**utoimmune **P**ost-infectious **P**ediatric **L**imited-time **E**vent (ADEM's **APPLE**), **P**rogressive **M**ultifocal **L**eukoencephalopathy will **PuMmeL** people who are immunocompromised, and Guillain–**Bare**-e syndrome will leave your peripheral nerves **bare**. Look for these patterns on boards and on wards when you suspect a demyelinating disease!

REVIEW QUESTIONS

1. A 42 y/o M who has lived in Nicaragua all his life immigrates to the United States. He makes an appointment to see a primary care doctor. At his first appointment, he reports difficulty walking for the past 2 years. He initially noticed weakness in his left lower limb while working as a construction worker. He said that this weakness would "come and go," with weeks where he had trouble walking interspersed with months where his strength was intact. However, he was always able to compensate for his weakness and never sought medical care. He denies sensory loss, visual abnormalities, or flu-like symptoms. A lumbar puncture shows oligoclonal bands in his cerebrospinal fluid. Which of the following argues most strongly *against* a diagnosis of multiple sclerosis at this time?
    A. Recurrent nature of neurologic deficits
    B. Neurologic deficits in only the left lower leg
    C. Male gender
    D. Upbringing in a tropical region
    E. Ability to work even after disease onset
    F. Presence of oligoclonal bands in cerebrospinal fluid

2. (Continued from previous question.) At his follow-up appointment one month later, the patient reports a tremor of his right hand along with an "hormigueo" (tingling) sensation in his right arm. He also reports difficulty swallowing which causes occasional coughing while eating. An MRI of his brain shows multiple plaques around the ventricles bilaterally as seen below:

    Which of the following is the best next step in management?
    A. Prescribing corticosteroids
    B. Prescribing glatiramer acetate
    C. Prescribing an interferon
    D. Prescribing natalizumab
    E. Arranging for plasmapheresis
    F. Administering intravenous immunoglobulins
    G. Referring to physical therapy

3. A 51 y/o M with a history of HIV infection presents to his infectious disease specialist reporting recent onset of difficulty walking and speaking. He has been treated for HIV for the past 15 years, although his particular strain of the virus is resistant to multiple types of antiviral medications, leading to recurrent treatment failures. His current CD4$^+$ count is less than 10 cells/µl. On exam, his speech is dysarthric, with difficulty enunciating words. His gait is ataxic. He has difficulty with finger-to-nose testing, and his Romberg sign is positive. At a follow-up visit two weeks later, he is in a wheelchair due to extreme difficulty walking. His speech is weak to the point of being unable to communicate. He is admitted to the hospital for supportive care. An MRI of the brain shows multiple areas of widespread demyelination as seen below:

Which of the following is the most likely explanation for his condition?
    A. Autoimmune demyelination
    B. Direct neurotoxicity of HIV
    C. Concurrent infection by more than one virus
    D. Post-infectious reactivation of the measles virus
    E. Inflammation of the spinal cord

4. A 15 y/o F is brought to the emergency department after 2 days of progressively worsening motor weakness in all 4 limbs. She had a case of "food poisoning" involving diarrhea and vomiting 2 weeks ago that had resolved without medical treatment. On exam, there is 1/5 motor function in each of her limbs. A nerve conduction study was performed which showed a predominantly demyelinating pattern. Which of the following additional findings is most likely to be seen on further examination?
    A. Active bloodstream bacterial infection
    B. Muscle spasticity to palpation
    C. Upgoing plantar responses
    D. Loss of pain and temperature sensation over both arms
    E. Areflexia in the biceps, patellar, and ankle jerk reflexes
    F. None of the above are likely to be found

1. **The best answer is B.** A diagnosis of multiple sclerosis requires that any neurologic signs or symptoms are disseminated in both time and space. This patient's relapsing and remitting course shows a pattern of dissemination in time (answer A), but the fact that his neurologic deficits are localized to a single area does not demonstrate dissemination in space. His gender (answer C) and upbringing in a tropical region (answer D) are both less common in multiple sclerosis, but they are not incompatible with the diagnosis. While some people with multiple sclerosis become functionally impaired by this disease, others are not (answer E). Finally, the presence of oligoclonal bands in cerebrospinal fluid is evidence in favor of a diagnosis of multiple sclerosis, not against it (answer F).

2. **The best answer is A.** Now that dissemination in space has been demonstrated for this patient's neurologic deficits, a diagnosis of multiple sclerosis can be confirmed. In the setting of an acute attack, steroids should be used as the first-line treatment. Glatiramer acetate and interferons are both effective treatments for multiple sclerosis, but they are generally used for long-term prevention of attacks rather than acute management (answers B and C). Natalizumab is a second-line treatment for multiple sclerosis and should not be used until other drugs have failed (answer D). Neither plasmapheresis nor intravenous immunoglobulins are first-line treatments for acute attacks of multiple sclerosis (answers E and F). Physical therapy is an important part of long-term management but is not the immediate priority (answer G).

3. **The best answer is C.** This vignette describes a case of progressive multifocal leukoencephalopathy, a potentially fatal demyelinating disease caused by the JC virus. While the JC virus is typically harmless, in people with a compromised immune system (such as this patient with HIV/AIDS) it can lead to severe neurologic dysfunction. Unlike multiple sclerosis and Guillain–Barré syndrome, an autoimmune mechanism is not thought to account for progressive multifocal leukoencephalopathy (answer A). While HIV itself can cause neuronal damage, on its own it would not lead to the rapidly progressive disease seen in this case (answer B). Post-infectious reactivation of the measles virus is related to acute disseminated encephalomyelitis (answer D), while inflammation of the spinal cord is seen in neuromyelitis optica (answer E).

4. **The best answer is E.** Guillain–Barré syndrome is a demyelinating disease that primarily affects the peripheral nervous system, including both motor and sensory neurons. Notably, unmyelinated neurons, such as those carrying pain and temperature sensation, are not affected (answer D). As Guillain–Barré syndrome affects the peripheral nervous system, lower motor neuron signs including areflexia should be seen, while upper motor neuron signs such as spasticity and a positive Babinski signs should be absent (answers B and C). Guillain–Barré syndrome is thought to be mediated by autoantibodies whose production is induced by exposure to the *Campylobacter jejuni* bacteria rather than being associated with an active bacterial infection (answer A).

22 PERIPHERAL NEUROPATHY

Disorders affecting the peripheral nervous system are known broadly as **peripheral neuropathies**. Peripheral neuropathies can take many forms. Dysfunction of a specific nerve is known as a **mononeuropathy**, while a generalized dysfunction of multiple nerves is known as **polyneuropathy**. There is variation in terms of which nerves are affected as well, with some peripheral neuropathies affecting only the **motor** component of nerves, others affecting only the **sensory** aspects, and still others affecting primarily **autonomic** functions. Many peripheral neuropathies will affect more than one of these functions at a time. Because of this variability, the presenting signs and symptoms of peripheral neuropathy can be completely different from one disorder to the next. Nevertheless, some general themes do emerge.

In a *mono*neuropathy, the specific nerve that is damaged will determine what parts of the body are affected. We discussed a few signs and symptoms associated with common mononeuropathies back in Chapter 8 (such as a wrist drop being related to a radial neuropathy or a winged scapula resulting from a long thoracic neuropathy). In cases of a *poly*neuropathy, the most common pattern is for the most distal parts of the nerves to be affected first, while more proximal areas are spared. This results in a characteristic "**stocking glove**" pattern in which the ends of the extremities (the hands and feet) are most severely affected.

Sensory disturbances resulting from peripheral neuropathy can involve not only the *absence* of *normal* sensations but also the *presence* of *abnormal* sensations. These sensations range from the merely uncomfortable (including recurrent tingling "pins and needles" sensations known as **paresthesias**) to the outright painful (including "burning," "stabbing," or "electrical" sensations known as **neuropathic**

pain). Sensory loss can be complete (meaning a total absence of all sensory signals coming from a particular part of the body) or can occur in some modalities but not others (such as someone who is unable to sense vibration or proprioception in their toes but can still feel pain and sense temperature). In some cases, this lack of sensation can lead to injury when the patient is unable to sense that they are damaging a part of their body.

Motor deficits are generally associated with **lower motor neuron** signs, which makes sense as it is the peripheral nerve (and not a higher up part of the chain like the motor cortex or basal ganglia) that is involved. Lower motor neuron signs should be familiar to you by now, but as a reminder they tend to involve flaccid paralysis, poor reflexes, low muscle tone, diminished power, and decreased bulk.

Autonomic dysfunction can involve basically any part of the sympathetic or parasympathetic nervous systems, including their ability to regulate vascular tone (often producing an inability to constrict the blood vessels in response to postural changes known as **orthostatic hypotension**), bowel and bladder functions (which can lead to constipation), and sexual function (which can result in impotence).

A specific form of localized neuropathy known as a **radiculopathy** occurs when the nerve is affected at its *root* just after exiting from the spinal cord. This often occurs due to an injury or degeneration of the spinal bones, resulting in a narrowing of the space through which the nerve travels on its way out of the spinal cord (radiculopathies are often called a "pinched nerve" for this reason). This has a tendency to cause pain, sensory loss, and weakness in a **strict dermatomal and myotomal distribution**. You can remember the association of **radi**culopathy with compression of the nerve **root** by thinking of a **radi**sh, a **root** vegetable.

A **radiculopathy** involves dysfunction of a **nerve root**, leading to **pain, numbness,** and **weakness** in the **dermatomes** and **myotomes** innervated by that nerve.

A **radish**-culopathy involves the nerve **root** (just like a **radish** is a **root** vegetable).

In some cases, dysfunction can affect areas that are not close together enough to be considered part of the same group of nerves but are not dispersed enough to be considered a generalized polyneuropathy. Instead, the affected nerves are almost randomly distributed throughout the body (as in a case of someone who develops simultaneous neuropathies in both the right thigh and left wrist). These cases are referred to as **mononeuritis multiplex** (with the "mono-" prefix referring to the fact that it seems to hit individual nerves and the "multi-" prefix suggesting that it is hitting multiple nerves at once). In many cases, mononeuritis multiplex represents a kind of "pre-polyneuropathy" in that it progresses and becomes more widespread to the point that it is mostly indistinguishable from a generalized polyneuropathy.

CAUSES OF PERIPHERAL NEUROPATHY

In many cases, peripheral neuropathy is a *finding* rather than a *disease* in and of itself. Peripheral neuropathies can have a wide variety of different causes, so a patient presenting with peripheral neuropathy should undergo a thorough work-up to determine where the damage is coming from. To remember all of the various causes of peripheral neuropathy, use the mnemonic **THIS DAMNED PAIN**:

T is for Toxins. A variety of chemicals can be toxic to neurons, making it essential to screen for environmental exposures in patients presenting with peripheral neuropathy. In particular, **heavy metals** such as lead, arsenic, mercury, and gold have been associated with various forms of nerve damage. However, by far the most common toxin associated with peripheral neuropathy is **alcohol**. Alcoholic neuropathy involves degeneration of both motor and sensory nerves throughout the body. It's unclear whether alcohol itself is directly responsible for the nerve damage or whether it results from the nutritional deficiencies that almost always accompany cases of chronic alcoholism. Nevertheless, abstinence from alcohol does appear to reduce the severity of alcoholic neuropathy, suggesting that there is some direct effect.

H is for Heredity. Several **heritable disorders** can cause damage to peripheral nerves. The one most classically associated with peripheral neuropathy is **Charcot–Marie–Tooth disease**, a condition involving a mutation in one or more of the genes that directly contribute to the myelin sheath. This leads to both motor and sensory deficits that begin during childhood and progressively get worse with age. Charcot–Marie–Tooth disease tends to be associated with certain physical abnormalities as well, including prominent **foot deformities** as seen in the following image:

Foot deformities related to Charcot–Marie–Tooth disease.

I is for Infections. We have already covered a few **infectious diseases** that affect the peripheral nervous system including **syphilis** and **Lyme disease**. Another common infectious culprit is **HIV/AIDS** which tends to cause a distal symmetric polyneuropathy in around a third of all patients with the disease (although this may partly be attributable to the drugs used to treat HIV, many of which can themselves cause peripheral neuropathy).

S is for Sarcoidosis. Sarcoidosis is a rheumatologic disease in which immune cells collect into discrete lumps known as **granulomas**. These granulomas can grow and cause problems in almost any area of the body, with the nervous system being no exception. Sarcoidosis has a tendency to affect the central nervous system and cranial nerves, although spinal nerves can be affected as well.

D is for Diabetes. Diabetes mellitus is the **single most common cause** of peripheral neuropathy. Uncontrolled levels of sugar in the bloodstream appear to directly injure the small blood vessels supplying nerves, leading to ischemic damage. Diabetic neuropathy can include not only damage to individual nerves but also widespread dysfunction of nerves across the body.

A is for Amyloidosis. Amyloidosis is a disease in which proteins known as amyloids deposit into various tissues throughout the body. Amyloidosis tends to produce a primarily *sensory* neuropathy that begins distally and moves in proximally. Unlike sarcoidosis, the central nervous system is generally not involved.

M is for Malignancy. Several forms of **cancer** can cause peripheral neuropathies, especially those that are based in the bloodstream rather than in a solid organ (such as **lymphomas** and **multiple myelomas**). Many forms of **chemotherapy** used to treat cancer can themselves damage peripheral nerves as well.

N is for Nutrition. Nutritional deficiencies can cause damage to peripheral nerves. In particular, a deficiency of **vitamin B₁₂** is well-known to cause a particular syndrome known as **subacute combined degeneration** in which both the dorsal and lateral columns of the spinal cord become damaged and dysfunctional. Recall that the dorsal columns carry **F**ine touch, **V**ibration, and **P**roprioception (the **F**eeling **V**ery **P**atient sensory modalities) while the lateral columns carry most of the **motor neurons** traveling in the corticospinal tract. For this reason, subacute combined degeneration leads to a gradual onset of *both* distal motor weakness *and* loss of epicritic sensation. Vitamin B_{12} deficiency can result from an inability to absorb this vitamin through the gut, or it can come from a restricted diet lacking in nutrients (with a classic boards-type question involving a patient with a "tea and toast" diet).

Peripheral neuropathy can also be caused by a deficiency in **vitamin B_6** (also known as **pyridoxine**). Vitamin B_6 is needed to synthesize a molecule that forms a part of nerve cell membranes, so a lack of this vitamin will lead to dysfunctional nerves.

E is for Endocrine. A common cause of peripheral neuropathy is **hypothyroidism**, especially if it has been untreated for a long time. It's unclear how hypothyroidism leads to nerve damage, although it has been suggested that the swelling that occurs in tissues as a result of this disease may compress and thereby damage nerves.

D is for Drugs. We've talked about how some **medications**, such as those used to treat HIV and cancer, can cause peripheral neuropathy, but unfortunately this is just the tip of the iceberg. All sorts of drugs can have the unfortunate side effect of damaging peripheral nerves, including those used for infections (metronidazole, nitrofurantoin, isoniazid, and chloroquine), seizures (phenytoin), heart conditions (amiodarone and digoxin), high blood pressure (hydralazine), hyperlipidemia (statins), and psychiatric conditions (lithium), just to name a few.

P is for Porphyria. Porphyrias are a group of diseases that all involve excessive levels of substances called **porphyrins** in the body. The peripheral neuropathy seen in cases of porphyria tends to present as **acute attacks of motor weakness** (rather than building up slowly as do most other causes of peripheral neuropathy). Other symptoms such as abdominal pain, vomiting, and vital sign instability often accompany these attacks as well.

A is for Autoimmune. We have covered Guillain–Barré syndrome and other **autoimmune diseases** in their own chapters, but many of these can be considered a form of peripheral neuropathy as well.

I is for Idiopathic. An upstream cause cannot be found in all patients presenting with peripheral neuropathy. These are known as **idiopathic** cases. Even when no cause can be found, however, peripheral neuropathies can still be just as painful and debilitating to the patient.

Idiopathic cases of peripheral neuropathy can affect a single nerve or can involve multiple nerves across the body. A particular mononeuropathy known as **trigeminal neuralgia** presents as severe pain in regions supplied by the trigeminal nerve, including all parts of the face. These can either occur in sudden "attacks"

lasting a few minutes or may be present in a more chronic form. Trigeminal neuralgia is one of the most painful conditions known. The exact cause is unclear, although it may be related to demyelination as higher rates of trigeminal neuralgia are seen in patients with multiple sclerosis.

N is for Nephrology. Finally, failure of the **kidneys** (the organs treated by nephrologists) to properly clear out waste products from the body can lead to peripheral neuropathy if these toxins build up excessively, a condition known as **uremic neuropathy**.

A **wide variety of medical conditions** can cause **peripheral neuropathy**.

THIS DAMNED PAIN:
Toxins
Heredity
Infections
Sarcoidosis
Diabetes
Amyloidosis
Malignancy
Nutrition
Endocrine
Drugs
Porphyria
Autoimmune
Idiopathic
Nephrology

DIAGNOSIS AND TREATMENT OF PERIPHERAL NEUROPATHY

Peripheral neuropathy most often presents with paresthesias and neuropathic pain in distal parts of the body. The **specific sensory modalities** affected (touch, pain, temperature, vibration, and/or proprioception) and their distribution throughout the body should be assessed. If weakness is present, it should be worked up to determine if it is resulting from upper and/or lower motor neuron damage. The **anatomic distribution** of any sensory or motor abnormalities should also be noted to determine the likely cause, as abnormalities in a strict dermatomal and myotomal distribution suggest a radiculopathy while those in a "stocking glove" pattern are more suggestive of a generalized polyneuropathy. A history of recent medical conditions, changes in medication, or toxic exposures can also help to identify some of the most common causes of peripheral neuropathy.

In many cases, careful history taking and a thorough physical exam can identify the likely culprit. In other cases, more thorough testing may be beneficial. **Nerve conduction studies** can demonstrate specific abnormalities in the ability of peripheral nerves to conduct an impulse, while **electromyography** can detect problems with both the muscle itself as well as the nerve supplying it.

Treatment of peripheral neuropathy involves identifying the underlying cause and addressing it (such as by getting blood sugar under better control in diabetes or reducing alcohol intake in alcoholic neuropathy). Some treatments can be used symptomatically to address specific symptoms like neuropathic pain, with **anticonvulsants** (such as gabapentin and topiramate), **antidepressants** (like amitriptyline and duloxetine), and **local anesthetics** (such as lidocaine and capsaicin) being particularly helpful. Non-pharmacologic treatments such as **physical therapy** and **orthotics** can help to provide support as well. A **transcutaneous electrical nerve stimulator** (or TENS) device can improve neuropathic pain by using electric signals to overwhelm peripheral nerves, resulting in decreased ability to transmit pain signals. All in all, make sure to consider **both drugs and non-pharmacologic strategies** for managing painful peripheral neuropathies!

PUTTING IT ALL TOGETHER

Peripheral neuropathy can be a diagnosis in and of itself, although more often it is a result of an underlying condition. Use the **THIS DAMNED PAIN** mnemonic to identify some of the most common culprits and treat them if possible. In cases of idiopathic peripheral neuropathy, don't give up! There is often still something that you can do to help, including both medications and other forms of intervention.

REVIEW QUESTIONS

1. A 57 y/o M living in Canada sees his primary care doctor reporting a slow but steady onset of pain in his feet and calves bilaterally. He describes the pain as "burning," saying, "It's like when you try to walk on hot concrete during the summer." He also describes a "pins and needles" sensation in his feet. The pain is particularly severe at night, resulting in poor sleep for several months. He denies any other symptoms of depression. His exam is notable for decreased plantar flexion of both feet, reduced ankle jerk reflexes, and diminished sensation for pain, temperature, vibration, and proprioception in both feet. Dry crusty skin with mild bruising in both sets of toes is apparent, as seen below:

Which of the following is the most likely explanation for his symptoms?
    A. Compression of a nerve root in the spinal cord
    B. Resistance to insulin
    C. Antibodies directed against his own nerves
    D. Damage to the anterior horn of the spinal cord
    E. Undiagnosed malignancy
    F. Idiopathic peripheral neuropathy

2. (Continued from previous question.) All of the following are likely to result in improvement in the patient's symptoms and quality of life *except*:
    A. Treatment of the underlying disorder
    B. Gabapentin, an anticonvulsant
    C. Capsaicin, a topical anesthetic
    D. Duloxetine, an antidepressant
    E. Physical therapy
    F. All of the above are likely to improve the patient's symptoms

3. A 71 y/o M experiences the loss of his wife due to cancer. For 6 months following her death, he becomes severely depressed and has little appetite, restricting his food intake to old crackers and other items he finds in the pantry. He drinks several bottles of beer per day and will sometimes drink vodka and other distilled drinks when he thinks of his wife. Several months later, he presents to his primary care nurse practitioner reporting difficulty walking without a cane. He has never had need of a cane previously and has no significant past medical history. He is not on any medications. On interview, he reports a feeling of "sharp" pain on the back of his left calf which worsens when he stands up from a chair. His vital signs are within normal limits. His exam is notable for left foot drop though all other muscles of the left leg are at full motor strength. There is diminished sensation to proprioception and vibration in the left foot. Which of the following is most likely to result in improvement of his symptoms?
    A. Treatment of his depression
    B. Expanded food selection
    C. Reduction in alcohol intake
    D. Improved glycemic control
    E. Spinal surgery

1. **The best answer is B.** The most common cause of peripheral neuropathy in developed countries is diabetes mellitus, as high levels of sugar in the blood are damaging to neurons, especially those in the most distal parts of the extremities. Autoimmune disorders (answer C) and malignancies (answer E) are both causes that should be considered as well, as should an idiopathic cause (answer F). A radiculopathy would be unlikely to cause bilateral findings (answer A), while damage to the anterior horn of the spinal cord would not present with sensory loss (answer D).

2. **The best answer is F.** Treatment of diabetic peripheral neuropathy should be comprehensive, involving not only medications but also physical therapy as well (answer E). A variety of medications have been shown to be effective in treating peripheral neuropathy including anticonvulsants (answer B) and topical anesthetics (answer C). Certain antidepressants, particularly those that interact with norepinephrine, are effective at reducing symptoms, even in patients who are not suffering from depression (answer D).

3. **The best answer is E.** This case describes an L5 radiculopathy as evidenced by pain in a dermatomal distribution with weakness in the corresponding myotome. An L5 radiculopathy is often related to a herniated disc for which a surgical discectomy may be performed. As there appears to be only a single nerve root involved, treatment of systemic causes of peripheral neuropathy such as vitamin B_{12} deficiency (answer B), excess alcohol intake (answer C), and diabetes mellitus (answer D) are unlikely to result in significant improvements. While some antidepressants can be used for symptomatic treatment of neuropathic pain, they would not address the nerve root compression that is the current cause of his symptoms (answer A).

23 HEADACHE

On the surface, a **headache** seems like a simple thing that requires little explanation. Most people have experienced a headache (and if they haven't yet they likely will in the future!). However, just because headaches are common doesn't make them any less irritating or disabling, and any health care provider will need to have a systematic way of assessing and treating headaches. When trying to learn about headaches, it's worth knowing that the *brain itself* does not feel pain! Instead, the sensation of pain during a headache tends to come from structures *in and around* the brain, including the meninges, the periosteum of the skull, and the skin of the scalp.

Headaches can either be a symptom of another disease or a disease in their own right. Headaches that occur on their own are called **primary headaches** while those that are related to another condition are known as **secondary headaches**. While secondary headaches can be associated with some pretty scary diseases (including cancer, infections, and bleeding), that does not make primary headaches any less deserving of medical attention.

For the rest of this chapter, we will focus first on the various ways that primary headaches can present, including **tension headaches**, **migraine headaches**, and **cluster headaches**. We will then look at some of the most common causes of secondary headaches. Some of these causes we have talked about already in previous chapters (such as a subarachnoid hemorrhage), but we will make reference to them again here.

PRIMARY HEADACHES

The vast majority of headaches (around 90%) are **primary headaches**. There are a number of different forms of primary headaches, but we will limit our discussion to the three most high-yield forms: tension headaches, migraine headaches, and cluster headaches. Of these, tension and migraine headaches are by far the most common, while cluster headaches are so severe that they have a tendency to show up frequently on standardized tests even if they are relatively rare in real life.

TENSION HEADACHES

A **tension headache** is the most common form of headache, with around 20% of people experiencing them on a regular basis. As their name implies, they are experienced as a sense of "tension" or "pressure," almost as if the head were being squeezed. Notably, tension headaches are **bilateral** and tend to be located in a **band-like** pattern around the forehead, the sides of the heads, or the back of the head near the neck. Tension headaches usually last for a **few hours** at a time. They are often precipitated by situational factors, including stress and poor sleep. While tension headaches can be uncomfortable or even painful, they are usually not incapacitating.

Treatment involves over-the-counter drugs such as **aspirin, acetaminophen**, and **NSAIDs** like ibuprofen or naproxen. However, these must be taken with caution, as excessive use may actually make headaches *worse* in the long-term (a condition known as a **medication overuse headache** or **rebound headache**). For people with chronic tension headaches who are at risk for medication overuse headaches, other approaches (such as anti-anxiety or muscle relaxant medications) may be tried, although the evidence for these is fairly poor. Because of the potential downsides of pharmacologic treatment of tension headaches, prevention should be the cornerstone of management. Lifestyle modifications such as stress management, sleep hygiene, and hydration may be helpful. In some cases, antidepressants can help reduce the frequency of tension headaches.

MIGRAINE HEADACHES

A **migraine headache** is the second most common form of headache, with around 15% of people being affected by them. They are often described as **paroxysmal**, meaning that they tend to come on episodically and are quite severe when they occur. To understand migraines, it can be helpful to understand how they differ from tension headaches. The word **POUND** can help you to do this:

P is for Pulsatile. Migraine headaches tend to have a "throbbing" or "pounding" quality, almost as if the brain is beating like a heart (which should help you to remember the mnemonic "POUND" itself).

O is for hOurs. The painful phase of a migraine often lasts around **4 hours**, although some people have intractable headaches that can last up to a few days at a time.

U is for Unilateral. Unlike the bilateral pain caused by tension headaches, migraines tend to be felt much more strongly on one side of the head or the other.

N is for Nausea. Nausea and vomiting frequently accompany migraine headaches, with over 90% of patients reporting this symptom during an attack. Vomiting is less common but still affects around a third of migraine sufferers.

D is for Disabling. Finally, migraine headaches are often disabling, and the patient is often unable to work or interact with others during an attack. Partly this is due to pain, although many people with migraines also report an intense sensitivity to lights and sounds (known as **photophobia** and **phonophobia**, respectively) that prevent them from functioning as well. For this reason, it is not uncommon for someone with a migraine to retreat to a dark, quiet room during an attack.

Migraines are a **disabling form** of **paroxysmal headache** that presents with **pulsatile unilateral pain** lasting **several hours**.

POUND:
Pulsatile
hOurs
Unilateral
Nausea
Disabling

A migraine does not involve only the headache itself but also distinct symptoms occurring both before and after the attack. Many people experience a **prodrome** for several hours or even days prior to the onset of a migraine which alerts them to the coming attack. The specific symptoms of a prodrome differ from person to person, but they can commonly consist of changes in mood, energy levels, toileting habits, and sensitivity to light and noise.

Some people also experience an **aura** that occurs before or during the headache. Despite both of them occurring before a migraine, an aura is distinct from a prodrome in that it is usually more transient (only a few minutes) and involves distinct **visual abnormalities**. Most often this takes the form of "blurry" or "flickering lights" sensations known as **scintillating scotomas**, as seen in the following picture. However, in some cases these visual abnormalities may even extend to vision loss, as in a hemianopsia. Non-visual sensory abnormalities are less common but can occur as well, including "pins-and-needles" **paresthesias** in the arms and face. In rare cases, even **motor weakness** may be observed as part of an aura.

*Depiction of a **scintillating scotoma** during a **migraine**.*

Following a migraine, a **postdromal state** may occur. These are often described as being "not unlike a hangover," with many people reporting fatigue, malaise, cognitive dulling, depressed mood, and soreness in the part of the head where they felt the pain most acutely. A migraine postdrome can last for several days.

Most people who experience one migraine will go on to have more attacks in the future. For this reason, treatment of migraines involves not only acute management of a headache (known as **abortive treatment**) but also **preventive treatment** aimed at reducing the likelihood of future episodes. In mild cases, the same over-the-counter medications that are used in tension headaches can be tried. In more severe cases, drugs known as **triptans** (so-named because many of their names end in -triptan, as in sumatriptan, rizatriptan, and zolmitriptan) can be used. Triptans are effective at reducing both headache and nausea in the majority of patients who take them. Like with over-the-counter pain medicines, however, care must be taken to avoid overuse which can lead to rebound headaches. For this reason, alternative strategies to prevent migraines should be used in people who experience frequent attacks. While the mechanism underlying their use in migraine prophylaxis is unclear, the two best-supported medication classes are **anticonvulsants** like topiramate and valproate and **beta-blockers** like propranolol and metoprolol. Lifestyle modifications and various forms of therapy may help to reduce migraine frequency and severity as well.

CLUSTER HEADACHES
Cluster headaches are an incredibly painful form of headache—so painful, in fact, that they are also known as "**suicide headaches**" because patients who experience them have been known to contemplate killing themselves rather than continuing to live with the unbearable agony of a cluster headache. The pain is often located around or above the eye on one side and is described as someone sticking a "hot poker behind my eye." More than just being painful, cluster headaches are associated with several other features that the word **CLUSTER** will help you to remember:

C is for Conjunctival injection. This is basically just a fancy way of saying "red eyes."

L is for Lacrimation. Cluster headaches are associated with excessive crying and nasal discharge, typically on the same side as the pain. However, other signs such as eyelid drooping or pupillary constriction can appear as well.

U is for Unilateral. Like a migraine (and *unlike* a tension headache), a cluster headache tends to be felt only on one side or the other.

S is for Speedy. Cluster headaches tend to come on quickly, with no prodrome or aura as may be found in a migraine. They also dissipate just as quickly, with most lasting less than an hour.

T is for Treatable. Cluster headaches are treatable. Interestingly, administering **high-flow oxygen** seems to produce improvements in the majority of people within 15 minutes. **Triptans** also appear to help stop an episode quickly. Preventive treatments include **verapamil**, a calcium channel blocker that is used as an antihypertensive. The mechanism by which these seemingly random treatments work in cluster headaches is not known.

E is for Eyelid drooping. Ptosis, or a drooping eyelid, is commonly seen on the affected side during a cluster headache.

R is for Recurrent. Finally, cluster headaches are highly recurrent, occurring at the same time each day for most patients. Some patients have even given them the nickname "alarm clock headaches" because of how precisely regular they are.

Cluster headaches are **highly recurrent headaches** that are experienced as **retro-orbital pain**. Autonomic signs such as **lacrimation** and **rhinorrhea** are often seen.

CLUSTER:
Conjunctival injection
Lacrimation
Unilateral
Speedy
Treatable
Eyelid drooping
Recurrent

Cluster headaches tend to begin in one's 20s and 30s. For unclear reasons, **men** are affected four times as often as women. The cause of cluster headaches is not known, although there appears to be a genetic component. The majority of people who experience cluster headaches have a history of **smoking**, although unfortunately smoking cessation does not lead to improvement in the headaches, making it unlikely that this is a direct cause.

SECONDARY HEADACHES

Secondary headaches, or those caused by another medical condition, represent a minority of all headaches seen in clinical practice, with only around 10% of headaches having a clear underlying cause. However, because of the potential seriousness of some of these causes, secondary headaches must always be on your differential! The key to picking up secondary headaches is to look for **red flags** that signal the need for a more thorough work-up. You can remember these red flags with the mnemonic **PAID 40 TAXMEN** (a situation that would give just about anyone a headache!):

P is for Papilledema. The presence of papilledema or any other signs of increased intracranial pressure could be suggestive of a brain tumor, an infection, or idiopathic intracranial hypertension.

A is for Abrupt. A headache that arrives with an abrupt and sudden onset (sometimes called a "thunderclap" headache) may be a sign of an intracranial bleed like a subarachnoid hemorrhage.

I is for Immunosuppressed. Cancer, HIV, steroid use, and other situations that result in an immunocompromised state increase the risk of central nervous system infections significantly, so a headache in these patients should be taken as a potential sign of a dangerous disease.

D is for Different than before. Someone who suddenly presents with a headache that feels completely different than anything they have experienced previously in their life should receive an additional work-up.

40 is for 40 years or older. It is unusual for someone above the age of 40 who has never experienced headaches before to suddenly start having them, so this may warrant further investigation.

T is for Trauma. While some degree of headache following a mechanical trauma such as a car crash or fall may be completely normal, it is still wise to order imaging to rule out an intracranial bleed.

A is for Altered mental status. A headache in the context of accompanying changes in one's mental status (including confusion, cognitive impairment, or unusual behavior) can be concerning for an infection, an inflammatory disease, or a tumor.

X is for eXertional. Heavy exertion or frequent coughing increases intracranial pressure, which may lead to bursting of a blood vessel with subsequent bleeding. Any headache that is triggered by this kind of exertion should prompt a work-up for a possible bleed.

M is for Morbid. Signs of morbid illness, including systemic signs and symptoms such as fever, rash, or abnormal vital signs, could indicate an infection or tumor.

E is for Escalating. Any recurrent headache that is steadily increasing in frequency and/or severity is worrying for a progressive disease process such as a brain tumor or subdural hematoma.

N is for Neurologic signs or symptoms. With some exceptions (primarily migraines), most primary headaches do not present with accompanying neurologic changes, so a headache with neurologic findings (including weakness, sensory changes, visual loss, or seizures) should prompt clinical concern for a secondary headache.

While **secondary headaches** are the **exception rather than the rule**, be on the look out for a variety of **red flags** that might signal the presence of an underlying cause.

PAID 40 TAXMEN:
Papilledema
Abrupt
Immunosuppressed
Different than before
40 years or older
Trauma
Altered mental status
eXertional
Morbid
Escalating
Neurologic signs or symptoms

Now that we have an understanding of when to look for upstream causes of headache, let's look at one cause of secondary headache that we haven't already addressed elsewhere.

GIANT-CELL ARTERITIS
Giant-cell arteritis (also known as **temporal arteritis**) is a rheumatologic disease involving inflammation of the temporal artery. It often presents as a **unilateral headache** overlying the temporal region (seen at right), although there are often other signs and symptoms as well including fever. This inflammation causes narrowing of nearby blood vessels which manifests as **claudication** (soreness and pain related to tissue ischemia) in the jaw and tongue when chewing. If the ischemia extends to the ophthalmic artery, **vision loss and blindness** can occur.
For this reason, giant-cell arteritis is considered to be a **medical emergency**, as permanent damage can occur if it is not diagnosed and treated urgently.

For unclear reasons, giant-cell arteritis tends to affect **men** more often than women. It almost exclusively begins in **older adults** above the age of 50. On exam, the skin over the temporal region may be tender to palpation, and there may be signs of poor perfusion (including decreased pulses and ischemic changes on ophthalmologic exam). Lab testing often shows elevated inflammatory markers, especially a high **erythrocyte sedimentation rate** (ESR). However, the gold standard for diagnosing giant-cell arteritis is a **temporal artery biopsy** which will show mononuclear cell infiltrates or multinucleate giant cells invading the tissues. However, given the risk of permanent damage, you don't need to wait for diagnostic testing results before administering treatment. Once giant-cell arteritis is suspected, treatment with **corticosteroids** should be administered promptly to reduce inflammation!

*Inflamed **temporal artery** in a patient with **giant-cell arteritis**.*

The mnemonic **TEMPL3** can assist in rapidly identifying the signs and symptoms of giant-cell arteritis. This should help you think of abnormalities in the **T**emporal artery (including tenderness or reduced pulse strength), an elevated **E**SR, **M**ononuclear cell infiltrates or **M**ultinucleate giant cells on biopsy, the presence of a **P**ainful new-onset localized headache, and a **L**ate in life onset (50 years or older). If at least **3** of these features are present, giant-cell arteritis should be high on your differential (and if less than 3 are present, then you can feel more comfortable that the diagnosis has been ruled out).

Giant-cell arteritis is an **inflammatory disease** that results in a **unilateral headache, jaw and tongue claudication**, and possibly even **vision loss**.

TEMPL3:
Temporal artery tenderness or reduced pulse strength
ESR elevated
Mononuclear cell infiltrates or Multinucleate giant cells on biopsy
Painful new-onset localized headache
Late in life onset (over 50 years)
At least 3 of these

PUTTING IT ALL TOGETHER

Any patient presenting with a headache should always receive additional questioning to get more information about what is going on. Even in primary headaches where no cause has been identified, knowing about the type of headache can help to identify the best treatments (such as triptans in migraine headaches or high-flow oxygen in cluster headaches). In cases where any of the red flags in the **PAID 40 TAXMEN** mnemonic are present, you may want to go beyond just a history and physical by considering lab testing and/or neuroimaging to rule out other more serious (and potentially even deadly) causes. Finally, take time to review conditions from previous chapters that can present as headaches, including **strokes** (Chapter 12), **intracranial bleeds** (Chapter 13), **hydrocephalus** (Chapter 13), **idiopathic intracranial hypertension** (Chapter 13), **post-ictal headaches** (Chapter 18), **brain tumors** (Chapter 19), and infections such as **meningitis** and **encephalitis** (Chapter 20).

REVIEW QUESTIONS

1. A 23 y/o F is seeing a neurologist for management of recurrent headaches. Several times per month, she experiences a severe headache on the left side of her head which she describes as "someone sticking my head in a bag and hitting it with a sledgehammer." These headaches generally last around 4 hours during which time she tries to lay down in a quiet dark room as "seeing any light is like staring into the sun." She often experiences nausea during these episodes and occasionally vomits as a result. During the appointment, she tells her neurologist that in the past week she has had 2 attacks. For half an hour prior to each attack, she noticed small "dots that change color" appearing in her field of view that were "kind of like looking through a kaleidoscope." These dots were then followed by complete loss of vision in one eye, although she notes that it was a different eye each time (left the first time, right the second time). Which of the following is the best explanation for her visual symptoms?
   A. Transient ischemic attacks
   B. Migraine headaches
   C. Mononeuritis multiplex
   D. Occipital lobe seizures
   E. Optic neuritis related to multiple sclerosis

2. A 71 y/o M presents to the emergency department with sudden vision loss accompanied by "the worst headache of my life." He reports that for the past month he has had recurrent headaches of an "agonizing" quality on the right side of his head. Over this same time period, he has had a few episodes of blurry vision in his right eye that have resolved on their own. Review of symptoms is positive for reduced food intake related to pain in his jaw while chewing. Vital signs are HR 102, BP 136/88, RR 14, and T 101.4°F. On exam, there is extreme tenderness to palpation of his right scalp with diminished pulse strength. Which of the following in the best next step?
   A. Ordering a CT scan of the head
   B. Ordering an MRI scan of the head
   C. Obtaining a tissue sample for biopsy
   D. Obtaining a blood sample to test the erythrocyte sedimentation rate
   E. Administering corticosteroids
   F. Administering tissue plasminogen activator
   G. Administering high flow oxygen

3. A 24 y/o M is brought to the emergency department by ambulance around 11:00 at night after telling his girlfriend he wanted to die. This is his third time coming to the hospital in the past month. On interview, he reports a desire to die related to severe retro-orbital pain on his right side "like someone is jabbing a knife directly into my eyeball over and over and over." He denies any plans to actively harm himself but says, "I can't keep living like this!" The pain began around 25 minutes ago and awakened him shortly after falling asleep. He is having trouble sitting still during the interview which he attributes to the pain. Which of the following features is *least* likely to be seen in this case?
    A. Unilateral eyelid drooping
    B. Impaired pupillary light reflex
    C. Progression to both eyes
    D. Spontaneous termination of symptoms
    E. Good response to treatment
    F. History of tobacco use

4. A 44 y/o F sees her primary care doctor for management of headaches. She has been having headaches "off and on" for over 10 years. Since changing jobs 4 months ago, however, her headaches have been "almost constant." The pain is located over her forehead and feels like "pressure." If she massages her forehead, it brings a small degree of relief but only temporarily. She also describes pain on her back between her neck and left shoulder. Over the past few months, she has taken various medications in an effort to relieve her pain, including caffeine, over-the-counter medications (ibuprofen, naproxen, acetaminophen, and some herbal supplements), antidepressants (amitriptyline), and anticonvulsants (gabapentin). Each one brought partial relief at the time the drug was started, but they slowly lost efficacy over time. In the past week, she has had episodes of nausea and vomiting which she has not experienced before. She also had an episode where she fell while walking up stairs at work, though she says, "It's probably because I was wearing high heels." Examination reveals increased muscle tone in her trapezius muscles bilaterally, though she is able to reduce this tone when asked. Motor strength is intact throughout exam for 4/5 strength in her right leg and 3/5 in her right ankle. Which of the following is the best next step?
    A. Starting lorazepam, a benzodiazepine
    B. Starting tramadol, an opioid
    C. Stopping her existing medications
    D. Referring for psychotherapy
    E. Ordering an MRI of the head
    F. None of the above

1. **The best answer is B.** While headaches are the hallmark symptom of migraines, they are not the only manifestation of this condition. Many people with migraines experience visual symptoms either before or during an attack, with scintillations, scotomas, and even blindness occurring. The patient's description of her headache matches the presentation of a migraine closely, with a pulsatile quality, nausea, vomiting, and photophobia. For this reason, it is unlikely that another condition is needed to explain her visual symptoms (answers A, C, D, and E).

2. **The best answer is E.** This case describes a classic presentation of giant-cell arteritis, an inflammatory disease affecting large blood vessels such as the temporal artery. It often presents as a unilateral headache in an elderly patient along with jaw claudication, visual abnormalities, and constitutional symptoms such as fever. Giant-cell arteritis is a medical emergency, as delays in treatment can lead to permanent vision loss. For this reason, treatment should not be delayed for diagnostic tests if there is a reasonably high degree of certainty about the diagnosis (answers A–D). Corticosteroids are the treatment of choice for giant-cell arteritis as they are effective at rapidly reducing the inflammatory state brought on by this disease. High flow oxygen is effective at treating cluster headaches (answer G). Given the gradual onset of the patient's symptoms, a stroke is less likely (answer F).

3. **The best answer is C.** Cluster headaches are also known as "suicide headaches," as their excruciatingly painful nature has been said to make death sound like an attractive option compared to experiencing them. Cluster headaches are associated with autonomic signs including ptosis (answer A) and constriction of the pupils (answer B). Most cluster headaches will end on their own in around 30 minutes (answer D), although during a cluster of attacks the recurrence rate is high. Cluster headaches are treatable using high flow oxygen or triptans (answer E). There is an association between smoking and cluster headaches, although the exact mechanism linking the two is not clear (answer F). Most cluster headaches are unilateral, so progression to both eyes is unlikely to be seen.

4. **The best answer is E.** This vignette describes what initially appears to be a tension headache with a possible contribution from medication overuse. However, there are several features of this case that are concerning for a secondary headache, including a distinct change in how her headaches present beginning 4 months ago, atypical symptoms such as nausea and vomiting, and focal neurologic deficits on exam. For this reason, other causes of headaches, such as a brain tumor, must be ruled out. If no primary cause is found, then stopping her existing medications would be an appropriate treatment for a medication overuse headache (answer C). Starting a new medication is not likely to provide lasting relief, and both benzodiazepines and opioids are prone to dependence (answers A and B). Psychotherapy can be a helpful adjunct for helping to cope with headaches but is not the highest priority compared to working up a potential brain tumor (answer D).

24 NEUROCUTANEOUS DISORDERS

Okay, we're almost done! In our next-to-final chapter, we will talk about a class of genetic diseases known as **neurocutaneous disorders** that have effects on both the **nervous system** ("neuro-") and the **skin** ("-cutaneous"). The link between these two organ systems isn't immediately obvious. However, if you consider that nerves and skin both derive from the **ectoderm**, or one of the three germ layers that form during early embryonic development, it starts to make more sense. In particular for our study of neurology, these diseases tend to increase one's risk of developing **nervous system tumors**, as we will discover here.

Because genes contribute in some way to just about everything in the body, it naturally follows that genetic diseases can have deleterious effects in multiple organ systems. For that reason, the disorders we will be studying in this chapter do not always make intuitive or logical sense and will instead require a lot of memorization. (Like, *a lot.*) But that's just the sort of situation that mnemonics were made for! So buckle up and strap in for the final ride of this book as we explore the world of neurocutaneous disorders.

NEUROFIBROMATOSIS TYPE I

The term **neurofibromatosis** refers not to a single disease but rather to a collection of diseases that are all characterized by rampant growth of tumors in the nervous system. Of note, these tumors arise not in the neurons themselves but rather in the supporting cast members (the **glial cells** we talked about back in Chapter 2). These tumors are known as **neurofibromas** and are generally made up of *non-myelinating* Schwann cells (or those that provide other forms of support to neurons in the peripheral nervous system).

Neurofibromatosis type I (NF1, or previously **von Recklinghausen disease**) is an **autosomal dominant disorder** caused by a mutation in the neurofibromin 1 gene on chromosome **17**. (Conveniently, "von Recklinghausen" is made up of 17 letters, which should help you remember this association.)

> **Neurofibromatosis type I** (previously known as **von Recklinghausen disease**) is an **autosomal dominant disease** caused by a mutation on **chromosome 17**.
>
> *"von Recklinghausen" has **17** letters which should help you remember chromosome **17**.*

Neurofibromatosis type I is characterized by a triad of **neurofibromas** (tumors of Schwann cells), **café-au-lait spots** (hyperpigmented birthmarks named after the French term for "coffee with milk," referencing their light brown color), and **Lisch nodules** (tumor-like aggregations known as **hamartomas** consisting of melanocytes, or pigment-producing cells, found in the iris of the eye).

Neurofibromas and café-au-lait spots on the skin of the back.

Hyperpigmented Lisch nodules in the iris.

Other signs of neurofibromatosis type I include freckling of the skin around the armpit and groin, skeletal deformities, and gliomas (or more tumors of glial cells) in the optic nerve. You can put all of these presenting signs and symptoms together into the mnemonic **CAFÉ SPOT** which stands for **C**afé-au-lait spots, **A**xillary/inguinal freckling, **F**ibromas, **E**ye hamartomas, **S**keletal deformities, **P**arent or other first-degree relative with the same disease, and an **O**ptic nerve **T**umor. Neurofibromatosis type I is quite variable in its severity, as many patients are only mildly affected while others are completely disabled. There is **no cure**, but care can still be provided to minimize symptoms and maximize functional ability.

Neurofibromatosis type I is characterized by a triad of **neurofibromas, café-au-lait spots,** and **Lisch nodules** as well as other associated signs.

CAFÉ SPOT:
Café-au-lait spots
Axillary/inguinal freckling
Fibromas
Eye hamartomas (Lisch nodules)
Skeletal deformities
Parent or other first-degree relative with the same disease
Optic nerve Tumor

NEUROFIBROMATOSIS TYPE II

Neurofibromatosis type II also goes by the name **MISME syndrome** which, conveniently, is also a mnemonic for what this condition involves! **MISME** stands for **M**ultiple **I**nherited **S**chwannomas, **M**eningiomas, and **E**pendymomas which pretty much sums up the clinical presentation of patients with this disease. The schwannomas are often found in the sheath around the **vesticulocochlear nerve** (which you'll recall from Chapter 19 is the most common location for schwannomas to hit) and tend to be **bilateral** (in contrast to sporadic schwannomas which are generally unilateral).

Neurofibromatosis type II involves **bilateral benign brain tumors**, particularly **bilateral schwannomas** as well as **meningiomas** and **ependymomas**.

MISME: Multiple Inherited Schwannomas, Meningiomas, and Ependymomas.

When it is inherited, neurofibromatosis type II involves a defect in the NF2 gene on chromosome 22. Like type I, it is inherited in an **autosomal dominant** fashion. In contrast to type I, however, it often presents a little later in life (usually around one's teenage years or early 20s). Treatment typically involves **surgical removal** of the schwannomas as well as **hearing aids** and other assistive devices if needed.

Neurofibromatosis type II is also an easy-to-remember condition because the **II** in its name can help to remind you of a lot of the features of the disease: the **bi**lateral occurrence of vestibular schwannomas, the location on chromosome **22**, and the onset around the age of **2**0.

Neurofibromatosis type II is inherited in an **autosomal dominant** fashion and is localized to the **NF2 gene** on **chromosome 22**.

Neurofibromatosis type II involves bilateral vestibular schwannomas, is located on chromosome 22, and begins around the age of 20.

TUBEROUS SCLEROSIS

Tuberous sclerosis is an **autosomal dominant** genetic disorder in which mutations of two **tumor suppressor genes** (specifically TSC1 and TSC2, both named after this disease) lead to the development of **multiple benign tumors** in various organs of the body. The main clinical features of tuberous sclerosis can be captured in the mnemonic **I ♥ TUBERS**:

I is for Intellectual disability. Cognitive deficits are seen in about half of all patients with tuberous sclerosis.

♥ is for Heart. One type of tumor seen commonly in tuberous sclerosis is a **cardiac rhabdomyoma**, or a tumor of the muscles cells of the heart. In fact, over half of all cardiac rhabdomyomas occur in the context of tuberous sclerosis.

TU is for TUmors. Lots of tumors.

B is for Brain. Tuberous sclerosis is associated with three types of brain tumors in particular: **giant cell astrocytomas**, **cortical tubers**, and **subependymal nodules**. It is believed that these tumors are the direct cause of the neuropsychiatric signs and symptoms observed in this syndrome.

E is for Epilepsy. Most patients with tuberous sclerosis suffer from recurrent **seizures** and generally require treatment with anticonvulsants.

R is for Renal. The majority of tuberous sclerosis cases involve benign tumors in the kidney known as **angiomyolipomas**, named for the combination of vascular ("angio"), muscular ("myo"), and fatty ("lipo") tissues seen in these tumors.

S is for Skin. As a neurocutaneous syndrome, it should come as no surprise that skin involvement in seen in almost all cases of tuberous sclerosis. Hypopigmented areas known as **ash leaf spots** are incredibly common (note that this is the *opposite* pattern from the *hyper*pigmented lesions seen in neurofibromatosis type I!). Another common finding is multiple **facial angiofibromas**, or small flesh-colored papules as seen in the image below:

Tuberous sclerosis is an **autosomal dominant neurocutaneous disorder** that involves the growth of **multiple benign tumors** in various organs of the body.

I ♥ TUBERS:
Intellectual disability
♥ (cardiac rhabdomyomas)
*Multiple benign **TU**mors*
***B**rain tumors*
***E**pilepsy*
***R**enal angiomyolipomas*
***S**kin findings (ash leaf spots and facial angiofibromas)*

Given that tuberous sclerosis is a complex syndrome involving many organ systems, treatment often involves a multidisciplinary team to address the various biological, psychological, and social aspects of the disease.

STURGE-WEBER SYNDROME

Sturge-Weber syndrome (also known as **encephalotrigeminal angiomatosis**—quite the mouthful!) is a neurocutaneous disorder characterized by dark red cutaneous hemangiomas known as **port-wine stains** that are found on the patient's face at birth. If this were the only anomaly associated with this condition, it wouldn't be quite so bad. However, babies with Sturge-Weber syndrome also present with a variety of other clinical manifestations including **seizures**, **unilateral muscle weakness**, and **glaucoma**. Most children with this condition end up with some degree of **intellectual disability**. Sturge-Weber syndrome is unique among most of the neurocutaneous diseases in that there does not appear to be a clear genetic cause; instead, most cases are **sporadic**. You can remember the features of Sturge-Weber syndrome by thinking of **Sturge** as **St. Urge**. This **S**aint had an evil **urge** to give wine to a baby! However, he ended up spilling it on the baby's face, giving it a **port-wine stain** and making it go into alcohol withdrawal (a common cause of seizures).

Sturge-Weber syndrome is a **sporadic neurocutaneous disease** seen at the time of birth involving **port-wine stains, seizures, unilateral hemiparesis, glaucoma**, and **intellectual disability**.

*This **St.** (saint) had an evil **urge**: to give **port-wine** to a **baby**!*

VON HIPPEL-LINDAU DISEASE

Von Hippel–Lindau disease is an **autosomal dominant** genetic disorder involving a mutation in a tumor suppressor gene on **chromosome 3**, leading to tumors popping up in multiple areas of the body. In the nervous system, **hemangioblastomas** in the cerebellum and spine are quite common, with many patients having more than one of these tumors at a time. Other common associated findings are **retinal angiomas**, **renal cell carcinomas** (often bilateral), and **pheochromocytomas** (or tumors of the adrenal glands producing excessive amounts of norepinephrine, which can mimic a state of sympathetic nervous system overactivation). These tumors can all occur on their own, but when they appear in children or as more than one tumor at a time, this is strongly suggestive of von Hippel–Lindau disease. You can remember the four most common manifestations of this condition by thinking of it as von **HARP**el—Lindau disease, which stands for **H**emangioblastomas, **A**ngiomatosis, **R**enal cell carcinomas, and **P**heochromocytomas.

Von Hippel–Lindau disease manifesting as multiple
hemangioblastomas in the brainstem and cerebellum.

Von Hippel–Lindau disease is an **autosomal dominant genetic disorder** resulting in multiple tumors across the body, including **hemangioblastomas, retinal angiomas, renal cell carcinomas**, and **pheochromocytomas**.

*von **HARP**el—Lindau disease:*
Hemangioblastomas
Angiomatosis
Renal cell carcinomas
Pheochromocytomas

ATAXIA TELANGIECTASIA

The last neurocutaneous disorder we will talk about is **ataxia telangiectasia**. Luckily, the two biggest manifestations of the disease (ataxia and multiple telangiectasias) are both written right into the name! We've talked about **ataxia** already in the context of cerebellar signs, and you should remember that it involves impaired balance and motor coordination. **Telangiectasia** might be a new word for you, but it refers to **small dilated blood vessels** located right under the surface of the skin that make small points of redness, as seen in the following image:

Telangiectasias on the lip.

While ataxia and telangiectasias are the core features of this disease, most people with ataxia telangiectasia also suffer from **immunodeficiency** and are at an increased risk for infections (particularly in the lungs). There is also an increased risk of various types of **cancer**, with lymphomas and leukemia being the most common.

Ataxia telangiectasia is an **autosomal recessive** genetic disease caused by a mutation in the **ATM gene** on **chromosome 11**. The ATM gene is involved in repairing broken DNA, which explains why people with ataxia telangiectasia are at an increased risk of cancer (due to their inability to repair DNA damage) and dysfunction of the immune system (as creation of antibodies requires rearranging DNA sequences that are normally put back together by ATM). The mechanism by which loss of the ATM gene leads to the ataxia and telangiectasias that are the hallmarks of this disease is not known, however. You can remember the mechanism of this disease by thinking of a situation in which someone **attacks ya tel**evision set. What do you do? **Repair IT**! This will help you associate "**ataxia tel**angiectasia" with DNA **repair** as well as the high risk of both **I**mmunodeficiency and **T**umors. You can also think of the antenna on top of the TV as being an **11** to associate it with chromosome **11**.

> **Ataxia telagiectasia** is an **autosomal recessive** disorder involving **malfunctioning DNA repair** that leads to **ataxia, telangiectasias, immunodeficiency**, and an increased risk of **cancer**.
>
> *What do you do when someone **attacks ya tel**evision set? **Repair IT**!*

PUTTING IT ALL TOGETHER

The diseases found in this chapter can admittedly come across as a hodgepodge of different conditions that have few, if any, unifying themes between them. However, try to remember the core pattern of both **nervous system** and **skin involvement** due to the origin of both of these organs in the **ectoderm**! From there, use the mnemonics provided to look for patterns that will help you to identify the exact cause of the patient's suffering (and hopefully ways to help as well!).

REVIEW QUESTIONS

1. A 27 y/o F has seen a primary care doctor for the past decade. She comes in today for a check-up. Her medical history is notable for blindness in her right eye due to radiation treatment of an optic nerve tumor as a child. She also underwent corrective surgery for scoliosis at the age of 12. Her physical exam is notable for several hyperpigmented areas on her back with small soft skin nodules dispersed across her body as seen below:

    These findings have all been noted by the doctor since the time he first saw her, and he does not believe there has been any change in their pattern or distribution. On interview, she reports increasing fatigue for the past 2 weeks, with nausea yesterday and today. She also reports occasional abdominal pain over the same time period. A urine pregnancy test is positive. Her partner has no significant personal or family history of disease. Which of the following is the most appropriate statement for the doctor to make at this time?
    - A. "The likelihood of your child inheriting this condition from you really depends on whether it is a boy or a girl."
    - B. "It is almost certain that your child will be affected by your condition."
    - C. "There is a 50% chance that you will pass your condition to your child."
    - D. "It is highly unlikely that your child will be affected."
    - E. "There is no chance that your child will develop your condition."

2. A 3 y/o M is brought to the hospital for fever and lethargy over the past 2 days. He has a history of recurrent ear infections, and his exam today is consistent with a repeat infection. His medical history is notable for developmental delays in both motor and speech milestones as well as a prior hospitalization for aspiration pneumonia. His pediatrician documented in his chart for the past several visits that his gait was unsteady, with a tendency to fall when walking more than a few feet at a time. His height and weight are appropriate for his age. Small dilated blood vessels are seen over his ears and nose but are particularly prominent on his sclerae as seen below:

Which of the following should most be avoided in this patient?
- A. CT scans of the chest to diagnose pulmonary infections
- B. MRI scans of the head to evaluate cerebellar volume
- C. Prophylactic antibiotics to prevent future infections
- D. Mechanical bracing of the legs to improve leg stability
- E. Feeding tubes to prevent aspiration

3. A 16 y/o F is brought to the hospital by her caregiver after she was seen having a generalized tonic-clonic seizure. She was born to parents belonging to a religious group that forbid contact with the government or health care providers, so her medical history is unknown. When her parents died 2 weeks ago, she became a ward of the state. She is currently living in a group home and was there when the seizure occurred. On interview, the patient appears to have difficulty producing verbal responses to questions asked. The caregiver provides results of recent testing showing her IQ to be in the range of severe intellectual disability. Her exam is notable for small growths on her cheeks extending onto her nose and her forehead as seen in the following image:

Which of the following is *least* likely to be of value in this patient's care?
- A. Starting an anticonvulsant
- B. Obtaining an MRI of the brain
- C. Drawing blood to evaluate renal function
- D. Arranging for electroencephalography
- E. Ordering an echocardiogram
- F. All of the above are likely to be of value

1. **The best answer is C.** This patient likely has neurofibromatosis type I given the presence of café-au-lait spots, neurofibromas, and several associated conditions including scoliosis and optic nerve tumors. Neurofibromatosis type I is an autosomal dominant disorder, so this patient has about a 50% chance of passing the disease to her offspring, not lower or higher (answers B, D, and E). Neurofibromatosis type I is not an X-linked condition (answer A).

2. **The best answer is A.** Patients with ataxia–telangiectasia have a mutation in the ATM gene, which normally produces a protein that is involved in repairing DNA damage. For this reason, exposure to radiation and other potential sources of DNA damage should be avoided to reduce the risk of developing cancer as much as possible (although in some cases the benefits of doing an x-ray or CT scan will outweigh this risk). MRI scans do not involve radiation and will not increase the risk of cancer (answer B). While overuse of antibiotics is a concern, for a patient who is at high risk of recurrent infections, prophylactic use may be appropriate (answer C). A feeding tube is an invasive procedure, although it may be appropriate if the patient is unable to eat by mouth without aspirating food (answer E). Mechanical bracing of the legs is an appropriate measure to improve mobility (answer D).

3. **The best answer is F.** This patient likely has tuberous sclerosis as evidenced by the characteristic triad of epilepsy, intellectual disability, and cutaneous findings. Tuberous sclerosis is a multi-system disorder that requires an interdisciplinary medical team for appropriate management. For this patient, ordering an EEG and starting an anticonvulsant are appropriate given her recent seizure (answers A and D). The patient is at high risk of brain tumors, so an MRI of the brain can help to rule those out (answer B). Tuberous sclerosis is associated with both renal angiomyolipomas and cysts, so evaluating renal function is essential (answer C). Finally, patients with this condition are at high risk of cardiac rhabdomyomas, so an echocardiogram should be obtained (answer E).

25 FINAL REVIEW

Okay, that's a wrap! At this point, we have covered many of the most common neurologic diseases found on exams and in the real world. We have also covered the foundational neuroanatomy that allows us to explain what we are seeing on a clinical level. This is not to say that we have gone over every possible detail of neurologic pathology, as such a feat would require volumes of books and a lifetime of learning. Because of this, it is possible that as you continue on in your clinical career, you will encounter neurologic diseases that we haven't explicitly covered here. Don't be put off by this! By keeping our neuroanatomical framework in mind, learning about new diseases doesn't have to be scary or confusing. Try to use everything you have learned so far about neuroanatomy to make predictions about what kinds of signs and symptoms you might observe with any new disease you come across—because you'll probably be right! This is because the nervous system is an understandable and predictable structure, and those that take the time to learn it will find themselves rewarded.

We will close out this book with a final set of review questions that will hopefully bring together much of what you have learned into a cohesive whole. After all, when practicing in the real world, patients will not come to you with their diseases neatly organized into discrete chapters. Instead, you will need to be prepared to see whatever pathology may come through the door at any given moment. Use this opportunity to make connections and comparisons between the various signs, symptoms, and clinical findings that are shared across different types of diseases so that you can come to the right diagnosis and treatment.

Good luck!

FINAL REVIEW QUESTIONS

1. A 10 y/o F is adopted from an orphanage in Laos and brought to live in the United States. Her medical history is unknown. At the age of 12, she is brought to a pediatrician for an evaluation after she develops intermittent jerking movements of her arms and legs. Her adopted mother says that over the same period of time her personality began to change and that the "bright sunny girl" she used to be has gone away. The pediatrician diagnoses her as having a tic disorder, says that her personality changes are a normal part of pre-adolescent development, and prescribes her a medication to treat her tics. Over the next several months, the jerky movements begin to happen more frequently and more violently. She begins to struggle in school, and she is much more irritable and withdrawn. She is brought to the hospital after she drops "like a rag doll" several times at school. She does not lose consciousness during these episodes. In the emergency department, her exam is notable for difficulty following simple commands such as being asked to raise her hand or hop on one leg. There is mild cogwheel rigidity in her upper extremities bilaterally. Her vital signs are within normal limits for her age. A lumbar puncture is performed which shows no abnormalities in cell counts, glucose, or protein. An MRI of the brain reveals abnormal signals in the white matter of the left frontal lobe as below:

The patient is admitted to the hospital. Which of the following is the most likely explanation for her presentation?
   A. Bacterial meningitis
   B. Viral encephalitis
   C. Fungal meningoencephalitis
   D. Childhood absence epilepsy
   E. Juvenile myoclonic epilepsy
   F. Lennox-Gastaut syndrome
   G. Pilocytic astrocytoma
   H. Acute disseminated encephalomyelitis
   I. Subacute sclerosing panencephalitis
   J. None of the above

2. An 18 y/o M plays football on his high school team. During a championship game, he sustains two hard hits to the head but does not lose consciousness. Worried about being ejected from the game, he does not tell his coach about this. Over the next 5 days, he begins to experience a progressive headache and increasing nausea with three episodes of vomiting. One week after the game, he tells his parents to take him to the hospital. In the emergency department, he is initially fully alert and oriented. However, as time passes he begins to look increasingly sedated and is unable to understand the questions being asked of him. Concerned, the emergency medicine team orders a head CT. Which of the following images is most likely to be seen?

3. A 58 y/o F with a history of hypertension and diabetes mellitus presents to the emergency department with left-sided weakness. When she awoke this morning, she noticed that her left arm was weak and that she was having difficulty speaking. Left leg weakness developed several hours later. She denies any loss of consciousness or changes in vision. Vital signs are HR 92, BP 182/114, RR 16, and T 99.1°F. Neurological exam is notable for an absent gag reflex, weakness of the left upper and lower extremities, loss of vibration and proprioception on the left, and deviation of the tongue to the right as seen in the following image:

No facial weakness or asymmetry is seen. Extraocular movements are intact for both eyes. Pain and temperature sensation are intact throughout. Which of the following arteries is most likely to reveal an occlusion?
   A.   Left anterior cerebral artery
   B.   Right anterior cerebral artery
   C.   Left middle cerebral artery
   D.   Right middle cerebral artery
   E.   Left posterior cerebral artery
   F.   Right posterior cerebral artery
   G.   Basilar artery
   H.   Left anterior inferior cerebellar artery
   I.   Right anterior inferior cerebellar artery
   J.   Left posterior inferior cerebellar artery
   K.   Right posterior inferior cerebellar artery
   L.   Left vertebral artery
   M.   Right vertebral artery
   N.   Anterior spinal artery

4.   A 19 y/o F with no significant past medical history presents to the emergency department complaining of severe headaches for the past 3 weeks along with blurry vision for the past 5 days. She describes her headaches as "throbbing" and continuous. She denies fever, chills, or muscle weakness but does note that she has felt more tired recently. Vital signs are HR 92, BP 130/84, RR 16, and T 99.1°F. Exam reveals a moderately obese young woman who is alert and oriented to person, place, time, and situation. Motor strength and sensation is intact in all four extremities. Gait is steady and balanced. Her Romberg test is negative. Cranial nerve exam reveals limited ability to look laterally in both eyes. Visual acuity is decreased with an enlarged blind spot bilaterally. Fundoscopic examination reveals blurring of the optic discs bilaterally as seen in the following image:

An MRI of the brain is ordered which shows no abnormalities. Which of the following is most likely to relieve her symptoms?
    A.   Short course of corticosteroids
    B.   Lumbar puncture
    C.   Ibuprofen
    D.   Neurosurgical tumor resection
    E.   Sumatriptan
    F.   Broad-spectrum antibiotics
    G.   High flow oxygen by nasal cannula
    H.   Full recovery is expected without treatment

5.   A 25 y/o right-handed M who is a graduate student in archaeology comes to the student health clinic reporting shaking of his right hand for the past several months. This shaking is most noticeable when he is writing and recently has resulted in him being unable to take written tests for his coursework. The shaking seems to "come and go," though at times it is so pronounced that his friends will ask him about it. He denies a history of excessive alcohol intake but says, "Now that you mention it, the shaking does seem to get better when I drink." A full neurological exam is unremarkable, with intact cranial nerves, full motor strength, no sensory deficits, and a steady gait. There is no resting tremor in his arms, but when asked to hold his arms out a tremor is seen in both hands, greater on the right than the left. The tremor increases in amplitude when asked to write his name and the date using a pencil, as seen below:

Which of the following is the best next step in management?
    A.   Genetic testing
    B.   MRI of the brain
    C.   PET scan of the brain
    D.   Prescribing a blood pressure medication
    E.   Injecting botulinum toxin
    F.   Electromyography of both upper extremities

6. A 28 y/o F is training to be a neurologist. She is reading the results of a genetic test that she recently ordered for one of her patients. The report says that her patient has an expansion of the trinucleotide repeat sequence GAA on chromosome 9. Which of the following is most likely to describe her patient?

    A. A 9 y/o F with an unsteady gait, absent reflexes, and an enlarged heart
    B. A 42 y/o M with involuntary swinging movements of the arms and legs
    C. A 15 y/o F with epilepsy, hyperpigmented spots, and skin nodules
    D. A 28 y/o M with bilateral hand weakness and slowed muscle relaxation
    E. A 50 y/o F with diffuse muscle weakness, spasticity, and atrophy
    F. None of the above

7. A 23 y/o M goes to the urgent care clinic reporting severe pain and a rash on his left chest. He has never had a rash like this before. He denies recent sick contacts or unsafe sexual practices. He is otherwise healthy and takes no medications. Vital signs are HR 74, BP 126/84, RR 14, and T 98.8°F. Exam reveals a linear grouping of red vesicles as seen below:

The remainder of the physical and neurological exam is completely normal. Viral particles are most likely to be found in which of the following spinal nerve roots?

    A. C5
    B. C7
    C. T1
    D. T4
    E. T7
    F. T10
    G. L2
    H. L4
    I. S1

8. An 18 y/o F with a history of epilepsy is brought to the emergency department after a generalized tonic-clonic seizure lasting 2 minutes. She regularly sees a neurologist in clinic and has been taking lamotrigine for the past several years. On interview, she appears tired but is alert and oriented to person, place, time,

and situation. Neurological exam reveals 2/5 motor strength in the left arm and leg. Her voice is soft and faint, though she is able to both speak and understand instructions. Vital signs are HR 114, BP 136/78, RR 18, and T 99.5°F. Which of the following is most likely to be seen on neuroimaging?

    A. Hemorrhage in the region of the right anterior cerebral artery
    B. Hemorrhage in the region of the left anterior cerebral artery
    C. Hemorrhage in the region of the right middle cerebral artery
    D. Hemorrhage in the region of the left middle cerebral artery
    E. Hemorrhage in the region of the right posterior cerebral artery
    F. Hemorrhage in the region of the left posterior cerebral artery
    G. Ischemia in the region of the right anterior cerebral artery
    H. Ischemia in the region of the left anterior cerebral artery
    I. Ischemia in the region of the right middle cerebral artery
    J. Ischemia in the region of the left middle cerebral artery
    K. Ischemia in the region of the right posterior cerebral artery
    L. Ischemia in the region of the left posterior cerebral artery
    M. None of the above

9. A 79 y/o F is brought to the hospital after being found on the floor by her daughter. It is unclear whether she had lost consciousness or how long she had been on the floor. Neurologic exam reveals intact motor strength and preservation of all sensory modalities throughout her extremities. The most notable finding is profoundly impaired visual acuity, as the patient is observed to walk directly into objects, ignore a plate of food that is placed directly in front of her, and ask for lights to be turned on during the daytime. On more thorough testing, visual acuity is lost in all four quadrants of both eyes. When asked about her vision, she adamantly denies visual loss. When the doctor asks her to name various objects that are being held in front of her, she gives seemingly random responses, calling a watch "a pen" and a clipboard "a bottle." Her pupillary light reflexes are intact bilaterally. There is no evidence of other neurologic deficits. Where is the most likely location of the injury accounting for her deficits?

    A. Eye
    B. Optic nerve
    C. Optic chiasm
    D. Optic tract
    E. Lateral geniculate nucleus
    F. Optic radiations
    G. Occipital lobe
    H. Medial longitudinal fasciculus
    I. Paramedian pontine reticular formation
    J. Frontal eye fields
    K. Edinger-Westphal nuclei

10. A 71 y/o right-handed F is brought to the hospital from a local pier after a passerby found her sitting on a bench looking confused. When asked questions, she did not respond but looked very frustrated and upset about her situation. She was able to follow commands such as "Hold up your right hand" or "Shake your

head." She was unable to write when given a paper and pencil. No other deficits are noted during a full neurological exam. Magnetic resonance angiography is most likely to reveal severe narrowing of which of the following arteries?

- A. Right anterior cerebral artery
- B. Left anterior cerebral artery
- C. Right middle cerebral artery
- D. Left middle cerebral artery
- E. Right posterior cerebral artery
- F. Left posterior cerebral artery
- G. None of the above

11. A 19 y/o M is brought to the hospital after not eating for the past 3 weeks related to a belief that all food has been poisoned. He calls his family members "deceivers" and claims that he cannot trust them as they have "all been replaced by demons." For the past 6 months, he has stopped bathing or going to work. He is given a diagnosis of schizophrenia and started on a medication that blocks dopamine receptors in the brain. Which of the following effects is *least* likely to be seen as a side effect of this medication?

- A. Difficulty initiating movements
- B. Increased muscular rigidity
- C. Decreased production of prolactin
- D. Decreased goal-directed behavior
- E. All of the above are likely to be observed

12. An 11 y/o F is brought to see an optometrist after she tells her parents she is having trouble reading. She has been increasingly accident prone over the past few months and has been hit in the side of the head by a ball during recess on two separate occasions. In both instances, she says that she did not see the ball coming before it hit her. Visual acuity testing reveals no refractive errors. However, there are significant deficits in her field of vision as seen below:

She is referred to an ophthalmologist for further evaluation. Her review of systems is positive for headache and increased thirst. Her weight is in the 12th percentile; she was in the 64th percentile one year ago. An MRI is ordered which shows the following:

Which of the following best explains the patient's presentation?
- A. Clonal expansion of glial cells in the central nervous system
- B. Tumor of cerebellar stem cells
- C. Growth of cerebrospinal fluid-producing cells in the ventricular system
- D. Neoplastic growth of the vascular system supplying the brain
- E. Growth of embryonic cell remnants in the pituitary gland
- F. None of the above

13. (Continued from previous question.) The patient is scheduled for surgical resection followed by radiation therapy. Both of these are successful, and the patient is deemed to be in remission. Over the next year, however, she is noted to have an increased appetite resulting in excessive weight gain. Within two years, her BMI is in the morbidly obese range, and she is diagnosed as having insulin resistance. Her change in appetite is most likely attributable to damage in which of the following areas?
- A. Ventral posterolateral nucleus of the thalamus
- B. Ventral posteromedial nucleus of the thalamus
- C. Lateral geniculate nucleus of the thalamus
- D. Medial geniculate nucleus of the thalamus
- E. Anterior nucleus of the hypothalamus
- F. Lateral nucleus of the hypothalamus
- G. Ventromedial nucleus of the hypothalamus
- H. Suprachiasmatic nucleus of the hypothalamus
- I. Supraoptic nucleus of the hypothalamus
- J. Paraventricular nucleus of the hypothalamus

14. A 53 y/o F with a history of poorly controlled diabetes mellitus type 2 presents to the emergency department complaining of new-onset double vision. She says that over the past week she has had blurriness of vision, with difficulty focusing on objects beginning yesterday. On exam, there are no focal motor or sensory deficits in her extremities. Her eyes are deviated in separate directions as seen in the following image:

Her pupils are equal and reactive bilaterally. Vital signs are within normal limits. Her blood glucose is elevated at 280 mg/dL. A CT scan of the brain shows no evidence of ischemic changes. Which of the following cranial nerves is most likely affected?

A. Oculomotor nerve
B. Trochlear nerve
C. Abducens nerve
D. Oculomotor and trochlear nerves
E. Oculomotor and abducens nerves
F. Trochlear and abducens nerves
G. Oculomotor, trochlear, and abducens nerves
H. None of the nerves

15. A 4 y/o F is brought to the hospital by her parents after she begins repeatedly falling to one side while walking "like she's drunk." Her medical history is unremarkable except for an episode of vomiting and diarrhea that occurred 5 days prior to this episode. Her parents do not believe she has ingested any alcohol, poisons, or other substances. She is up to date on her immunizations. Her vital signs are entirely within normal limits with no fever. There are no deficits in either motor strength or any sensory modality noted on neurological exam. There is no facial asymmetry or nystagmus. Her mental status appears to be grossly intact, and her parents deny any episodes of lost consciousness. CT and MRI scans of the head are ordered, and both show no focal abnormalities. Urine toxicology testing is negative for all substances including alcohol. Within 2 weeks, her gait has returned to normal. What is the most likely etiology?

A. Acute cerebellar ataxia
B. Acute disseminated encephalomyelitis
C. Subacute sclerosing panencephalitis
D. Encephalitis
E. Meningitis
F. Guillain–Barré syndrome
G. Multiple sclerosis
H. Hydrocephalus
I. Atonic seizures

16. A 24 y/o F gives birth to a healthy baby boy after a 39-week gestation. The mother lives in a rural area and objects to medical care, so she gives birth at home. One week after birth, the infant begins crying inconsolably and refuses to nurse. After several hours, the mother is sufficiently concerned and takes him to the emergency department. On exam, the patient is noted to have increased muscle tone throughout his body leading to an arched position as seen below:

The exam is also notable for a malodorous purulent discharge from his umbilicus. No abnormalities in the fontanelles are observed. The patient is afebrile. Which of the following is the most likely cause of the patient's presentation?
   A. Group B *Streptococci*
   B. *Escherichia coli*
   C. *Clostridium tetani*
   D. *Clostridium botulinum*
   E. Genetic defect in the SMN1 gene
   F. None of the above

17. A 30 y/o F clutches her head and cries out suddenly while at work. She appears to be in a panic, so a nearby coworker calls 911. Upon initial evaluation in the hospital, she is completely unresponsive. Her body shows decerebrate extensor posturing. A CT is ordered which shows an acute left subdural hematoma. A follow-up MRI shows transtentorial herniation as below:

Which of the following is most likely to be seen on examination?
- A. Fixed constricted pupils bilaterally
- B. Downward and outward positioning of right eye
- C. Upward and inward drift of the left eye
- D. Outward drift of both eyes
- E. Linear areas of bleeding in the midbrain and upper pons
- F. None of the above

18. A 70 y/o F is referred to a neurologist after she develops slurring of her speech gradually over a period of one year. Her past medical history is significant for hypertension and diabetes both of which are well controlled with medications and lifestyle changes. While speaking with the patient, the neurologist notes that the patient's emotions will vacillate wildly from one moment to the next, and she switches between laughing and crying several times. Her emotional expression does not appear to correlate with the topic of the conversation. After additional evaluation, the patient is diagnosed with primary lateral sclerosis. Which of the following is most likely to be found on further examination?
- A. Absent gag reflex
- B. Tongue atrophy
- C. Urinary incontinence
- D. Rapid functional decline and death within several months
- E. Difficulty swallowing
- F. None of the above

19. A 72 y/o M with a history of poorly controlled hypertension and hyperlipidemia presents to the hospital after a sudden onset of headache with a "spinning" sensation. When he tried to walk around after this, he felt that he was perpetually falling to the left. On the way to the hospital, he developed severe nausea with several episodes of vomiting. On initial evaluation, his vital signs are within normal limits. Neurological exam is normal except for a slow unsteady gait, rapid darting eye movements when looking to the left, and inability to flip his hands over repeatedly when asked. While his visual acuity is intact, during the exam he notes that his vision is "not keeping up" with his eyes. He is unable to elaborate further when asked about this. The cranial nerve exam is otherwise intact. There is full motor strength and sensation in all four extremities. His memory and cognition are grossly normal. Which of the following is the most likely explanation for his symptoms?
- A. Thromboembolic occlusion of the anterior cerebral circulation
- B. Thickening of the inner lining of the vertebral artery
- C. Acute blockage of the ventricular system
- D. Buildup of fluid in the endolymphatic compartment of the inner ear
- E. Viral infection of the vestibular nerve
- F. None of the above

20. A 37 y/o M sees his primary care doctor after he awoke with severe low back pain and numbness in both legs. When he tried to get out of bed, his legs could not support his weight, and he collapsed onto the floor. On interview, he reports that

several days ago he developed shooting pains in his back while lifting weights at the gym, but these resolved on their own. On exam, the patient is alert and oriented. His vital signs are within normal limits. Motor strength is intact in both upper extremities but is significantly decreased in the left lower extremity, with mild weakness in the thigh, moderate weakness in the calf, and complete paralysis in the foot. The left patellar reflex and bilateral Achilles reflexes are all absent. Sensory numbness is noted in the scrotum and perianal area. Urine is seen soaking his pants. When asked about this, the patient reports that he has had dribbling of urine since this morning. Magnetic resonance imaging of the back is most likely to reveal a herniated disk in which region of the spine?

    A. Cervical
    B. Thoracic
    C. Lumbar
    D. Sacral
    E. Coccygeal

21. A 36 y/o M with a history of migraines goes to the emergency department complaining of double vision. At first he thought that his visual changes were related to a migraine, so he took a dose of rizatriptan. However, this did not result in improvement in his symptoms. When asked to look to the right, both eyes move synchronously. When asked to look to the left, however, his right eye remains in the middle while his left eye moves laterally, as seen below:

The patient exclaims, "That made everything go *really* double!" While looking to the left, his left eye is seen making quick darting movements back and forth in the horizontal axis. Visual acuity, pupillary light reflexes, convergence, and eyelid strength are all intact. Fundoscopic exam reveals normal-sized and symmetric optic discs. He demonstrates full motor strength and sensory function throughout all four limbs. A lesion is most likely to be found in which of the following structures?

    A. Optic nerve
    B. Oculomotor nerve
    C. Trochlear nerve
    D. Abducens nerve
    E. Medial longitudinal fasciculus
    F. Paramedian pontine reticular formation
    G. Frontal eye fields

22. A 18 y/o F college student is spending a semester abroad. On her first day, she goes to dinner with her host family at a local restaurant. She is offered a dish that she does not recognize. Not wanting to be rude, she takes a bite. However, she is immediately repulsed by the taste and gags on the food, spitting it back out. She then feels nauseous and on the verge of vomiting for the next several minutes. Which of the following neural structures is *least* involved in these processes?
    A. Facial nerve
    B. Glossopharyngeal nerve
    C. Vagus nerve
    D. Hypoglossal nerve
    E. Edinger-Westphal nuclei
    F. Nucleus solitarius
    G. Nucleus ambiguus
    H. Area postrema

23. A 21 y/o M comes to the emergency department reporting a 4-day history of increasing nausea. His initial examination is unremarkable, with no focal neurologic deficits. Vital signs are HR 66, BP 124/76, RR 16, and T 98.2°F. He is given fluid hydration, with plans made for discharge. However, when the nurse enters the room to give him his paperwork, she notices that he appears somnolent and confused. Repeat vital signs are HR 38, BP 168/90, RR 18, and T 98.8°F. His exam is now notable for a slow unsteady gait and a positive Romberg sign. A third set of vital signs show HR 36, BP 190/100, RR 8, and T 99.0°F. Which of the following is the most likely explanation for his rapidly changing condition?
    A. Thromboembolism leading to ischemic brain damage
    B. Ruptured artery leading to increased intracranial pressure
    C. Viral infection leading to widespread inflammation of the brain
    D. Epileptic activity leading to alteration of consciousness
    E. Autoimmune attack leading to central nervous system demyelination

24. A 70 y/o M with no past medical history presents to his primary care doctor after he was told by a friend that his walking was "abnormal" while golfing. On exam, his cranial nerves are all intact. There are no signs of weakness or sensory deficits in any of his extremities. No tremor or rigidity is seen. He is able to perform finger-to-nose, heel-to-shin, and rapid alternating movement testing. The patient's gait is slowed, and he finds himself needing to place his hand on the wall to steady himself. His performance on the MoCA, a cognitive screening test, shows no signs of mental decline. Labs are all within normal limits, and an MRI of the head shows no significant findings outside of some mild cerebral atrophy which is considered normal for his age. His primary care doctor is unable to arrive at a diagnosis and suggests monitoring his symptoms without treatment for now. Over the next 6 months, the patient's gait progressively worsens to the point where he cannot walk without a cane. He begins to have frequent urination including several episodes where he soils himself. He stops playing games with friends at his senior center as he finds himself confused and unable to remember the rules. He returns for his follow-up visit with his primary medical doctor with the results of a new MRI which shows only "enlargement of the ventricles consistent with cerebral

volume loss." He asks his doctor, "What's happening to me? Am I dying?" Which of the following is the most appropriate response at this time?

    A. "This is a treatable condition. Let me prescribe you a new medication."
    B. "This is a treatable condition. Let me refer you to a neurosurgeon."
    C. "The disease you have is related to loss of neurons in the substantia nigra. It is slowly progressive, with no known cure."
    D. "You likely have a form of dementia. Medications may be able to help, although they cannot reverse the deficits you have already suffered."
    E. "You may have suffered a stroke in your cerebellum. The important thing now is to focus on preventing future strokes."

25. A 71 y/o F is brought to the hospital following an unwitnessed fall at her nursing home. On arrival to the emergency department, she appears lethargic but is able to follow commands. A CT scan is obtained showing an intracerebral bleed with subfalcine herniation as seen below:

Which of the following is most likely to be seen secondary to arterial compression by herniation of the brain across the falx cerebri?

    A. Weakness of the legs and urinary incontinence
    B. Weakness of the arms and expressive aphasia
    C. Contralateral homonymous hemianopsia with macular sparing
    D. Unsteady wide-based gait
    E. Full body weakness without sensory disturbance
    F. Absent sensation in all extremities with full motor strength

26. A 42 y/o M is involved in a motor vehicle accident in which he was the driver. The right side of his head hit the steering wheel, resulting in a large bruise above his right ear. He did not lose consciousness but did report a headache and "dizzy" feelings for several minutes following the crash. In the emergency department,

his pupils are equal and reactive. His right eye shows full range of movement, but his left eye is divergent as seen below:

The affected cranial nerve exits from which part of the central nervous system?
- A. Brain
- B. Midbrain
- C. Pons
- D. Medulla oblongata
- E. Cervical spine
- F. None of the above

27. A 34 y/o M working as a physician assistant decides to become trained in administering injections of botulinum toxin. Which of the following patients is *not* likely to benefit from his training?
- A. A 68 y/o F retiree with muscle spasticity following a stroke
- B. A 19 y/o M college student with excessive underarm sweating
- C. A 38 y/o F cartoonist with recurrent cramping of her right hand
- D. A 55 y/o M lawyer with overactive bladder and occasional incontinence
- E. A 13 y/o F student with inward misalignment of the eyes
- F. All of these patients are likely to benefit from botulinum toxin injections

28. A 60 y/o F wakes up in the morning and notices "stiffness" on her right side. When she gets up to go to the bathroom, she feels that her gait is slow, and she finds that she needs to steady herself on the wall and nearby objects to avoid falling. Concerned, she calls an ambulance. On evaluation in the emergency department, she is fully alert and oriented. She reports no past medical history outside of hypertension. Vital signs are HR 90, BP 160/88, RR 16, and T 99.5°F. Her neurological exam is notable for limb rigidity on the right, cogwheeling in the right elbow, and a slow shuffling gait with forward leaning of her upper body. There are no motor or sensory deficits in the head or any of her extremities. Finger-to-nose testing and rapid alternating movements are both intact. Her MoCA cognitive screen is 30/30, although her writing is noticeably small. An MRI is ordered. An ischemic lesion is most likely to be seen in which of the following structures?

29. A 12 y/o M is brought to the emergency department after a witnessed generalized tonic-clonic seizure. His mother reports that he has been complaining of daily headaches and a tingling sensation in his hands for the past 2 weeks. On exam, there is limited abduction of the right eye and impaired hearing on the left. There is full motor strength throughout his body, with no sensory deficits. Finger-to-nose testing is impaired, though his gait is intact. Fundoscopic exam reveals bilateral swelling of the optic discs, prompting the doctor to order an MRI which is seen below:

He is diagnosed with two tumors arising from the vascular system within the cerebellum and brainstem. Which of the following laboratory abnormalities is most likely to be seen on testing?
 A. Elevated red blood cell count
 B. Decreased white blood cell count
 C. Elevated platelets
 D. Decreased sodium
 E. Elevated glucose
 F. None of the above

30. (Continued from previous question.) He is sent for genetic testing which reveals an autosomal dominant genetic disorder involving a mutation in a tumor suppressor gene on chromosome 3. Based on these findings, he is at risk for developing all of the following *except*:
 A. Proliferation of capillaries in the retinas
 B. Neoplastic growth of cells lining the renal tubules
 C. Episodes of excess release of epinephrine and norepinephrine from the adrenal medulla
 D. Benign tumor of striated muscle in the heart
 E. All of the above are likely to be seen

31. A 64 y/o F presents to her primary care doctor complaining of weakness. She first noticed this 4 months ago when she began having difficulty getting up from her chair at night to go to bed. However, her weakness has progressed to the point where she has extreme difficulty climbing stairs or reaching for high objects in her kitchen cupboards. On exam, there is decreased motor strength in her shoulders, hips, and knees bilaterally, with preservation of the muscles of the hands and feet. Her exam is also notable for skin atrophy with punctate red dots over her joints on the backs of her fingers as seen below:

Which of the following is most likely to be seen on further investigation?
 A. Fatiguing pattern on repetitive nerve stimulation testing
 B. Mononuclear white blood cells between muscle cells on biopsy
 C. Oligoclonal bands in cerebrospinal fluid on lumbar puncture
 D. Decreased creatine kinase concentration on laboratory testing
 E. Scarring of the internal capsule on magnetic resonance imaging
 F. None of the above

32. A 70 y/o M is brought to the emergency department by his wife after he was found looking confused while at the bank. His wife was waiting in the car while the patient went to withdraw money from the ATM. However, when the patient did not return for 15 minutes, his wife went to go see what was taking so long. When his wife found him, he was staring at the computer screen on the ATM and appeared frustrated and confused about what was happening. The patient denies other symptoms. He has a past medical history of hypertension, hyperlipidemia, and atrial fibrillation. His neurological exam is notable for right homonymous hemianopsia. There are no deficits in motor or sensory function. His gait is steady. Testing of his speech reveals intact expression, comprehension, and repetition. While undergoing brief cognitive testing, the patient is unable to follow instructions that are handed to him on a piece of paper. He is able to write a sentence when asked, although he is then unable to read that same sentence aloud. An MR angiogram is most likely to reveal ischemic damage in the territory of which artery?

33. A 71 y/o F with a history of osteoporosis falls during a game of tennis and is brought to an urgent care clinic. She undergoes a full examination which reveals no neurologic deficits. She is diagnosed with a compression fracture and discharged home. At a follow-up appointment 2 weeks later, she complains of severe pain in her neck and upper back. Examination continues to reveal no focal neurologic deficits. She is scheduled for vertebral augmentation surgery to

relieve her pain. After the operation, she awakens to find that she is unable to move the muscles in her lower limbs, though motor strength in her upper limbs is preserved. Further testing reveals a loss of pain and temperature sensation in the lower limbs, though both vibration and proprioception are intact. Her deep tendon reflexes are intact in the upper extremities, with hyporeflexia in the patellar joints and areflexia in the ankle joints bilaterally. Which of the following best explains the patient's post-operative findings?

    A.   Hypotensive ischemia in the basal ganglia
    B.   Surgical injury of the posterior spinal cord
    C.   Embolism in the anterior spinal artery
    D.   Unilateral hemorrhage in the lateral spinal cord
    E.   Compression of spinal nerve roots
    F.   None of the above

34. A 55 y/o M presents to the hospital with weakness of his right arm and leg. He first noticed this one month ago but did not seek care until today. He notes that the weakness has worsened over time to the point where he has difficulty raising his right arm and leg against gravity. A CT scan in the emergency department reveals the following:

A diagnosis of a brain metastasis is made. Which of the following is *least* likely to be the source organ in this case?

    A.   Breast
    B.   Colon
    C.   Kidney
    D.   Lung
    E.   Skin
    F.   Stomach

35. (Continued from previous question.) The patient is admitted to the hospital. When the doctor informs him of the poor prognosis for his diagnosis, he does not react with any emotion. Later, when his nurse asks him, "How are you holding up with the news?" he responds by saying, "What news?" He is later seen attempting to eat the remote control to his television. The next morning, the nurse comes in the room and finds him masturbating. She shrieks and runs out, but he continues his behavior as though nothing had happened. His current presentation is most consistent with damage to which of the following structures?
    A. Anterior cingulate cortex
    B. Thalamus
    C. Amygdala
    D. Paraventricular hypothalamic nucleus
    E. Subthalamic nucleus
    F. Mammillary bodies
    G. Hippocampus

36. A 25 y/o F is brought to the hospital after becoming non-responsive following a chiropractic treatment earlier in the day. She presented for her treatment in the morning and then went to work immediately after. Upon arriving to work, she appeared confused and dizzy. An ambulance was called after she stumbled and passed out on her way to the bathroom. In the emergency department, she is alert but appears puzzled. She remains unsteady in her gait. Cerebellar testing reveals an inability to perform finger-to-nose, heel-to-shin, and rapid alternating movement testing on the left side. MRI reveals an acute infarction in the territory of the left posterior inferior cerebellar artery. Which of the following findings is *not* likely to be seen in this patient?
    A. Deficits in pain and temperature sensation in the right limbs
    B. Deficits in pain and temperature sensation in the left face
    C. Absent gag reflex
    D. Difficulty swallowing
    E. Drooping eyelid on the left
    F. All of the above are likely to be seen

37. A 16 y/o F is brought to see her pediatrician for a recent change in her personality. Previously she was a bright and engaged student, but for the past several months she has appeared very tired and has been failing her schoolwork. She is a talented softball player, but over the past month she has been benched due to poor performance. On exam, there is a mild but noticeable tremor in both hands that increases in intensity during active motion. Her gait is slowed but steady. Her facial expression appears "frozen" to the doctor, and her speech is monotone. Examination of her eyes reveals decreased visual acuity and bilateral cataracts as seen in the following image:

Which of the following statements is most appropriate to make to her parents at this time?

A. "This is normal behavior for her age. Don't worry about it too much."
B. "This is a treatable condition. Let me give you a prescription and a referral for a dietician."
C. "This is a treatable condition. Let me give you a prescription and a referral for a psychiatrist."
D. "This is a treatable condition. Let me give you a prescription and a referral for a transplant surgeon."
E. "This is an untreatable condition, but we can do our best to manage it with physical and occupational therapy."
F. "This is an untreatable condition, and it will likely only get worse from now on."

38. A 40 y/o F comes to her nurse practitioner complaining of right arm weakness and pain for the past month. The pain is localized primarily in the right forearm on the radial side but radiates into her hand as well. There is also a "tingling" sensation in the same distribution. She reports difficulty with movements in her right hand, saying, "I can't open jars anymore." On exam, there is diffuse numbness in the right thumb, index finger, and middle finger. Grip strength is reduced in the right hand compared to the left, with flaccid paralysis of the involved muscles. Hyporeflexia of the biceps reflex is appreciated on the right. On further exam, there is hyperreflexia in the patellar and ankle jerk reflexes on the right, with spasticity in the calf and ankle flexors. Which of the following explanations best accounts for these findings?

A. Demyelinated plaques in the left primary motor cortex
B. Ischemic damage to the posterior limb of the internal capsule
C. Whiplash injury at the level of the pyramidal decussation
D. Compressive arthritis in the cervical spine
E. Infectious damage to the anterior horn of the spinal cord
F. None of the above

39. A 45 y/o M is brought to a publicly funded hospital after he was found wandering on a hot desert road. On initial evaluation in the emergency department, he appears confused and does not know his name, though he is able to follow simple commands. His physical exam is notable for enlarged cervical and inguinal lymph nodes as well as a healed ulcer on his penis. The venereal disease research laboratory (VDRL) and rapid plasma reagin (RPR) tests, which evaluate for the presence of syphilis, are both positive. Which of the following findings is *least* likely be found on exam?
    A. Pupil constriction in response to light
    B. Pupil constriction in response to a nearby object
    C. Impaired vibration and proprioceptive sensation
    D. Poor performance on cognitive testing
    E. None of the above are likely to be found

40. A 47 y/o F presents for follow-up with her neurologist. She was diagnosed with amyotrophic lateral sclerosis a year ago after she began having weakness in her legs. The diagnosis was frustrating to her, but it did not come as a surprise as she had two immediate family members who were also diagnosed with the disease. She is now reliant on a wheelchair for mobility. Since her last appointment one month ago, she has developed new swinging movements of her arms that occur constantly. She maintains that these movements are involuntary, saying through a weak voice, "Sometimes I feel like one of those flailing tube men they have outside of car dealerships." Cognitive testing is performed and is within normal limits. What is the most likely explanation for her new movements?
    A. Neuronal loss in the subthalamus
    B. Upper motor neuron degeneration in the anterior horns
    C. Epileptiform activity in the primary motor cortex
    D. Exposure to dopamine-blocking medications
    E. Physician misdiagnosis of amyotrophic lateral sclerosis
    F. Patient misrepresentation of voluntary movements
    G. None of the above

41. A 25 y/o M with no prior medical history presents to a primary care doctor with a 6 month history of a "ringing" sound in his ears and a sense that he cannot hear things as well as he used to. He works as a DJ and has played several parties each week for the past few years without ear protection. A Weber test reveals equal sound intensity in both ears, while a Rinne test reveals air conduction greater than bone conduction in both ears. His gait is unsteady. A Romberg test is positive. The remainder of his neurological exam is normal, with no motor or sensory deficits. An MRI is ordered which reveals the following:

Which of the following is the most likely cause of this patient's presentation?
- A. Physiological hearing loss due to aging
- B. Sensorineural hearing loss due to latent infection
- C. Conductive hearing loss due to ear canal occlusion
- D. Progressive hearing loss due to a genetic mutation
- E. Environmental hearing loss due to loud noise exposure
- F. None of the above

42. A 7 y/o F is brought to the hospital following a "fit." The patient was sleeping in her bed when her mother heard "choking noises" from outside the door. Upon entering the room, the mother saw the patient's face twisting and contorting repeatedly. The patient's entire body then became stiff for several seconds followed by a period of shaking lasting approximately 2 minutes. The episode had ended by the time the patient arrived in the emergency department. Her neurological exam shows no focal abnormalities. Vital signs are entirely within normal limits. A 24-hour EEG reveals centrotemporal spikes during sleep. The mother is worried about her daughter and wants to know what will happen next. Which of the following is the most appropriate statement to make?
- A. "This seizure occurred as the result of neuronal damage in the brain. As long as the damage is there, she will be at risk of further seizures."
- B. "This seizure is the result of a brain tumor. The prognosis is good, but we need to operate right away."
- C. "There's nothing to be worried about. This condition tends to get better even without treatment. This may be the last seizure she'll ever have."
- D. "Unfortunately this condition does not just involve seizures. She is at high risk of developing an intellectual disability."
- E. "This was not a seizure. I think your daughter may be trying to get your attention."
- F. None of the above

43. A 38 y/o F presents to the emergency department complaining of headache and chills for the past several months. Around 6 months ago she had "the flu" for several weeks which resolved on its own. She has a history of opioid dependence and has scars on her arm suggestive of intravenous drug use. Vital signs are HR 78, BP 140/92, RR 16, and T 101.3°F. Her exam is notable for drooping of her right eyelid as well as weakness of her left arm and leg. An MRI with contrast is ordered which reveals a ring-enhancing lesion as seen below:

Serological testing is positive for antibodies against *Toxoplasma gondii*. Which of the following most likely accounts for the patient's presentation?
   A. Recent change in immune system function
   B. Exposure to cat feces
   C. Handling of undercooked meat
   D. Undetected pregnancy
   E. Transmission through intravenous injection
   F. None of the above

44. A 3 m/o M is brought to the emergency department after he is seen having several tonic-clonic seizures involving the right half of his body. On exam, a deep purple patch of skin is noticeable on the left side of the patient's face as seen below:

Which of the following conditions is this patient at risk for later in life?
   A.   Recurrent seizures
   B.   Increased intraocular pressure leading to damage of the optic nerve
   C.   Delayed attainment of motor and speech milestones
   D.   Weakness of right-sided muscles
   E.   All of the above
   F.   None of the above

45.   A 77 y/o F comes to the emergency department complaining of repeated attacks of sharp pain in her head behind her right eye. She denies a history of any recent head trauma. On exam, there is noticeable drooping of her right upper eyelid, with a downward and outward displacement of her right eye. Her right pupil is dilated compared to the left. The rest of her neurological exam is normal, with intact motor strength, sensation, and coordination throughout. CT angiography is ordered which shows the following:

A focal outpouching in which of the following blood vessels is most likely responsible for her presenting signs and symptoms?
   A.   Anterior communicating artery
   B.   Left anterior cerebral artery
   C.   Right anterior cerebral artery
   D.   Left middle cerebral artery
   E.   Right middle cerebral artery
   F.   Left posterior cerebral artery
   G.   Right posterior cerebral artery
   H.   Left posterior communicating artery
   I.   Right posterior communicating artery
   J.   None of the above

46. (Continued from previous question.) While in the emergency department, the patient suddenly cries out. She reports the onset of a "10 out of 10" headache located "all over my head." She develops nausea and vomiting several minutes later. Her mental status is unchanged, as she is fully oriented and is able to obey verbal commands. A repeat CT scan is most likely to show which of the following images?

47. A 22 y/o F comes to the student health clinic reporting headaches of increasing intensity, duration, and frequency over the past 3 months to the point where they are near constant. She has also had difficulty sleeping over the past month and feels that she is not tired at night but then "super tired during the day." The nurse at the clinic is concerned and refers her for urgent neurological evaluation. At her appointment with the neurologist one week later, she reports a recent onset of blurry vision and severe nausea. She is not certain whether the blurry vision and nausea are related to her headaches. Neurological exam is notable for downward trending eyes with weakness of upward gaze. A CT scan reveals asymmetric expansion of the ventricles and a well-circumscribed lesion as seen in the following image:

Which of the following best explains her presentation?
- A. Autoimmune-mediated inflammation of the optic nerve
- B. Toxin-related dysfunction of the oculomotor nerves bilaterally
- C. Abducens nerve palsy due to compression at the level of the pons
- D. Trochlear nerve ischemia due to arterial narrowing
- E. Central herniation of the cerebrum through the tentorium cerebelli
- F. Dysfunction of the epithalamus due to unregulated cell growth
- G. Focal plaques of demyelination in the central nervous system
- H. Atrophy of the suprachiasmatic nucleus in the hypothalamus
- I. None of the above

48. A 57 y/o right-handed F with a history of diabetes and hyperlipidemia experiences a sudden sensation of coldness in the left half of her body "almost like someone turned me on my side and dipped me into the ocean." She notes that her left side is numb as well, as she is unable to feel her clothes. She is able to perceive some sensation with vigorous rubbing of her hand against her left arm and leg, but even then the sensation feels "distant." After several hours without a change in status, she calls 911. In the emergency department, she is alert and fully oriented. Her vital signs are HR 102, BP 176/98, RR 18, and T 98.9°F. She reports that the feeling of coldness now feels like "burning." Her neurological exam is notable for absent touch and pinprick sensation in the left face, arm, and leg. Her motor strength, reflexes, and gait are all normal. Which of the following mechanisms best accounts for this patient's presentation?

A. Occlusion of the right middle cerebral artery
B. Ischemic stroke in the right thalamus
C. Infarction of the spinothalamic tract at the level of the medulla
D. Damage to the right cervical spinal cord
E. Narrowing of the posterior spinal artery
F. None of the above

49. A 43 y/o F goes to the emergency department for evaluation of double vision. She reports that for the past 9 months she has had intermittent episodes of her vision losing focus which seem to happen most often when reading, saying, "It's like there's a ghost of each letter lurking just behind it." She previously had perfect vision. Attempts at using corrective eyeglasses to fix the problem have not been helpful. A head CT in the emergency department shows no focal abnormalities. After further workup is unrevealing, she is discharged with an outpatient referral to see a neurologist. By the time of her appointment 2 weeks later, her vision has improved. On interview, she notes that this is the general pattern, saying, "My visual stuff comes and goes like it has a mind of its own." However, she does report fatigue over the same time period that is persistent rather than episodic. Her fatigue increases throughout the day to the point where even sitting upright to work on her computer in the evening is a struggle. Which of the following is *least* likely to be helpful at finding the cause of this patient's symptoms?
    A. Laboratory testing of blood
    B. Lumbar puncture
    C. Computed tomography
    D. Magnetic resonance imaging
    E. Electromyography
    F. Full neurological exam

50. (Continued from previous question.) The patient is sent for various tests, with a plan to return in 2 weeks. However, 5 days later she is admitted to the hospital for difficulty breathing. Vital signs are HR 102, BP 138/84, RR 24, T 99.6°F, and decreased oxygen saturation at 85%. She is intubated and put on assisted ventilation. The treatment team reviews her chart. She was able to complete some but not all of the ordered tests prior to her respiratory decompensation. The MRI showed no focal abnormalities, while repetitive nerve stimulation showed a fatiguing pattern. Which of the following treatments should be administered at this time?
    A. A short course of oral corticosteroids
    B. An inhibitor of the enzyme responsible for metabolizing acetylcholine
    C. A drug with a molecular resemblance to myelin basic protein
    D. An antidote against the offending bacterial toxin
    E. A mixture of donated antibodies from healthy volunteers
    F. None of the above

51. A 10 y/o M is brought to the hospital after a generalized tonic-clonic seizure. He is awake but poorly responsive. Vital signs are HR 112, BP 104/60, RR 20, and T 102.0°F. Per his parents, he recently returned from a camping trip in the woods

near the Appalachian Mountains. Since his return, he has been complaining of chills and headache, with an episode of vomiting this morning. On exam, he is not able to follow instructions. However, he does cry out when his neck is flexed and when the doctor attempts to examine his pupils with a pen light. Sensing the patient's pain, the doctor does not examine his optic discs. He is placed on his side in preparation for a lumbar puncture. He again cries out when his legs are drawn up towards his chest prior to the needle being inserted into his back. A lumbar puncture is performed which shows an elevated opening pressure, a cloudy appearance, decreased glucose, elevated protein, and a high lymphocyte count. Which of the following causative organisms is most likely to be seen in his cerebrospinal fluid?

    A.   *Neisseria meningitidis*
    B.   *Streptococcus pneumoniae*
    C.   *Haemophilus influenza*
    D.   *Herpes simplex virus*
    E.   *Lyssaviruses*
    F.   *Coccidioides immitis*
    G.   *Blastomyces dermatitidis*
    H.   *Taenia solium*

52. (Continued from previous question.) Fifteen minutes after undergoing a lumbar puncture, the patient's mental status suddenly deteriorates, and he becomes comatose. Repeat vital signs are HR 44, BP 160/90, RR 14, and T 102.3°F. Exam reveals fixed dilated pupils bilaterally and decerebrate posturing in his extremities. Corneal and gag reflexes are absent. The patient is quickly intubated. Imaging reveals bilateral downward displacement of the cerebellar tonsils. Which of the following is most likely to have prevented this outcome?

    A.   Proper sterile technique prior to needle insertion
    B.   Earlier radiographic imaging of the head
    C.   Rapid administration of tissue plasminogen activator
    D.   Surgical removal of the blood clot under the dura mater
    E.   Strict blood pressure control
    F.   None of the above could have prevented this outcome

53. A 38 y/o F who is 39-weeks pregnant desires to give birth at home. During her delivery, she is seen losing large amounts of blood. Concerned, her husband drives her to the hospital where she receives several liters of transfused blood. She is discharged home the next day after her vital signs stabilize. One week later, while caring for her infant, she suddenly feels faint and collapses. She is brought back to the hospital and resuscitated. Magnetic resonance imaging of her brain reveals an abnormal signal in the pituitary gland suggestive of ischemic damage. Which of the following findings is *least* likely to be seen in this patient?

    A.   Lack of milk production
    B.   Low blood sugar
    C.   Lack of urination
    D.   Hypothyroidism
    E.   Lack of a feeling of bonding with her child

1. **The best answer is I.** This vignette describes a case of subacute sclerosing panencephalitis, a devastating condition that affects some people who were infected by measles earlier in life. The patient's earlier medical history is unknown, though earlier in life she lived in an area where the prevalence of measles was significantly higher than in the United States. Subacute sclerosing panencephalitis often presents as changes in cognition and personality, with subsequent development of focal neurologic signs including myoclonic jerks and atonic seizures. The diagnosis could likely be confirmed by testing for the presence of anti-measles antibodies. Meningitis and/or encephalitis are unlikely given the patient's normal vital signs and lack of cerebrospinal fluid findings (answers A—C). While the patient is presenting with myoclonic and atonic seizures, an epilepsy syndrome is unlikely as seizures alone cannot explain the presence of personality changes, cognitive decline, and lesions on neuroimaging (answers D—F). A brain tumor would likely be seen on MRI and is more likely to be found in an infratentorial location in a child (answer G). Acute disseminated encephalomyelitis tends to occur weeks after an infection, not years as in subacute sclerosing panencephalitis, and would present with central nervous system demyelination (answer H). *(Chapter 20—Central Nervous System Infections and Chapter 21—Central Demyelinating Diseases)*

2. **The best answer is B.** This vignette describes a case of a subdural hematoma which is consistent with the history of head trauma, subacute onset of symptoms, and progressive nature of symptoms including headache and nausea. A subdural hematoma often presents as a crescent-shaped strip of blood between the brain and the skull on CT. Epidural hematomas can present similarly but are often much faster in their progression and tend to involve an immediate loss of consciousness (answer C). Subarachnoid hemorrhages tend to involve a sudden "thunderclap" headache and neck irritation (answer D). Signs and symptoms of an intracerebral hemorrhage tend to come on much more quickly as well (answer A). The clinical history here is not suggestive of either a brain tumor (answer E) or hydrocephalus (answer F). *(Chapter 13—Intracranial Bleeds)*

3. **The best answer is N.** This vignette describes a case of right medial medullary syndrome which is most often related to a stroke in the anterior spinal artery. We can determine the location of this stroke in the medulla by looking at what cranial nerves are involved. The presence of tongue deviation implicates the 12th cranial nerve which exits the brainstem at the level of the medulla, while the presence of intact extraocular movements argues against either midbrain or pons involvement as the 3rd, 4th, and 6th cranial nerves exit from these two regions. To determine whether the lesion is medial or lateral, consider the presence of both motor weakness and loss of epicritic sensation. This shows that the corticospinal tract and medial lemniscus, both of which travel medially in the medulla, are involved. Notably, protopathic sensation is intact, arguing against a lateral medullary syndrome which tends to be involved in a stroke in the posterior inferior cerebellar artery (answers J and K). The presence of cranial nerve involvement localizes the lesion to the brainstem, arguing against a stroke in the anterior, middle, or posterior cerebral arteries (answers A—F). Strokes in the

region of the vertebral and basilar arteries more often present with cerebellar signs (answers G, L, and M). Anterior inferior cerebellar artery strokes are more associated with lateral pontine syndrome which would present with facial weakness and/or asymmetry (answers H and I). *(Chapter 12—Brainstem Strokes)*

4.   **The best answer is B.** Idiopathic intracranial hypertension often presents with headache and visual abnormalities in an obese but otherwise healthy young woman. Papilledema is classically seen on fundoscopic exam. The first step in management is often a lumbar puncture which not only helps to confirm the diagnosis but also provides immediate relief of symptoms by rapidly reducing the intracranial pressure. This case is unlikely to be a primary headache such as a tension headache, cluster headache, or migraine given the presence of papilledema and focal neurologic deficits, so treatments like nonsteroidal anti-inflammatory drugs, oxygen, or triptans will likely not be effective (answers C, E, and G). The MRI showed no evidence of a tumor, so neurosurgical resection is not necessary (answer D). The patient is afebrile and shows no other signs of bacterial infection (answer F). Steroids would help if this were a case of giant-cell arteritis, but the patient's presenting symptoms and demographics make this unlikely (answer A). *(Chapter 13—Idiopathic Intracranial Hypertension and Chapter 23—Secondary Headaches)*

5.   **The best answer is D.** This vignette describes a prototypical case of essential tremor as evidenced by the presence of an intention tremor that improves with alcohol with onset in a young person. Essential tremor is often a clinical diagnosis, and in the absence of any other neurologic signs, neuroimaging is not required to rule out other potential causes of tremor such as Parkinson's disease (answers B and C). Essential tremor does appear to run in families with an autosomal dominant pattern, but a specific gene has not been identified (answer A). Initial management of essential tremor often involves prescribing a beta-blocker. Botulinum toxin is generally used for focal dystonias and is rarely used for treatment of essential tremor unless if multiple other treatments have been ineffective (answer E). Electromyography is unlikely to reveal any abnormalities in the absence of motor or sensory deficits (answer F). *(Chapter 17—Tremor)*

6.   **The best answer is A.** An expansion of the trinucleotide repeat sequence GAA on chromosome 9 is consistent with a diagnosis of Friedreich's ataxia which often presents with ataxia, peripheral neuropathy, and hypertrophic cardiomyopathy. Huntington's disease is associated with the repeat sequence CAG (answer B), while myotonic dystrophy is associated with the repeat sequence CTG (answer D). Neither neurofibromatosis type 1 (answer C) nor amyotrophic lateral sclerosis (answer E) are associated with trinucleotide repeat sequences. *(Chapter 5—Friedreich's Ataxia, Chapter 14—Muscular Dystrophies, and Chapter 17—Huntington's Disease)*

7. **The best answer is E.** A vesicular rash in a dermatomal distribution is classic for shingles, an infectious disease caused by the varicella zoster virus. Knowing your dermatomal landmarks is essential for localizing the infection to a specific spinal nerve root. Two important landmarks on the torso are the nipples at T4 and the belly button at T10. As this patient's infection is between these two, T7 is the best answer. *(Chapter 8—Spinal Nerves and Chapter 20—Peripheral Nervous System Infections)*

8. **The best answer is M.** Postictal paralysis, also known as Todd's paralysis, is known to affect around 10% of all patients following a generalized tonic-clonic seizure. In a young patient with no significant medical history presenting with focal neurologic deficits immediately after a seizure, there is little reason to suspect a concurrent stroke, as no additional pathology is necessary to explain these findings (answers A—L). *(Chapter 18—Generalized Seizures)*

9. **The best answer is G.** This vignette describes a case of Anton's syndrome, a condition in which someone experiences blindness but does not admit to this and will even confabulate to fill in for the missing sensory input. Anton's syndrome is associated with injury to the primary visual cortex in the occipital lobe. The presence of an intact pupillary light reflex bilaterally rules out any injury to more anterior portions of the visual pathway, as does the loss of visual acuity in all quadrants rather than a hemianopsia or quadrantanopsia (answers A—F). The medial longitudinal fasciculus, paramedian pontine reticular formation, frontal eye fields, and Edinger-Westphal nuclei are all involved in control over extraocular muscles, not visual acuity (answers H—K). *(Chapter 9—Vision)*

10. **The best answer is D.** This patient is suffering from an expressive aphasia, also known as Broca's aphasia, as evidenced by her inability to speak or write despite intact language comprehension. Expressive aphasias are most often related to damage in Broca's area which lies in the frontal lobe of the dominant hemisphere in an area supplied by the middle cerebral artery. As the patient is right-handed, it is most likely that her dominant lobe is on the left, not the right (answer C). The anterior and posterior cerebral arteries do not supply Broca's area (answers A, B, E, and F). *(Chapter 3—Language Centers and Chapter 12—Cortical Strokes)*

11. **The best answer is C.** Dopamine is a neurotransmitter that is involved in a variety of processes in the brain. It is highly involved in modulating movements in the basal ganglia, so someone taking a dopamine-blocking medication is likely to experience increased muscular rigidity and difficulty initiating movements as a result of its effects here (answers A and B). Dopamine is involved in goal-directed behavior through its action in the ventral tegmental area (answer D). Finally, dopamine is involved in prolactin production, but its effect here is to *decrease* the release of prolactin, so someone taking a dopamine-blocking medication would instead see *increased* production of prolactin as a result. *(Chapter 4—The Basal Ganglia and The Pituitary Gland, Chapter 6—The Midbrain, and Chapter 17—Parkinson's Disease)*

12. **The best answer is E.** Craniopharyngiomas often present with bitemporal hemianopsia due to their typical location above the optic chiasm. Other features of this patient's presentation are related to dysfunction of the pituitary gland itself, as decreased levels of growth hormone and vasopressin can lead to growth restriction and diabetes insipidus, respectively. The MRI shows the characteristic location of the tumor in the brain. Craniopharyngiomas represent neoplastic growth of Rathke's pouch, which is the embryonic precursor of the anterior pituitary gland. Pilocytic astrocytomas (answer A), medulloblastomas (answer B), ependymomas (answer C), and hemangioblastomas (answer D) all have different presentations. *(Chapter 19—Pediatric Brain Tumors and Chapter 4—The Pituitary Gland)*

13. **The best answer is G.** Cases of severe obesity have been documented following treatment for a craniopharyngioma, as surgery and radiation can damage nearby structures such as the hypothalamus. In particular, damage to the ventromedial hypothalamic nucleus, which normally responds to the presence of leptin by inducing a state of satiety and reducing food intake, can lead to dramatic increases in food intake. In contrast, the lateral hypothalamic nucleus produces feelings of hunger, so damage here would likely *decrease* food intake, not increase it (answer F). The thalamus is involved in processing sensory information and does not play a large role in appetite (answers A—D). The anterior hypothalamic nucleus is involved in thermoregulation and autonomic regulation (answer E), the suprachiasmatic nucleus is involved in the circadian rhythm (answer H), the supraoptic nucleus produces vasopressin (answer I), and the paraventricular nucleus produces oxytocin (answer J). *(Chapter 4—The Hypothalamus)*

14. **The best answer is A.** Hyperglycemia related to diabetes mellitus is the most common cause of oculomotor nerve palsy in adults. This classically presents as an acute onset of diplopia and unilateral ptosis. Because the oculomotor nerve controls 4 of the 6 extraocular muscles, the actions of the unopposed lateral rectus and superior oblique muscles lead to a characteristic "down and out" deviation of the affected eye as seen in this image. While muscles controlling pupil size travel on the oculomotor nerve, these are typically spared in cases of oculomotor nerve palsy related to diabetes mellitus. There is no evidence in this vignette suggestive of either trochlear or abducens nerve involvement (answers B—G). *(Chapter 9—Vision)*

15. **The best answer is A.** We have not talked about acute cerebellar ataxia directly, so this question is more about ruling out the other causes than your knowledge of this condition in particular. Acute cerebellar ataxia is an inflammatory central nervous system disease involving a rapid onset of ataxia with subsequent recovery. It is most often seen in young children following a viral illness. Most patients recover within several weeks without long-lasting deficits, so the goal here is to rule out any other explanations that would require more intensive treatment. Acute cerebellar ataxia is frequently confused for acute disseminated encephalomyelitis, as both are post-infectious inflammatory diseases. However,

acute disseminated encephalomyelitis tends to present with focal neurologic findings as well as abnormalities on brain imaging (answer B). Subacute sclerosing panencephalitis is also post-infectious and may involve ataxia, but it is generally characterized by a much more dramatic presentation, including behavioral abnormalities, changes in mental status, seizures, loss of vision, and progressive cognitive decline (answer C). Encephalitis and meningitis are both less likely given the patient's normal vital signs, lack of focal neurologic findings, and stable mental status (answers D and E). Guillain–Barré syndrome is tempting as it is also post-infectious, but this would specifically involve findings in the peripheral nervous system such as motor weakness or sensory abnormalities (answer F). Multiple sclerosis is highly unlikely in a young child and should not be diagnosed based on a single episode given the requirement for dissemination in both space and time (answer G). Hydrocephalus would be observable on brain imaging (answer H). Finally, atonic seizures would present with loss of consciousness which was not present in this patient (answer I). *(Chapter 5— Cerebellar Dysfunction, Chapter 13—Hydrocephalus, Chapter 18—Generalized Seizures, Chapter 20—Multiple Sections, and Chapter 21—Autoimmune Diseases)*

16. **The best answer is C.** A neonate presenting with generalized muscle rigidity and an opisthotonus position is concerning for either tetanus or meningitis. In this case, the lack of fever or bulging fontanelles makes meningitis less likely (answers A and B). The tetanus toxin blocks the release of inhibitory neurotransmitters in the neuromuscular junction, leading to widespread excitation of muscles. It is normally preventable through vaccination of the mother, though in this case the mother's objections to medical care have made it so that she was not immunized. Botulism (answer D) and spinal muscular atrophy (answer E) would both be expected to produce generalized muscle *weakness*, not rigidity. *(Chapter 15— Neuromuscular Junction Diseases, Chapter 20—Meningitis, and Chapter 16—Motor Neuron Diseases)*

17. **The best answer is E.** Transtentorial herniation can be caused by a variety of conditions that increase intracranial pressure. In this case, a spontaneous rupture of an artery led to a subdural hematoma with subsequent herniation. Transtentorial herniation most often compresses the oculomotor nerve, leading to fixed *dilated* pupils (answer A) and a "down and out" positioning of the ipsilateral eye. In this case, the subdural hematoma was on the left, so the oculomotor nerve palsy would be on the left, not the right (answer B). Palsies of either the trochlear nerve (answer C) or abducens nerve (answer D) are not commonly seen in a transtentorial herniation. In contrast, Duret hemorrhages are often seen and reflect the traumatic displacement of the midbrain across the tentorium. *(Chapter 13—Brain Herniation)*

18. **The best answer is E.** Primary lateral sclerosis is a motor neuron disease that affects upper motor neurons exclusively, leaving lower motor neurons intact. For this reason, lower motor neuron signs such as absent reflexes (answer A) and muscle atrophy (answer B) are absent, replaced by an exaggerated gag reflex and tongue spasticity, respectively. Dysphagia is common due to involvement of the

brainstem. In contrast to amyotrophic lateral sclerosis, primary lateral sclerosis has a much better prognosis, and most people die from unrelated causes (answer D). Urinary incontinence is uncommon, though a state of *emotional* incontinence known as pseudobulbar affect is seen in this case (answer C). *(Chapter 16—Motor Neuron Diseases)*

19. **The best answer is B.** Vertigo has a wide variety of possible causes that are often categorized into central causes (those involving a lesion in the cerebellum or brainstem) and peripheral causes (those involving the vestibular system of the inner ear). In this case, the patient presented with an acute onset of vertigo along with several cerebellar signs including dysdiadochokinesia, nystagmus, and ataxia. These all make a central cause of vertigo more likely than a peripheral cause, as patients with peripheral vertigo tend to perform well on finger-to-nose, heel-to-shin, rapid-alternating movements, and other tests of cerebellar function (answer E). Ménière's disease is even more unlikely given the absence of hearing loss or ringing in the ears (answer D). An acute blockage of the ventricular system leading to obstructive hydrocephalus could cause symptoms of cerebellar dysfunction, although most cases of hydrocephalus tend to have a slower onset and would present with changes in mental status and other signs of increased intracranial pressure (answer C). There are no cortical signs such as motor deficits, sensory loss, or impaired cognition to suggest a stroke in the anterior cerebral circulation (answer A). *(Chapter 5—Cerebellar Dysfunction, Chapter 9—Balance, and Chapter 12—Cerebellar Strokes)*

20. **The best answer is C.** This patient has developed cauda equina syndrome as evidenced by the presence of low back pain, saddle anesthesia, weakness and numbness in the legs, and urinary incontinence. The cauda equina represents the bundle of spinal nerves that continues even after the spinal cord ends in the lumbar region. Recall that, although nerves from the cauda equina *exit* in the lumbar, sacral, and coccygeal regions, the cauda equina itself is located in lumbar spine (answers D and E). Cervical nerves innervate the neck and arms which are not involved in this case (answer A), while thoracic nerves innervate the arms and chest (answer B). *(Chapter 7—Spinal Cord Pathology and Chapter 8—Spinal Nerves)*

21. **The best answer is E.** This case describes a typical presentation of internuclear ophthalmoplegia as evidenced by impaired adduction of one eye with intact abduction and nystagmus of the other eye. Internuclear ophthalmoplegia is related to dysfunction of the medial longitudinal fasciculus in the brainstem. The medial longitudinal fasciculus coordinates between the oculomotor nerve, trochlear nerve, abducens nerve, and the paramedian pontine reticular formation, though an injury in any one of these individual components will generally not produce internuclear ophthalmoplegia (answers B, C, D, and F). The optic nerve is intact as evidenced by full visual acuity and pupillary light reflexes (answer A). Damage to the frontal eye fields produces conjugate gaze towards the side of the lesion but would not result in diplopia (answer G). *(Chapter 9—Vision)*

22. **The best answer is E.** Several neuroanatomical structures are involved in tasting and reacting to food. The hypoglossal nerve is used to move the food inside the mouth (answer D), while the nucleus ambiguus contains the cell bodies of neurons involved in swallowing (answer G). The facial and glossopharyngeal nerves (answers A and B) carry taste sensations from the anterior and posterior aspects of the tongue, respectively, to the nucleus solitarius (answer F). When it senses food that it wants to reject, the nucleus solitarius sends signals to the area postrema to induce nausea and vomiting (answer H). In addition, the vagus nerve activates the pharyngeal muscles responsible for gagging (answer C). Of the listed options, only the Edinger-Westphal nuclei are not directly involved in these processes. Instead, the Edinger-Westphal nuclei play a role in the pupillary light reflex. *(Chapter 6—The Medulla Oblongata, Chapter 8—Cranial Nerves, and Chapter 9—Taste)*

23. **The best answer is B.** This patient is demonstrating Cushing's triad of irregular breathing, a slow heart rate, and elevated blood pressure. Cushing's triad is classically associated with a sudden increase in intracranial pressure as would occur due to a ruptured artery. Viral encephalitis could lead to similar alterations in consciousness but would likely present with fever as well (answer C). Neither an ischemic stroke nor a seizure would produce the sudden changes in vital signs seen here (answers A and D). Finally, autoimmune demyelination tends to move at a much slower pace, causing changes in presentation over weeks or months rather than hours (answer E). *(Chapter 13—Signs and Symptoms of Intracranial Hypertension)*

24. **The best answer is B.** This vignette describes a case of normal pressure hydrocephalus, a disease characterized by a triad of gait instability, incontinence, and cognitive deficits. Of these, gait instability is the most common sign and is typically the first presentation of the illness, with incontinence and cognitive deficits occurring later. Normal pressure hydrocephalus is a treatable condition, with surgical placement of a shunt resulting in rapid improvements for the majority of patients. Medication does not play a large role in management of this disease (answer A). Normal pressure hydrocephalus is often misdiagnosed. It can be diagnosed as dementia, especially as the enlargement of the ventricular spaces seen on imaging can resemble the hydrocephalus *ex vacuo* caused by cerebral atrophy; however, in dementia gait disturbance is typically a late finding, not the initial presenting complaint (answer D). The presence of gait disturbance puts Parkinson's disease on the differential, although a lack of tremor or rigidity is not characteristic (answer C). Finally, a cerebellar stroke may impact gait but would not be expected to lead to cognitive deficits or urinary incontinence (answer E). *(Chapter 12—Cerebellar Strokes, Chapter 13—Hydrocephalus, and Chapter 17—Parkinson's Disease)*

25. **The best answer is A.** Subfalcine herniation occurs when the brain is displaced under the anterior edge of the falx cerebri due to increased intracranial pressure. For this reason, frontal structures in the brain including the anterior cerebral artery are at risk of compressive injury in a subfalcine herniation. Compression of

the anterior cerebral artery leads to weakness of the lower limbs as well as urinary incontinence. Compression of the middle cerebral artery would lead to arm weakness and expressive aphasia (answer B), while compression of the posterior cerebral artery would lead to contralateral homonymous hemianopsia with macular sparing (answer C). Ataxia is more likely to be related to compression of the arteries supplying the cerebellum (answer D). Pure motor or pure sensory strokes are more often seen in lacunar than cortical strokes (answers E and F). *(Chapter 13—Brain Herniation and Chapter 12—Cortical Strokes)*

26. **The best answer is B.** This image shows an upward and inward drift of the left eye which is consistent with a trochlear nerve palsy. The trochlear nerve exits from the midbrain along with the oculomotor nerve, while the abducens nerve exits from the pons (answer C). The cranial nerves exit in groups of four, with the first four exiting from the brain (answer A) and midbrain, the middle four exiting from the pons, and the final four exiting from the medulla oblongata (answer D). Cranial nerves by definition do not exit from the spinal cord (answer E). *(Chapter 8—Vision and Chapter 6—The Midbrain)*

27. **The best answer is F.** Botulinum toxin works by preventing the release of acetylcholine into synapses, and it is effective at reducing activation of acetylcholine receptors wherever they are found. Injection of botulinum toxin can be an effective treatment for a variety of disorders characterized by overactive muscles, including muscle spasticity (answer A) and focal dystonia (answer C). It can be an effective treatment for some cases of strabismus, or misalignment of the eyes, by relaxing specific extraocular muscles to allow for the gaze to become aligned again (answer E). Botulinum toxin can also be effective for non-skeletal muscles such as those in the bladder, as acetylcholine is the neurotransmitter used here (answer D). Finally, while sweating is a function of the sympathetic nervous system, it uses acetylcholine as its neurotransmitter, so botulinum toxin injections can be effective at addressing this as well (answer B). *(Chapter 2—The Autonomic Nervous System and Chapter 15—Neuromuscular Junction Diseases)*

28. **The best answer is E.** This patient is presenting with clear signs of Parkinsonism including rigidity, cogwheeling, and a forward-flexed shuffling gait. While most cases of idiopathic Parkinson's disease have a slow insidious onset, there are reports of vascular Parkinsonism related to ischemic injury that can be much more sudden in their onset. Imaging in vascular Parkinsonism often shows damage to the substantia nigra which is located in the midbrain. The other labeled structures are the frontal cortex (answer A), corpus callosum (answer B), thalamus (answer C), hypothalamus (answer D), pons (answer F), medulla (answer G), and cerebellum (answer H). *(Chapter 17—Parkinson's Disease and Chapter 6—The Midbrain)*

29. **The best answer is A.** This patient has tumors in the brainstem and cerebellum that have been diagnosed as hemangioblastomas, which are tumors not of the nervous tissue itself but of the vasculature supplying it. Hemangioblastomas have an association with polycythemia, or increased red blood cell count, due to excess production of the hormone erythropoietin. Leukopenia (answer B), thrombocythemia (answer C), hyponatremia (answer D), and hyperglycemia (answer E) do not have known associations with hemangioblastomas. *(Chapter 19—Pediatric Brain Tumors)*

30. **The best answer is D.** This patient has von Hippel–Lindau disease, a genetic disorder with manifestations in various organs throughout the body, including hemangioblastomas, angiomatosis (answer A), renal cell carcinomas (answer B), and pheochromocytomas (answer C). In contrast, there is no association with cardiac rhabdomyomas which are instead seen more commonly in tuberous sclerosis. *(Chapter 24—Neurocutaneous Disorders)*

31. **The best answer is B.** The presence of proximal muscle weakness combined with skin rashes is highly suggestive of dermatomyositis. Diagnosing dermatomyositis often involves laboratory testing, electromyography, and a muscle biopsy, the latter of which will show white blood cells invading the space *between* muscle fibers, which is in contrast to the cells being *within* muscle fibers as occurs in polymyositis. Creatine kinase concentrations are generally *increased*, not decreased (answer D). A fatiguing pattern on repetitive nerve stimulation is more suggestive of myasthenia gravis (answer A), while oligoclonal bands suggest a diagnosis of multiple sclerosis (answer C). Damage to the internal capsule can lead to motor weakness, though this would be unlikely to show a pattern of exclusively proximal weakness as seen in this case (answer E). *(Chapter 14—Inflammatory Myopathies)*

32. **The best answer is F.** A homonymous hemianopsia in combination with alexia without agraphia is highly suggestive of a stroke in the left posterior cerebral artery. Keep in mind that head imaging is displayed as though you are looking at the patient's brain from their feet, so the *left* posterior cerebral artery is found on the *right* side of the page, not the left (answer E). A stroke in the anterior cerebral arteries (answers A and B) would result in motor weakness in the lower extremities while a stroke in the middle cerebral arteries would result in motor weakness in the upper extremities (answers C and D). *(Chapter 10—Cerebral Blood Supply and Chapter 12—Cortical Strokes)*

33. **The best answer is C.** An anterior spinal artery syndrome is a rare complication of spinal surgery. Paraplegia in the lower extremities with loss of protopathic sensation should immediately bring to mind the anterior spinal cord, as the structures containing these neurons both travel in the front parts of the cord. In contrast, epicritic sensation travels posteriorly in the spinal cord and would not be affected (answer B). Unilateral damage to the lateral spinal cord would produce Brown-Séquard syndrome (answer D). A radiculopathy would be unilateral and would likely only produce deficits in the distribution of a single

nerve rather than in both legs (answer E). Finally, damage to the basal ganglia would produce a movement disorder rather than sudden onset of weakness (answer A). *(Chapter 7—Spinal Cord Pathology and Chapter 12—Spinal Cord Strokes)*

34. **The best answer is F.** The most common sources of brain metastases include the lungs, breasts, skin, kidneys, and colon. In contrast, brain metastases from a primary malignancy of the stomach are rarely seen clinically, for unclear reasons. *(Chapter 19—Brain Metastases)*

35. **The best answer is C.** This vignette describes a case of Klüver–Bucy syndrome which is characterized by docility, amnesia, hypersexuality, and hyperorality. Docility and amnesia are the key features localizing this disorder to the amygdala, as the amygdala is responsible both for activating the fear response (such as the fear most people would feel about engaging in sexual behavior in a public place) and for assigning emotional meaning to experiences (such as learning about a devastating diagnosis). Damage to the other areas involved in memory including the hippocampus and mammillary bodies would also produce these memory failures but would not likely lead to these types of behavior (answers F and G). In contrast, damage to the anterior cingulate cortex may lead to socially unacceptable behavior but would not produce the memory failures (answer A). The thalamus (answer B) and subthalamic nucleus (answer E) are involved in sensory and motor processes, respectively, and would not produce the syndrome described here when damaged. The paraventricular nucleus of the hypothalamus produces oxytocin which tends to promote prosocial, rather than antisocial, behavior (answer D). *(Chapter 3—The Limbic System)*

36. **The best answer is F.** Lateral medullary syndrome, also known as Wallenberg's syndrome, can occur following a stroke in the posterior inferior cerebellar artery or vertebral artery. It affects structures that are found to the side of the medulla, resulting in contralateral loss of protopathic sensation from involvement of the spinothalamic tract (answer A), an absent gag reflex from involvement of the glossopharyngeal and vagus nerves (answer C), and dysphagia from involvement of the nucleus ambiguus (answer D). Protopathic sensation from the face is carried on the trigeminal nerve which exits out of the pons; however, the nucleus of the trigeminal nerve lies within the medulla, so a stroke here can produce ipsilateral loss of protopathic sensation as well (answer B). Loss of facial muscles is more typically associated with a stroke in the *anterior* inferior cerebellar artery and lateral pontine syndrome; however, recall that nerve fibers belonging to the sympathetic nervous system travel through the lateral medulla as well, so it is possible to see ptosis in lateral medullary syndrome (answer E), although other muscles of facial expression should be intact. *(Chapter 12—Brainstem Strokes)*

37. **The best answer is B.** This patient is showing signs of a movement disorder including a slowed gait, tremor, and a mask-like face. Any young person presenting with a movement disorder should have Wilson's disease high on the differential, as in general movement disorders are primarily found in older

individuals. Kayser-Fleischer rings, as seen in the image, are caused by the accumulation of copper in the cornea and are considered to be diagnostic for Wilson's disease. Wilson's disease is associated with a poor prognosis if untreated (answer A), but fortunately there are effective treatments available (answers E and F). Treatment involves use of penicillamine, a drug that helps to clear excess copper from the system. Dietary avoidance of high copper foods can also be effective. While Wilson's disease can present with psychiatric manifestations, psychiatric medications are not the first line of treatment (answer C). In rare cases, liver transplantation may be considered; however, this is reserved for patients with fulminant liver failure who have not responded to conventional treatments (answer D). *(Chapter 17—Wilson's Disease)*

38. **The best answer is D.** The presence of both upper motor neuron and lower motor neuron findings at the same time is highly suggestive of a lesion at the level of the spine, as the spine is the only area in which both upper and lower motor neuron signs can be produced by the same lesion. In this case, arthritis of the spine is compressing not only the C5 spinal nerve root but also the spinal cord itself. The radiculopathy causes sensory loss and lower motor neuron signs in the C5 distribution, while the spinal cord compression leads to upper motor neuron signs in the legs. Damage to motor neurons in the cerebral cortex (answer A), internal capsule (answer B), medulla (answer C), or anterior horn (answer E) would all produce exclusively upper *or* lower motor neuron signs. *(Chapter 22— Peripheral Neuropathy, Chapter 15—Motor Neuron Disease, and Chapter 7—Spinal Cord Anatomy)*

39. **The best answer is A.** If left untreated, syphilis can wreak havoc on the nervous system, with several conditions resulting from with this. General paresis refers to the psychiatric manifestations of neurosyphilis which often include cognitive deficits (answer D). Tabes dorsalis refers to demyelination of the dorsal columns of the spinal cord leading to impaired vibration and proprioceptive sensation (answer C). Argyll Robertson pupils will constrict when the patient focuses on a nearby object (answer B) but notably will not constrict when exposed to a bright light. *(Chapter 7—Spinal Cord Pathology, Chapter 9—Vision, and Chapter 20— Central Nervous System Infections)*

40. **The best answer is A.** Involuntary flailing movements of the limbs are known as hemiballismus. Hemiballismus is most often caused by a stroke in the area of the subthalamic nucleus, but any disease that causes neuronal damage in this area can lead to hemiballismus, including amyotrophic lateral sclerosis. While upper motor neuron damage can lead to muscle spasticity, it would not lead to the dramatic ballistic movements described here (answer B). The constant nature of these movements argues against a seizure (answer C). Dopamine-blocking medications can cause extrapyramidal symptoms, but hemiballismus is not one of them (answer D). While hemiballismus is a rare outcome of amyotrophic lateral sclerosis, there is no reason to suspect that the diagnosis is incorrect (answer E) or that the patient is feigning illness (answer F). *(Chapter 4—The Basal Ganglia, Chapter 17—Huntington's Disease, and Chapter 16—Motor Neuron Diseases)*

41. **The best answer is D.** Hearing loss has a wide variety of causes. Some degree of hearing loss with age is expected, especially if the patient has been chronically exposed to loud noises. However, the presence of ataxia and an unsteady gait are strongly suggestive of a more pathological process (answers A and E). A sensorineural or conductive hearing loss would not account for these findings (answers B and C). In this case, the largest clue comes from the MRI which reveals bilateral schwannomas in the nerve sheath of the vestibulocochlear nerve. Because they are symmetrical, an observer may assume they are normal, but don't make this mistake—those two tumors should not be there. Bilateral vestibular schwannomas are diagnostic for neurofibromatosis type II, a genetic disorder that can either be inherited in an autosomal dominant fashion or develop through *de novo* mutations. *(Chapter 24—Neurocutaneous Disorders, Chapter 19—Adult-Onset Brain Tumors, and Chapter 9—Hearing)*

42. **The best answer is C.** This vignette describes a case of benign Rolandic epilepsy as evidenced by the focal onset of the seizure during sleep and the characteristic centrotemporal spikes on EEG. Benign Rolandic epilepsy has a good prognosis, and many patients with this condition will not need treatment. There is no association between structural damage in the brain and this condition like there is with temporal lobe epilepsy and mesial temporal sclerosis (answer A). There is no evidence of a brain tumor at this time, with the presence of centrotemporal spikes and absence of neurologic deficits making this a remote possibility (answer B). Benign Rolandic epilepsy does not involve intellectual disability as other forms of epilepsy such as Lennox–Gastaut syndrome do (answer D). Finally, positive findings on EEG argue strongly against psychogenic non-epileptic seizures in this patient (answer E). *(Chapter 18—Epilepsy Syndromes)*

43. **The best answer is A.** It is estimated that up to half of the world's population is infected by *Toxoplasma gondii*. However, toxoplasmosis generally produces symptoms only in patients with compromised immune systems. In this case, the patient's intravenous drug use provides a mechanism for contracting HIV. While exposure to cat feces (answer B) and handling of undercooked meat (answer C) are common means of transmission of toxoplasmosis, they would not lead to a symptomatic state in and of themselves without the change in immune status. While pregnancy is a concern for someone with toxoplasmosis, this is due to the effect it would have on the infant, as pregnancy itself does not predispose the mother to developing active toxoplasmosis (answer D). Transmission of toxoplasmosis is generally oral or congenital rather than intravenous (answer E). *(Chapter 20—Central Nervous System Infections)*

44. **The best answer is E.** The combination of infantile seizures with a port-wine stain is characteristic of Sturge–Weber syndrome, a neurocutaneous disorder that affects multiple organ systems. Patients with Sturge–Weber syndrome are at risk for recurrent seizures (answer A), glaucoma (answer B), intellectual disability (answer C), and unilateral hemiparesis (answer D), the latter of which notably tends to occur on the opposite side of the body as the port-wine stain. *(Chapter 24—Neurocutaneous Disorders)*

45. **The best answer is I.** The oculomotor nerve and the posterior communicating artery are right next to each other, so an aneurysm of this artery can lead to compressive dysfunction in that nerve. In fact, posterior communicating artery aneurysms are so common that an acute painful oculomotor nerve palsy with pupil dilation is often assumed to be a posterior communicating artery aneurysm unless proven otherwise. The oculomotor nerve palsy is ipsilateral to the side of the aneurysm, so the aneurysm is on the right, not the left (answer H). The anterior communicating artery is a common site for aneurysms, but it is not located near the oculomotor nerve (answer A). The anterior, middle, and posterior cerebral arteries are not located near the oculomotor nerve, nor do they supply oxygen to the nerve (answers B—G). *(Chapter 13—Intracranial Bleeds and Chapter 9—Vision)*

46. **The best answer is D.** When aneurysms become large enough to compress nearby structures and produce neurologic symptoms, it suggests a high degree of instability in the arterial wall. Unstable aneurysms are prone to rupturing and causing a subarachnoid hemorrhage which often presents as the sudden "thunderclap" onset of a severe headache (answer A). While an intracerebral hemorrhage can present similarly, it is less likely given the presence of a known unstable aneurysm and a lack of recent head trauma. A lack of recent head trauma also argues against either a subdural hematoma (answer B) or an epidural hematoma (answer C). A brain tumor (answer E) or hydrocephalus (answer F) both tend to come on more slowly compared to the acute onset described here. *(Chapter 13—Intracranial Bleeds)*

47. **The best answer is F.** This vignette describes a tumor of the pineal gland in the epithalamus leading to an obstructive hydrocephalus, melatonin insufficiency, and Parinaud's syndrome (or a weakness of upward gaze related to compression of the vertical gaze center in the medial longitudinal fasciculus). Upward gaze is mediated by the superior rectus muscle which is controlled by the oculomotor nerve; however, the oculomotor nerve also controls several other extraocular muscles, so dysfunction of the nerve itself would not lead to an isolated upward gaze palsy (answer B). The trochlear and abducens nerves do not control upward gaze (answers C and D). Central herniation can produce "sunset eyes" as well, but this would likely present with a sudden onset of coma due to compression of vital structures in the brainstem (answer E). The suprachiasmatic nucleus does regulate sleep, but a lesion here would not account for Parinaud's syndrome and would likely present with other signs of hypothalamic dysfunction as well (answer H). Optic neuritis would result in impaired vision rather than weakness in

extraocular movements (answer A). Finally, multiple sclerosis is an unlikely cause of hydrocephalus (answer G). *(Chapter 4—The Epithalamus, Chapter 9—Vision, and Chapter 10—Hydrocephalus)*

48. **The best answer is B.** This case describes a pure sensory stroke which is most often related to a lacunar infarct in the thalamus on the side contralateral to the observed deficits. A pure sensory stroke can present not only with numbness but also paresthesias and pain as well. A stroke in the territory of the middle cerebral artery would tend to produce motor deficits in addition to sensory loss (answer A). A lesion in the spinothalamic tract at the level of the medulla would not produce the facial numbness seen in this case (answer C). Damage to the right spinal cord would produce Brown-Séquard syndrome and would not involve the face (answer D). Finally, occlusion of the posterior spinal artery would primarily affect the dorsal columns leading to deficits in vibration and proprioceptive sensation, not pain and temperature as seen here (answer E). *(Chapter 12—Lacunar Strokes)*

49. **The best answer is C.** For a patient presenting with neurologic symptoms in a relapsing-remitting pattern, consideration should be given to a diagnosis of multiple sclerosis. However, a patient with diplopia and fatigue that worsens in the evening is also suggestive of myasthenia gravis. This patient's history is not immediately diagnostic of one or the other, so steps should be taken to evaluate further. A diagnosis of multiple sclerosis would be supported by the presence of oligoclonal bands on lumbar puncture (answer B) or the characteristic plaques on MRI (answer D), while a diagnosis of myasthenia gravis would be supported by identifying antibodies against the acetylcholine receptor in the blood (answer A) or abnormal action potential patterns on electromyography (answer E). Only a CT scan would not have diagnostic value in either multiple sclerosis or myasthenia gravis, as it is primarily used for identifying infarctions, bleeds, tumors, and bone abnormalities. A neurological exam is always of diagnostic value in working up a neurologic complaint (answer F). *(Chapter 21—Central Demyelinating Diseases and Chapter 15—Neuromuscular Junction Diseases)*

50. **The best answer is E.** This patient's MRI and fatiguing pattern on repetitive nerve stimulation are both suggestive of myasthenia gravis. She has now developed weakness of her respiratory muscles known as a myasthenic crisis, which is a medical emergency requiring immediate treatment. While acetylcholinesterase inhibitors are effective treatments for myasthenia gravis, they do not work quickly enough in a potentially life-threatening situation (answer B). Instead, either plasmapheresis or intravenous immunoglobulins (IVIGs) should be administered to rapidly clear the offending antibodies from the system. Steroids (answer A) and glatiramer acetate (answer C) are both treatments used for multiple sclerosis, not myasthenia gravis. Myasthenia gravis is an autoimmune disease and is not related to toxins as with botulism or tetanus (answer D). *(Chapter 15—Neuromuscular Junction Diseases)*

51. **The best answer is G.** Fever, headache, photophobia, a positive Brudzinski's sign, and a positive Kernig's sign are all highly suggestive of meningitis. The attributes of the cerebrospinal fluid on lumbar puncture can help to narrow down the possible infectious agents that could be causing his presentation. The presence of significant abnormalities in opening pressure, the elevated protein concentration, and the low glucose help to rule out an aseptic or viral meningitis (answer D). Fungal and bacterial meningitis both have these findings, so the best way of differentiating between them is to look at the cell predominance. Bacterial meningitis presents with a neutrophilic predominance while fungal meningitis presents with a lymphocytic predominance. In this case, the high number of lymphocytes argues against a bacterial cause of meningitis (answers A—C). The two fungi listed have different geographic distributions, with *Coccidioides* being found in the American southwest and *Blastomyces* being seen more in the eastern United States. In this case, the patient went camping in the woods in the Appalachian mountains, making *Blastomyces* more likely that *Coccidioides* (answer F). *Lyssaviruses* (answer E) are responsible for rabies while *Taenia solium* (answer H) is the parasite responsible for neurocysticercosis; neither are common causes of meningitis. *(Chapter 20—Meningitis)*

52. **The best answer is B.** Cerebral herniation following a lumbar puncture is a rare event, but given the morbidity and mortality associated with it, it is important to keep in mind. As a rule, it is not necessary to order a CT scan prior to performing a lumbar puncture. However, in certain cases, such as a young patient presenting with seizures, it may have helped to identify a source of increased intracranial pressure that would make herniation more likely if a lumbar puncture is performed. In this case, it is possible that there may have been other signs of increased intracranial pressure, although because the fundoscopic exam was skipped it is difficult to say. As this was not a stroke, administration of either tissue plasminogen activator or antihypertensives is unlikely to have been of benefit (answers C and E). The patient had signs of meningeal infection prior to the lumbar puncture, so the quality of sterile technique is unlikely to account for this outcome (answer A). While a subdural hematoma can lead to brain herniation in some cases, the lack of focal head trauma and a clear alternative explanation in meningitis makes this a much less likely source (answer D). *(Chapter 11—Lumbar Puncture and Chapter 13—Brain Herniation)*

53. **The best answer is C.** This vignette describes a case of postpartum pituitary gland necrosis, also known as Sheehan's syndrome. The pituitary gland is sensitive to ischemic damage, so in cases of severe blood loss the pituitary gland can stop functioning, leading to deficits in many of its endocrine functions. These include milk production from prolactin (answer A), release of glucose in the bloodstream from adrenocorticotropic hormone (answer B), proper thyroid function from thyroid-stimulating hormone (answer D), and a feeling of bonding with the child from oxytocin (answer E). Damage to the posterior pituitary can result in lack of vasopressin release, which would make the frequency of urination likely to *increase*, not decrease. *(Chapter 4—The Pituitary Gland)*

ATTRIBUTIONS

The fonts **Oswald** and Source Sans Pro were used for the cover and inside text, respectively. They were accessed from Google Fonts under an open-source license.

With the following exceptions, all images displayed in this book are in the public domain and/or are not associated with any known copyright restrictions. Most images have been modified for formatting. Use of this content does not suggest that the content's original creator(s) endorse this book or its author in any way.

COVER AND BACK
- Cover and back design by Stephen Sauer (SingleFinDesign.com).
- Images and icons designed by Iconfinder.

CHAPTER 2 | THE NERVOUS SYSTEM
- "HE stain of brain autopsy specimen (formalin-fixated, paraffin embedded) showing oligodendrocytes with fried-egg appearance." Credit: Jensflorian (Creative Commons Attribution-Share Alike 4.0 International license).
- "Typing consciousness." Credit: Akiyao and LucasVB; modified by Cangjie6 (Creative Commons Attribution-Share Alike 3.0 Unported license).
- "Shows termination of nerve in muscle." Credit: Wellcome Images (Creative Commons Attribution 4.0 International license).
- "Comment utiliser cette latrines." Credit: SuSanA Secretariat (Creative Commons Attribution 2.0 Generic license).
- "Divisions of the nervous system." Credit: Fuzzform at English Wikipedia (Creative Commons Attribution-Share Alike 3.0 Unported license).

CHAPTER 3 | THE CEREBRAL CORTEX
- "Motor homunculus." Credit: ralf@ark.in-berlin.de (Creative Commons Attribution-Share Alike 4.0 International license).
- "Sensory homunculus." Credit: btarski (Creative Commons Attribution-Share Alike 4.0 International license).
- "The classical Wernicke-Lichtheim-Geschwind model of the neurobiology of language." Credit: Peter Hagoort (Creative Commons Attribution 3.0 Unported license).
- "Optic tract and optic nerve." Credit: Anatomist90 (Creative Commons Attribution-Share Alike 3.0 Unported license).

CHAPTER 4 | THE CEREBRAL SUBCORTEX
- "12 Line Field Telephone Switchboard." Credit: Sam Stokes (Creative Commons Attribution-ShareAlike 2.0 Generic license).
- "Basal Nuclei Connections." Credit: OpenStax (Creative Commons Attribution 4.0 International license).
- "Parinaud syndrome." Credit: Luciobgomes (Creative Commons Attribution-Share Alike 4.0 International license).
- "The Hypothalamus-Pituitary Complex." Credit: OpenStax College (Creative Commons Attribution 3.0 Unported license).

- "A giant and a dwarf, London, 1927." Credit: Wellcome Images (Creative Commons Attribution 4.0 International license).

CHAPTER 5 | THE CEREBELLUM
- "Push-up-with-feet-on-an-exercise-ball." Credit: Everkinetic (Creative Commons Attribution-Share Alike 3.0 Unported license).
- "Cerebellar Peduncles." Credit: OpenStax College (Creative Commons Attribution 3.0 Unported license).
- "Major Regions of the Cerebellum." Credit: OpenStax College (Creative Commons Attribution 3.0 Unported license).
- "Surgical result after ventral fusion of scoliosis." Credit: Weiss HR, Goodall D (Creative Commons Attribution 2.0 Generic license).

CHAPTER 6 | THE BRAINSTEM
- None.

CHAPTER 7 | THE SPINAL CORD
- "The human body in anatomical position." Credit: Osteomyoamare (Creative Commons Attribution 3.0 Unported license).
- "Apparatus for the treatment of paralysis." Credit: Wellcome Images (Creative Commons Attribution 4.0 International license).

CHAPTER 8 | THE PERIPHERAL NERVOUS SYSTEM
- "2nd nerve-figure, by Vesalius." Credit: Wellcome Images (Creative Commons Attribution 4.0 International license).
- "Trigeminal nerve." Credit: Harrygouvas (Creative Commons Attribution-Share Alike 3.0 Unported license).
- "Diagram showing the parts of the inner ear." Credit: Cancer Research UK (Creative Commons Attribution-Share Alike 4.0 International license).
- "Automatic Innervation." Credit: OpenStax College (Creative Commons Attribution 3.0 Unported license).
- "Bells palsy diagram." Credit: Patrick J. Lynch, medical illustrator (Creative Commons Attribution 2.5 Generic license).
- "Reflexo da tosse." Credit: Ericneuro (Creative Commons Attribution-Share Alike 4.0 International license).
- "Autonomic Nervous System." Credit: Paul Walker (Creative Commons Attribution-ShareAlike 2.0 Generic license).
- "highwire." Credit: yumikrum (Creative Commons Attribution 2.0 Generic license).
- "Pancoast Tumor." Credit: Jmarchn (Creative Commons Attribution-Share Alike 1.0 Generic license).

CHAPTER 9 | THE SPECIAL SENSES
- "Optical Fields." Credit: OpenStax College (Creative Commons Attribution 3.0 Unported license).
- "Cranial nerve III visceral." Credit: Patrick J. Lynch, medical illustrator (Creative Commons Attribution 2.5 Generic license).
- "Dilated and Undilated Pupil." Credit: National Eye Institute Creative Commons

Attribution 2.0 Generic license).

- "Symptoms and Findings in Multiple Sclerosis." Credit: Guido4 (Creative Commons Attribution-Share Alike 4.0 International license).
- "Rinneversuch." Credit: FOX 52 (Creative Commons Attribution-Share Alike 4.0 International license).
- "falling." Credit: Lovelorn Poets (Creative Commons Attribution 2.0 Generic license).
- "Anatomy and physiology of animals Olfactory organ the sense of smell." Credit: Sunshineconnelly at English Wikibooks (Creative Commons Attribution 3.0 Unported license).

CHAPTER 10 | THE KITCHEN SINK

- "Carotidian pulse." Credit: Rama (Creative Commons Attribution-ShareAlike 3.0 license).
- "Vesalius, figure of the brain." Credit: Wellcome Images (Creative Commons Attribution 4.0 International license).
- "MRA Circle of Willis." Credit: © Nevit Dilmen (Creative Commons Attribution-Share Alike 3.0 Unported license).
- "Oedema." Credit: Klaus D. Peter (Creative Commons Attribution-Share Alike 1.0 Generic license).

CHAPTER 11 | THE NEUROLOGICAL EXAM

- "A doctor skating past a group of people whilst inspecting their tongues and running down a street throwing pills to patients in houses." Credit: Wellcome Images (Creative Commons Attribution 4.0 International license).
- "Moro Reflex." Credit: Ashley Arbuckle (Creative Commons Attribution 2.0 Generic license).
- "Rooting Reflex." Credit: Ashley Arbuckle (Creative Commons Attribution 2.0 Generic license).
- "Palmar Grasp Reflex." Credit: Ashley Arbuckle (Creative Commons Attribution 2.0 Generic license).
- "Romberg." Credit: Gonad (Creative Commons Attribution-Share Alike 1.0 Generic license).
- "Trendelenburg's sign." Credit: Foto H.-P.Haack (Creative Commons Attribution-Share Alike 3.0 Unported license).
- "CT and MRI of cerebral hemorrhages and effective T2 MRI of subsequent hemosiderosis." Credit: Hongwei Zhao, Jin Wang, Zhonglie Lu, Qingjie Wu, Haijuan Lv, Hu Liu, Xiangyang Gong (Creative Commons Attribution 4.0 International license).

CHAPTER 12 | STROKE

- "Ischemic Stroke." Credit: ElinorHunt (Creative Commons Attribution-Share Alike 4.0 International license).
- "A patient paying a dentist after having a tooth removed with gas." Credit: Wellcome Images (Creative Commons Attribution 4.0 International license).
- "FLAIR MRI of cerebral infarction." Credit: Shazia Mirza and Sankalp Gokhale (Creative Commons Attribution 4.0 International license).

- "Cerebellum arteries." Credit: Petit B (Creative Commons Attribution-Share Alike 4.0 International license).
- "Arteries entering spinal canal." Credit: Wellcome Images (Creative Commons Attribution 4.0 International license).
- "Arteries at base of brain and anterior spinal arteries." Credit: Wellcome Images (Creative Commons Attribution 4.0 International license).
- "Neuroimaging in Acute Stroke." Credit: Shazia Mirza and Sankalp Gokhale (Creative Commons Attribution 4.0 International license).
- "TOF MRI angiography of right middle cerebral artery stenosis." Credit: Shazia Mirza and Sankalp Gokhale (Creative Commons Attribution 4.0 International license).
- "Oculomotor nerve palsy." Credit: Wang Y, Wang XH, Tian MM, Xie CJ, Liu Y, Pan QQ, Lu YN (Creative Commons Attribution 4.0 International license).
- "Palatine Uvula." Credit: Luigithemetal64 (Creative Commons Attribution-Share Alike 3.0 Unported license).

CHAPTER 13 | INTRACRANIAL PRESSURE
- "Epidurale Blutung in der Computertomographie rechts." Credit: Hellerhoff (Creative Commons Attribution-Share Alike 3.0 Unported license).
- "Large left sided frontal parietal subdural hematoma with associated midline shift." Credit: James Heilman, MD (Creative Commons Attribution-Share Alike 3.0 Unported license).
- "A subarachnoid hemorrhage." Credit: James Heilman, MD (Creative Commons Attribution-Share Alike 3.0 Unported license).
- "An intra parenchymal bleed with surrounding edema." Credit: James Heilman, MD (Creative Commons Attribution-Share Alike 4.0 International license).
- "Ruptured 7mm left vertebral artery aneurysm." Credit: James Heilman, MD (Creative Commons Attribution-Share Alike 4.0 International license).
- "Skull and brain human normal." Credit: Patrick J. Lynch, medical illustrator (Creative Commons Attribution 2.5 Generic license).
- "Brain herniation types." Credit: Delldot, with derivative work by RupertMillard (Creative Commons Attribution-Share Alike 3.0 Unported license).
- "Hydrocephalus with sunset eyes." Credit: شهاب (Creative Commons Attribution-Share Alike 4.0 International license).
- "Papilledema Stages." Credit: Ambika S., Arjundas D., Noronha V. (Creative Commons Attribution-Share Alike 2.0 Generic license).
- "Anterior communicating artery aneurysm before and after GDC coil embolization." Credit: J Neal Rutledge (Creative Commons Attribution-ShareAlike 3.0 license).
- "Brain atrophy from vascular dementia." Credit: James Heilman, MD (Creative Commons Attribution-Share Alike 4.0 International license).

CHAPTER 14 | MYOPATHY
- "Polymyositis HE." Credit: Jensflorian (Creative Commons Attribution-Share Alike 3.0 Unported license).
- "High magnification micrograph of dermatomyositis, a type of inflammatory myopathy. H&E stain." Credit: Nephron (Creative Commons Attribution-Share

Alike 3.0 Unported license).
- "Dermatomyositis." Credit: Elizabeth M. Dugan, Adam M. Huber, Frederick W. Miller, Lisa G. Rider (Creative Commons Attribution-Share Alike 3.0 Unported license).
- "Patient with DMD enlarged calf muscles." Credit: Sohail A, et al. (Creative Commons Attribution license).

CHAPTER 15 | NEUROMUSCULAR JUNCTION DISEASE
- "Shows termination of nerve in muscle." Wellcome Images (Creative Commons Attribution 4.0 International license).
- "Botox Injections from Dr Braun." Credit: Dr. Braun (Creative Commons Attribution-ShareAlike 2.0 Generic license).
- "Myasthenia gravis ptosis reversal." Credit: Mohankumar Kurukumbi, Roger L Weir, Janaki Kalyanam, Mansoor Nasim, Annapurni Jayam-Trouth (Creative Commons Attribution 2.0 Generic license).

CHAPTER 16 | MOTOR NEURON DISEASE
- "A boy affected by konzo, causing a spastic paraparesis with walking difficulties. It also shows the upper motor neuron, the suspected site of the neurodamage." Credit: Thorkild Tylleskar (Creative Commons Attribution-Share Alike 3.0 Unported license).
- "Chin-ups-1." Credit: Everkinetic (Creative Commons Attribution-Share Alike 3.0 Unported license).
- "Amyotrophic lateral sclerosis." Credit: Frank Gaillard (Creative Commons Attribution-Share Alike 3.0 Unported license).

CHAPTER 17 | MOVEMENT DISORDERS
- "Spiral drawing - essential tremor." Credit: Undescribed/Pharexia (Creative Commons Attribution-Share Alike 4.0 International license).
- "Kayser-Fleischer ring." Credit: Herbert L. Fred, MD, Hendrik A. van Dijk (Creative Commons Attribution 3.0 Unported license).

CHAPTER 18 | SEIZURES
- "A group of people standing around a man having an epileptic fit." Credit: Wellcome Images (Creative Commons Attribution 4.0 International license).
- "Attaque: Periode Epileptoide. Planche XVII." Credit: Wellcome Images (Creative Commons Attribution 4.0 International license).
- "Human EEG with prominent alpha-rhythm." Credit: Andrii Cherninskyi (Creative Commons Attribution-Share Alike 4.0 International license).
- "Frontal lobe tumor." Credit: Roland Schmitt et al (Creative Commons Attribution 2.0 Generic license).
- "A figure with four arms and four legs." Credit: Wellcome Images (Creative Commons Attribution 4.0 International license).
- "Generalized 3 Hz spike and wave discharges in a child with childhood absence epilepsy." Credit: Der Lange (Creative Commons Attribution-Share Alike 2.0 Generic license).
- "Normal axial T2-weighted MR image of the brain." Credit: Novaksean (Creative

CHAPTER 19 | NEOPLASMS

CHAPTER 20 | INFECTIONS

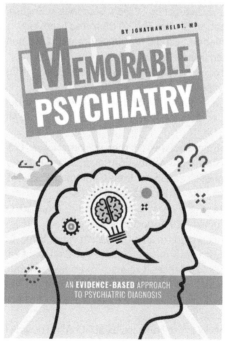

INTERESTED IN LEARNING MORE?

Get *Memorable Psychopharmacology* and *Memorable Psychiatry*,
both available now from the same author!

Now that you have a solid background in the anatomy, function, and pathology of the nervous system, build upon that foundation by exploring psychiatric disorders and the medications used to treat them. Both *Memorable Psychopharmacology* and *Memorable Psychiatry* feature the same conversational tone, helpful mnemonics, visual aids, and practice questions as *Memorable Neurology* to ensure that you not only learn the material but retain it far into the future. For anyone preparing to meet the mental health needs of their patients, these books are an indispensable review!

BOTH AVAILABLE NOW ON AMAZON.COM!

ABOUT THE AUTHOR

Jonathan Heldt is currently on faculty at the UCLA Semel Institute for Neuroscience & Human Behavior. He completed his Bachelor's degree in Biochemistry at Pacific Union College, his medical degree at the Loma Linda University School of Medicine, and his residency at the UCLA Psychiatry Residency Training Program. He is interested in both mental health and medical education and hopes that this book will inspire these interests in others. He has no conflicts of interest to disclose.

*For questions, comments, and updates, please visit **memorablepsych.com** or email **memorablepsych@gmail.com**.*

Made in the USA
Middletown, DE
24 March 2023

27546734R00245